KU-070-118

lonely planet

Discover
Ireland

Experience the best
of Ireland

This edition written and researched by

Catl

4 1 0074048 1

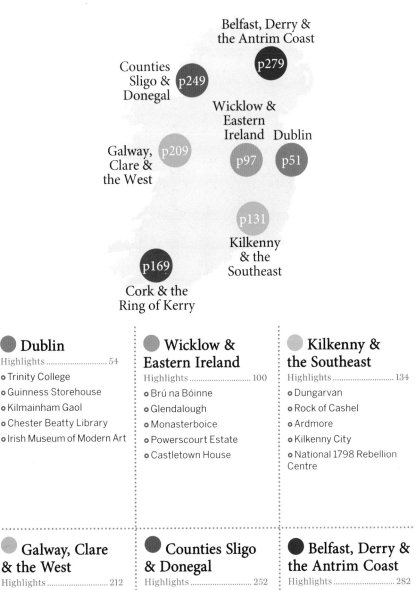

Contents

Contents

On the Road

Belfast, Derry & the Antrim Coast   279

This is Ireland

For a small country, Ireland gets huge billing. Its praises are sung in song and described in prose; its many charms are evoked to delicious perfection by artists on canvas and poets in verse. Part of that is down to the Irish diaspora, whose attachment to the land of their ancestors gets stronger with each passing generation.

But much of the credit goes to Ireland itself. Despite the trappings of modernity and the fickle hand of fortune, Ireland remains one of the world's most beautiful countries, and is worth every effort you make to explore it. From the postcard-perfect peninsulas of the southwest to the brooding loneliness of Connemara, Ireland's hold on the imagination remains as strong as ever. Brave the raging Atlantic on a crossing to the Aran Islands or spend a summer's evening in the yard of a thatched cottage pub and you'll experience a country that has changed little in generations – this is most likely the Ireland you came to see.

Céad míle fáilte **– a hundred thousand welcomes.** Why a hundred thousand when one is perfectly adequate everywhere else? Everyone has heard of Irish friendliness, and once you arrive you'll gladly discover it's not a myth. A bit of friendly banter and the offer of a helping hand – to make sense of garbled directions or share a pint (it's a sin to drink alone!) – are never far from the first hello, for the Irish consider hospitality to be their greatest asset. A hundred thousand welcomes. It seems excessive, but in Ireland, excess is fine, so long as it's practised in moderation.

And when we say Ireland, we mean the whole island. The North, for so long scarred by conflict, is fully engaged in the process of recovery and is once again parading its stunning self to a world that, until recently, knew of it only through the stories on the evening news.

> **66**
> Ireland's hold on the imagination remains as strong as ever
> **99**

Coastline, County Donegal (p262)
TRAVELPIX LTD/GETTY IMAGES ©

Ireland

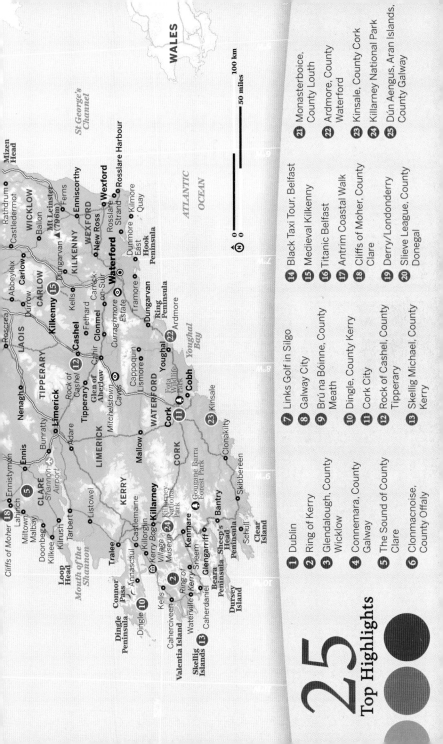

WALES

St George's Channel

Mizen Head

ATLANTIC OCEAN

N

0   50 miles
0   100 km

25 Top Highlights

1. Dublin
2. Ring of Kerry
3. Glendalough, County Wicklow
4. Connemara, County Galway
5. The Sound of County Clare
6. Clonmacnoise, County Offaly
7. Links Golf in Sligo
8. Galway City
9. Brú na Bóinne, County Meath
10. Dingle, County Kerry
11. Cork City
12. Rock of Cashel, County Tipperary
13. Skellig Michael, County Kerry
14. Black Taxi Tour, Belfast
15. Medieval Kilkenny
16. Titanic Belfast
17. Antrim Coastal Walk
18. Cliffs of Moher, County Clare
19. Derry/Londonderry
20. Slieve League, County Donegal
21. Monasterboice, County Louth
22. Ardmore, County Waterford
23. Kinsale, County Cork
24. Killarney National Park
25. Dún Aengus, Aran Islands, County Galway

25 Ireland's Top 25 Highlights

Dublin

Ireland's capital and largest city (p60) by some stretch is the main gateway into the country, but it has enough distractions to keep visitors mesmerised for at least a few days. From world-class museums and entertainment, superb dining and top-grade hotels, Dublin has all the baubles of a major international metropolis. But the real clinchers are the Dubliners themselves, who are friendlier, more easy-going and welcoming than the burghers of virtually any other European capital. And it's the home of Guinness. Spire of Dublin, O'Connell St

RICHARD I'ANSON/GETTY IMAGES ©

The Ring of Kerry

Driving around the Ring of Kerry (p196), a 179km tourist charm bracelet enveloping the Iveragh Peninsula just west of Killarney, is an unforgettable experience. Along its winding, weaving (and often narrow) roads you'll see everything you came to Ireland for: mesmerising mountain views, vertiginous cliffs, tranquil lakes, historic towns and colourful villages. This is Ireland of the postcard and the song, as beautiful as it is popular. Prepare your camera! Gap of Dunloe (p194)

Glendalough, County Wicklow

St Kevin knew a thing or two about magical locations. When he chose a remote cave on a glacial lake nestled at the base of a forested valley as his monastic retreat, he inadvertently founded a settlement that would later prove to be one of Ireland's most dynamic universities and, in our time, one of the country's most beautiful ruined sites (p107). The remains of the settlement (including an intact round tower), coupled with the stunning scenery, are unforgettable. St Kevin's Kitchen (p109)

The Best...
Ancient Monuments

BRÚ NA BÓINNE
Neolithic passage graves older than the pyramids (p118).

CLONMACNOISE
Once one of Europe's greatest universities... before universities even existed. (p230)

ROCK OF CASHEL
Thousand-year-old castle, abbey and cathedral straddling a rock above the town. (p161)

SKELLIG MICHAEL
Monastic settlement clinging to a rock since the 6th century. (p198)

GLENDALOUGH
Beautiful monastic ruins in the serenest of settings (p107).

The Best...
Places for Irish History

KILMAINHAM GAOL
Blood, guts and gore behind prison walls. (p92)

NATIONAL 1798 REBELLION CENTRE
The history of rebellion in bloody and magnificent detail. (p150)

DUNBRODY FAMINE SHIP
Full-scale replica of a 19th-century 'famine ship'. (p148)

ULSTER FOLK MUSEUM
The fascinating lives of ordinary people in 18th and 19th century Ulster. (p299)

4 Connemara, County Galway

A filigreed coast of tiny coves and beaches is the Connemara Peninsula's (p225) beautiful border with the wild waters of the Atlantic. Wandering characterful roads take you from one village to another, each with trad pubs and restaurants serving seafood chowder cooked from recipes that are family secrets. Inland, the scenic drama is even greater. In fantastically desolate valleys, green hills, yellow wildflowers and wild streams reflecting the blue sky provide elemental beauty. Mannin Bay

5 The Sound of County Clare

Western Europe's most vibrant folk music is Irish traditional music. It may have earned worldwide fame thanks to the likes of Riverdance but is best expressed in a more sedate setting, usually an old-fashioned pub. You'll find these throughout County Clare (p232), from the county's capital, Ennis, to the villages of Ennistymon, Doolin and Kilfenora. You won't be asked to join in, but there's nothing stopping you tapping your foot! O'Connor's (p241), Doolin

Clonmacnoise, County Offaly

The once-enormous ecclesiastical city of Clonmacnoise (p230) may be long past its pre-medieval prime, but these magnificent ruins, in the ideal location overlooking the River Shannon, still pay a fine tribute to its former glory. In the centuries before the established universities of England, France or Italy, this was one of Europe's premier centres of education.

Links Golf in Sligo

If Scotland is the home of golf, then Ireland is where golf goes on holiday. And the best vacation spots are along the sea, where the country's collection of seaside links are dotted in a steady string along virtually the entire Irish coastline, each more revealed than carved in the undulating, marram-grass-covered landscapes. One of the finest examples is the breathtaking County Sligo Golf Course (p259), laid out in the shadow of magnificent Benbulben, the peak that inspired WB Yeats.

Galway City

One word to describe Galway city (p218)? Craic! Ireland's liveliest city literally hums through the night at music-filled pubs where you can hear three old guys playing spoons and fiddles or a hot, young band. Join the locals as they bounce from place to place, never knowing what fun lies ahead but certain of the possibility. Add in local bounty such as the famous oysters and nearby adventure in the Connemara Peninsula and the Aran Islands and the fun never ends.

The Best...
Traditional Pubs

JOHN MULLIGAN'S
The classic Dublin pub. (p86)

TYNAN'S BRIDGE HOUSE
A rural country pub in the middle of a big town. (p143)

CROWN LIQUOR SALOON
The most famous of Belfast's Victorian pubs. (p298)

SÉHÁN UA NEÁCHTAIN
Galway's most celebrated – and photographed – pub. (p220)

OLDE GLEN BAR & RESTAURANT
A perfect boozer in a remote corner of the country. (p273)

Brú na Bóinne, County Meath

Looking at once ancient and yet eerily futuristic, Newgrange's immense, round, white stone walls topped by a grass dome is one of the most extraordinary sights you'll ever see. Part of the vast Neolithic necropolis Brú na Bóinne (p118; the Boyne Palace), it contains Ireland's finest Stone Age passage tomb, predating the Pyramids by some six centuries. Most extraordinary of all is the tomb's precise alignment with the sun at the time of the winter solstice.

The Best...
Scenic Drives

SKY ROAD
A spectacular Connemara loop. (p227)

RING OF KERRY
Ireland's most popular drive (p196).

HEALY PASS
Spectacular border crossing between Cork and Kerry (p199).

LOUGH INAGH VALLEY
In the shadow of the brooding Twelve Bens (p232).

GLENGESH PASS
A touch of the Alps in Donegal (p265).

10 Dingle, County Kerry

Dingle is the name of both the picturesque peninsula (p203) jutting into the Atlantic from County Kerry, strewn with ancient ruins, and its delightful main town (p204), the peninsula's beating heart. Fishing boats unload fish and shellfish that couldn't be any fresher if you caught it yourself, many pubs remain untouched since their earlier incarnations as old-fashioned shops, artists sell their creations (including beautiful jewellery with Irish designs) at intriguing boutiques, and toe-tapping trad sessions take place around roaring pub fires. Dingle Peninsula

Cork City

The Republic's second city (p178) is second only in terms of size – in every other respect it will bear no competition. A tidy, compact city centre is home to an enticing collection of art galleries, museums and – most especially – places to eat. From cheap cafes to top-end gourmet restaurants, Cork city excels, though it's hardly a surprise given the county's exceptional foodie reputation. At the heart of it is the simply wonderful English Market (p179), a covered produce market that is an attraction unto itself. English Market

OLIVER STREWE/GETTY IMAGES ©

Rock of Cashel, County Tipperary

Soaring up from the green Tipperary pastures, this ancient fortress (p161) takes your breath away at first sight. The seat of kings and churchmen who ruled over the region for more than a thousand years, it rivalled Tara as a centre of power in Ireland for 400 years. Entered through the 15th-century Hall of the Vicars Choral, its impervious walls guard an awesome enclosure with a complete round tower, a 13th-century Gothic cathedral and the most magnificent 12th-century Romanesque chapel in Ireland.

Skellig Michael, County Kerry

Brace yourself for the experience of a lifetime as you brave the choppy crossing to clamber about the jagged rocks of Skellig Michael (p198), where early Christian monks lived in splendid isolation from the 6th to 12th century, perched 150m above the raging sea in bare, beehive cells. The only difference now is the monks are gone and a small guard rail is in place.

GARETH MCCORMACK/GETTY IMAGES ©

Black Taxi Tour, Belfast

No trip to Northern Ireland is complete without visiting the Republican and Loyalist murals of Belfast's Falls and Shankhill districts (p294). But for an outsider, the city's bitterly divided society can be hard to get your head around. Without a local guide to provide some background and explanation, the murals can be just so much garish paint. Belfast's black taxi tours (p296) are justifiably famous because they provide that context, with drivers who are both insightful and darkly humorous without making light of a serious and often tragic situation.

The Best...
Local Activities

CLIMB CROAGH PATRICK
A three-hour climb rewards with superb views and a touch of spiritual enlightenment. (p246)

LEARN SOME MUSIC ON INISHEER
Learn the basics of the bodhrán at the Craiceann Inis Oírr International Bodhrán Summer School. (p239)

COOKING IN CORK
Learn the nuances of fine Irish cuisine at the country's most famous cooking school. (p186)

CATCH A FISH
Tackle the sea with some angling off the coast of Kilmore Quay. (p145)

COUNTY SLIGO GOLF COURSE
Go for par on one of Ireland's most beautiful links, in the shadow of Benbulben. (p259)

The Best...
Festival Frolics

KILKENNY ARTS FESTIVAL
Medieval Kilkenny shows its artistic side. (p144)

CAT LAUGHS COMEDY FESTIVAL
Comics from the world over descend upon Kilkenny every year for fits and giggles. (p144)

WILLIE CLANCY IRISH MUSIC FESTIVAL
You'll hear some of the best traditional music in the world at this annual festival on the Clare coast. (p237)

GALWAY ARTS FESTIVAL
The city goes arts-and-fun crazy for two weeks. (p224)

GALWAY INTERNATIONAL OYSTER FESTIVAL
Locally fished oysters washed down with Guinness to a lively musical soundtrack. (p224)

15

Medieval Kilkenny

From its regal castle to its soaring medieval cathedral, Kilkenny (p140) exudes a permanence and culture that have made it an unmissable stop on journeys to the south and west. Its namesake county boasts scores of artisans and craftspeople and you can browse their wares at Kilkenny's classy shops and boutiques. Chefs eschew Dublin in order to be close to the source of Kilkenny's wonderful produce and you can enjoy the local brewery's namesake brew at scores of delightful pubs.

Above: Kilkenny city;
Left: Jerpoint Abbey (p143)

LEFT: GAVIN HELLIER/GETTY IMAGES ©; TOP: DESIGN PICS/THE IRISH IMAGE COLLECTION/GETTY IMAGES ©

Titanic Belfast

16

The construction of the world's most famous ocean liner is celebrated in high-tech, multimedia glory at this wonderful new museum (p289). Not only can you explore virtually every detail of the *Titanic*'s construction (including a simulated 'fly-through' of the ship from keel to bridge) but you can place yourself in the middle of the industrial bustle that were Belfast's shipyards at the turn of the 20th century. The experience is heightened by the use of photography, audio and the only footage of the actual Titanic still in existence.

Antrim Coastal Walk

17

Stretching for 16 scenic kilometres between the swaying Carrick-a-Rede Rope Bridge (p303) and the geological flourish of the Giant's Causeway (p304), this is coastal hiking at its best. It offers an ever-changing vista of cliffs and islands, sandy beaches and ruined castles, framed by scenic, seabird-haunted Rathlin Island (p306) at one end and the cheering prospect of a dram or two at the Old Bushmills Distillery (p303) at the other

Carrick-a-Rede Rope Bridge

Cliffs of Moher, County Clare

Bathed in the golden glow of the late afternoon sun, the iconic Cliffs of Moher (p238) are one of the splendours of the west coast and one of the country's most popular natural attractions. Witnessed from a boat bobbing below, the towering stone faces – rising 203m from the churning waves – have a jaw-dropping, dramatic beauty that is enlivened by scores of sea birds, including cute little puffins. A vast visitor centre set into the side of the hill provides all the information.

The Best...
Leg Stretchers

GLENDALOUGH
Fabulous walks around this monastic site are part of the 117km Wicklow Way. (p107)

KILLARNEY NATIONAL PARK
You've seen these views on a thousand postcards – now you can see them for yourself. (p193)

DUBLIN CITY CENTRE
Who says you need greenery for a good walk? Try Dublin's Georgian architecture instead. (p60)

ARDMORE CLIFFS
Walk part of the ancient St Declan's Way across green fields and alongside stunning cliff views. (p159)

Derry/ Londonderry

19

History runs deep in Northern Ireland's second city (p307). From the 17th-century city walls built to protect Protestant settlers, to the bipartite Republican/Loyalist name, Derry/Londonderry, symbols of the country's sectarian past are evident. But a new bridge spanning the River Foyle is a symbol of an attempt to bridge that divide and to look to the future as a city filled with a restless creative energy, expressed in its powerful murals, vibrant music scene and numerous art galleries. *Hands Across the Divide by Maurice Harron*

GARETH MCCORMACK/GETTY IMAGES ©

The Best...
Seaside Villages

KILMORE QUAY
Great spot to relax and watch the fishermen pull in their nets. (p145)

DUNFANAGHY
Elegant village fronted by a huge strand. (p269)

ROUNDSTONE
Colourful terrace houses and a boat-filled harbour complete this Connemara gem. (p226)

CUSHENDUN
Cornish-style houses make this one of the delights of the Antrim Coast. (p306)

ARDMORE
Quiet and relatively undiscovered, Ardmore's beach is a well-kept secret. (p158)

20 Slieve League, County Donegal

The Cliffs of Moher may be more famous and get all the tourist kudos, but the cliffs at Slieve League (p266) in County Donegal are taller – the highest in Europe in fact. Sail beneath them aboard a diminutive 12-seater boat, or head up to the top to see the stark, otherworldly rock face tumbling 600m into the Atlantic Ocean. The cliffs are particularly scenic at sunset when the waves crash dramatically far below and the ocean reflects the last rays of the day.

SIMON GREENWOOD/GETTY IMAGES ®

Monasterboice, County Louth

Home to two of the finest Celtic High Crosses in the country, an imposing round tower and a pair of church ruins, the remains of the 5th-century monastery at Monasterboice (p129) have retained the air of monastic stillness that once encouraged the contemplative life. If you visit in the evening, just before sunset, the crowing ravens give the whole place an atmospherically eerie feeling that will linger long in the memory.

Ardmore, County Waterford

Occupying a relatively undiscovered headland at the bottom of County Waterford is the wonderful seaside village of Ardmore (p158), which is blessed by the wide arc of a superb beach. Along the cliffs just north of the village is one of the oldest Christian sites in Ireland, a fabulous hotel and the start of a bracing cliffside loop that brings you right back into town. And with relatively few visitors at any time of year it's all yours for the asking! View from St Declan's Way (p159)

Kinsale, County Cork

This is one of Ireland's most popular coastal towns (p184), its cluster of brightly coloured houses stretching up the hill from the busy harbour. Indeed, it is the harbour that is responsible for the town's reputation as the unofficial gourmet capital of the south – some of the country's best restaurants (specialising in seafood, of course) can be found here; even the pubs have gotten in on the act, serving up some of the most delicious pub grub you'll eat anywhere.

The Best...
Places for Food

DUBLIN
The capital's range of cuisines is the best in the country. (p60)

BELFAST
From pub grub to gourmet feasts, Belfast's foodie rep is growing. (p288)

CORK CITY
Gourmet capital of Ireland, Cork is renowned for its emphasis on local produce. (p178)

KINSALE
Fishy Fishy Cafe in Kinsale is one of the best seafood restaurants in Ireland – although the food is superb everywhere else, too. (p184)

DUNGARVAN
Great farmers markets provide local restaurateurs with the raw ingredients to fashion their magic. (p156)

29

Killarney National Park, County Kerry

Surrounding the peaty waters of three stunning lakes is the expanse of Killarney National Park (p193), 10,000-odd hectares of such beauty that it has the Unesco stamp of protection. Inside, you'll find castle ruins, stately homes, restorative walks and Ireland's only wild herd of native red deer, who've lived here continuously for the last 12,000 years. Energetic visitors can ascend Carrantuohill, Ireland's highest peak. Ross Castle (p19:

The Best...
Places to Stay

CLIFF HOUSE HOTEL
Modern refurb of an old hotel that has been an un-qualified success. (p159)

LOUGH ESKE CASTLE
Award-winning hotel epito-mises elegant country living. (p264)

MERRION
Georgian elegance in the birthplace of the Duke of Wellington. (p81)

WATERFORD CASTLE
A 19th-century turreted castle on its private island. (p153)

ASHFORD CASTLE
Grand style accommo-dation on Connemara's edge. (p245)

Dún Aengus, Aran Islands, County Galway

You have to make an effort to get here, crossing the sometimes choppy sea from Galway or Clare, but once you set foot on Inishmór, you'll see that it's more than worth it. Perched perilously at the edge of a wind- and ocean-lashed cliff, the Iron Age fort of Dún Aengus (p223) is a tribute to the imagination, forbearance and building skills of its Celtic constructors. It has withstood both time and weather to remain standing after 2000 years.

Ireland's Top Itineraries

Dublin & Around
Capital Highlights

5 DAYS

Short on time? Dublin has enough to entertain you for at least three days, leaving you two days to devote to trips from the capital. Even on a quick trip here you'll see some of the country's top highlights.

COUNTY MEATH

DUBLIN

Irish Sea

COUNTY WICKLOW

① Dublin (p60)

Start with the city's big hitters – Trinity College, the Book of Kells and the Guinness Storehouse. Then take in a collection or two: the Chester Beatty Library is worth an hour at least, as is the National Museum – Archaeology & History. On day two, amble through St Stephen's Green before checking out the National Gallery. In the afternoon, head west and visit the Irish Museum of Modern Art and/or the fabulous Kilmainham Gaol. On day three, explore the north side of the city – a walk down O'Connell St will lead you to the Dublin City Gallery – The Hugh Lane. In the evening, take in a performance at either the Abbey Theatre or the Gate.

DUBLIN ◯ COUNTY WICKLOW
🚗 **One hour** Along M11, then right on R755.
🚌 **Four hours** Organised bus tour from Dublin Tourism, includes Powerscourt Estate.

② County Wicklow (p106)

Immediately south of Dublin is the wild countryside of County Wicklow. If you only have one day, we recommend a guided tour during which you'll visit the county's showpiece attractions and be back in time for dinner. On top of the pile are the monastic ruins at Glendalough and the broad expanse of Powerscourt Estate. Along the way you'll pass through the beautiful Wicklow Mountains.

DUBLIN ◯ COUNTY MEATH
🚗 **One hour** Along M1, left on N51. 🚌 **Four hours** Organised bus tour with Dublin Tourism.

③ County Meath (p118)

On day five, head north into County Meath and prehistory by visiting the stunning Neolithic passage grave complex of Brú na Bóinne, which predates Stonehenge and the pyramids of Egypt. If you're on an organised tour, you can also visit Tara, where the high kings of Ireland resided in Celtic times, and the Battle of the Boyne site, where the bloody showdown in 1690 between Protestant and Catholic forces would determine the course of Irish history for the next 300 years.

Brú na Bóinne (p118)
STEPHEN O'KANE[TBSTEVE@FLICKR]/GETTY IMAGES ©

5 DAYS

Dublin to Killarney
Ireland in a Nutshell

If you've only got five days and you must see the best of the country, you won't have time to linger too long anywhere – but if you manage it correctly, you'll leave with the top highlights in your memory and on your memory card.

ATLANTIC OCEAN

NORTHERN IRELAND

GALWAY ②

DUBLIN ①

CLIFFS OF MOHER ③

④ DINGLE

⑤ KILLARNEY

St George's Channel

① Dublin (p60)

A one-day whistle-stop tour of the capital should include visits to Trinity College and the Book of Kells, the National Museum – Archaeology & History and the Guinness Storehouse. Make sure to sample a pint of Guinness in one of the city's superb pubs.

DUBLIN ◆ GALWAY
🚗 **Three hours** Along M6. 🚌 **3½ hours** From Dublin's Busaras to Galway Bus Station. 🚆 **Three hours** From Dublin's Heuston Station to Galway's Ceannt Station.

② Galway (p218)

On day two, cross the island and make for the capital of the west, Galway city. The journey should take no longer than three hours. Once settled in, take a drive into Connemara: you won't get far but the drive to Oughterard will give you more than a taste of the region's stunning beauty. In the late afternoon, return to Galway and soak in the city's delights: a meal followed by a drink (or four) and a live céilidh (session of traditional music and dancing) in a traditional old pub such as Tig Cóilí.

GALWAY ◆ CLIFFS OF MOHER
🚗 **One hour** Along N18. 🚌 **80 minutes** From Galway Bus Station to Ennis Bus Station. 🚆 **80 minutes** From Galway's Ceannt Station to Ennis Station.

③ Cliffs of Moher (p238)

On day three, go south through the Burren towards the Cliffs of Moher, where the crowds are a small price to pay for some of the most stunning views you'll see anywhere. A good base for the evening is Ennis, County Clare's largest town, where you'll find decent hotels and some excellent music bars. We recommend Brogan's, unassuming by day but livened up by traditional music at night.

CLIFFS OF MOHER ◆ DINGLE
🚗 **2½ hours** Along N18 to Limerick, N21 to Tralee and N86 to Dingle.

④ Dingle (p204)

Moving south again, cross into County Kerry through the beautiful Connor Pass and make for Dingle, on its eponymous peninsula. The town itself has plenty to keep you there, but it would be a shame to miss the peninsula itself, especially Slea Head and its stunning prehistoric monuments – not to mention the views!

DINGLE ◆ KILLARNEY
🚗 **80 minutes** Along N86 to Tralee and N22 to Killarney.

⑤ Killarney (p188)

On day five, head south once more to storied Killarney, which you should use as a base for the equally renowned Ring of Kerry, a much-trafficked loop around the Iveragh Peninsula.

By day's end you should feel exhausted and in need of another holiday; the good news is that there's plenty more to see and do in Ireland when you next return.

Slea Head (p206)
JOHN ELK/GETTY IMAGES ©

10 DAYS

Dublin to Doolin
East to West

Ten days is ample time to explore the country's midriff from east to west, beginning in Dublin and wending your way to the west coast, where Galway, Connemara and the natural and musical bounty of County Clare awaits.

ATLANTIC OCEAN

NORTHERN IRELAND

CLIFDEN ④

CLONMACNOISE ②

DUBLIN ①

GALWAY ③

DOOLIN ⑤

① Dublin (p60)

Spend a couple of days in the capital visiting Trinity College and the Book of Kells, the National Museum – Archaeology & History and the Guinness Storehouse. On day two, be sure to visit the Chester Beatty Library and St Patrick's Cathedral before visiting the neighbouring attractions of the Irish Museum of Modern Art and Kilmainham Gaol.

DUBLIN ➲ CLONMACNOISE
🚗 1½ hours Along M4 and M6.

② Clonmacnoise (p230)

As you move west across the midlands, stop at the Neolithic passage graves at Loughcrew in County Meath, rarely visited but fascinating nonetheless. Then head for the 6th-century ruins of Clonmacnoise, majestically positioned overlooking the mighty Shannon – a fitting location for the country's most important monastic site. From here, cross into County Galway and head for Galway City.

CLONMACNOISE ➲ GALWAY
🚗 50 minutes Along M6.

③ Galway (p218)

In Galway city you can shop for Claddagh rings, enjoy the local life around Shop Street and the Spanish Arch and, most memorably, the nightlife in one of the city's collection of outstanding traditional bars, where you will hear some terrific tunes. It's also the perfect base from which to explore Connemara and North Clare.

GALWAY ➲ CLIFDEN
🚗 75 minutes Along N59. 🚌 1½ hours From Galway Bus Station to Clifden.

Kilmainham Gaol (p92)
IIC/ AXIOM/GETTY IMAGES ©

④ Clifden (p227)

Head west, into the wilds of Connemara, exploring seaside villages such as Roundstone, driving through scenic wonderlands like the Lough Inagh Valley, and sneaking some R & R in Victorian Clifden before perhaps making a day trip to the Aran Islands. Inishmór is the most popular of the islands thanks to the presence of the prehistoric fort of Dún Aengus.

CLIFDEN ➲ DOOLIN
🚗 75 minutes Along N18 to Kilcolgan and N67 to Doolin. 🚌 1½ hours From Galway Bus Station to Doolin Hostel. 🚢 1½ hours From Inishmór (Aran Islands).

⑤ Doolin (p241)

From the Aran Islands you can hop on a boat across to Doolin, which is the perfect spot to begin exploring County Clare. If you're looking for authentic traditional music, Doolin, along with other villages including Miltown Malbay, are some of the best places in the country to hear outstanding musicians. Clare's other attractions are geographic: the Cliffs of Moher are justifiably one of the country's outstanding tourist attractions, while the lunar-like landscape of the Burren is a haven for birdlife.

10 DAYS

Belfast to Donegal
Northern Delights

One of the benefits of a more peaceful Northern Ireland is that the province has been able to showcase its outstanding visitor attractions and superb scenery. Worth including on your travels is County Donegal, one of Ireland's most beautiful counties and a favourite with vacationing northerners.

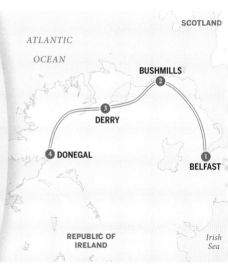

SCOTLAND

ATLANTIC OCEAN

BUSHMILLS ②

③ DERRY

④ DONEGAL

① BELFAST

REPUBLIC OF IRELAND

Irish Sea

① Belfast (p288)

Start in Belfast, where you should take a black taxi tour of West Belfast and then a visit to Titanic Belfast. You should also be sure to pay a visit to one of the city's famed Victorian pubs; the most well-known of them is the Crown Liquor Saloon. On your second day, visit the Ulster Transport Museum and the Ulster Folk Museum in the town of Holywood, just outside Belfast.

BELFAST ⊙ BUSHMILLS

🚗 **70 minutes** Along Antrim Coast. 🚌 **Three hours** From Belfast Europa Bus Station via Portstewart, Portrush & Antrim Coast.

② Bushmills (p302)

Head north toward the Antrim Coast, visiting Cushendun before challenging your vertigo with a crossing of the Carrick-a-Rede Rope Bridge. Nearby is the Unesco World Heritage Site of Giant's Causeway – which shouldn't be missed by any visitor to Northern Ireland – and, just beyond it, the fascinating village of Bushmills, home to the famous distillery.

BUSHMILLS ⊙ DERRY

🚗 **One hour** Along B17 to Coleraine and A2 to Derry. 🚌 **Two hours** Bushmills via Coleraine to Derry Foyle St.

③ Derry (p307)

Derry city should be your next stop, where you can walk the city's 17th-century walls before exploring its more recent past with a visit to the Bogside neighbour-hood, home to some of the most famous murals in Northern Ireland and a powerful example of the efforts of urban regeneration. Be sure to step in to the Museum of

Old Bushmills Distillery (p303)
PAUL HARRIS/GETTY IMAGES ©

Free Derry for a full-bodied history of how the Troubles affected this district.

DERRY ⊙ DONEGAL

🚗 **One hour** Along A38 to Lifford and N15 to Donegal Town. 🚌 **1½ minutes** Derry Foyle St to Abbey Hotel, Donegal Town.

④ Donegal (p262)

Cross the invisible border into the Republic by visiting County Donegal. Your first stop should be the Inishowen Peninsula; as you venture further west, the savage beauty of the land becomes ever more apparent as you skirt the coastline past handsome Dunfanaghy, imposing Errigal Mountain and the beguiling Poisoned Glen. In Donegal's southwestern corner there are the surfing meccas of Rossnowlagh and Bundoran, as well as the weaving centre of Ardara, where you can observe genuine Irish woollens and tweeds being fashioned in front of your very eyes – and then you can buy them. Near here, through the lovely Glengesh Pass, are the stunning sea cliffs at Slieve League – the tallest in Europe.

2 WEEKS

Belfast to Dublin
The Long Way Round

This tourist trail takes you past some of Ireland's most famous attractions and through spectacular countryside. It's only about 500km in length, so you could manage it in a few days, but what would be the point of rushing? You won't be disappointed on this route.

❶ Belfast (p288)

Start at the mind-blowing Neolithic necropolis at Brú na Bóinne, built before the Great Pyramids were even a twinkle in the Pharaoh's eye. Continue north to Mellifont Abbey, Ireland's first Cistercian abbey, before crossing the border into Northern Ireland. Once you've landed in Belfast, visit Titanic Belfast.

BELFAST ➲ DUNFANAGHY

🚗 **3½ hours** Along A44 & A2, via Derry/Londonderry. 🚌 **3½ hours** Belfast Europa Bus Station to Dunfanaghy, via Derry/Londonderry.

❷ Dunfanaghy (p269)

Go northwest along the Antrim Coast to the Unesco World Heritage site of Giant's Causeway, best enjoyed at sunset but wonderful at any time of the day or year. Be sure to stop off at Bushmill's Distillery, home of one of the finest Irish whiskeys available. Continue through the outskirts of Derry/Londonderry and around the stunning coastline of north Donegal, stopping at gorgeous Dunfanaghy.

DUNFANAGHY ➲ SLIGO

🚗 **Two hours** Along N56 & N15, via Letterkenny. 🚌 **Two hours, 15 minutes** Dunfanaghy to Sligo Institute of Technology, via Donegal Town.

❸ Sligo (p258)

Head south past the mighty sea cliffs of Slieve League and into lively Sligo, from where you can climb the Stone Age passage grave Carrowkeel for panoramic views of Lough Arrow or tee off in the shadow of Benbulben at the simply superb County Sligo Golf Club at Rosses Point.

SLIGO ➲ KENMARE

🚗 **Five hours** Along N17 & N18, via the Burren, to N71.

❹ Kenmare (p202)

Make your way to the southwest via Connemara, visiting at least one of the Aran Islands as you go. Marvel at the Burren and check out some lively traditional music in Doolin before crossing into County Kerry and setting up base in Dingle to explore the Dingle Peninsula. Go through Killarney on

Beara Peninsula (p199)
TRISH PUNCH/GETTY IMAGES ©

⑥ Ardmore (p158)

Explore the often-ignored beauty of County Waterford from the handsome seaside village of Ardmore. Visit Dungarvan Castle and then pay a visit to the Waterford Museum of Treasures. Cross the border into County Wexford and explore the 1798 Rebellion Centre in Enniscorthy. Go northwards through Thomastown and visit medieval Kilkenny.

ARDMORE ➲ DUBLIN

🚗 1½ hours Along M9. 🚌 2½ hours Ormonde Rd, Kilkenny, to Busaras, Dublin. 🚆 Two hours MacDonagh Station, Kilkenny, to Heuston Station, Dublin.

⑦ Dublin (p60)

Visit Castletown House in County Kildare before cutting east through the Wicklow Mountains to visit stunning Glendalough in the middle of Wicklow Mountains National Park. Head back to Dublin and settle in to a well-deserved pint of Guinness in John Mulligan's to toast the end of your Irish adventure.

your way round the Ring of Kerry, and step offshore and into a different century with a visit to Skellig Michael. Make your camp in handsome Kenmare.

KENMARE ➲ CORK

🚗 1½ hours Along R569 & N22. 🚌 Four hours Darcy's in Kenmare to Parnell Place, Cork.

⑤ Cork (p178)

Test the county's foodie credentials by buying some black pudding in Clonakilty and sampling the fine dining in the gourmet capital of Kinsale – a love of seafood is definitely a plus. Wind your way east and explore Ireland's second city, Cork, making sure to pay a visit to the Victorian English Market. From Cork, head east to Midleton for a picnic and a visit to the Old Jameson Distillery.

CORK ➲ ARDMORE

🚗 Two hours, 45 minutes Along N25 via Dungarvan & R676/696.

Month by Month

February

⭐ **Six Nations Rugby**
Ireland, winners of the 2009 Grand Slam, play their three home matches at the Aviva Stadium in the Dublin suburb of Ballsbridge. The season runs from February to April.

✦ **Jameson Dublin International Film Festival**
Most of Dublin's cinemas participate in the country's biggest film festival (www.jdiff.com). This two-week showcase of new films by Irish and international directors features local flicks, arty international films and advance releases of mainstream movies.

March

✦ **St Patrick's Day**
Ireland erupts into one giant celebration on 17 March (www.stpatricksday.ie), but Dublin throws a five-day party around the parade (attended by 600,000 people), involving gigs and festivities that leave the city with a giant hangover.

April

⭐ **Circuit of Ireland International Rally**
Northern Ireland's most prestigious rally race – known locally as the 'Circuit' (www.circuitofireland.net) – sees over 130 competitors throttle and turn through some 550km of Northern Ireland and parts of the Republic over two days at Easter.

(left) March Face-painting, St Patrick's Day
IAN CONNELLAN/GETTY IMAGES ©

☆ Irish Grand National

Ireland loves horse racing, and the race that's loved the most is the Grand National, the showcase of the national hunt season that takes place at Fairyhouse (www.fairyhouseraces.ie) in County Meath on Easter Monday.

☆ World Irish Dancing Championships

There's far more to Irish dancing than Riverdance. Every April, some 4500 competitors from all over the world gather to test their steps and skills against the very best. The location varies from year to year; see www.irishdancingorg.com for details.

May

☆ Cork International Choral Festival

One of Europe's premier choral festivals (www.corkchoral.ie), with the winners going on to the Fleischmann International Trophy Competition. It's held over four days at the beginning of May.

☆ Cathedral Quarter Arts Festival

Belfast's Cathedral Quarter hosts a multidisciplinary arts festival (www.cqaf.com) including drama, music, poetry and street theatre over 10 days at the beginning of the month.

☆ North West 200

Ireland's most famous road race (www.northwest200.org) is also the country's biggest outdoor sporting event; 150,000-plus people line the triangular route to cheer on some of the biggest names in motorcycle racing. Held mid-May.

☆ Fleadh Nua

The third week of May sees the cream of the traditional music crop come to Ennis, County Clare, for one of the country's most important festivals (www.fleadhnua.com).

☆ Listowel Writers' Week

Well-known writers engaged in readings, seminars and storytelling are the attraction at the country's premier festival for bibliophiles (www.writersweek.ie), which runs over five days in the County Kerry town of Listowel at the end of the month. There's also poetry, music and drama.

June

☆ Cat Laughs Comedy Festival

Kilkenny gets very, very funny in early June with the country's premier comedy festival (www.thecatlaughs.com), which draws comedians both known and unknown from the four corners of the globe.

☆ Irish Derby

Wallets are packed and fancy hats donned for the best flat-race festival (www.curragh.ie) in the country, run during the first week of the month.

☆ Bloomsday

Edwardian dress and breakfast of 'the inner organs of beast and fowl' are but two of the elements of the Dublin festival celebrating 16 June, the day on which James Joyce's *Ulysses* takes place. The real highlight is retracing Leopold Bloom's steps.

☆ Mourne International Walking Festival

The last weekend of the month plays host to a walking festival (www.mournewalking.co.uk) in the Mourne Mountains of County Down, designated an Area of Outstanding Natural Beauty.

Oxegen

Ireland's version of Glastonbury (albeit for a younger crowd) is a three-day supergig (www.oxegen.ie) in mid-July at Punchestown Racecourse in County Kildare, featuring some of the big names in dance music and pop.

Killarney Summerfest

From kayaking to street theatre and gigs by international artists, this week-long extravaganza, held in late July, offers something for everybody (www.killarney summerfest.com).

August

Galway Race Week

The biggest horse-racing festival west of the Shannon is not just about the horses, it's also a celebration of Irish culture, sporting gambles and elaborate hats (www.galwayraces.com).

Mary From Dungloe

Ireland's second-most important beauty pageant (www.maryfromdungloe.com) takes place in Dungloe, County Donegal, at the beginning of the month. Although it's an excuse for a giant party, the young women really do want to be crowned the year's 'Mary'.

Féile An Phobail

The name translates simply as the 'people's festival' and it is just that: Europe's largest community arts festival (www.feilebelfast. com) takes place on the Falls Road in West Belfast over two weeks.

Fleadh Cheoil na hÉireann

The mother of all Irish music festivals (www.comhaltas.ie), usually held at the end of the month, attracts in excess of 250,000 music lovers and revellers to whichever town is playing host – there's some great music amid the drinking.

July

Willie Clancy Summer School

Inaugurated to celebrate the memory of a famed local piper, this exceptional festival of traditional music (p237) sees the world's best players show up for gigs, pub sessions and workshops over nine days in Miltown Malbay, County Clare.

Galway Film Fleadh

Irish and international releases make up the program at one of the country's premier film festivals (www.galwayfilm fleadh.com). Held early July.

Galway Arts Festival

Music, drama and other artistic endeavours are on show at Ireland's most important arts festival (www.galwayartsfestival.com), which sees Galway go merriment mad for the last two weeks of the month.

Above: August Galway Race Week
HOLGER LEUE/GETTY IMAGES ©

Puck Fair

Ireland's oldest festival (www.puckfair. ie) is also its quirkiest: crown a goat king and celebrate for three days. Strange idea, brilliant festival that takes place in Killorglin, County Kerry in mid-August.

Rose of Tralee

The Irish beauty pageant sees wannabe Roses plucked from Irish communities throughout the world to compete for the ultimate prize. It's a big party.

September

Galway International Oyster Festival

Over the last weekend of the month Galway kicks off its oyster season with a festival celebrating the local catch (www. galwayoysterfest.com). Music and beer have been the accompaniment since its inception in 1953.

Dublin Fringe Festival

Upwards of 100 different performances take the stage, the street, the bar and the car in the fringe festival (www.fringefest. com) that is unquestionably more innovative than the main theatre festival that follows it.

All-Ireland Finals

The second and fourth Sundays of the month see the finals of the hurling and Gaelic football championships respectively, with 80,000-plus crowds thronging into Dublin's Croke Park for the biggest sporting days of the year.

October

Dublin Theatre Festival

The most prestigious theatre festival (www.dublintheatrefestival.com) in the country sees new work and new versions of old work staged in theatres and venues throughout the capital.

Belfast Festival at Queen's

Northern Ireland's top arts festival (www. belfastfestival.com) attracts performers from all over the world for the second half of the month; on offer is everything from visual arts to dance.

Wexford Opera Festival

Opera fans gather in the Wexford Opera House, which is the country's only theatre built for opera, to enjoy Ireland's premier lyric festival (www.wexfordopera.com). This festival tends to eschew the big hits in favour of showcasing lesser-known works.

Guinness Cork Jazz Festival

Ireland's best-known jazz festival (www. guinnessjazzfestival.com) sees Cork taken over by more than a thousand musicians and their multitude of fans during the last weekend of the month.

December

Christmas

Christmas is a quiet affair in the countryside, though on 26 December (St Stephen's Day) the ancient custom of Wren Boys is re-enacted, most notably in Dingle, County Kerry, when groups of children dress up and go about singing hymns.

Christmas Dip

A traditional Christmas Day swim at the Forty Foot in the Dublin suburb of Sandycove sees a group of very brave swimmers go for a 20m swim to the rocks and back.

What's New

For this new edition of Discover Ireland, our authors hunted down the fresh, the transformed, the hot and the happening. Here are a few of our favourites. For up-to-the-minute recommendations, see lonelyplanet.com/ireland.

1 **REMEMBERING THE TITANIC**
To mark the 2012 centenary of the world's most famous ocean liner, there's a brand new multimedia museum (p289) in Belfast, the city where the *Titanic* was built. Cobh in County Cork, which was the liner's last port of call before disappearing in the north Atlantic, marked the anniversary with the opening of the Titanic Experience (☎ 021-481 4412; www.titanicexperiencecobh.ie; 20 Casement Sq; adult/child €9.50/4.75; ◷ 9am-6pm). It is located in the original office of White Star, the company that owned the *Titanic*.

2 **CROKE PARK SKYLINE, DUBLIN**
The newest part of the Croke Park Experience is the Skyline (www.skyli-necrokepark.ie; Croke Park; adults/students/children €25/20/15; ◷ 11am & 2pm May-Sep, Fri-Sun only Oct-Apr; 🚌 3, 11, 11A, 16, 16A or 123 from O'Connell St), a guided tour around the stadium's roof.

3 **MEDIEVAL MUSEUM, WATERFORD**
The newest of Waterford's trio of museums (known collectively as the Waterford Museum of Treasures) is devoted to exploring the city's 1000-year history. (p152)

4 **GIANT'S CAUSEWAY VISITOR EXPERIENCE**
A new ecofriendly visitor centre dedicated to Northern Ireland's most famous natural attraction. (p304)

5 **CRUMLIN ROAD GAOL, BELFAST**
Belfast's most notorious prison is now a brilliant museum. (p293)

6 **DINGLE BREWING COMPANY**
A new craft brewery in a converted creamery offers guided tours. (p203)

7 **JACKIE CLARKE COLLECTION, BALLINA**
The superb efforts of one extraordinary collector are on display in a new museum, which is housed in a converted 19th-century bank (www.clarkecollection.ie; Pearse St; ◷ 10am-5pm Tue-Sat Apr-Sep, tours 11.30am & 2.30pm).

8 **ATHLONE CASTLE VISITOR CENTRE**
A new visitor centre with an eclectic collection of exhibits. (p236)

9 **CAMPAGNE, KILKENNY**
Garrett Byrne's exquisite restaurant earned itself a well-deserved Michelin star in 2013. (p142)

Get Inspired

📖 Books

○ **Strumpet City** (James Plunkett, 1969) Classic portrayal of Dublin during the 1913 Lockout.

○ **The Butcher Boy** (Patrick McCabe, 1992) Boy retreats into a violent fantasy life as his small-town world collapses.

○ **Paddy Clarke Ha Ha Ha** (Roddy Doyle, 1993) Booker Prize winner about the trials of a Dublin child.

○ **Angela's Ashes** (Frank McCourt, 1996) Pulitzer Prize–winning memoir about working-class Limerick.

○ **Reading in the Dark** (Seamus Deane, 1996) Young Belfast boy's view of growing up during the Troubles.

🎞 Films

○ **Bloody Sunday** (Paul Greengrass, 2002) Superb film about the events of 30 January 1972.

○ **The Dead** (John Huston, 1987) Based on James Joyce's fantastic story *Dubliners*.

○ **Garage** (Lenny Abrahamson, 2007) A lonely man attempts to come out of his shell.

○ **The Crying Game** (Neil Jordan, 1992) This classic explores violence, gender and the IRA.

○ **The Magdalene Sisters** (Peter Mullan, 2002) Harrowing portrayal of life in the infamous asylum.

🎵 Music

○ **The Joshua Tree** (U2) Many's favourite record by the Dublin superstars.

○ **I Do Not Want What I Haven't Got** (Sinead O'Connor) Powerful album by a superb singer.

○ **Becoming a Jackal** (Villagers) The band's knockout debut album.

○ **St Dominic's Preview** (Van Morrison) Lesser known but still brilliant.

○ **Live & Dangerous** (Thin Lizzy) Excellent live album by beloved Irish rockers.

🔖 Websites

○ **Fáilte Ireland** (www.discoverireland.com) The Republic's tourist site has practical info and a huge accommodation database.

○ **Irish Times** (www.irishtimes.com) Ireland's newspaper of record.

○ **Lonely Planet** (www.lonelyplanet.com) Comprehensive travel information and advice.

○ **Northern Ireland Tourism** (www.nitb.com) Official tourist information site, with activities and accommodation.

Short on time?

This list will give you an instant insight into Ireland.

Read *Angela's Ashes* painted a sorry picture of Limerick but did wonders for the author!

Watch *Bloody Sunday*, Paul Greengrass' documentary-style drama, is gripping.

Listen *Becoming a Jackal* is a great record by Conor O'Brien, one of Ireland's top contemporary musicians.

Log on Visit Ireland (www.discoverireland.ie) has everything you need for your Irish holiday.

Marjorie Fitzgibbon's *James Joyce*, Dublin
INGOLF POMPE/GETTY IMAGES ©

●●● Need to Know

Currency
Republic of Ireland: euro (€); Northern Ireland: pound sterling (£)

Languages
English and Irish

Visas
Not required for most citizens of Europe, Australia, NZ, the US and Canada.

Money
ATMs widely available. Chip-and-PIN credit cards accepted almost everywhere except smaller B&Bs.

Mobile Phones
Most foreign phones work in Ireland (beware roaming charges). Local SIM cards cost from €10; SIM and a basic phone from €40.

Wi-Fi
Common in most hotels and some restaurants; generally free. Also free on trains and some private bus services.

Internet Access
Most towns have an internet cafe (€4–8 per hour).

Tipping
Not required, but 10–15% is expected for good service.

When to Go

Warm to hot summers, mild winters

Belfast
GO May–Sep

Dublin
GO any time

Galway
GO May–Sep

Kerry
GO May–Sep

Cork
GO May–Sep

High Season (Jun–Aug)
○ Ireland's weather is at its best.

○ Accommodation rates at their highest (especially August).

○ Tourist peak in Dublin, Kerry, and southern and western coasts.

Shoulder (Easter to end May, mid-Sep to end Oct)
○ Weather often good; sun and rain in May. 'Indian summers' often warm September.

○ Crowds and accommodation rates drop off.

Low Season (Nov–Feb)
○ Reduced opening hours October to Easter; some places shut down.

○ Cold, wet, foggy weather throughout the country.

○ Sights in big cities (Dublin, Cork, Galway, Belfast) operate as normal.

Advance Planning

○ **Two months ahead** Book accommodation and any special activities.

○ **One month ahead** Book your rental car and make reservations for top-end restaurants.

○ **Two weeks ahead** Confirm opening times and prices for visitor attractions.

○ **One week ahead** Check the weather forecast (but plan for it to be wrong).

Your Daily Budget

Budget Less than €60
- Dorm bed: €12–20
- Cheap meal in cafe or pub: €6–12
- Intercity bus travel: €12–25 for 200km journey
- Pint: €4.50–5

Midrange €60–120
- Midrange hotel or B&B: €40–100 (Dublin €60–130) per double room
- Main course in midrange restaurant: €10–18
- Car rental: from €40 per day
- Three-hour train journey: €65

Top End Over €120
- Accommodation in four-star hotel: from €150
- Three-course meal in good restaurant: around €50 per person
- Round of golf at respected course: from €80 midweek

Exchange Rates

Australia	A$1	€0.75
Canada	C$1	€0.71
Japan	¥100	€0.94
New Zealand	NZ$1	€0.57
UK	£1	€1.15
USA	US$1	€0.72

For current exchange rates see www.xe.com.

What to Bring

- **Good walking shoes** Rubber soles and weatherproof uppers an advantage.
- **Rain jacket** It really could rain at any minute.
- **UK/Ireland electrical adaptor** Those three-pin plugs are quite devilish!
- **A good sense of humour** The Irish express affection by making fun of each other – and you.
- **A hollow leg** How else can you last the night in a pub?

Arriving in Ireland

Dublin Airport
Private coach Every 15 minutes to city centre (€7).
Taxi Allow 30–45 minutes to city centre (€20–25).

Dun Laoghaire Ferry Port
Bus Takes about 45 minutes to city centre.
Train DART (suburban rail) About 25 minutes to city centre.

Dublin Port Terminal
Bus Timed to meet arrivals and departures (€2.50).

Getting Around

- **Air** Besides the main hubs, Donegal, Kerry, Knock and Waterford have regional airports.
- **Bus** Bus Éireann has the most extensive network; local operators offer regular – and often cheaper – regional services.
- **Train** The train network is limited and expensive, but the easiest way to travel between major urban centres.
- **Car** Your own car will let you reach those out-of-the-way spots; petrol is expensive and traffic can be challenging.

Accommodation

- **B&Bs** Ubiquitous and varying in standard. Many rural ones accept only cash.
- **Guesthouses** Large family homes with boutique-hotel comfort. Most accept credit cards.
- **Hotels** Ranging from local pubs to five-star castles; priced accordingly. Business chain hotels are clean, comfortable and characterless.

Be Forewarned

- **Public holidays** *Everything* (including pubs) closes on Good Friday and Christmas Day in the Republic. Avoid Northern Ireland on 12 July, the climax of the Loyalist marching season.
- **Pub restrictions** Under 16s aren't allowed in pubs after 7pm, even if accompanied by parents (enforced less strictly in rural areas).
- **Traffic jams** A fact of life in big towns and cities during rush hours.

Dublin

Sultry rather than sexy, Dublin exudes personality as only those who've managed to turn careworn into carefree can. The halcyon days of the Celtic Tiger, when cash cascaded like a free-flowing waterfall, have long since disappeared and the city has once again been forced to grind out a living. But Dubliners still know how to enjoy life. They do so through their music, art and literature – things which Dubs often take for granted but, once reminded, generate immense pride.

There are world-class museums, superb restaurants and the best range of entertainment available anywhere in Ireland – and that's not including the pub, the ubiquitous centre of the city's social life and an absolute must for any visitor. And should you wish to get away from it all, the city has a handful of seaside towns at its edges that make for wonderful day trips.

SEAN CAFFREY/GETTY IMAGES ©

Grafton Street (p91)

JOHN ELK/GETTY IMAGES ©

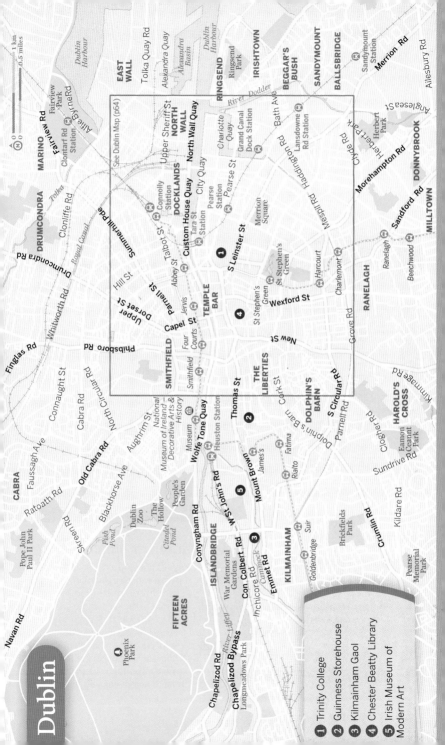

Dublin

0 — 1 km
0 — 0.5 miles

Navan Rd

CABRA

Fausaugh Ave
Ratoath Rd
Skreen Rd

Pope John
Paul II Park

Old Cabra Rd
Blackhorse Ave

Connaught St
North Circular Rd
Cabra Rd

Finglas Rd
Whitworth Rd

DRUMCONDRA
Drumcondra Rd
Clonliffe Rd

Tolka

MARINO

Fairview Rd
Fairview Park
Clontarf Rd
Station

Alfie Byrne Rd

Dublin Harbour

Summerhill Pde
Royal Canal

Phibsboro Rd

Upper Dorset St
Parnell St
Hill St

Capel St

Connolly Station
Talbot St
Abbey St
Custom House Quay
Jervis

Tolka Quay Rd

EAST WALL

Upper Sheriff St
NORTH WALL
North Wall Quay

Alexandra Quay
Alexandra Basin

Dublin Harbour

See Dublin Map (p64)

SMITHFIELD
Four Courts
Smithfield

DOCKLANDS

City Quay
Pearse Station
Tara St Station

Pearse St

TEMPLE BAR ❹

S Leinster St ❶

Merrion Square

River Dodder

Charlotte Quay
Grand Canal Dock Station

Bath Ave

RINGSEND
Ringsend Park

IRISHTOWN

BEGGAR'S BUSH

SANDYMOUNT
Sandymount Station

BALLSBRIDGE
Merrion Rd

Anglesea St
Herbert St
Herbert Park

Lansdowne Rd Station
Haddington Rd
Northumberland Rd
Mespil Rd

DONNYBROOK
Morehampton Rd
Sandford Rd

MILLTOWN

Aylesbury Rd

FIFTEEN ACRES

Phoenix Park ❻

River Liffey

Chapelizod Rd
Chapelizod Bypass
Longmeadows Park

Dublin Zoo
The Hollow
Fish Pond
Citadel Pond

People's Garden

Conyngham Rd

ISLANDBRIDGE
War Memorial Gardens
Con Colbert Rd
Inchicore Rd

KILMAINHAM
Emmet Rd
Camac Rd

National Museum of Ireland – Decorative Arts & History
Museum
Wolfe Tone Quay
Heuston Station

W St John's Rd
Mount Brown ❺

James's
Thomas St ❷

THE LIBERTIES
New St
Cork St

DOLPHIN'S BARN
Dolphin's Barn
Fatima
Rialto
Parnell Rd

Goldenbridge
Suir

Crumlin Rd
Brickfields Park

Sundrive Rd
Eamon Ceannt Park
Clogher Rd

HAROLD'S CROSS
Kimmage Rd

Pearse Memorial Park
Kildare Rd

St Stephen's Green
Wexford St
Harcourt
Charlemont
Grove Rd

RANELAGH
Ranelagh
Beechwood
Charlemont

❶ Trinity College
❷ Guinness Storehouse
❸ Kilmainham Gaol
❹ Chester Beatty Library
❺ Irish Museum of Modern Art

Dublin's Highlights

Trinity College

Ireland's most prestigious university (p60) is also its most beautiful, a 16-hectare masterpiece of Victorian architecture and landscaping. Trinity College was granted its charter in 1592 by Queen Elizabeth I in the hope that the city's youth would not be 'infected with popery', and indeed it remained exclusively Protestant until 1793. No such exclusions exist today, and it now has a reputation as one of the best universities in the world. Regent House entrance, College Green

Guinness Storehouse

For Guinness lovers and those merely curious about Ireland's most famous beer, the Guinness Storehouse (p78) is a must: an old grain silo on the grounds of the brewery has been converted into a multimedia museum devoted to all aspects of the black gold. Not only will you learn the history of the beer, but more importantly you'll learn how to pour it before enjoying a pint.

RICHARD I'ANSON/GETTY IMAGES ©

Kilmainham Gaol

MARTIN MOOS/GETTY IMAGES ©

Ireland's tempestuous and torturous path to independence is vividly documented in the former prison (p92), whose list of (reluctant) residents reads like a roll call of Irish patriots and revolutionaries. A visit here is as close to Irish history as you can get in Dublin, especially when standing in the yard where the leaders of the 1916 Rising were executed.

Chester Beatty Library

The Chester Beatty Library (p71) was originally the private library of its founder, Alfred Chester Beatty; today it is one of Ireland's national cultural icons. A selection of the Library's remarkable treasures is on display in two permanent exhibition galleries, and occasional temporary exhibitions are held throughout the year.

Eastern religions display

Irish Museum of Modern Art

Whatever you happen to think of modern art, a visit to the Irish Museum of Modern Art (p71) in Kilmainham should leave you thoroughly satisfied – if not for the magnificent range of contemporary art hanging on its walls, then for the exquisite surroundings of its building, styled after Les Invalides in Paris. It was also once used as a hospital for veterans.

Dublin's Best…

Places to Eat

○ **Chapter One** Top-rated Irish cuisine. (p86)

○ **Restaurant Patrick Guilbaud** Best in the country? (p84)

○ **Musashi Noodles & Sushi Bar** Superb Japanese. (p85)

○ **Fade Street Social** Fabulous tapas. (p84)

○ **Fumbally Cafe** A beautiful cafe. (p85)

Spots to Wet Your Beak

○ **John Mulligan's** Classic traditional bar. (p86)

○ **Stag's Head** Victorian classic. (p87)

○ **Cobblestone** For fiddles and bodhráns. (p89; p89)

○ **Fallon's** For mixing with Dubliners. (p88)

○ **37 Dawson St** To see and be seen. (p87)

Uniquely Dublin

○ **Bloomsday** Get Edwardian every 16 June. (p43)

○ **Guinness Storehouse** Home of the world's most famous beer. (p78)

○ **Ha'penny Bridge** Get a snap of Dublin's most iconic bridge. (p66)

○ **Little Museum of Dublin** Museum devoted to the city's history. (p70)

○ **St Patrick's Cathedral** Visit Jonathan Swift's tomb. (p70)

Georgian Classics

◦ **Leinster House** Ireland's parliament was once the city's most handsome residence. (p69)

◦ **Custom House** James Gandon's first Irish masterpiece. (p77)

◦ **Four Courts** Gandon's greatest building is an appellant's nightmare. (p75)

◦ **Merrion** The Duke of Wellington's birthplace is now a top hotel. (p81)

◦ **Old Library** Thomas Burgh's masterpiece has a stunning interior. (p60)

Need to Know

ADVANCE PLANNING

◦ **Two months before** Sort out your hotel room.

◦ **Two weeks before** Work on your hollow leg.

◦ **One week before** Make high-end restaurant reservations.

RESOURCES

◦ **Visit Dublin** (www.visitdublin.com) The main event.

◦ **Dublinlinks** (www.dublinks.com) One-stop guide for all manner of goings-on.

◦ **Le Cool** (www.lecool.com/cities/dublin) Listings, reviews and events.

EMERGENCY NUMBERS

◦ **Police, Fire & Ambulance** (☏999)

GETTING AROUND

◦ **Bus** Good for sightseeing; not good for traffic.

◦ **Walk** The easiest way to get around town.

◦ **Cycle** If you're not overly worried about cars.

◦ **Luas** The best way to visit the southern suburbs.

BE FOREWARNED

◦ **Sightseeing** Cut costs on entrance charges and skip the queues with the **Dublin Pass** (www.dublinpass.ie; adult/child 1 day €35/19, 2 day €55/31, 3 day €65/39, 6 day €95/49).

◦ **Restaurants** You'll need to book for top-end establishments.

◦ **Public transport** You'll need exact change if you're getting a bus.

◦ **Rounds system** In the pub, you take it in turns to buy rounds of drinks for your party.

Left: St Patrick's Cathedral (p70);
Above: Four Courts (p75) on the River Liffey

(LEFT) EOIN CLARKE/GETTY IMAGES ©;
(ABOVE) CHARLES BOWMAN/GETTY IMAGES ©

The Dublin Crawl Walking Tour

Dubliners of old would assure their 'bitter halves' that they were 'going to see a man about a dog' before beating a retreat to the nearest watering hole. Treat this walking tour as a sociological study...and with great care!

WALK FACTS

- **Start** Lower Camden St
- **Finish** Crown Alley
- **Distance** 2.5km
- **Duration** One hour to two days

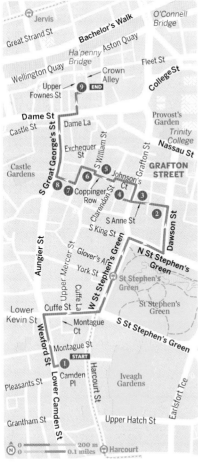

1 Anseo

Start in the always excellent Anseo on Lower Camden St, where hipsters rub shoulders with the hoi polloi and everyone toe-taps to the great bag of DJ tunes.

2 37 Dawson St

Head deep into the city centre and become a character in *Mad Men* at the whiskey bar at the back of Dublin's newest trendy bar, 37 Dawson St (p87).

3 Kehoe's

Sink an equally glorious pint of plain (Guinness) in the snug at South Anne St's Kehoe's (p86), one of the city centre's most atmospheric bars and a must-stop for all visitors to the city.

4 Bruxelles

Find a spot out the front of Bruxelles: the bronze statue of Thin Lizzy's Phil Lynott outside is testament to the bar's reputation as a great spot for rock music.

5 Pygmalion

Directly across the street in the basement of the Powerscourt Townhouse Centre is Pygmalion, the 'in' place with the cool kids for much of 2013.

6 Grogan's Castle Lounge

Discuss the merits of that unwritten masterpiece with a clutch of frustrated writers and artists in Grogan's Castle Lounge (p88) on Castle Market.

7 No Name Bar

A couple of streets away is the appropriately named No Name Bar. Occupying the upstairs floor of an old townhouse, this is one of the city centre's most pleasant and handsome watering holes.

8 Hogan's

At the corner with South Great George's St, Hogan's (p87) has been one of the most popular watering holes in the city for longer than most of its clientele has been alive.

9 Vintage Cocktail Club

Finally, make your way into Temple Bar and ring the doorbell to access the Vintage Cocktail Club, which is upstairs behind a plain steel door on Crown Alley. If you've followed the tour correctly, it's unlikely that you'd now be referring to this guide. How many fingers?

Dublin In...

TWO DAYS

If you only have two days, start with Trinity College (p60) and the Book of Kells before venturing into the Georgian heartland. Amble through St Stephen's Green (p70) and Merrion Square (p83), but be sure to visit the National Museum of Ireland – Archaeology (p67). The next day go west, stopping at the Chester Beatty Library (p71) on your way to the Guinness Storehouse (p78). If you still have legs for it, the Irish Museum of Modern Art (p71) and Kilmainham Gaol (p92) will round off your day perfectly.

FOUR DAYS

Follow the two-day itinerary, but stretch it out by refuelling between stops at some of the city's better pubs. Visit the Dublin City Gallery – The Hugh Lane (p74). Become a whiskey expert at the Old Jameson Distillery (p76) and a literary (or beer) one with a Dublin Literary Pub Crawl (p80). Explore the north side's blossoming foodie scene and dine at Musashi Noodles & Sushi Bar (p85). Oh, and don't forget Temple Bar (p66) – there are distractions there for every taste.

Sculpture by Arnaldo Pomodoro, Trinity College (p60)

SFERA CON SFERA, 1982–3, BRONZE, Ø 200 CM, BERKELEY LIBRARY, TRINITY COLLEGE, UNIVERSITY OF DUBLIN. © ARNALDO POMODORO/ JOHN SONES SINGING BOWL MEDIA/GETTY IMAGES ©

Discover Dublin

Temple Bar (p66)
RICHARD I'ANSON/GETTY IMAGES ©

⊙ Sights

GRAFTON STREET & AROUND

Trinity College   Historic Building
(Map p64; ☏ 01-896 1000; www.tcd.ie; ⊗ 8am-
10pm; ☐ all city centre) FREE This calm and
cordial retreat from the bustle of contemporary Dublin is not just Ireland's most
prestigious **university**, but a throwback to
those far-off days when a university education was the preserve of a very small elite
who spoke passionately of the importance
of philosophy and the need for empire.
Today's alumni are an altogether different
bunch, but Trinity still looks the part, and on
a summer's evening, when the crowds thin
and the chatter subsides, there are few
more delightful places to be.

A great way to see the grounds is
on a **walking tour** (Map p64; ☏ 01-
896 1827; admission €5, incl Book of
Kells €10; ⊗ every 40min 10.15am-
3.40pm Mon-Sat, to 3pm Sun mid-
May–Sep), which depart from
the **Regent House entrance**
on College Green.

Old Library   Library
(Map p64; Library Sq; ☐ all city
centre) To the south of Library
Sq is the Old Library, built in a
rather severe style by Thomas
Burgh between 1712 and 1732.
Despite Ireland's independence, the Library Act of 1801 still
entitles Trinity College Library,
along with four libraries in Britain, to
a free copy of every book published in
the UK. Housing this bounty requires nearly
another 1km of shelving every year and the
collection amounts to around 4.5 million
books. Of course, these cannot all be kept
at the college library, so there are now
additional library storage facilities dotted
around Dublin.

County Dublin

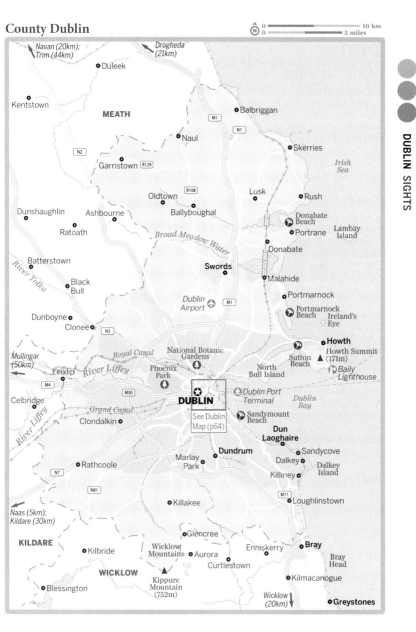

Long Room Notable Building
(Map p64; East Pavilion, Library Colonnades;
adult/student/child €9/8/free; ⏰9.30am-5pm
Mon-Sat year-round, noon-4.30pm Sun Oct-Apr,
9.30am-4.30pm Sun May-Sep; 🚌all city centre)
Trinity's greatest treasures are kept in
the Old Library's stunning 65m Long
Room, which houses about 250,000 of
the library's oldest volumes, including the
breathtaking **Book of Kells**. Your entry
ticket includes admission to temporary
exhibitions on display in the East Pavilion.

Trinity College, Dublin

STEP INTO THE PAST

Ireland's most prestigious university, founded on the order of Queen Elizabeth I in 1592, is an architectural masterpiece, a cordial retreat from the bustle of modern life in the middle of the city. Step through its main entrance and you step back in time, the cobbled stones transporting you to another era, when the elite discussed philosophy and argued passionately in favour of empire.

Standing in Front Square, the 30m-high **Campanile** ❶ is directly in front of you with the **Dining Hall** ❷ to your left. On the far side of the square is the Old Library building, the centrepiece of which is the magnificent **Long Room** ❸, which was the inspiration for the computer- generated imagery of the Jedi Archive in Star Wars Episode II: Attack of the Clones. Here you'll find the university's greatest treasure, the **Book of Kells** ❹. You'll probably have to queue to see this masterpiece, and then only for a brief visit, but it's very much worth it.

Just beyond the Old Library is the very modern **Berkeley Library** ❺, which nevertheless fits perfectly into the campus' overall aesthetic: directly in front of it is the distinctive **Sphere Within a Sphere** ❻, the most elegant of the university's sculptures.

Campanile
Trinity College's most iconic bit of masonry was designed in the mid-19th century by Sir Charles Lanyon; the attached sculptures were created by Thomas Kirk.

Chapel

Main Entrance

DON'T MISS

» Douglas Hyde Gallery, the campus' designated modern art museum.

» Cricket match on pitch, the most elegant of pastimes.

» Pint in the Pavilion Bar, preferably while watching the cricket.

» Visit to the Science Gallery, where science is made completely relevant.

Dining Hall
Richard Cassels' original building was designed to mirror the Examination Hall directly opposite on Front Square: the hall collapsed twice and was rebuilt from scratch in 1761.

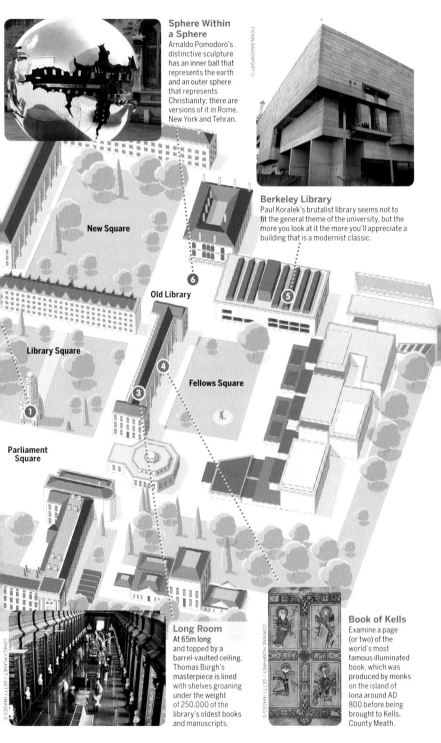

Sphere Within a Sphere
Arnaldo Pomodoro's distinctive sculpture has an inner ball that represents the earth and an outer sphere that represents Christianity; there are versions of it in Rome, New York and Tehran.

FIONN DAVENPORT ©

Berkeley Library
Paul Koralek's brutalist library seems not to fit the general theme of the university, but the more you look at it the more you'll appreciate a building that is a modernist classic.

New Square

Old Library

Library Square

Fellows Square

Parliament Square

Long Room
At 65m long and topped by a barrel-vaulted ceiling, Thomas Burgh's masterpiece is lined with shelves groaning under the weight of 250,000 of the library's oldest books and manuscripts.

LONELY PLANET / GETTY IMAGES ©

CORINNE HUMPHREY / GETTY IMAGES ©

Book of Kells
Examine a page (or two) of the world's most famous illuminated book, which was produced by monks on the island of Iona around AD 800 before being brought to Kells, County Meath.

Dublin

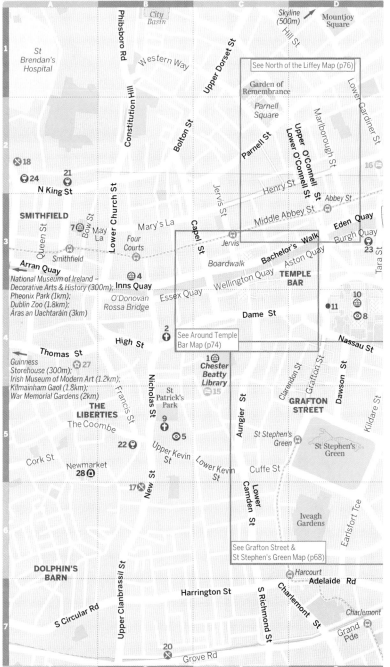

See North of the Liffey Map (p76)

See Around Temple Bar Map (p74)

See Grafton Street & St Stephen's Green Map (p68)

St Brendan's Hospital

Philsboro Rd

City Basin

Skyline (500m)

Mountjoy Square

Hill St

Upper Dorset St

Western Way

Constitution Hill

Bolton St

Garden of Remembrance

Parnell Square

Parnell St

Upper O'Connell St
Lower O'Connell St

Marlborough St

Lower Gardiner St

N King St

Jervis St

Henry St

Abbey St

16

SMITHFIELD

Bow St

May La

Mary's La

Capel St

Jervis

Middle Abbey St

Eden Quay

Burgh Quay

23

Queen St

Lower Church St

Four Courts

Boardwalk

Bachelor's Walk

Aston Quay

Tara St

Smithfield

Arran Quay

National Museum of Ireland –
Decorative Arts & History (300m);
Pheonix Park (1km);
Dublin Zoo (1.8km);
Áras an Uachtaráin (3km)

Inns Quay

O'Donovan Rossa Bridge

Essex Quay

Wellington Quay

TEMPLE BAR

Dame St

10

11

8

High St

Nassau St

Thomas St

Guinness Storehouse (300m);
Irish Museum of Modern Art (1.2km);
Kilmainham Gaol (1.8km);
War Memorial Gardens (2km)

THE LIBERTIES

The Coombe

Francis St

Nicholas St

St Patrick's Park

Chester Beatty Library

15

Clarendon St

Grafton St

Dawson St

Kildare St

GRAFTON STREET

Aungier St

St Stephen's Green

St Stephen's Green

Cork St

Newmarket

Upper Kevin St

Lower Kevin St

Cuffe St

Iveagh Gardens

Earlsfort Tce

DOLPHIN'S BARN

S Circular Rd

Upper Clanbrassil St

New St

Lower Camden St

Harcourt

Adelaide Rd

Harrington St

S Richmond St

Charlemont St

Charlemont

Grand Pde

Grove Rd

18

24

21

7

4

2

27

22

28

17

9

5

1

20

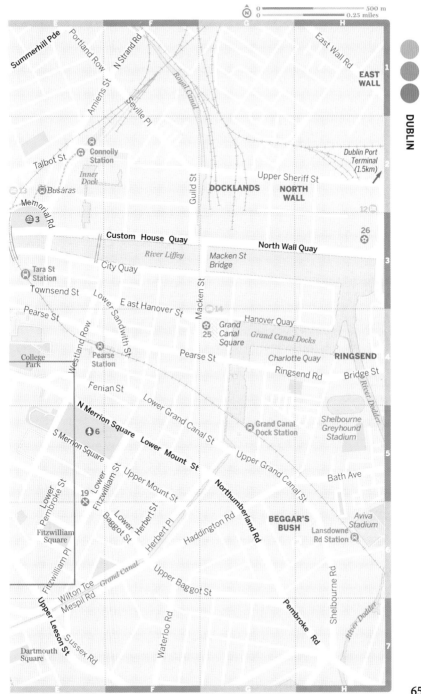

EAST WALL

East Wall Rd

Summerhill Pde

Portland Row

N Strand Rd

Amiens St

Seville Pl

Royal Canal

Talbot St

Connolly Station

Inner Dock

23 Busáras

Memorial Rd

3

Tara St Station

Townsend St

Pearse St

Custom House Quay

City Quay

River Liffey

Lower Sandwith St

East Hanover St

Westland Row

Pearse Station

Fenian St

College Park

S Merrion Square

N Merrion Square

6

Lower Mount St

Lower Pembroke St

19

Lower Fitzwilliam St

Upper Mount St

Herbert St

Fitzwilliam Square

Fitzwilliam Pl

Lower Baggot St

Herbert Pl

Lower Grand Canal St

Upper Grand Canal St

Northumberland Rd

Haddington Rd

Wilton Tce

Mespil Rd

Upper Baggot St

Grand Canal

Upper Leeson St

Sussex Rd

Dartmouth Square

Waterloo Rd

Pembroke Rd

Guild St

DOCKLANDS

Upper Sheriff St

NORTH WALL

Dublin Port Terminal (1.5km)

12

26

North Wall Quay

Macken St Bridge

Macken St

14

25

Grand Canal Square

Hanover Quay

Grand Canal Docks

RINGSEND

Charlotte Quay

Ringsend Rd

Bridge St

River Dodder

Grand Canal Dock Station

Shelbourne Greyhound Stadium

BEGGAR'S BUSH

Lansdowne Rd Station

Aviva Stadium

Bath Ave

Shelbourne Rd

River Dodder

Pembroke Rd

0 ——— 500 m
0 ——— 0.25 miles

Dublin

The ground-floor Colonnades was originally an open arcade, but was enclosed in 1892 to increase the storage area. Other displays include a rare copy of the **Proclamation of the Irish Republic**, which was read out by Pádraig Pearse at the beginning of the Easter Rising in 1916. Also here is the so-called **harp of Brian Ború**, which was definitely not in use when the army of this early Irish hero defeated the Danes at the Battle of Clontarf in 1014. It does, however, date from around 1400, making it one of the oldest harps in Ireland.

Temple Bar   Neighbourhood
(Map p74) Many weekend visitors will barely venture beyond the cobbled borders of Dublin's so-called 'cultural quarter', a maze of streets and alleys sandwiched between Dame St and the Liffey, running from Trinity College to Christ Church Cathedral.

Meeting House Square is one of the real success stories of Temple Bar. On one side is the excellent **Gallery of Photography** (Map p74; www.galleryofphotography.ie; ⊙11am-6pm Mon-Sat; 🚌all city centre) FREE, hosting temporary exhibitions of contemporary local and international photographers. The other side of the square is home to the **National Photographic Archive** (Map p74; ⊙10am-

4.45pm Mon-Sat, noon-4.45pm Sun; 🚌all city centre) FREE, a magnificent resource for anyone interested in a photographic history of Ireland. On Saturdays it hosts a popular **food market**.

Merchant's Arch leads to the **Ha'penny Bridge** (Map p74), named after the ha'penny (half-penny) toll once needed to cross. The **Stock Exchange** (Map p74) is on Anglesea St, in a building dating from 1878.

Dublin Castle   Historic Building
(Map p74; ☎01-677 7129; www.dublincastle.ie; Dame St; adult/child €4.50/2; ⊙10am-4.45pm Mon-Sat, noon-4.45pm Sun; 🚌50, 54, 56a, 77, 77a) If you're looking for a turreted castle straight out of central casting you'll be disappointed; the stronghold of British power in Ireland for 700 years is principally an 18th-century creation that is more hotch-potch palace than medieval castle. Only the **Record Tower** (Map p74), completed in 1258, survives from the original Anglo-Norman fortress commissioned by King John from 1204.

The 45-minute guided tours (departing every 20 to 30 minutes, depending on numbers) are pretty dry, but they're included in the entry fee. You get to visit the State Apartments, many of which are decorated in dubious taste. You will also see St Patrick's Hall, where Irish

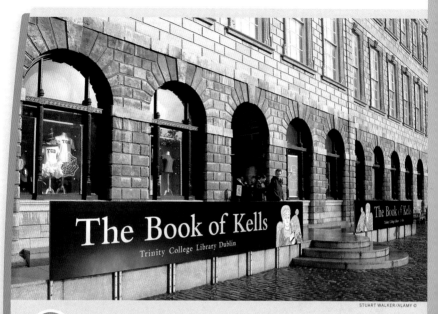

STUART WALKER/ALAMY ©

⭐ Don't Miss
The Book of Kells

More than half a million visitors stop in each year to see Trinity's top show-stopper, the world-famous **Book of Kells**. This illuminated manuscript, dating from around AD 800 and therefore one of the oldest books in the world, was probably produced by monks at St Colmcille's Monastery on the remote island of Iona, off the western coast of Scotland. Repeated looting by marauding Vikings forced the monks to flee to the temporary safety of Kells, County Meath, in AD 806, along with their masterpiece. Around 850 years later, the book was brought to the college for safekeeping and has remained here since.

To really appreciate the book, you can buy your own reproduction copy for a mere €22,000. Failing that, the library bookshop stocks a plethora of souvenirs and other memorabilia, including Otto Simm's excellent *Exploring the Book of Kells* (€12.95), a thorough guide with attractive colour plates, and a popular DVD-ROM (€31.95) showing all 800 pages. Kids looking for something a little less stuffy might enjoy the animated *Secret of Kells* (2009), which is more fun than accurate in its portrayal of how the gospel was actually put together.

NEED TO KNOW

Map p64; Long Room, East Pavilion, Library Colonnades; adult/student/child €9/8/free; ⊘9.30am-5pm Mon-Sat year-round, noon-4.30pm Sun Oct-Apr, 9.30am-4.30pm Sun May-Sep; 🖵all city centre)

presidents are inaugurated and foreign dignitaries toasted, and the room in which the wounded James Connolly was tied to a chair while convalescing after the 1916 Easter Rising – brought back to health to be executed by firing squad.

National Museum of Ireland – Archaeology   Museum

(Map p68; www.museum.ie; Kildare St; ⊘10am-5pm Tue-Sat, 2-5pm Sun; 🖵all city centre) FREE
The mother of Irish museums and the country's most important cultural institu-

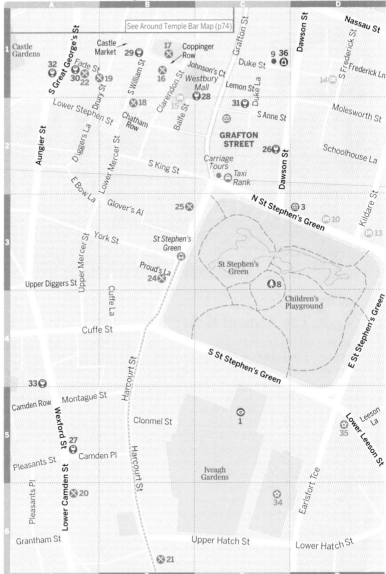

tion was established in 1977 as the primary repository of archaeological treasures. The collection, however, has expanded beyond the walls of this superb, purpose-built building next to the Irish parliament into three other separate museums – the

stuffed beasts of the Museum of Natural History (p69), the decorative arts section at **Collins Barracks** and a **country life museum** (www.museum.ie; off N5, Turlough Park; ☺10am-5pm Tue-Sat, 2-5pm Sun) **FREE** in County Mayo, on Ireland's west coast.

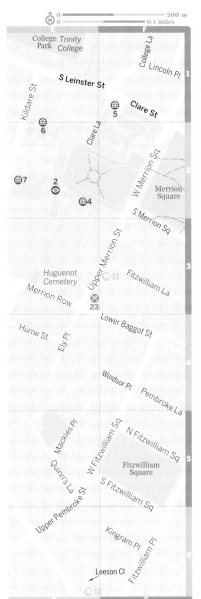

prehistoric and Viking artefacts, and a few interesting items relating to Ireland's fight for independence.

National Gallery
Museum

(Map p68; www.nationalgallery.ie; West Merrion Sq; ☺9.30am-5.30pm Mon-Wed, Fri & Sat, to 8.30pm Thu, noon-5.30pm Sun; ☐7 & 44 from city centre) **FREE** A magnificent Caravaggio and a breathtaking collection of works by Jack B Yeats – William Butler's younger brother – are the main reasons to visit the National Gallery, but not the only ones. Its excellent collection is strong in Irish art, but there are also high-quality collections of every major European school of painting. There are free tours at 3pm on Saturdays and at 2pm, 3pm and 4pm on Sundays.

Leinster House
Notable Building

(Oireachtas Éireann; Map p68; ☏tour information 01-618 3271; www.oireachtas.ie; Kildare St; ☺observation gallery 2.30-8.30pm Tue, 10.30am-8.30pm Wed, to 5.30pm Thu Nov-May, tours 10.30am, 11.30am, 2.30pm & 3.30pm Mon-Fri when parliament is in session; ☐all city centre) All the big decisions are made – or rubber-stamped – at Oireachtas Éireann (Irish Parliament). This magnificent Palladian mansion was built as a city residence for James Fitzgerald, the Duke of Leinster and Earl of Kildare, by Richard Cassels between 1745 and 1748 – hence the name by which it's still known. Its Kildare St facade looks like a townhouse (which inspired Irish architect James Hoban's designs for the US White House), whereas the Merrion Sq frontage was made to resemble a country mansion.

Museum of Natural History
Museum

(National Museum of Ireland – Natural History; Map p68; www.museum.ie; Merrion St; ☺10am-5pm Tue-Sat, 2-5pm Sun; ☐7 & 44 from city centre) **FREE** Dusty, weird and utterly compelling, this window into Victorian times has barely changed since Scottish explorer Dr David Livingstone opened it in 1857 – before disappearing into the African jungle for a meeting with Henry Stanley. Compared to the multimedia-this and interactive-that of virtually every

They're all fascinating, but the star attractions are all here, mixed up in Europe's finest collection of Bronze and Iron Age gold artefacts, the most complete collection of medieval Celtic metalwork in the world, fascinating

Grafton Street & St Stephen's Green

COLIN PALMER PHOTOGRAPHY/ALAMY ©

Don't Miss
Chester Beatty Library

This world-famous library, in the grounds of Dublin Castle, houses the collection of mining engineer Sir Alfred Chester Beatty (1875–1968), bequeathed to the Irish State on his death. And we're immensely grateful for Chester's patronage: spread over two floors, the breathtaking collection includes more than 20,000 manuscripts, rare books, miniature paintings, clay tablets, costumes and other objects of artistic, historical and aesthetic importance.

NEED TO KNOW
Map p64; ☎01-407 0750; www.cbl.ie; Dublin Castle; ⏰10am-5pm Tue-Fri, 11am-5pm Sat, 1-5pm Sun year-round, 10am-5pm Mon May-Sep, free tours 1pm Wed, 3pm & 4pm Sun; 🚌50, 51B, 77, 78A or 123

Christ Church Cathedral Cathedral (Church of the Holy Trinity; Map p64; www.cccdub. ie; Christ Church Pl; adult/child €6/2; ⏰9.30am-5pm Mon-Sat & 12.30-2.30pm Sun year-round, longer hours Jun-Aug; 🚌50, 50A or 56A from Aston Quay, 54 or 54A from Burgh Quay) Its hilltop location and eye-catching flying buttresses make this the most photogenic by far of Dublin's three cathedrals as well as one of the capital's most recognisable symbols.

Throughout much of its history, Christ Church vied for supremacy with nearby St Patrick's Cathedral but it also fell on hard times in the 18th and 19th centuries (earlier, the nave had been used as a market and the crypt had housed taverns) and was virtually derelict by the time restoration took place. Today, both Church of Ireland cathedrals are outsiders in a largely Catholic nation.

Irish Museum of Modern Art   Museum
(IMMA; www.imma.ie; Military Rd; ⏰10am-5.30pm Tue & Thu-Sat, 10.30am-5.30pm Wed, noon-5.30pm Sun, tours 2.30pm Tue-Sun, noon Sat; 🚌Heuston) FREE Ireland's most important

71

National Museum of Ireland

NATIONAL TREASURES

Ireland's most important cultural institution is the National Museum, and its most important branch is the original one, housed in this fine neoclassical (or Victorian Palladian) building designed by Sir Thomas Newenham Deane and finished in 1890. Squeezed in between the rear entrance of Leinster House – the Irish parliament – and a nondescript building from the 1960s, it's easy to pass by the museum. But within its fairly cramped confines you'll find the most extensive collection of Bronze and Iron Age gold artefacts in Europe and the extraordinary collection of the Treasury. This includes the stunning **Ardagh Chalice** ❶ and the delicately crafted **Tara Brooch** ❷. Amid all the lustre, look out for the **Broighter Gold Collar** ❸ and the impressively crafted **Loughnashade War Trumpet** ❹, both extraordinary examples of Celtic art. Finally, pay a visit to the exquisite **Cross of Cong** ❺, which was created after the other pieces but is just as beautiful.

As you visit these treasures – all created after the arrival of Christianity in the 5th century – bear in mind that they were produced with the most rudimentary of instruments.

LUNCH BREAK

Enjoy homemade pasta along with a nice glass of Italian red at the very authentic Dunne & Crescenzi (14–16 South Frederick St), or a pancake on the go from Lemon (Dawson St).

First Floor

Ground Floor

Main Entrance

VIKING DUBLIN

Archaeological excavations in Dublin between 1961 and 1981 unearthed evidence of a Viking town and cemeteries along the banks of the River Liffey. The graves contained weapons such as swords and spears, together with jewellery and personal items. Craftsmen's tools, weights and scales, silver ingots and coins show that the Vikings, as well as marauding and raiding, were also engaged in commercial activities. The Viking artefacts are now part of the National Museum's collection.

Cross of Cong
Made in 1123 to encase a fragment of the True Cross that was touring the country at the time, it was kept by the Augustinian monks at their friary in Cong, County Galway. The exquisite gold filigree on both the front and back are testament to the important role the cross was designed to have.

NATIONAL MUSEUM OF IRELAND ©

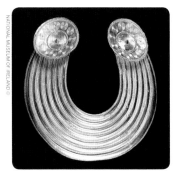

Broighter Gold Collar
The most exquisite element of the larger Broighter Hoard, this beautiful gold neck ornament (called a torc) is decorated in the elaborate curved patterns of high Celtic art, called La Tène style.

Tara Brooch
Designed around AD 700 as a clasp for a cloak, this is the second superstar of the collection – its delicate craftsmanship has become a symbol of the excellence of Irish art.

③
② ①
⑤   ④

Loughnashade War Trumpet
One of four bronze trumpets found in a dried-up lake in County Armagh, this magnificent war trumpet is a masterpiece of skilled riveting; the bell-end is beautifully decorated in a lotus-bud motif, and the sound it made terrified all who heard it.

Ardagh Chalice
Made of gold, silver, bronze, brass, copper and lead, the 12th-century Ardagh Chalice is the finest example of Celtic art ever found.

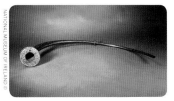

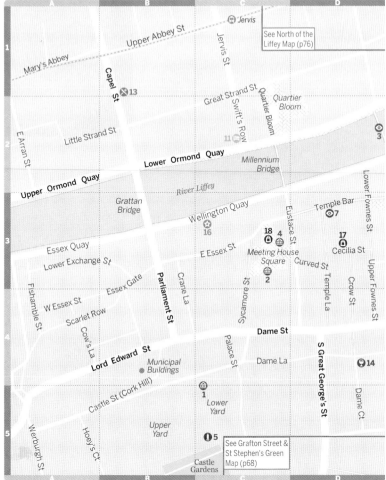

collection of modern and contemporary Irish art is housed in the elegant, airy expanse of the Royal Hospital at Kilmainham, which in 1991 became a magnificent exhibition space and was almost completely refurbished in 2012–13.

There are free guided tours (2.30pm Wednesday, Friday and Sunday) of the museum's exhibits throughout the year, but we strongly recommend the free seasonal heritage tours (50 minutes) of the building itself, which run from July to September.

NORTH OF THE LIFFEY

Dublin City Gallery – The Hugh Lane
Gallery

(Map p76; ☎ 01-222 5550; www.hughlane.ie; 22 North Parnell Sq; ☺ 10am-6pm Tue-Thu, to 5pm Fri & Sat, 11am-5pm Sun; ☲ 3, 7, 10, 11, 13, 16, 19, 46A, 123) **FREE** Whatever reputation Dublin has as a repository of world-class art has a lot to do with the simply stunning collection at this exquisite gallery, housed in the equally impressive Charlemont House, designed by William Chambers in 1763.

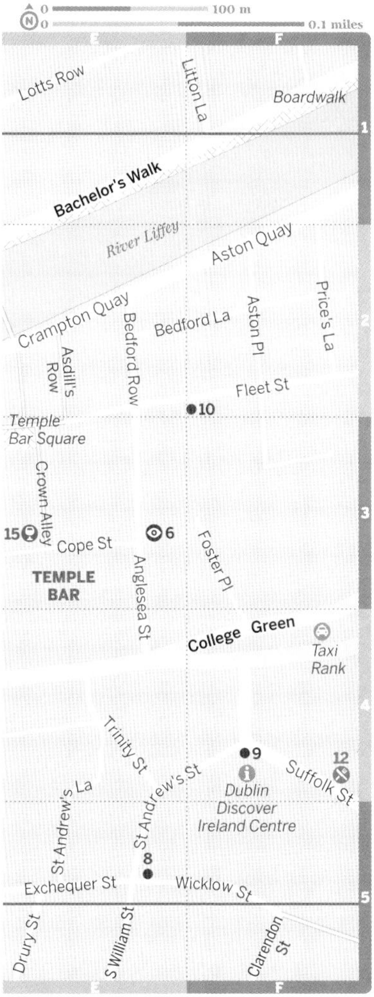

Around Temple Bar

Sights

1	Dublin Castle	C5
2	Gallery of Photography	C3
3	Ha'penny Bridge	D2
4	National Photographic Archive	C3
5	Record Tower	C5
6	Stock Exchange	E3
7	Temple Bar	D3

Activities, Courses & Tours

8	1916 Rebellion Walking Tour	E5
9	Dublin Bus Tours	F4
10	Dublin Musical Pub Crawl	F2

Sleeping

11	Morrison Hotel	C2

Eating

12	Avoca	F4
13	Musashi Noodles & Sushi Bar	B1

Drinking & Nightlife

14	Stag's Head	D4
15	Vintage Cocktail Club	E3

Entertainment

16	Workman's Club	C3

Shopping

	Avoca Handweavers	(see 12)
17	Claddagh Records	D3
18	Temple Bar Farmers Market	C3

A modernist extension, which opened in 2006, has seen the addition of 13 bright galleries spread across three floors of the old National Ballroom.

The collection (known as the **Hugh Lane Bequest 1917**) was split in a complicated 1959 settlement that sees some of the paintings moving back and forth. The conditions of the exchanges are in the midst of negotiation, but for now the gallery has Manet's *La Musique Aux Tuileries*, Degas' *Bains de Mer*, and *Lavacourt under Snow* by Monet.

Impressionist masterpieces notwithstanding, the gallery's most popular exhibit is the **Francis Bacon Studio**, which was painstakingly moved, in all its shambolic mess, from 7 Reece Mews, South Kensington, London, where the Dublin-born artist (1909–92) lived for 31 years.

Four Courts Historic Building

(Map p64; Inns Quay; 9am-5pm Mon-Fri; 25, 66, 67 or 90 from city centre, Four Courts)

FREE This masterpiece of James Gandon (1743–1823) is a mammoth complex stretching 130m along Inns Quay, as fine an example of Georgian public architecture as there is in Dublin. Despite the construction of a brand new criminal courts building further west along the Liffey, the Four Courts is still the enduring symbol of Irish law going about its daily business.

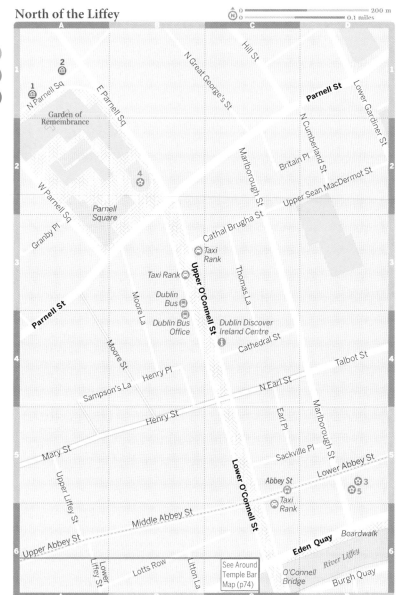

Old Jameson Distillery Museum
(Map p64; www.jamesonwhiskey.com; Bow St;
adult/child €14/7.70; ☉9am-6pm Mon-Sat,
10am-6pm Sun; ☐ 25, 66, 67 or 90 from city
centre, ☐ Smithfield) Smithfield's biggest
draw is devoted to *uisce beatha* (*ish*-kuh

ba-ha, 'the water of life'), the Irish for
whiskey. To its more serious devotees,
that is precisely what whiskey is, although
they may be put off by the slickness of
the museum (occupying part of the old
distillery that stopped production in

North of the Liffey

1971), which shepherds visitors through a compulsory tour of the re-created factory (the tasting at the end is a lot of fun) and into the ubiquitous gift shop.

National Museum of Ireland – Decorative Arts & History
Museum

(www.museum.ie; Benburb St; ☉10am-5pm Tue-Sat, 2-5pm Sun; 🚌25, 66, 67 or 90 from city centre, 🚋Smithfield) **FREE** Once the world's largest military barracks, this splendid early neoclassical grey-stone building on the Liffey's northern banks is now home to the Decorative Arts & History collection of the National Museum of Ireland.

Inside the imposing exterior lies a treasure trove of artefacts ranging from silver, ceramics and glassware to weaponry, furniture and folk-life displays – and an exquisite exhibition dedicated to iconic Irish designer **Eileen Gray** (1878–1976). Some of the best pieces are gathered in the **Curator's Choice** exhibition, which is a collection of 25 objects hand-picked by different curators, and displayed alongside an account of why they were chosen.

DOCKLANDS

Custom House
Museum

(Map p64; ☉10am-5pm Mon-Fri, 2-5pm Sat & Sun; 🚌all city centre) Georgian genius James Gandon (1743–1823) announced his arrival on the Dublin scene with this magnificent building (1781–91), constructed just past Eden Quay at a wide stretch in the River Liffey. It's a colossal, neoclassical pile that stretches for 114m topped by a copper dome, beneath which the **Visitor Centre** (Custom House Quay; admission €1; ☉10am-12.30pm Mon-Fri, 2-5pm Sat & Sun mid-Mar–Oct, closed Mon-Tue & Sat Nov–mid-Mar) features a small museum on Gandon and the history of the building.

View along the River Liffey

RICHARD I'ANSON/GETTY IMAGES ©

Don't Miss
Guinness Storehouse

This beer-lover's Disneyland is a multimedia homage to the country's most famous export and the city's most enduring symbol. More than any beer produced anywhere in the world, Guinness has transcended its own brand and is considered a substance with near spiritual qualities, at least by its legions of devotees the world over.

www.guinness-storehouse.com

St James's Gate, South Market St

adult/student/child €16.50/10.50/6.50, Conoisseur Experience €25, discounts apply for online bookings

⊙9.30am-5pm Sep-Jun, to 7pm Jul-Aug

🚌21a, 51b, 78, 78a or 123 from Fleet St, 🚉St James's

Martello Tower, Sandycove

They halted while Haines surveyed the tower and said at last:
-- Rather bleak in wintertime, I should say. Martello you call it?
Billy Pitt had them built, Buck Mulligan said, when the French were on the sea. But ours is the omphalos.

Grain Storehouse & Brewery

The old grain storehouse, the only part of the massive, 26-hectare St James's Gate Brewery open to the public, is a suitable cathedral in which to worship the black gold; shaped like a giant pint of Guinness, it rises seven impressive storeys high around a stunning central atrium. At the top is the head, represented by the Gravity Bar, with a panoramic view of Dublin. Immediately below it is the brewery itself, founded in 1759 by Arthur Guinness and once the employer of over 5000 people: the gradual shift to greater automatisation has reduced the workforce to around 300.

The Perfect Pour

As you work your way to the top and your prize of arguably the nicest Guinness you could drink anywhere, you'll explore the various elements that made the beer the brand that it is and perhaps understand a little better the efforts made by the company to ensure its quasi-mythical status. From the (copy of) the original 9000-year lease (in a glass box embedded in the ground floor) to the near-scientific lesson in how to pour the perfect pint, everything about this place is designed to make you understand that Guinness isn't just any other beer.

Arthur Guinness

One fun fact you will learn is that genius can be inadvertent: at some point in the 18th century, a London brewer accidentally burnt his hops while brewing ale, and so created the dark beer we know today. It's name of 'porter' came because the dark beer was very popular with London porters. In the 1770s, Arthur Guinness, who had until then only brewed ale, started brewing the dark stuff to get a jump on all other Irish brewers. By 1799 he decided to concentrate all his efforts on this single brew. He died four years later, aged 83, but the foundations for world domination were already in place.

Local Knowledge

Guinness Storehouse

BY MARK MCGOVERN,
MEDIA RELATIONS MANAGER
AT THE GUINNESS STOREHOUSE

1 **GUINNESS ACADEMY**
Visitors on this tour are offered a hands-on experience as they are invited behind the bar and taught the six-step guide to how to pour the perfect pint of Guinness.

2 **TASTING ROOMS**
Guinness has four distinct aromas. There's two kinds of barley smell: roasted and malted, with the latter having a sweet, biscuity aroma. The bitterness comes from hops, while the 'beer' smell is yeast, which is present in all beers. The four aromas are emitted by the columns in the Guinness White Room – and you'll also understand why it's important to drink Guinness *through* the head (so many sip the head and then drink the darker stuff at the bottom.

3 **GUINNESS FIVE**
Guinness doesn't have to be enjoyed in purely liquid form. On the third floor, you'll learn about the various dishes that use the beloved beer, from the well-known beef and Guinness stew to more surprising dishes such as mussels in a Guinness cream sauce and even a Guinness chocolate mousse.

4 **GUINNESS HISTORY & ADVERTISING**
The fourth floor is home to the Guinness Archive, where visitors can trace the family trees and genealogy of over 20,000 employees of the company dating back to 1870. Also on display is the first Guinness Book of Records and the iconic ads that made the company famous.

5 **GRAVITY BAR**
It's hard to beat the stunning views of the city from the rooftop Gravity Bar – but what makes it a really special experience is the glass of perfectly poured Guinness that accompanies it.

If You Like...
Libraries

If you enjoy the collections at the Chester Beatty Library (p71) and Trinity College's Old Library (p60), you should check out the following repositories of the written word.

1 DUBLIN WRITERS MUSEUM
(Map p76; www.writersmuseum.com; 18 North Parnell Sq; adult/child €7.50/4.70; ⊙10am-5pm Mon-Sat, 11am-5pm Sun; ⬚3, 7, 10, 11, 13, 16, 19, 46A, 123) Interesting collection of vaguely literary ephemera associated with some of the city's most recognisable names (Samuel Beckett's phone; Brendan Behan's union card).

2 MARSH'S LIBRARY
(Map p64; www.marshlibrary.ie; St Patrick's Close; adult/child €2.50/free; ⊙9.30am-1pm & 2-5pm Mon & Wed-Fri, 10am-1pm Sat; ⬚50, 50A or 56A from Aston Quay, 54 or 54A from Burgh Quay) Ireland's oldest extant library with over 25,000 ancient books, rare manuscripts and precious tomes.

3 NATIONAL LIBRARY
(Map p68; www.nli.ie; Kildare St; ⊙9.30am-9pm Mon-Wed, 10am-5pm Thu & Fri, to 1pm Sat; ⬚all city centre) The National Library's beautiful reading room features in James Joyce's *Ulysses*.

Tours

A plethora of tours offer a range of exploring options; you can walk (or crawl, if you opt for a drinking tour), get a bus or hop aboard an amphibious vehicle. There are lots of themed tours too, while some companies will combine a city tour with trips further afield. You'll save a few euros booking online.

1916 Rebellion Walking Tour
Walking Tour

(Map p74; ☎086 858 3847; www.1916rising.com; 23 Wicklow St; per person €12; ⊙11.30am Mon-Sat, 1pm Sun Mar-Oct) Superb two-hour tour starting in the International Bar, Wicklow St. Lots of information, humour and irreverence to boot. The guides – all Trinity graduates – are uniformly excellent and will not say no to the offer of a pint back in the International at tour's end.

Dublin Literary Pub Crawl
Walking Tour

(Map p68; ☎01-670 5602; www.dublin-pubcrawl.com; 9 Duke St; adult/student €12/10; ⊙7.30pm daily Apr-Oct, 7.30pm Thu-Sun Nov-Mar) A tour of pubs associated with famous Dublin writers is a sure-fire recipe for success, and this 2½-hour tour/performance by two actors – which includes them acting out the funny bits – is a riotous laugh. There's plenty of drink taken, which makes it all the more popular. It leaves from the Duke on Duke St; get there by 7pm to reserve a spot for the evening tour.

Dublin Musical Pub Crawl
Walking Tour

(Map p74; ☎01-478 0193; www.discoverdublin.ie; Oliver St John Gogarty's, 58-59 fleet St; adult/student €12/10; ⊙7.30pm daily Apr-Oct, 7.30pm Thu-Sat Nov-Mar) The story of Irish traditional music and its influence on contemporary styles is explained and demonstrated by two expert musicians in a number of Temple Bar pubs over 2½ hours. Tours meet upstairs in the Oliver St John Gogarty pub and are highly recommended.

Sleeping

GRAFTON STREET & AROUND

Trinity Lodge
Guesthouse €

(Map p68; ☎01-617 0900; www.trinitylodge.com; 12 South Frederick St; s/d from €56/70; ⏜; ⬚all city centre, ⬚St Stephen's Green) Martin Sheen's grin greets you upon entering this cosy, award-winning guesthouse, which he declared his favourite spot for an Irish stay. Marty's not the only one: this place is so popular that they've added a second townhouse across the road, which has also been kitted out to the highest standards. Room 2 of the original house has a lovely bay window.

Radisson Blu Royal Hotel Hotel €€
(Map p64; ☎01-898 2900; www.radissonblu.ie/royalhotel-dublin; Golden Lane; r €110-220; @ 📶; 🚌all city centre, 🚊St Stephen's Green) Our favourite hotel in this price range is an excellent example of how sleek lines and muted colours combine beautifully with luxury, ensuring a memorable night's stay. From hugely impressive public areas to sophisticated bedrooms – each with flat-screen digital TV embedded in the wall to go along with all the other little touches – this hotel will not disappoint.

Cliff Townhouse Guesthouse €€
(Map p68; ☎01-638 3939; www.thecliff townhouse.com; 22 St Stephen's Green North; r from €99; @ 📶; 🚌all city centre, 🚊St Stephen's Green) As *pied-à-terres* go, this is a doozy: there are 10 exquisitely appointed bedrooms spread across a wonderful Georgian property whose best views overlook St Stephen's Green. Downstairs is Sean Smith's superb restaurant **Cliff Townhouse** (Map p68; ☎01-638 3939; www.thecliff townhouse.com; 22 North St Stephen's Green; mains €19-35; ⏰noon-2.30pm & 6-11pm Mon-Sat, noon-4pm & 6-10pm Sun; 🚌all city centre).

Number 31 Guesthouse €€€
(Map p68; ☎01-676 5011; www.number31.ie; 31 Leeson Close; s/d/tr incl breakfast €180/260/300; 📶; 🚌all city centre) The city's most distinctive property is the former home of modernist architect Sam Stephenson, who successfully fused '60s style with 18th-century grace. Its 21 bedrooms are split between the retro coach house, with its fancy rooms, and the more elegant Georgian house, where rooms are individually furnished with tasteful French antiques and big comfortable beds.

Gourmet breakfasts with kippers, homemade breads and granola are served in the conservatory. Yeah, baby!

Merrion Hotel €€€
(Map p68; ☎01-603 0600; www.merrionhotel.com; Upper Merrion St; r/ste from €485/995; @ 📶 🏊; 🚌all city centre) This resplendent five-star hotel, in a terrace of beautifully restored Georgian townhouses, opened in 1988 but looks like it's been around a lot

Georgian house, Merrion Square (p83)

TRAVEL INK/GETTY IMAGES ©

Detour:
Phoenix Park

Dubliners are rightly proud of this humungous **park** (www.phoenixpark.ie; ⊙24hr; 🚌10 from O'Connell St, 25 or 26 from Middle Abbey St then Phoenix Park Shuttle Bus from Parkgate St entrance) **FREE** at the northwestern edge of the city centre, a short skip from Heuston Station and the Liffey quays. The hugely impressive 709 hectares that comprise the park make up one of the largest set of inner-city green lungs in the world. To put it into perspective, it dwarfs the measly 337 hectares of New York's Central Park and is larger than all of the major London parks put together. The park is home to the residence of the Irish president, **Áras an Uachtaráin** (Phoenix Park; ⊙guided tours hourly 10am-4pm Sat; 🚌10 from O'Connell St, 25 & 26 from Middle Abbey St) **FREE**, as well as the American ambassador and a shy herd of fallow deer who are best observed – from a distance – during the summer months. It is also where you'll find Europe's oldest **zoo** (www.dublinzoo.ie; Phoenix Park; adult/child/family €16/11.50/45.50; ⊙9.30am-6pm Mar-Sep, to dusk Oct-Feb; 🚌10 from O'Connell St, 25 & 26 from Middle Abbey St), not to mention dozens of playing fields for all kinds of sport. How's that for a place to stretch your legs?

Chesterfield Ave runs northwest through the length of the park from the Parkgate St entrance to the Castleknock Gate. Near the Parkgate St entrance is the 63m-high **Wellington Monument** obelisk, completed in 1861. Nearby is the **People's Garden**, which dates from 1864, and the bandstand in the Hollow. Across Chesterfield Ave from the Áras an Uachtaráin – and easily visible from the road – is the massive **Papal Cross**, which marks the site where Pope John Paul II preached to 1¼ million people in 1979. In the centre of the park the **Phoenix Monument**, erected by Lord Chesterfield in 1747, looks so unlike a phoenix that it's often referred to as the Eagle Monument.

Bus No 10 from O'Connell St or bus Nos 25 or 26 from Middle Abbey St will get you here. The best way to get around the park is via the **Phoenix Park Shuttle Bus** (adult/child €2/1; ⊙hourly 7am-5pm Mon-Fri, 10am-5pm Sat & Sun), which goes from just outside the Parkgate St gate.

longer. Try to get a room in the old house (with the largest private art collection in the city), rather than the newer wing, to sample its truly elegant comforts.

Located opposite Government Buildings, its marble corridors are patronised by politicos, visiting dignitaries and the odd celeb. Even if you don't stay, come for the superb afternoon tea (€36), with endless cups of tea served out of silver pots by a raging fire.

Westbury Hotel   Hotel €€€
(Map p68; ☎01-679 1122; www.doylecollection. com; Grafton St; r/ste from €199/299; @ 🛜; 🚌all city centre) Visiting celebs looking for some quiet time have long favoured the

Westbury's elegant suites, where they can watch TV from the Jacuzzi before retiring to a four-poster bed. Mere mortals tend to make do with the standard rooms, which are comfortable enough but lack the sophisticated grandeur promised by the luxurious public spaces – which are a great spot for an afternoon drink.

Shelbourne   Hotel €€€
(Map p68; ☎01-676 6471; www.theshelbourne.ie; 27 St Stephen's Green North; r from €220; @ 🛜; 🚌all city centre, 🚊St Stephen's Green) Dublin's most iconic hotel, founded in 1824, was bought out by the Marriott group, who spent a ton of money restoring its rooms and public spaces to their former

grandeur, a few years ago. The refurb was successful, but their management style has been criticised as being somewhat short of its five-star reputation.

NORTH OF THE LIFFEY

Morrison Hotel
Hotel €€€

(Map p74; ☏ 01-887 2400; www.morrison hotel.ie; Ormond Quay; r from €199; @ 🛜; ⌨ all city centre, 🚇 Jervis) A buyout by Russian billionaire Elena Baturina has breathed new life into this quayside hotel, courtesy of a €7m refurbishment that has seen the rooms given a contemporary makeover and the already elegant public spaces a facelift. King-size beds (with Serta mattresses), 40" LED TVs, free wi-fi and Crabtree & Evelyn toiletries are just some of the hotel's offerings.

Townhouse Hotel
Inn €€€

(Map p64; ☏ 01-878 8808; www.townhouse-ofdublin.com; 47-48 Lower Gardiner St; s/d/tr €140/199/219; ⌨ 36 or 36A, 🚇 Connolly) The ghostly writing of Irish-Japanese author Lafcadio Hearn may have influenced the Gothic-style interior of his former home. A dark-walled, gilt-framed foyer with jingling chandelier leads into 82 individually designed comfy (but cramped) rooms. It shares a dining room with the **Globetrotters Tourist Hostel** (Map p64; ☏ 01-878 8088; www.globetrottersdublin.com; 46-48 Lower Gardiner St; dm €16; ⌨ all city centre, 🚇 Connolly) next door.

DOCKLANDS

Gibson Hotel
Hotel €€

(Map p64; ☏ 01-618 5000; www.thegibsonhotel. ie; Point Village; r from €120; @ 🛜; ⌨ 151 from city centre, 🚇 Grand Canal Dock) Built for business travellers and out-of-towners taking in a gig at the O2 next door, the Gibson is undoubtedly impressive: 250-odd ultramodern rooms decked out in snazzy Respa beds, flat-screen TVs and internet work stations. The public areas are bright, big and airy – lots of muted colours and floor-to-ceiling glass – and you might catch last night's star act having breakfast the next morning.

If You Like...
Gardens

If you like the bucolic charms of St Stephen's Green, you'll enjoy these other bits of greenery.

1 IVEAGH GARDENS
(Map p68; ⏱ dawn-dusk year-round; ⌨ all city centre, 🚇 St Stephen's Green) Behind the walls is one of the city centre's loveliest spots to relax in on a summer's day.

2 MERRION SQUARE
(Map p64; ⏱ dawn-dusk; ⌨ 7 & 44 from city centre) Beautifully tended flower beds and carefully sculpted shrubbery in this elegant square.

3 WAR MEMORIAL GARDENS
(www.heritageireland.ie; South Circular Rd, Islandbridge; ⏱ 8am-dusk Mon-Fri, from 10am Sat & Sun; ⌨ 25, 25A, 26, 68 or 69 from city centre) Skirting the Liffey, these Lutyens-designed gardens are a fabulous retreat from city life.

Marker
Hotel €€€

(Map p64; ☏ 01-687 5100; www.themarkerhotel-dublin.com; Grand Canal Sq; r from €200; @ 🛜; ⌨ 56a & 77A, 🚇 Grand Canal Dock) Dublin's newest designer digs is impressive from the outside – the shell is a stunning building created by Manuel Aires Mateus. The recession put paid to it for a couple of years, but it finally opened in 2013 with 187 ultraswish bedrooms, a ground-floor cocktail lounge and a decent restaurant. The rooftop bar has great views.

Eating

GRAFTON STREET & AROUND

Green Nineteen
Irish €

(Map p68; ☏ 01-478 9626; www.green19.ie; 19 Lower Camden St; mains €10-14; ⏱ 10am-11pm Mon-Sat, noon-6pm Sun; ⌨ all city centre) A firm favourite on Camden St's corridor of cool is this sleek restaurant that specialises in locally sourced, organic grub – without the fancy price tag. Braised lamb chump,

If You Like...
Fine Dining

If you enjoy the Michelin-starred fare in Patrick Guilbaud (p84), Chapter One (p86) or L'Ecrivain (p85), the following restaurants are just as good.

1 THORNTON'S
(Map p68; ☎01-478 7000; www.thorntonsrestaurant.com; 128 West St Stephen's Green; midweek 3-course lunch €45, dinner tasting menus €76-120; ☺12.30-2pm & 7-10pm Tue-Sat; ☐all city centre) Chef Kevin Thornton's signature restaurant is French with an Irish twist – so good it's got a Michelin star.

2 LOCK'S BRASSERIE
(Map p64; ☎01-420 0555; www.locksbrasserie.com; 1 Windsor Tce; mains €25-32; ☺lunch Thu-Sun, dinner daily; ☐128, 14, 142, 14a, 15, 15a, 15b, 15e, 15f, 65, 65b, 74, 74a, 83 from city centre) A lovely canalside spot in Dublin specialising in Irish cuisine.

3 SHANAHAN'S ON THE GREEN
(Map p68; ☎01-407 0939; www.shanahans.ie; 119 West St Stephen's Green; mains €46-49; ☺from 6pm Mon-Thu & Sat & Sun, from noon Fri; ☐all city centre) No Michelin star, but this is the best steakhouse in Ireland by a country mile.

corned beef, pot roast chicken and the ubiquitous burger are but the meaty part of the menu, which also includes salads and veggie options. We love it.

Fade Street Social   Modern Irish €€
(Map p68; ☎01-604 0066; www.fadestreetsocial.com; Fade St; mains €19-29, tapas €8-12; ☺lunch & dinner Mon-Fri, dinner Sat & Sun; ☐all city centre) Two eateries in one, courtesy of renowned chef Dylan McGrath: at the front, the buzzy Gastro Bar, which serves up gourmet tapas from a beautiful open kitchen. At the back, the more muted Restaurant does Irish cuts of meat – from veal to rabbit – served with homegrown,

organic vegetables. Designed to impress; it does. Reservations suggested.

Coppinger Row   Mediterranean €€
(Map p68; www.coppingerrow.com; Coppinger Row; mains €18-25; ☺noon-5.30pm & 6-11pm Mon-Sat, 12.30-4pm & 6-9pm Sun; ☐all city centre) Virtually all of the Mediterranean basin is represented on the ever-changing, imaginative menu. Choices include the likes of pan-fried sea bass with roast baby fennel, tomato and olives; or rump of lamb with spiced aubergine and dried apricots. A nice touch are the filtered still and sparkling waters (€1), where 50% of the cost goes to cancer research.

Damson Diner   American Fusion €€
(Map p68; www.damsondiner.com; 52 South William St; mains €12.50-25; ☺noon-midnight; ☐all city centre) Behind the glass-fronted entrance is a superb new eatery, where the menu offers up a mix of Asian dishes (fennel *bhaji*, *ssam* duck or pork) and American classics (Boston chowder, chilli con carne). Damson is also home to the best cheeseburger in town, where the beef is *stuffed* with cheese. Great food, great fun and superb music.

L'Gueuleton   French €€
(Map p68; www.lgueuleton.com; 1 Fade St; mains €19-26; ☺12.30-4pm & 6-10pm Mon-Sat, 1-4pm & 6-9pm Sun; ☐all city centre) Dubliners have a devil of a time pronouncing the name (which means 'a gluttonous feast' in French) and have had their patience tested with the no-reservations-get-in-line-and-wait policy, but they just can't get enough of this restaurant's robust (read: meaty and filling) take on French rustic cuisine that makes twisted tongues and sore feet a small price to pay.

Restaurant Patrick Guilbaud   French €€€
(Map p68; ☎01-676 4192; www.restaurantpatrickguilbaud.ie; 21 Upper Merrion St; 2-/3-course set lunch €40/50, dinner mains

€38-56; ⏰12.30-2.30pm & 7.30-10.30pm Tue-Sat; 🚌7 & 44 from the city centre) Its devotees have long proclaimed this exceptional restaurant the best in the country and Guillaume Lebrun's French haute cuisine the most exalted expression of the culinary arts, an opinion that has found favour with the good people at Michelin, who have put two stars in its crown. The lunch menu is an absolute steal, at least in this stratosphere.

L'Ecrivain
French €€€

(Map p64; ☎ 01-661 1919; www.lecrivain.com; 109A Lower Baggot St; 3-course lunch menu €35, 10-course tasting menu €90, mains €40-47; ⏰lunch Mon-Fri, dinner Mon-Sat; 🚌38 & 39 from city centre) A firm favourite with the bulk of the city's foodies, L'Ecrivain trundles along with just one Michelin star to its name, but the plaudits keep coming. Head chef Derry Clarke is considered a gourmet god for the exquisite simplicity of his creations, which put the emphasis on flavour and the use of the best local ingredients – all given the French once over and turned into something that approaches divine dining.

THE LIBERTIES & KILMAINHAM

Fumbally Cafe
Cafe €

(Map p64; Fumbally Lane; mains €5-8; ⏰8am-5pm Mon-Sat; 🚌49, 54a & 77x from city centre) Part of the new, trendy Fumbally Development is this terrific warehouse cafe. The superb menu has a range of pastries, homemade sandwiches, healthy breakfasts and daily lunch specials. The avocado sandwich is divine. A cut above the rest.

NORTH OF THE LIFFEY

Musashi Noodles & Sushi Bar
Japanese €€

(Map p74; ☎ 01-532 8057; www.musashidublin.com; 15 Capel St; mains €15-25; ⏰lunch & dinner; 🚌all city centre, 🚇Jervis) A lovely, low-lit room, this new spot is the most authentic Japanese restaurant in the city, serving up freshly crafted sushi to an ever-growing number of devotees. The lunch *bento* deals are a steal, and if you don't fancy raw fish they also do a wide range of other Japanese specialties. It's BYOB (corkage charged). Evening bookings recommended.

The fry (p329; a full Irish breakfast)

OLIVER STREWE/GETTY IMAGES ©

Chapter One Modern Irish €€€
(Map p76; ☎01-873 2266; www.chapteroneres-
taurant.com; 18 North Parnell Sq; 2-course lunch
€29, 4-course dinner €65; ⏱12.30-2pm Tue-Fri,
6-11pm Tue-Sat; 🚌3, 10, 11, 13, 16, 19 or 22
from city centre) Michelin-starred Chapter
One is our choice for city's best eatery
because it successfully combines flawless
haute cuisine with a relaxed, welcoming
atmosphere that is at the heart of Irish
hospitality. The food is French-inspired
contemporary Irish, the menus change
regularly and the service is top-notch. The
three-course pre-theatre menu (€36.50)
is a favourite with those heading to the
Gate around the corner.

🍺 Drinking & Nightlife

If there's one constant about life in Dublin,
it's that Dubliners will always take a drink.
Come hell or high water, the city's pubs
will never be short of customers, and we
suspect that exploring a
variety of Dublin's legendary
pubs and bars ranks pretty high on
the list of reasons you're here.

GRAFTON STREET & AROUND

John Mulligan's Pub
(Map p64; 8 Poolbeg St; 🚌all city centre) This
brilliant old boozer was established in
1782 and has barely changed over the
years. In fact, the last time it was renovated was when Christy Brown and his
rowdy clan ran amok here in the film *My
Left Foot*. It has one of the finest pints of
Guinness in Dublin and a colourful crew of
regulars. It's just off Fleet St, outside the
eastern boundary of Temple Bar.

Kehoe's Pub
(Map p68; 9 South Anne St; 🚌all city centre)
This is one of the most atmospheric pubs
in the city centre and a favourite with all
kinds of Dubliners. It has a beautiful Victorian bar, a wonderful snug, and plenty of
other little nooks and crannies. Upstairs,

drinks are served in what was once the publican's living room – and looks it!

Stag's Head
Pub

(Map p74; 1 Dame Ct; ☐ all city centre) The Stag's Head was built in 1770, remodelled in 1895 and thankfully not changed a bit since then. It's a superb pub: so picturesque that it often appears in films and also featured in a postage-stamp series on Irish bars. A bloody great pub, no doubt.

Long Hall
Pub

(Map p68; 51 South Great George's St; ☐ all city centre) Luxuriating in full Victorian splendour, this is one of the city's most beautiful and best-loved pubs. Check out the ornate carvings in the woodwork behind the bar and the elegant chandeliers. The bartenders are experts at their craft, an increasingly rare attribute in Dublin these days.

37 Dawson St
Contemporary Bar

(Map p68; ☎ 01-672 8231; www.37dawsonstreet. ie; 37 Dawson St; ☐ all city centre) Antiques, eye-catching art and elegant bric-a-brac adorn this new bar that has quickly established itself as a favourite with the trendy crowd. At the back is the new Whiskey Bar, a 50s-style bar that Don Draper & co would feel comfortable sipping a fine scotch at; upstairs is an elegant restaurant that serves a terrific brunch.

Whelan's
Bar

(Map p68; www.whelanslive.com; 25 Wexford St) The bar of one of the city's most beloved live-music venues is always full of earnest young things on a good night out. The bar is done up like a traditional pub, the crowd is fun and the music is all kinds of rock, folk and contemporary.

Hogan's
Bar

(Map p68; 35 South Great George's St) Once an old-style traditional bar, Hogan's is now a gigantic boozer spread across two floors. Midweek it's a relaxing hang-out for young professionals and restaurant and bar workers on a night off. But come the weekend the sweat bin downstairs pulls them in for some serious music courtesy of the usually excellent DJs.

Pouring the Perfect Pint

Like the Japanese Tea Ceremony, pouring a pint of Guinness is part ritual, part theatre and part logic. It's a six-step process that every decent Dublin bartender will use to serve the perfect pint.

THE GLASS

A dry, clean 20oz (568ml) tulip pint glass is used because the shape allows the nitrogen bubbles to flow down the side, and the contour 'bump' about halfway down pushes the bubbles into the centre of the pint on their way back up.

THE ANGLE

The glass is held beneath the tap at a 45-degree angle – and the tap faucet shouldn't touch the sides of the glass.

THE POUR

A smooth pour should fill the glass to about three-quarters full, after which it is put on the counter 'to settle'.

THE HEAD

As the beer flows into the glass its passes through a restrictor plate at high speed that creates nitrogen bubbles. In the glass, the agitated bubbles flow down the sides of the glass and – thanks to the contour bump – back up through the middle, settling at the top in a nice, creamy head. This should take a couple of minutes to complete.

THE TOP-OFF

Once the pint is 'settled', the bartender will top it off, creating a domed effect across the top of the glass with the head sitting comfortably just above the rim. Now it's the perfect pint.

WHERE TO FIND IT?

Now that you know what you're looking for, it's time to find it. The pint in the Gravity Bar is good, but it's missing one key ingredient: atmosphere, the kind found only in a traditional pub:

Kehoe's (p86) Stalwart popular with locals and tourists.

John Mulligan's (p86) Perfect setting for a perfect pint.

Grogan's Castle Lounge (Map p68; 15 South William St) Great because the locals demand it!

Fallon's (below) Centuries of experience.

THE LIBERTIES & KILMAINHAM

Fallon's   Traditional Pub
(Map p64; ☎ 01-454 2801; 129 The Coombe;
🚍 123, 206 or 51B from city centre) Just west of the city centre, in the heart of medieval Dublin, this is a fabulously old-fashioned bar that has been serving a great pint of Guinness since the end of the 17th century. Prize fighter Dan Donnelly, the only boxer ever to be knighted, was head bartender here in 1818. It's a genuine Irish bar filled with Dubs.

NORTH OF THE LIFFEY

Cobblestone   Pub

(Map p64; North King St; 🚊 Smithfield) This pub in the heart of Smithfield has a great atmosphere in its cosy upstairs bar, where superb nightly music sessions are performed by traditional musicians (especially Thursday) and up-and-coming folk acts.

Walshe's   Pub

(Map p64; 6 Stoneybatter; 🚌 25, 25A, 66, 67 from city centre, 🚊 Museum) If the snug is free, a drink in Walshe's is about as pure a traditional experience as you'll have in any pub in the city; if it isn't, you'll have to make do with the old-fashioned bar, where the friendly staff and brilliant clientele (a mix of locals and hipster imports) are a treat. A proper Dublin pub.

⭐ Entertainment

ROCK & POP

Dublin's love affair with popular music has made it one of the preferred touring stops for all kinds of musicians, who seem to relish the unfettered manner in which audiences embrace their favourite artists.

Workman's Club   Live Music

(Map p74; 🕿 01-670 6692; www.theworkmansclub.com; 10 Wellington Quay; 🚌 all city centre) A 300-capacity venue and bar in the former workingmen's club of Dublin, this new spot puts the emphasis on keeping away from the mainstream, which means a broad range of performers, from singer-songwriters to electronic cabaret.

Vicar Street

Live Music
(Map p64; 🕿 01-454 5533; www.vicarstreet.com; 58-59 Thomas St; 🚌 13, 49, 54a, 56a from city centre) Smaller performances

take place at this intimate venue (capacity of 1000) near Christ Church Cathedral, between its table-serviced group seating downstairs and theatre-style balcony. It offers a varied program, with a strong emphasis on soul, folk, jazz and foreign music.

O2   Live Music

(Map p64; 🕿 01-819 8888; www.theo2.ie; East Link Bridge, North Wall Quay; 🚊 Point Village) The premier indoor venue in the city has a capacity of around 10,000 and plays host to the very brightest stars in the firmament: Rihanna, Bryan Adams and the cast of *Glee* are just some of the acts that have brought their magic to its superb stage.

Whelan's   Live Music

(Map p68; 🕿 01-478 0766; www.whelanslive.com; 25 Wexford St; 🚌 bus 16, 122 from city centre) Perhaps the city's most beloved live venue is this mid-sized room attached to a traditional bar. This is the singer-songwriter's spiritual home: when they're done pouring out the contents of their hearts on stage, you can find them filling up in the bar along with their fans.

Pulling pints of Guinness at Gravity Bar (p79), Guinness Storehouse.
RICHARD I'ANSON/GETTY IMAGES ©

Sugar Club — Live Music

(Map p68; ☎ 01-678 7188; 8 Lower Leeson St; ⛔ St Stephen's Green) There's live jazz, cabaret and soul music at weekends in this comfortable theatre-style venue on the corner of St Stephen's Green.

CLASSICAL

Classical music concerts and opera take place in a number of city-centre venues. There are also occasional performances in churches; check the press for details.

Bord Gáis Energy Theatre — Theatre

(Map p64; ☎ 01-677 7999; www.grandcanaltheatre.ie; Grand Canal Sq; ⛔ Grand Canal Dock) Forget the uninviting sponsored name: Daniel Liebeskind's masterful design is a three-tiered, 2000-capacity auditorium where you're as likely to be entertained by the Bolshoi or a touring state opera as you are to see Disney on Ice or Barbra Streisand. It's a magnificent venue – designed for classical, paid for by the classics.

National Concert Hall — Live Music

(Map p68; ☎ 01-417 0000; www.nch.ie; Earlsfort Tce; ⛔ all city centre) Ireland's premier orchestral hall hosts a variety of concerts year-round, including a series of lunchtime concerts from 1.05pm to 2pm on Tuesdays, June to August.

THEATRE

Dublin's theatre scene is small but busy. Theatre bookings can usually be made by quoting a credit-card number over the phone, then you can collect your tickets just before the performance. Expect to pay anything between €12 and €25 for most shows, with some costing as much as €30. Most plays begin between 8pm and 8.30pm. Check www.irishtheatre online.com to see what's playing.

Gate Theatre — Theatre

(Map p76; ☎ 01-874 4045; www.gatetheatre.ie; 1 Cavendish Row; ⛔ all city centre) The city's most elegant theatre, housed in a late-18th-century building, features a generally unflappable repertory of classic American and European plays. Orson Welles' first professional performance was here, and James Mason played here early in his career. Even today it is the only theatre in town where you might see established international movie stars work on their credibility with a theatre run.

National Concert Hall

DESIGN PICS/GEORGE MUNDAY/GETTY IMAGES ©

Farmers & Organic Markets

Dublin Food Co-op (Map p64; www.dublinfoodcoop.com; 12 Newmarket; ⊙2-8pm Thu, 9.30am-4.30pm Sat; 🚌49, 54a & 77x from city centre) A buzzing community market specialising in organic veg, homemade cheeses and organic wines. There's also a bakery and even baby-changing facilities.

Coppinger Row Market (Map p68; Coppinger Row; ⊙9am-7pm Thu) It's small – only a handful of stalls – but it packs a proper organic punch, attracting punters with the waft of freshly baked breads, delicious hummus and other goodies.

Harcourt Street Food Market (Map p68; www.irishfarmersmarkets.ie; Park Pl, Station Bldgs, Upper Hatch St; ⊙10am-4pm Thu; 🚌all city centre) Organic vegies, cheeses, olives and meats made into dishes from all over the world.

Temple Bar Farmers Market (Map p74; Meeting House Sq; ⊙9am-4.30pm Sat; 🚌all city centre) This great little market is a fabulous place to while away a Saturday morning, sampling and munching on organic gourmet goodies bound by the market's only rule: local producers only. From cured meats to wildflowers, you could fill an entire pantry with their selection of delights.

For more info, check out www.irishfarmersmarkets.ie, www.irishvillagemarkets. com or local county council sites such as www.dlrcoco.ie/markets.

Abbey Theatre   Theatre

(Map p76; 🕿01-878 7222; www.abbeytheatre. ie; Lower Abbey St; 🚌all city centre, 🚊Abbey) Ireland's renowned national theatre, founded by WB Yeats in 1904, has been reinvigorated in recent years by director Fiach MacConghaill, who has introduced lots of new blood to what was in danger of becoming a moribund corpse. The current programme has a mix of Irish classics (Synge, O'Casey etc), established international names (Shepard, Mamet) and new talent (O'Rowe, Carr et al).

Work by up-and-coming writers and more experimental theatre is staged in the adjoining **Peacock Theatre** (Map p76; 🕿01-878 7222; 🚌all city centre, 🚊Abbey).

🔒 Shopping

If it's made in Ireland – or pretty much anywhere else – you can find it in Dublin. Grafton Street is home to a range of largely British-owned high-street chain stores, but you'll find the best local boutiques in the surrounding streets, selling everything from cheese to Irish designer clothing and streetwear.

Avoca Handweavers   Irish Crafts

(Map p74; 🕿01-677 4215; www.avoca.ie; 11-13 Suffolk St; ⊙9.30am-6pm Mon-Wed & Sat, 9.30am-7pm Thu & Fri, 11am-6pm Sun; 🚌all city centre) Combining clothing, homewares, a basement food hall and an excellent top-floor **cafe**, Avoca promotes a stylish but homey brand of modern Irish life – and is one of the best places to find an original present. Many of the garments are woven, knitted and naturally dyed at its Wicklow factory. The children's section, with unusual knits, bee-covered gumboots and dinky toys, is fantastic.

Cathach Books   Books

(Map p68; 🕿01-671 8676; www.rarebooks.ie; 10 Duke St; ⊙9.30am-5.45pm Mon-Sat; 🚌all city centre) Our favourite bookshop in the city stocks a rich and remarkable collection of Irish-interest books, with a particular emphasis on 20th-century literature and a large selection of first editions, including rare ones by the big guns: Joyce, Yeats, Beckett and Wilde.

Detour:
Kilmainham Gaol

Kilmainham Gaol (www.heritageireland.com; Inchicore Rd; adult/child €6/2; ⊙9.30am-6pm Apr-Sep, 9.30am-5.30pm Mon-Sat, 10am-6pm Sun Oct-Mar; 🚌23, 25, 25A, 26, 68 or 69 from city centre) If you have *any* desire to understand Irish history – especially the juicy bits about resistance to English rule – then a visit to this former prison is an absolute must. This threatening grey building, built between 1792 and 1795, has played a role in virtually every act of Ireland's painful path to independence.

An excellent audiovisual introduction to the building is followed by a thought-provoking tour of the eerie prison, the largest unoccupied building of its kind in Europe. Sitting incongruously outside in the yard is the *Asgard,* the ship that successfully ran the British blockade to deliver arms to Nationalist forces in 1914. The tour finishes in the gloomy yard where the 1916 executions took place.

Claddagh Records   Music

(Map p74; 📞01-677 0262; 2 Cecilia St; 🚌all city centre) An excellent collection of good-quality traditional and folk music is the mainstay at this centrally located record shop. The profoundly knowledgable staff should be able to locate even the most elusive recording for you.

ℹ️ Information

You'll find everything you need to kick-start your visit at the **Dublin Discover Ireland Centre** (Map p74; www.visitdublin.com; St Andrew's Church, 2 Suffolk St; ⊙9am-5.30pm Mon-Sat, 10.30am-3pm Sun). Besides general visitor information on Dublin and Ireland, it also has a free accommodation booking service, a concert-booking agent, local and national bus information, rail information, and tour information and bookings. There are also branches at Dublin Airport and **O'Connell St** (Map p76; 14 O'Connell St; ⊙9am-5pm Mon-Sat).

ℹ️ Getting There & Away

Air

Dublin Airport (📞01-814 1111; www.dublinairport.com), 13km north of the centre, is Ireland's major international gateway airport. It has two terminals: most international flights (including all US flights) use the new Terminal 2; Ryanair and select others use Terminal 1. Both terminals have the usual selection of pubs, restaurants, shops, ATMs and car-hire desks.

Boat

Dublin has two ferry ports: the **Dun Laoghaire ferry terminal** (📞01-280 1905; Dun Laoghaire), 13km east of the city, serves Holyhead in Wales and can be reached by DART to Dun Laoghaire, or bus 7, 7A or 8 from Burgh Quay or bus 46A from Trinity College; and the **Dublin Port terminal** (📞01-855 2222; Alexandra Rd), 3km northeast of the city centre, serves Holyhead and Liverpool.

Buses from Busáras are timed to coincide with arrivals and departures: for the 9.45am ferry departure from Dublin Port, buses leave Busáras at 8.30am. For the 9.45pm departure, buses depart from Busáras at 8.30pm. For the 1am sailing to Liverpool, the bus departs from Busáras at 11.45pm. All bus trips cost adult/child €2.50/1.25.

Bus

Busáras (Map p64; 📞01-836 6111; Store St), the main bus station, is just north of the river behind Custom House, and serves as the main city stop for **Bus Éireann** (www.buseireann.ie), which has a countrywide network.

Car & Motorcycle

The main rental agencies, which also have offices at the airport, include the following:

Avis Rent-a-Car (📞01-605 7500; www.avis.ie; 35 Old Kilmainham Rd)

Budget Rent-a-Car (📞01-837 9611, airport 01-844 5150; www.budget.ie; 151 Lower Drumcondra Rd)

Europcar (📞01-648 5900, airport 01-844 4179; www.europcar.com; 1 Mark St)

Hertz Rent-a-Car (☎01-709 3060, airport 01-844 5466; www.hertz.com; 151 South Circular Rd)

Thrifty (☎01-844 1944, airport 01-840 0800; www.thrifty.ie; 26 Lombard St East)

Train

Dublin has two main train stations: **Heuston Station** (☎01-836 5421), on the western side of town near the Liffey, which serves the southern half of the country; and **Connolly Station** (☎01-836 3333), a short walk northeast of Busáras, behind the Custom House, which covers the west and north. Heuston Station has left-luggage lockers of three sizes, costing €6 to €10 for 24 hours. At Connolly Station the facility costs €6.

Connolly Station is a stop on the DART line into town; the Luas Red Line serves both Connolly and Heuston stations.

ⓘ Getting Around

To/From the Airport

There is no train service to/from the airport, but there are bus and taxi options.

Bus

Aircoach (www.aircoach.ie; one-way/return €7/12) Private coach service with two routes from the airport to 18 destinations throughout the city, including the centre's main streets. Coaches run every 10 to 15 minutes between 6am and midnight, then hourly from midnight until 6am.

Airlink Express Coach (☎01-873 4222; www.dublinbus.ie; adult/child €6/3) Bus 747 runs every 10 to 20 minutes from 5.45am to 11.30pm between the airport, the central bus station (Busáras) and the Dublin Bus office on Upper O'Connell St; bus 748 runs every 15 to 30 minutes from 6.50am to 10.05pm between the airport and Heuston and Connolly Stations.

Dublin Bus (Map p76; ☎01-873 4222; www.dublinbus.ie; 59 Upper O'Connell St; ⊙9am-5.30pm Mon-Fri, to 2pm Sat) A number of buses serve the airport from various points in Dublin, including buses 16A (Rathfarnham), 746 (Dun Laoghaire) and 230 (Portmarnock); all cross the city centre on their way to the airport.

Taxi

There is a taxi rank directly outside the arrivals concourse. A taxi should cost about €20 from the airport to the city centre, including a supplementary charge of €2.50 (not applied going to the airport). Make sure the meter is switched on.

Lower Abbey St

RICHARD I'ANSON/GETTY IMAGES ©

Fare-Saver Passes

Fare-saver passes include:

Freedom Ticket (adult/child €28/12) Three-day unlimited travel on all bus services, including Airlink and Dublin Bus Hop-On, Hop-Off tours.

Adult (Bus & Rail) Short Hop (one/three days €12/24.50) Valid for unlimited travel on Dublin Bus, DART and suburban rail, but not Nitelink or Airlink.

Bus/Luas Pass (one/seven days €8.10/32.80) Unlimited travel on both bus and Luas.

Family One-Day Short Hop (€17.70) Valid for travel for one day for a family of two adults and two children aged under 16 on all bus and rail services except Nitelink, Airlink, ferry services and tours.

Rambler Pass (one/three/five days €6.90/15/25) Valid for unlimited travel on all Dublin Bus and Airlink services, except Nitelink.

10 Journey Travel 90 (adult €25) Valid for 10 90-minute journeys on all Dublin Bus and Airlink services, except Nitelink.

Bicycle

Dublin By Bike

One of the most popular ways to get around the city is with the blue bikes of Dublinbikes (www. dublinbikes.ie), a pay-as-you-go service similar to the Parisian Vélib system: cyclists purchase a €10 Smart Card (as well as pay a credit-card deposit of €150) – either online or at any of the 40 stations throughout the city centre – before 'freeing' a bike for use, which is then free of charge for the first 30 minutes and €0.50 for each half-hour thereafter.

Car & Motorcycle

Traffic in Dublin is a nightmare and parking is an expensive headache. There are no free spots to park anywhere in the city centre during business hours (7am to 7pm Monday to Saturday), but there are plenty of parking meters, 'pay & display' spots (€2.50 to €5 per hour) and over a dozen sheltered and supervised car parks (around €5 per hour).

Clamping of illegally parked cars is thoroughly enforced, and there is an €80 charge for removal. Parking is free after 7pm Monday to Saturday, and all day Sunday, in most metered spots and on single yellow lines.

Car theft and break-ins are a problem, and the police advise visitors to park in a supervised car park. Cars with foreign number plates are prime targets; never leave your valuables behind. When

you're booking accommodation, check on parking facilities.

The Automobile Association of Ireland (AA; ☏01-617 9999, breakdown 1800 667 788; www. aaireland.ie; 56 Drury St) is located in the city centre.

Public Transport

Bus

The office of Dublin Bus (Map p76; ☏01-872 0000; www.dublinbus.ie; 59 Upper O'Connell St; ⊙9am-5.30pm Mon-Fri, 9am-2pm Sat) has free single-route timetables of all its services.

Buses run from around 6am (some start at 5.30am) to 11.30pm. Fares are calculated according to stages:

● one to three stages: €1.65
● four to seven stages: €2.15
● eight to 13 stages: €2.40
● 14 to 23 stages: €2.80
● more than 23 stages: €2.80 (inside Citizone; outer suburban journeys cost €4.40)

Train

The Dublin Area Rapid Transport (DART; ☏01-836 6222; www.irishrail.ie) provides quick train access to the coast as far north as Howth (about 30 minutes) and as far south as Greystones in County Wicklow. Pearse Station is convenient for central Dublin south of the Liffey, and Connolly Station for north of the Liffey. There are services every 10 to 20 minutes, sometimes even more frequently, from around 6.30am to midnight Monday to Saturday; services are less frequent on Sunday. Dublin to Dun Laoghaire takes about 15 to 20 minutes. A one-way DART ticket from Dublin to Dun Laoghaire or Howth costs €2.30; to Bray it's €2.75.

There are also suburban rail services north as far as Dundalk, inland to Mullingar and south past Bray to Arklow.

Luas

The Luas light-rail system has two lines: the green line (running every five to 15 minutes) connects St Stephen's Green with Sandyford in south Dublin via Ranelagh and Dundrum; the red line (every 20 minutes) runs from Lower Abbey St to Tallaght via the north quays and Heuston Station. There are ticket machines at every stop or you can buy a ticket from newsagents in the city centre; a typical short-hop fare (around four stops) is €2. Services run from 5.30am to 12.30am Monday to Friday, from 6.30am to 12.30am Saturday and from 7am to 11.30pm Sunday.

Taxi

All taxi fares begin with a flag-fall fare of €4.10 (€4.45 from 10pm to 8am), followed by €1.03/km thereafter from 8am to 10pm (€1.35/km from 10pm to 8am). In addition to these there are a number of extra charges – €1 for each extra passenger and €2 for telephone bookings. There is no charge for luggage.

Taxis can be hailed on the street and found at taxi ranks around the city, including on the corner of Abbey and O'Connell Sts (Map p76); College Green (Map p74), in front of Trinity College; and St Stephen's Green at the end of Grafton St. There are numerous taxi companies that will dispatch taxis by radio including City Cabs (☎01-872 2688) and National Radio Cabs (☎01-677 2222; www.radiocabs.ie).

Phone the Garda Carriage Office (☎01-475 5888) if you have any complaints about taxis or queries regarding lost property.

Wicklow & Eastern Ireland

South of Dublin is Wicklow – scenic and wild. Its most imposing natural feature is a gorse-and-bracken mountain spine that provides one of Ireland's most stunning landscapes, replete with dramatic glacial valleys, soaring mountain passes and some of the country's most important archaeological treasures, from breathtaking early-Christian sites to the elegant country homes of Ireland's 18th-century nobility.

To the west is pastoral Kildare, the home of Irish horse racing and some of Ireland's richest farmland. What it lacks in history it more than makes up for in beautiful countryside.

North and northwest of Dublin is Meath, once one of the five provinces of ancient Ireland. The 'Middle Kingdom' attracted Ireland's first settlers, who left their mark in the magnificent Neolithic monuments of the Boyne Valley. Slightly north again is the 'Wee County', but while Louth may be small, it still packs a scenic punch – the ruins of Mellifont and Monasterboice are but two of the county's big attractions.

Lough Dan (p109), Wicklow Mountains
EOIN CLARKE/GETTY IMAGES ©

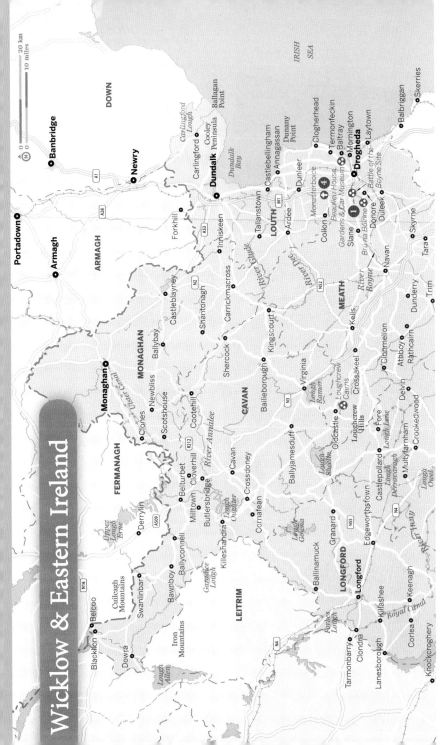

Wicklow & Eastern Ireland's Highlights

Brú na Bóinne

Newgrange and its surrounding tombs of Knowth and Dowth – known in Irish mythology as Brú na Bóinne, the home of the God Dagda and his wife Bóinne (the river Boyne) and later the burial place of the pagan kings of Tara – is one of only three World Heritage sites in Ireland (p118).

Glendalough

The simply extraordinary monastic remains at Glendalough (p107) are reason enough to make the visit, but once you're there, you'll see why St Kevin chose this particular spot to set up shop. Nestled in a tree-dotted glacial valley and bordered by two lakes, Glendalough is without a doubt one of the most beautiful corners of the whole country. St Kevin's Kitchen

STEPHEN SAKS/GETTY IMAGES ©

GARETH MCCORMAC/GETTY IMAGES ©

Powerscourt Estate

3

For a sense of how well the powerful and mighty Anglo-Normans lived, wander the magnificent Italianate gardens of Powerscourt Estate (p112), soak up the superb views of nearby Sugarloaf and then peek inside the former home of the Power family. This isn't how the other half lived, but how the other half a percent lived.

JOE CORNISH/GETTY IMAGES ©

4

Monasterboice

Most Irish monastic sites are soaked in atmosphere, but Monasterboice (p129) has an extra-special hue. The ancient church ruins, the near-perfect round tower and the exquisite high crosses dotted around a grass-covered cemetery make this site at the end of a country lane one of Ireland's most beautiful. Best of all, it doesn't get nearly as many visitors as its competitors.

5

Castletown House

William Conolly was Speaker of the Irish House of Commons and, conveniently, Ireland's richest man, so he commissioned the construction of a home to befit his elevated status – the breathtaking Castletown House (p116), near Maynooth in County Kildare. Its classical Palladian style would influence the architects of the soon-to-be-constructed Washington, DC. 18th-century interior moulding

101

Wicklow & Eastern Ireland's Best...

Beauty Spots

○ **Sally Gap** Cut across the Wicklow Mountains. (p109)

○ **Avondale House** Where Charles Parnell would retreat to. (p115)

○ **Powerscourt Estate** The most beautiful garden in Ireland? (p112)

○ **Hill of Tara** Ireland's most sacred turf. (p123)

○ **Loughcrew Cairns** Superb views from the top of the hill. (p126)

Gourmet Experiences

○ **Ghan House** Superb restaurant, magnificent surroundings. (p125)

○ **Tinakilly Country House & Restaurant** Fine Irish cuisine in an Italianate mansion. (p125)

○ **Strawberry Tree** Excellent organic dining in an idyllic setting. (p129)

○ **Kitchen** Drogheda's finest eatery. (p127)

○ **Ballyknocken House** Learn to cook like a gourmet chef. (p125)

Historical Spots

○ **Battle of the Boyne Site** King James got whupped here by his son-in-law, King William of Orange, in 1690. (p123)

○ **Hill of Tara** Home of the High Kings. (p123)

○ **Monasterboice** One of Ireland's most important monasteries. (p129)

○ **Avondale House** Parnell's country pile. (p115)

○ **Russborough House** A thieves' paradise? (p113)

Need to Know

Things for Free

o **Glendalough** Monastic magic in the valley. (p107)

o **Battle of the Boyne Site** The eye of Irish history's storm. (p123)

o **Old Mellifont Abbey** Handsome ruins of a mighty Cistercian abbey. (p128)

o **Monasterboice** Marvellous high crosses. (p129)

o **Loughcrew Cairns** Little-visited Neolithic passage graves. (p126)

ADVANCE PLANNING

o **Ten months before** Put your name into the Winter Solstice lottery at Brú na Bóinne.

o **Three months before** Book your spot at one of the cooking schools.

o **One month before** Sort out your accommodation.

o **Two weeks before** Check out the weather forecast. Then ignore it.

RESOURCES

o **Wicklow National Park** (www.wicklownationalpark. ie) All the info on the national park, including walks and visits to Glendalough.

o **Heritage Ireland** (www.heritageireland. ie) The Heritage Service is responsible for Glendalough, Brú na Bóinne and other sites of historical and archaeological importance.

o **Bus Eireann** (www. buseireann.ie) Official site for the national bus service, which is handy for getting around the region.

o **Battle of the Boyne** (www.battleoftheboyne.ie) Stacks of info on one of the most decisive battles of Irish history.

GETTING AROUND

o **Bus** Good bus networks cover most of the East Coast.

o **Train** Good service along the coast only – fine for coastal Wicklow and up to Drogheda.

o **Car** The best way of getting around; watch out for commuter traffic!

BE FOREWARNED

o **Crowds** Be prepared for summer crowds and traffic jams, especially in the Wicklow Mountains and the N11 south through Wicklow.

o **School tours** Brú na Bóinne is not just spectacular but educational and very popular with school outings.

o **Weather** The Wicklow Mountains ain't high, but they can get very cold. Come prepared.

Left: Cycling from Sally Gap (p109);
Above: Standing stone, Hill of Tara (p123)
(LEFT) © DAVID LYONS/ALAMY; (ABOVE) © GEORGE MUNDAY/ALAMY

Wicklow & Eastern Ireland Itineraries

Counties Wicklow, Kildare and Meath each have a distinctive character and plenty to offer visitors, from active hiking to ancient history. You can stay overnight, but all make for easy day trips from Dublin, too.

3 DAYS

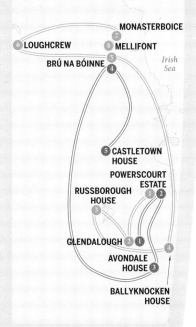

MONASTERBOICE

LOUGHCREW   MELLIFONT

BRÚ NA BÓINNE   *Irish Sea*

CASTLETOWN HOUSE

POWERSCOURT ESTATE

RUSSBOROUGH HOUSE

GLENDALOUGH

AVONDALE HOUSE

BALLYKNOCKEN HOUSE

GLENDALOUGH TO CASTLETOWN HOUSE
IN & OUT FROM DUBLIN

Start in the Wicklow Mountains, taking in the glacial ❶ **Glendalough** valley (p107), home to 6th-century monastic ruins, a pair of beautiful lakes and some of the finest walks in the county. Then head over to ❷ **Powerscourt Estate** (p112), the one-time demesne of the Power family, now a favourite with garden and scenery lovers – the view of Wicklow's most distinctive peak, the Sugarloaf, is magnificent. In the afternoon, wend your way south to Rathdrum and pay a visit to ❸ **Avondale House** (p115), former home of the 'uncrowned king' of Ireland, the brilliant and damned Charles Stewart Parnell, one of the most important figures in Irish history (it's also accessible by public transport). On the second day, explore the magnificent Neolithic passage tomb of ❹ **Brú na Bóinne** (p118) and marvel at the mathematical sophistication of its construction; be sure to take the tour that includes a simulation of the shaft of light illuminating the tomb on the winter solstice. On day three, visit Ireland's finest Palladian mansion, ❺ **Castletown House** (p116).

Top Left: Avondale House (p115), Rathdrum;
Top Right: Maynooth, County Kildare (p117)
(TOP LEFT) STEPHEN SAKS/GETTY IMAGES ©; (TOP RIGHT) IIC/AXIOM/GETTY IMAGES ©

5 DAYS

WICKLOW TO LOUTH

HEARTH & HISTORY

This five-day route begins with a visit to the ❶**Powerscourt Estate** (p112) before proceeding on to explore the ❷**Glendalough** valley (p107). Cut across the mountains and visit ❸**Russborough House** (p113) – the West Wing is one of the most luxurious abodes in the county. If you fancy some hands-on R&R, put on the apron at ❹**Ballyknocken House** (p125) and learn the essentials of Irish gourmet cooking. After a couple of days, head northwest and explore the passage tombs at ❺**Brú na Bóinne** (p118) before exploring the quieter network of tombs at ❻**Loughcrew**. Finish your visit with trips to the monastic ruins at ❼**Monasterboice** (p129) and ❽**Mellifont** (p128) before returning to Dublin.

Discover Wicklow & Eastern Ireland

COUNTY WICKLOW

Just south of Dublin, Wicklow (Cill Mhantáin) is the capital's favourite playground, a wild pleasure garden of coastline, woodland and a daunting mountain range through which runs the country's most popular walking trail.

Enniskerry & Powerscourt Estate

POP 2670

Tours

All tours that take in Powerscourt start in Dublin.

Dublin Bus Tours Bus Tour
(Map p74; ☎ 01-872 0000; www.dublinbus. ie; adult/child €24/12; ☉11am) A visit to Powerscourt is included in the four-hour South Coast & Gardens tour, which takes in the stretch of coastline between Dun Laoghaire and Killiney before turning inland to Wicklow and on to Enniskerry. Admission to the gardens is included.

Irish Sightseeing Tours Bus Tour
(☎ 01-872 9010; www.irishcitytours. com; Suffolk St; adult/student/ child €26/24/20; ☉10am Fri-Sun) Wicklow's big hits – Powerscourt, Glendalough and the lakes and a stop at Avoca, then Dun Laoghaire and Dalkey (includes admission to Glendalough visitor centre and Powerscourt, but not coffee). Tours depart from the Discover Ireland Dublin Centre.

Wild heather on the Wicklow Mountains
CHRIS HILL/GETTY IMAGES©

Eating

Johnnie Fox Seafood **€€**
(☎01-295 5647; www.jfp.ie; Glencullen; mains
€12-20; ⏱noon-10pm) Busloads of tourists
fill the place nightly throughout the
summer, mostly for the knees-up, faux-
Irish floorshow of music and dancing.
But there's nothing contrived about the
seafood, which is so damn good we'd
happily sit through yet another chorus
of *Danny Boy* and even consider joining in the jig. The pub is 3km northwest of Enniskerry in Glencullen.

❶ Getting There & Away

Enniskerry is 18km south of Dublin, just 3km
west of the M11 along the R117. Getting to
Powerscourt House under your own steam is
not a problem (it's 500m from the town), but
getting to the waterfall is tricky.
Dublin Bus (☎01-872 0000, 01-873 4222;
www.dublinbus.ie) Service 44 (€2.50, every
20 minutes) takes about 1¼ hours to get to
Enniskerry from Hawkins St in Dublin.

Glendalough

POP 280

If you've come to Wicklow, chances are
that a visit to Glendalough (Gleann dá
Loch, 'Valley of the Two Lakes') is one of
your main reasons for being here. And
you're not wrong, for this is one of the
most beautiful corners of the whole country and the epitome of the kind of rugged,
romantic Ireland that probably drew you
to the island in the first place.

HISTORY

In AD 498 a young monk named Kevin arrived in the valley looking for somewhere
to kick back, meditate and be at one with
nature. He pitched up in what had been
a Bronze Age tomb on the southern side
of the Upper Lake and for the next seven
years slept on stones, wore animal skins,
maintained a near-starvation diet and –
according to the legend – became bosom
buddies with the birds and animals.
Kevin's ecofriendly lifestyle soon attracted a bunch of disciples, all seemingly

If You Like…
Castles

If you like powerful fortifications such as
Trim Castle (p126), then you'll enjoy the
following.

1 SLANE CASTLE
(☎041-982 4080; www.slanecastle.ie; guided
tours adult/student €7/5, whiskey-tasting tour incl
castle tour €17, minimum 12 people; ⏱guided tours
noon-5pm Sun-Thu Jun-Aug) The private residence
of Earl of Mountcharles, Slane is popular for guided
tours and its yearly music concerts.

2 DUNSANY CASTLE
(☎046-902 5198; www.dunsany.com;
Dunsany; adult/child/under 9yr €20/10/free; ⏱by
appointment) The residence of the lords of Dunsany
is one of the oldest continually inhabited buildings
in Ireland.

3 MAYNOOTH CASTLE
(☎01-628 6744; ⏱10am-6pm Mon-Fri,
1-6pm Sat & Sun Jun-Sep, to 5pm Sun Oct) You
can visit the ruined gatehouse, keep and great
hall of this 13th-century castle, home of the
Fitzgerald family.

unaware of the irony that they were flock-
ing to hang out with a hermit who wanted
to live as far away from other people as
possible. Over the next couple of centuries his one-man operation mushroomed
into a proper settlement and by the 9th
century Glendalough rivalled Clonmacnoise as the island's premier monastic
city. Thousands of students studied and
lived in a thriving community that was
spread over a considerable area.

Inevitably, Glendalough's success
made it a key target for Viking raiders,
who sacked the monastery at least
four times between 775 and 1071. The
final blow came in 1398, when English
forces from Dublin almost destroyed it.
Efforts were made to rebuild and some
life lingered on here as late as the 17th
century when, under renewed repression,
the monastery finally died.

Glendalough

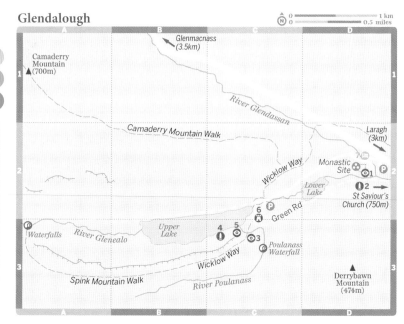

Glendalough

◉ Sights

UPPER LAKE

The original site of St Kevin's settlement, **Teampall na Skellig** is at the base of the cliffs towering over the southern side of the Upper Lake and is accessible only by boat; unfortunately, there's no boat service to the site and you'll have to settle for looking at it across the lake. The terraced shelf has the reconstructed ruins of a church and early graveyard. Rough wattle huts once stood on the raised ground nearby. Scattered around are some early grave slabs and simple stone crosses.

Just east of here and 10m above the lake waters is the 2m-deep artificial cave called **St Kevin's Bed**, said to be where Kevin lived. The earliest human habitation of the cave was long before St Kevin's era – there's evidence that people lived in the valley for thousands of years before the monks arrived. In the green area just south of the car park is a large circular wall thought to be the remains of an early Christian **stone fort** (caher).

Follow the lakeshore path southwest of the car park until you come to the considerable remains of **Reefert Church** above the tiny River Poulanass. It's a small, plain, 11th-century Romanesque nave-and-chancel church with some reassembled arches and walls. Traditionally, Reefert (literally 'Royal Burial Place') was the burial site of the chiefs of the local O'Toole family. The surrounding graveyard contains a number

Detour:
Sally Gap

One of the two main east–west passes across the Wicklow Mountains, the Sally Gap is surrounded by some spectacular countryside. From the turn-off on the lower road (R755) between Roundwood and Kilmacanogue near Bray, the narrow road (R759) passes above the dark and dramatic **Lough Tay**, whose scree slopes slide into **Luggala** (Fancy Mountain). This almost fairy-tale estate is owned by one Garech de Brún, member of the Guinness family and founder of Claddagh Records, a leading producer of Irish traditional and folk music. The small River Cloghoge links Lough Tay with **Lough Dan** just to the south. It then heads up to the Sally Gap crossroads, where it cuts across the Military Rd and heads northwest for Kilbride and the N81, following the young River Liffey, still only a stream.

of rough stone crosses and slabs, most made of shiny mica schist.

Climb the steps at the back of the churchyard and follow the path to the west and you'll find, at the top of a rise overlooking the lake, the scant remains of **St Kevin's Cell** (W of Reefert Churchyard), a small beehive hut.

LOWER LAKE

While the Upper Lake has the best scenery, the most fascinating buildings lie in the lower part of the valley east of the Lower Lake, huddled together in the heart of the ancient **monastic site**.

Just round the bend from the Glendalough Hotel is the stone arch of the **monastery gatehouse**, the only surviving example of a monastic entranceway in the country. Just inside the entrance is a large slab with an incised cross.

Beyond that lies a **graveyard**, which is still in use. The 10th-century **round tower** is 33m tall and 16m in circumference at the base. The upper storeys and conical roof were reconstructed in 1876. Near the tower, to the southeast, is the **Cathedral of St Peter and St Paul** with a 10th-century nave. The chancel and sacristy date from the 12th century.

At the centre of the graveyard to the south of the round tower is the **Priest's House**. This odd building dates from 1170

but has been heavily reconstructed. It may have been the location of shrines of St Kevin. Later, during penal times, it became a burial site for local priests – hence the name. The 10th-century **St Mary's Church**, 140m southwest of the round tower, probably originally stood outside the walls of the monastery and belonged to local nuns. It has a lovely western doorway. A little to the east are the scant remains of **St Kieran's Church**, the smallest at Glendalough.

Glendalough's trademark is **St Kevin's Kitchen** or **Church** at the southern edge of the enclosure. This church, with a miniature round towerlike belfry, protruding sacristy and steep stone roof, is a masterpiece. How it came to be known as a kitchen is a mystery as there's no indication that it was anything other than a church. The oldest parts of the building date from the 11th century – the structure has been remodelled since but it's still a classic early Irish church.

At the junction with Green Rd as you cross the river just south of these two churches is the **Deer Stone** in the middle of a group of rocks. Legend claims that when St Kevin needed milk for two orphaned babies, a doe stood here waiting to be milked. The stone is actually a *bullaun* (a stone used as a mortar for grinding medicines or food). Many such stones are thought to be prehistoric,

Glendalough

WALKING TOUR

A visit to Glendalough is a trip through ancient history and a refreshing hike in the hills. The ancient monastic settlement founded by St Kevin in the 5th century grew to be quite powerful by the 9th century, but it started falling into ruin from 1398 onwards. Still, you won't find more evocative clumps of stones anywhere.

Start at the **Main Gateway ❶** to the monastic city, where you will find a cluster of important ruins, including the (nearly perfect) 10th-century **Round Tower ❷**, the **Cathedral ❸** dedicated to **Sts Peter and Paul**, and **St Kevin's Kitchen ❹**, which is really a church. Cross the stream past the famous **Deer Stone ❺**, where Kevin was supposed to have milked a doe, and turn west along the path. It's a 1.5km walk to the **Upper Lake ❻**. On the lake's southern shore is another cluster of sites, including the **Reefert Church ❼**, a plain 11th-century Romanesque church where the powerful O'Toole family buried their kin, and **St Kevin's Cell ❽**, the remains of a beehive hut where Kevin is said to have lived.

ST KEVIN

St Kevin came to the valley as a young monk in AD 498, in search of a peaceful retreat. He was reportedly led by an angel to a Bronze Age tomb now known as St Kevin's Bed. For seven years he slept on stones, wore animal skins, survived on nettles and herbs and – according to legend – developed an affinity with the birds and animals. One legend has it that, when Kevin needed milk for two orphaned babies, a doe stood waiting at the Deer Stone to be milked.

Kevin soon attracted a group of disciples and the monastic settlement grew, until by the 9th century Glendalough rivalled Clonmacnoise as Ireland's premier monastic city. According to legend, Kevin lived to the age of 120. He was canonised in 1903.

St Kevin's Cell
This beehive hut is reputedly where St Kevin would go for prayer and meditation; not to be confused with St Kevin's Bed, a cave where he used to sleep.

Deer Stone
The spot where St Kevin is said to have truly become one with the animals is really just a large mortar called a *bullaun*, used for grinding food and medicine.

St Kevin's Kitchen
This small church is unusual in that it has a round tower sticking out of the roof – it looks like a chimney, hence the church's nickname.

Reefert Church

Its name derives from the Irish *right fearta*, which means 'burial place of the kings'. Seven princes of the powerful O'Toole family are buried in this simple structure.

Upper Lake

The site of St Kevin's original settlement is on the banks of the Upper Lake, one of the two lakes that gives Glendalough its name – the 'Valley of the Lakes'.

⑧

⑦

⑥

Round Tower

Glendalough's most famous landmark is the 33m-high Round Tower, which is exactly as it was when it was built a thousand years ago except for the roof; this was replaced in 1876 after a lightning strike.

②

③

①

← NORTH

INFORMATION

At the eastern end of the Upper Lake is the National Park Information Point, which has leaflets and maps on the site, local walks, etc. The grassy spot in front of the office is a popular picnic spot in summer.

Cathedral of Sts Peter & Paul

The largest of Glendalough's seven churches, the cathedral was built gradually between the 10th and 13th centuries. The earliest part is the nave, where you can still see the *antae* (slightly projecting column at the end of the wall) used for supporting a wooden roof.

Main Gateway

The only surviving entrance to the ecclesiastical settlement is a double-arch; notice that the inner arch rises higher than the outer one in order to compensate for the upward slope of the causeway.

RICK GERHARTER/GETTY IMAGES ©

Powerscourt Estate

One of the big draws in the whole of County Wicklow is the Palladian mansion and gardens that make up the Powerscourt Estate. The house was built by Richard Cassels between 1731 and 1743. An extra story was added in 1787 and other alterations were made during the 19th century, but the whole place was gutted by fire in 1974. Restoration of the house has been painfully slow, so you're limited to exploring the ground floor – which is home to a decent **cafe** and an outlet of the popular **Avoca** handicrafts chain.

If you can deal with the crowds (summer weekends are the worst) or, better still, avoid the worst of them and visit midweek, you're in for a real treat. Easily the biggest drawcards of the whole pile are the simply magnificent 20-hectare formal gardens and the breathtaking views that accompany them.

Originally laid out in the 1740s, the gardens were redesigned in the 19th century by Daniel Robinson, who had as much fondness for the booze as he did for horticultural pursuits: he liked (needed?) to be wheeled around in a wheelbarrow after a certain point in the day. Perhaps this influenced his largely informal style, which resulted in a magnificent blend of landscaped gardens, sweeping terraces, statuary, ornamental lakes, secret hollows, rambling walks and walled enclosures with more than 200 types of trees and shrubs, all beneath the stunning natural backdrop of the Great Sugarloaf Mountain to the southeast. Tickets come with a map laying out 40-minute and hour-long tours of the gardens.

The main entrance is 500m south of the village square.

NEED TO KNOW

www.powerscourt.ie; near Enniskerry; admission to house free, gardens adult/child €8.50/5; ⊙9.30am-5.30pm Mar-Oct, to dusk Nov-Feb

and they were widely regarded as having supernatural properties: women who bathed their faces with water from the hollow were supposed to keep their looks forever. The early churchmen brought the stones into their monasteries, perhaps hoping to inherit some of their powers.

The road east leads to **St Saviour's Church**, with its detailed Romanesque carvings. To the west, a nice woodland trail leads up the valley past the Lower Lake to the Upper Lake.

Tours

Bus Éireann
Bus Tour

(01-836 6111; www.buseireann.ie; Busáras; adult/child/student €29/23/25; departs 10am mid-Mar–Oct) Includes admission to the visitor centre and a visit to Powerscourt Estate in this whole-day tour, which returns to Dublin at about 5.45pm. The guides are good but impersonal.

Wild Wicklow Tour
Bus Tour

(01-280 1899; www.wildwicklow.ie; adult €28, student & child €25; departs 9am) Award-winning tours of Glendalough, Avoca and the Sally Gap that never fail to generate rave reviews for atmosphere and all-round fun, but so much craic has made a casualty of informative depth. The first pick-up is at the Shelbourne and then the tourist office, but there are a variety of pick-up points throughout Dublin; check the point nearest you when booking. The tour returns to Dublin about 5.30pm.

Sleeping

Most B&Bs are in or around Laragh, a village 3km east of Glendalough, or on the way there from Glendalough.

Glendalough Hotel
Hotel €€

(0404-45135; www.glendaloughhotel.com; s/d from €90/140; @ 🛜 ♿) There's no mistaking Glendalough's best hotel, conveniently located next door to the visitor centre. There is no shortage of takers for its 44 fairly luxurious bedrooms.

Eating

Wicklow Heather
International €€

(0404-45157; www.thewicklowheather.com; Main St, Laragh; mains €16-26; noon-8.30pm) This is the best place for anything substantial. The menu offers Wicklow lamb, wild venison, Irish beef and fresh fish (the trout is excellent) – most of it sourced locally and all of it traceable from farm to fork. Next door is the owners' **B&B** (s/d €35/70), where there are five well-appointed rooms, all en suite.

Getting There & Away

St Kevin's Bus (01-281 8119; www.glendaloughbus.com; one-way/return €13/20) departs from outside the Mansion House on Dawson St in Dublin at 11.30am and 6pm Monday to Saturday, and 11.30am and 7pm Sunday (one-way/return €13/20, 1½ hours). It also stops at the Town Hall in Bray. Departures from Glendalough are at 7.15am and 4.30pm Monday to Saturday. During the week in July and August the later bus runs at 5.30pm, and there is an additional service at 9.45am.

Blessington

POP 4018

Lined with pubs, shops and 17th- and 18th-century townhouses, Blessington makes a convenient exploring base for the surrounding area. The main attraction is Russborough House.

Sights

Russborough House
Historic Building

(045-865 239; www.russboroughhouse.ie; Blessington; adult/child guided tour €10/6, 3D exhibition €6/4; 10am-6pm daily May-Sep, Sun & bank holidays Apr & Oct) Magnificent Russborough House is one of Ireland's finest stately homes, a Palladian pleasure palace built for Joseph Leeson (1705–83), later the first Earl of Milltown and, later still, Lord Russborough. It was built between 1741 and 1751 to the design of Richard Cassels, who was at the height of his fame as an architect.

The house remained in the Leeson family until 1931. In 1952 it was sold to Sir Alfred Beit, the eponymous nephew of the co-founder of the de Beers diamond-mining company. An avid art collector, he lined his walls with paintings by Velázquez, Vermeer, Goya and Rubens among others.

The admission price includes a 45-minute tour of the house, decorated in typical Georgian style, and all the important paintings, which, given the history, is a monumental exercise in staying positive. A recent addition is the 3D exhibition on Sir Alfred's life and travels.

🛏 Sleeping

West Wing　　　Self-Catering €€€
(Russborough House; www.irishlandmark.com; Russborough House, Blessington; 3-nights Beit Residence €1200, 2-nights Garden Apt €650) The Beit family lived in the west wing of Russborough House until 2005: their former digs have now been converted into two luxury self-catering apartments managed by the Irish Landmark Trust. The Garden

Apartment is big – it sleeps seven comfortably across three bedrooms – but the Beit Residence is simply *huge*: eight people can live in the kind of luxury available only to the 1%. The Garden Apartment has a minimum stay of two nights; you'll have to spend three nights if you want the Beit Residence.

🍴 Eating

Grangecon Café　　International €€
(☎ 045-857 892; Tullow Rd; mains €11-18; ⊗ 10am-5pm Tue-Sat) Salads, home-baked dishes and a full menu of Irish cheeses are the staples at this tiny, terrific cafe in a converted schoolhouse. Everything here, from the pasta to the delicious apple juice, is made on the premises and many of the ingredients are organic. A short but solid menu represents the best of Irish cooking.

ℹ Getting There & Away

Blessington is 35km southwest of Dublin on the N81. There are regular daily services by **Dublin Bus** (☎ 01-873 4222, 01-872 0000); catch bus

Left: Wicklow Mountains (p109);
Below: Russborough House (p113), Blessington

(LEFT) GARETH MCCORMACK/GETTY IMAGES ©;
(BELOW) DESIGN PICS/THE IRISH IMAGE COLLECTION/GETTY IMAGES ©

65 from Eden Quay in Dublin (€4.40, 1½ hours, every 1½ hours). **Bus Éireann** (☏01-836 6111; www. buseireann.ie) operates express bus 005 to and from Waterford, with stops in Blessington two or three times daily; from Dublin it's pick-up only and from Waterford drop-off only.

Southern Wicklow

RATHDRUM

POP 2123

The quiet village of Rathdrum at the foot of the Vale of Clara comprises little more than a few old houses and shops, but in the late 19th century it had a healthy flannel industry and a poorhouse. It's not what's in the town that's of interest to visitors, however, but what's just outside it.

The small **tourist office** (☏0404-46262; 29 Main St; ⏰9am-5.30pm Mon-Fri) has leaflets and information on the town and its surrounding area, including the Wicklow Way.

⊙ Sights

Avondale House   House

(☏0404-46111; adult €5, student & child €4; ⏰11am-6pm May-Aug, Sat & Sun only Apr, by appointment only rest of year) Avondale House, a fine Palladian mansion surrounded by a marvellous 209-hectare estate, was the birthplace and Irish headquarters of Charles Stewart Parnell. Designed by James Wyatt in 1779, the house's many highlights include a stunning vermilion-hued library (Parnell's favourite room) and beautiful dining room.

✕ Eating

Bates Inn   Pub €€

(www.batesrestaurant.com; 3 Market Sq, Rathdrum; mains €19-25; ⏰6-9.30pm Tue-Sat, 12.30-3pm & 6-9pm Sun) Housed in a coaching inn that first opened its doors in 1785 is this outstanding restaurant that puts a

CHRIS HILL/GETTY IMAGES ©

⭐ Don't Miss
Castletown House

The magnificent Castletown House simply has no peer. It is Ireland's largest and most imposing Georgian estate, and a testament to the vast wealth enjoyed by the Anglo-Irish gentry during the 18th century. The house was built between the years 1722 and 1732 for William Conolly (1662–1729), speaker of the Irish House of Commons and, at the time, Ireland's richest man. Born into relatively humble circumstances in Ballyshannon, County Donegal, Conolly made his fortune through land transactions in the uncertain aftermath of the Battle of the Boyne (1690).

The original '16th-century Italian palazzo' design of the house was by the Italian architect Alessandro Galilei (1691–1737) in 1718. In 1724 the project was entrusted to Sir Edward Lovett Pearce (1699–1733). Inspired by the work of Andrea Palladio, Pearce enlarged the original design of the house and added the colonnades and the terminating pavilions. A highlight of the opulent interior is the Long Gallery, replete with family portraits and exquisite stucco work by the Francini brothers.

Conolly didn't live to see the completion of his wonder-palace. His widow, Katherine, lived in the unfinished house after his death in 1729, and instigated many improvements. Her main architectural contributions were the curious 42.6m **obelisk**, known as the Conolly Folly, and the Heath Robinson-esque (or Rube Goldberg-esque) **Wonderful Barn** (📞01-624 5448; Leixlip; 🕒closed to the public), six teetering storeys wrapped by an exterior spiral staircase, on private property just outside Leixlip.

Buses 120 and 123 run from Dublin to Celbridge (€3.50; 30 minutes; every half-hour Monday to Friday, hourly Saturday, six buses Sunday).

NEED TO KNOW

📞01-628 8252; www.castletownhouse.ie; Celbridge; adult/child €4.50/3.50; 🕒10am-4.45pm Tue-Sun Easter-Oct

premium on exquisitely prepared meat dishes (the chargrilled beef options are particularly good). One of the better options in southern Wicklow. Bookings recommended for weekend evenings.

ⓘ Getting There & Away

Bus Éireann (☏01-836 6111; www.buseireann.ie) Service 133 goes to Rathdrum from Dublin (one-way/return €12.50/19.50, 1¾ hours, 10 daily) on its way to Arklow.

Iarnród Éireann (☏01-836 6222) Trains serve Rathdrum from Dublin on the main Dublin to Rosslare Harbour line (one-way/return €15.50/20.50, 1½ hours, five daily).

COUNTY KILDARE

Kildare Town

POP 7538

Built around a compact, triangular square fronting its impressive cathedral, Kildare is a busy enough place, even if there aren't a lot of attractions within the town itself. It is closely associated with Ireland's second-most important saint, Brigid.

◎ Sights

St Brigid's Cathedral   Cathedral

(☏045-521 229; Market Sq; admission by donation, round tower admission €6; ⊙10am-1pm & 2-5pm Mon-Sat, 2-5pm Sun May-Sep) The solid presence of 13th-century St Brigid's Cathedral looms over Kildare Sq. Look out for a fine stained-glass window inside that depicts the three main saints of Ireland: Patrick, Brigid and Colmcille. The church also contains the restored tomb of Walter Wellesley, Bishop of Kildare, which disappeared soon after his death in 1539 and was only found again in 1971. One of its carved figures has been variously interpreted as an acrobat or a sheila-na-gig (a carved female figure with exaggerated genitalia).

The 10th-century **round tower** in the grounds is Ireland's second highest at 32.9m, and one of the few that you can

climb, provided the guardian is around. Its original conical roof has been replaced with an unusual Norman battlement. Near the tower is a **wishing stone** – put your arm through the hole and touch your shoulder and your wish will be granted. On the north side of the cathedral are the heavily restored foundations of an ancient **fire temple**.

Irish National Stud & Gardens   Gardens

(☏045-521 617; www.irishnationalstud.ie; Tully; adult/student/child €12.50/9.50/7; ⊙9am-6pm mid-Feb–Dec, last admission 5pm) With highlights like the 'Teasing Shed', the Irish National Stud, about 3km south of town, is the big attraction in the locality – horse-mad Queen Elizabeth II dropped in during her historic 2011 visit. The stud was founded by Colonel Hall Walker (of Johnnie Walker whiskey fame) in 1900. Today the immaculately kept centre is owned and managed by the Irish government. It breeds high-quality stallions to mate with mares from all over the world.

There are **guided tours** (many of the guides have a real palaver) of the stud every hour on the hour, with access to the intensive-care unit for newborn foals. If you visit between February and June, you might even see a foal being born. Alternatively, the foaling unit shows a 10-minute video with all the action. You can wander the stalls and go eye-to-eye with famous stallions. Given that most are now geldings, they probably have dim memories of their time in the aforementioned Teasing Shed, the place where stallions are stimulated for mating, while dozens look on. The cost: tens of thousands of euros for a top horse.

Also disappointing are the much-vaunted **Japanese Gardens** (part of the complex), considered to be the best of their kind in Europe – which doesn't say much for other contenders. Created between 1906 and 1910, they trace the journey from birth to death through 20 landmarks, including the Tunnel of Ignorance, the Hill of Ambition and the Chair of Old Age. When in bloom the flowers are beautiful, but the gardens are too small and bitty to really impress.

🛏 Sleeping

Martinstown House Hotel €€
(📞045-441 269; www.martinstownhouse.com; The Curragh; s/d from €90/150; ⊙mid-Jan–mid-Dec) This beautiful 18th-century country manor is built in the frilly Strawberry Hill Gothic style and set in a 170-acre estate and farm surrounded by trees. The house has four rooms filled with antiques; children are banned – darn. You can arrange for memorable dinners in advance (€55); ingredients are drawn from the kitchen garden.

🍴 Eating

Agape Cafe €
(📞045-533 711; Station Rd; meals €6-12; ⊙9am-6pm Mon-Sat) Just off Market Sq, this trendy little cafe has a fine range of homemade food. There's a full coffee bar and a menu of salads, soups, sandwiches and tasty hot specials.

❶ Getting There & Away

There is frequent Bus Éireann service between Dublin Busáras and Kildare (single/return €12.50/19.50, 1¾ hours). Some Dublin buses also service the Stud.

The Dublin–Kildare train (📞01-836 6222) runs from Heuston train station and stops in Kildare (€16.50, 35 minutes, one to four per hour). This is a major junction and trains continue to numerous places including Ballina, Galway, Limerick and Waterford.

COUNTY MEATH

Brú na Bóinne

The vast Neolithic necropolis known as Brú na Bóinne (the Boyne Palace) is one of the most extraordinary sites in Europe. A thousand years older than Stonehenge, it's a powerful and evocative testament to the mind-boggling achievements of prehistoric humankind.

The complex was built to house the remains of those who were at the top of the social heap and its tombs were the largest artificial structures in Ireland until

Knowth (122)

UIG VIA GETTY IMAGES/GETTY IMAGES ©

the construction of the Anglo-Norman castles 4000 years later. The area consists of many different sites; the three principal ones are Newgrange, Knowth and Dowth.

Over the centuries the tombs decayed, were covered by grass and trees, and were plundered by everybody from Vikings to Victorian treasure hunters, whose carved initials can be seen on the great stones of Newgrange. The countryside around the tombs is home to countless other ancient tumuli (burial mounds) and standing stones.

◉ Sights

Newgrange
Historic Site

(www.newgrange.com; adult/student incl visitor centre €6/3; ⊙9am-5pm Nov-Jan, 9.30am-5.30 Feb-Apr, 9am-6.30pm May, to 7pm Jun-Sep, 9.30am-5.30pm Oct) Even from afar, you know that Newgrange is something special. Its white round stone walls topped by a grass dome have an otherworldly appearance, and even just the size is impressive: 80m in diameter and 13m high. But underneath it gets even better. Here lies the finest Stone Age passage tomb in Ireland, and one of the most remarkable prehistoric sites in Europe. It dates from around 3200 BC, pre-dating the pyramids by some six centuries.

You can walk down the narrow 19m passage, lined with 43 stone uprights (some of them engraved), which leads into the tomb chamber about one-third of the way into the colossal mound. The chamber has three recesses, and in these are large basin stones that held cremated human bones. As well as the remains, the basins would have held funeral offerings of beads and pendants, but these were stolen long before the archaeologists arrived.

Above, the massive stones support a 6m-high corbel-vaulted roof. A complex drainage system means that not a drop of water has penetrated the interior in 40 centuries.

Local Knowledge

Brú na Bóinne

BY MARY GIBBONS, HERITAGE TOUR SPECIALIST (WWW. HERITAGEIRELAND.IE)

1 GREAT STONE CIRCLE
The great stone circle surrounding Newgrange is the largest of its kind in Ireland; although only 12 are left, there were once 35-odd standing stones. It's believed to have been an astronomical calendar, with shadows dividing the year.

2 THE KERBSTONES
The kerbstones built into the outside of the passage tomb are part of a Neolithic art tradition which spanned over a thousand years. The most magnificent is at the entrance, forming a symbolic barrier between the living and the dead.

3 THE PASSAGE
The 19m stone tunnel passage leading into the mound has some of the most beautifully executed Neolithic art anywhere in the world. Individually decorated stones alternate with undecorated ones. Just before the inner chamber is one of the most famous pieces of Neolithic art in Ireland: a triple spiral framed by triple lines in a chevron pattern.

4 THE INNER CHAMBER
The inner chamber, rediscovered in 1699 by one of the victors of the Battle of the Boyne, is a corbelled, cruciform-shaped space over 6m high, with three heavily decorated recesses; one has a triple spiral regarded by Dr Geraldine Stout, the foremost authority on Newgrange, as 'the most exquisite carving to be found in the entire corpus of European megalithic art'.

5 WINTER SOLSTICE EVENT
For 17 minutes of magic on the morning of 21 December, the light of the rising sun funnels through a light box above the main passage entrance and illuminates the passageway and the main chamber to reveal one of the world's most extraordinary prehistoric art galleries.

Brú na Bóinne

All visits start at the visitor centre ❶, which has a terrific exhibit that includes a short context-setting film. From here, you board a shuttle bus that takes you to Newgrange ❷, where you'll go past the kerbstone ❸ into the main passage ❹ and the burial chamber ❺. If you're not a lucky lottery winner for the solstice, fear not – there's an artificial illumination ceremony that replicates it. If you're continuing on to tour Knowth ❻, you'll need to go back to the visitor centre and get on another bus; otherwise, you can drive directly to Dowth ❼ and visit, but only from outside (the information panels will tell you what you're looking at).

Newgrange interior passage
The passage is lined with 43 orthostats, or standing stones, averaging 1.5m in height: 22 on the left (western) side, 21 on the right (eastern) side.

Newgrange

Knowth
Roughly one third of all megalithic art in Western Europe is contained within the Knowth complex, including more than 200 decorated stones. Alongside typical motifs like spirals, lozenges and concentric circles are rare crescent shapes.

Newgrange entrance kerbstone
Newgrange is surrounded by 97 kerbstones (24 of which are still buried), numbered sequentially from K1, the beautifully decorated entrance stone.

TOP TIP

Best time to visit is early morning mid-week during summer, when there are fewer tourists and no school tours.

Dowth

Like Newgrange, Dowth's passage grave is designed to allow for a solar alignment during the winter solstice. The crater at the top was due to a clumsy attempt at excavation in 1847.

ARCHAEO IMAGES / ALAMY ©

BRÚ NA BÓINNE VISITOR CENTRE ©

FACT FILE

The winter solstice event is witnessed by a maximum of 60 people selected by lottery. In 2012, 29,570 people applied.

⑦

Newgrange burial chamber

The corbelled roof of the chamber has remained intact since its construction, and is considered one of the finest of its kind in Europe.

❶

Brú na Bóinne Visitor Centre

Opened in 1997, the modern visitor centre was heavily criticised at first as being unsuitable but then gained plaudits for the way it integrated into the landscape.

Visiting Brú na Bóinne

In an effort to protect the tombs and their mystical surroundings, all visits to Brú na Bóinne start at the **Brú na Bóinne Visitor Centre** (☏ 041-988 0300; www. heritageireland.ie; Donore; adult/student visitor centre €3/2; visitor centre & Newgrange €6/3; visitor centre & Knowth €5/3; visitor centre, Newgrange & Knowth €11/6; ☺ 9am-5pm Nov-Jan, 9.30am-5.30 Feb-Apr, 9am-6.30pm May, to 7pm Jun-Sep, 9.30am-5.30pm Oct) from where there is a shuttle bus to the tombs. Built in a spiral design echoing Newgrange, the centre houses interactive exhibits on prehistoric Ireland and its passage tombs, and has regional tourism info, an excellent cafeteria, plus a book and souvenir shop. Upstairs, a glassed-in observation mezzanine looks out over Newgrange.

Allow plenty of time: an hour's visit for the visitor centre alone, two hours to include a trip to Newgrange or Knowth, and half a day to see all three (Dowth is closed to tourists).

In summer, particularly at weekends, Brú na Bóinne can be very crowded; on peak days over 2000 people can show up. As there are only 750 tour slots, you may not be guaranteed a visit to either of the passage tombs. Tickets are sold on a first-come, first-served basis (no advance booking) so the best advice is to arrive early in the morning or visit midweek and be prepared to wait.

The Brú na Bóinne Visitor Centre is well signposted from all directions. Tours are primarily outdoors with no shelter so bring rain gear, just in case.

Knowth   Historic Site

(adult/student incl visitor centre €5/3; ☺ 9am-5pm Nov-Jan, 9.30am-5.30 Feb-Apr, 9am-6.30pm May, to 7pm Jun-Sep, 9.30am-5.30pm Oct) Northwest of Newgrange, the burial mound of Knowth was built around the same time and seems set to surpass its better-known neighbour in both its size and the importance of the discoveries made here. It has the greatest collection of passage-grave art ever uncovered in Western Europe, and has been under intermittent excavation since 1962.

The excavations soon cleared a passage leading to the central chamber which, at 34m, is much longer than the one at Newgrange. Further excavations are likely to continue for the next decade at least, so you may see archaeologists at work when you visit.

Dowth   Historic Site

The circular mound at Dowth is similar in size to Newgrange – about 63m in diameter – but is slightly taller at 14m high. It has suffered badly at the hands of everyone from road builders and treasure hunters to amateur archaeologists, who scooped out the centre of the tumulus in the 19th century. For a time, Dowth even had a tearoom ignobly perched on its summit. Because it's unsafe, Dowth is closed to visitors, though the mound can be viewed from the road between Newgrange and Drogheda. Serious excavations began in 1998 and will continue for years to come.

North of the tumulus are the ruins of **Dowth Castle** and **Dowth House**.

🎫 Tours

Brú na Bóinne is one of the most popular tourist attractions in Ireland, and there are plenty of organised tours. Most depart from Dublin.

Mary Gibbons Tours   Guided Tour

(☏ 086 355 1355; www.newgrangetours.com; tour per adult/student €35/30) Tours depart from numerous Dublin hotels, beginning at 9.30am Monday to Friday, 7.50am Saturday and Sunday, and take in the whole of the Boyne Valley including Newgrange and the Hill of Tara. The expert guides offer a fascinating insight into Celtic and pre-Celtic life in Ireland. Pay cash on the bus (no credit cards).

Over the Top Tours Guided Tour
(01-860 0404; www.overthetoptours.com; tour per adult/student €28/25) Offers a Celtic Experience day tour that concentrates on the Boyne Valley, as well as an intriguing 'Mystery' Tour.

❶ Getting There & Away

Bus Éireann has a service linking the Brú na Bóinne Visitor Centre with Drogheda's bus station (one way/return €4/7, 20 minutes, two daily Monday to Saturday), with connections to Dublin.

The Battle of the Boyne

More than 60,000 soldiers of the armies of King James II and King William III fought in 1690 on this patch of farmland on the border of Counties Meath and Louth. In the end, William prevailed and James sailed off to France.

Today, the **battle site** (www.battleoftheboyne.ie; adult/child €4/2; ⏰10am-6pm May-Sep, 9.30am-5.30pm Mar & Apr, 9am-5pm Oct-Feb; 👫) is part of the Oldbridge Estate farm. At the visitor centre you can watch a short show about the battle, see original and replica weaponry of the time and explore a laser battlefield model.

The battle site is 3km north of Donore, signposted off the N51. From Drogheda, it's 3.5km west along Rathmullan Rd (follow the river).

Tara

The **Hill of Tara** is Ireland's most sacred stretch of turf occupying a place at the heart of Irish history, legend and folklore. It was the home of the mystical druids, the priest-rulers of ancient Ireland, who practised their particular form of Celtic paganism under the watchful gaze of the all-powerful goddess Maeve (Medbh). Later it was the ceremonial capital of the high kings, all 142 of them, who ruled until the arrival of Christianity in the 5th century. It is also one of the most important ancient sites in Europe, with a Stone Age passage tomb and prehistoric burial mounds that date back up to 5000 years.

Cannon on the Battle of the Boyne site

DAVID LYONS/GETTY IMAGES ©

Although little remains other than humps and mounds on the hill, its historic and folkloric significance is immense.

HISTORY

The Celts believed that Tara was the sacred dwelling place of the gods and the gateway to the otherworld. The passage grave was thought to be the final resting place of the Tuatha dé Danann, the mythical fairy folk. They were real enough, but instead of pixies and brownies, they were earlier Stone Age arrivals on the island.

When the early Christians hit town in the 5th century, they targeted Tara straight away. The arrival of Christianity marked the beginning of the end for Celtic pagan civilisation, and the high kings began to desert Tara, though the kings of Leinster continued to be based here until the 11th century.

◉ Sights

Rath of the Synods   Historic Site

The names applied to Tara's various humps and mounds were adopted from ancient texts, and mythology and religion intertwine with the historical facts. The Protestant church grounds and graveyard spill onto the remains of the Rath of the Synods, a triple-ringed fort where some of St Patrick's early synods (meetings) supposedly took place. Excavations of the enclosure suggest that it was used between AD 200 and 400 for burials, rituals and living quarters. Originally the ring fort would have contained wooden houses surrounded by timber palisades.

Excavations have uncovered Roman glass, shards of pottery and seals, showing links with the Roman Empire even though the Romans never extended their power to Ireland.

Royal Enclosure   Historic Site

To the south of the church, the Royal Enclosure is a large, oval Iron Age hill fort, 315m in diameter and surrounded by a bank and ditch cut through solid rock under the soil. Inside the Royal Enclosure are several smaller sites.

The **Mound of the Hostages**, a bump in the northern corner of the enclosure, is the most ancient known part of Tara, but is closed to the public. A treasure trove of artefacts was unearthed, including ancient Mediterranean beads of amber and faience (glazed pottery). More than 35 Bronze Age burials were found here, as well as extensive cremated remains from the Stone Age.

Although two other earthworks within the enclosure, the **Royal Seat** and **Cormac's House**, look similar, the Royal Seat is a ring fort with a house site in the centre, while Cormac's House is a barrow (burial mound) in the side of the circular bank. There are superb views of the Boyne and Blackwater Valleys.

Atop Cormac's House is the phallic **Stone of Destiny** (originally located

Trim Castle (p126)
STEPHEN SAKS/GETTY IMAGES ©

near the Mound of the Hostages), which represents the joining of the gods of the earth and the heavens. It's said to be the inauguration stone of the high kings, although alternative sources suggest that the actual coronation stone was the Stone of Scone, which was removed to Edinburgh, Scotland, and used to crown British kings. The would-be king stood on top of the Stone of Destiny and, if the stone let out three roars, he was crowned.

Enclosure of King Laoghaire
Historic Site

South of the Royal Enclosure is this large but worn ring fort where the king, a contemporary of St Patrick, is supposedly buried standing upright and dressed in his armour.

Banquet Hall
Historic Site

North of the churchyard is Tara's most unusual feature, a rectangular earthwork measuring 230m by 27m along a north-south axis. Tradition holds that it was built to cater for thousands of guests during feasts.

Gráinne's Fort
Historic Site

Gráinne was the daughter of King Cormac, the most lauded of all high kings. Betrothed to Fionn McCumhaill (Finn McCool), she eloped with Diarmuid, one of the king's warriors, on her wedding night. This became the subject of the epic *The Pursuit of Diarmuid and Gráinne*. Gráinne's Fort and the northern and southern **Sloping Trenches** to the northwest are burial mounds.

ℹ Information

Tara Visitor Centre (☑ 046-902 5903; www.heritageireland.ie; adult/child €3/1; ☺10am–6pm end May–mid-Sep) A former Protestant church (with a window by acclaimed stained glass artist, the late Evie Hone) is home to Tara's visitor centre and a 20-minute audiovisual presentation about the site.

ℹ Getting There & Away

Tara is 10km southeast of Navan, off the Dublin-Cavan road (R-147). It's well signposted.

♥ If You Like…
Country Homes

If you like Brook Lodge (p129) or the West Wing (p114) at Russborough House, you'll like these other fabulous country houses.

1 BALLYKNOCKEN HOUSE & COOKERY SCHOOL
(☑0404-44627; www.ballyknocken.com; s/d from €150/300, dinner mains €14-22) Beautiful ivy-clad Victorian home with stunning rooms and Catherine Fulvio's popular cookery school.

2 TINAKILLY COUNTRY HOUSE & RESTAURANT
(☑0404-69274; www.tinakilly.ie; Rathnew; r €115-200, dinner mains €22-29) Gorgeous country house hotel just outside Rathnew.

3 GHAN HOUSE
(☑042-937 3682; www.ghanhouse.com; Main Rd, Carlingford, County Louth; d from €130; @ 🛜) Eighteenth-century Georgian house with 12 rooms surrounded by flower-filled gardens.

Bus Éireann (www.buseireann.ie) services link Dublin to within 1km of the site (€9.10, 40 minutes, hourly Monday to Saturday and four times on Sunday). Ask the driver to drop you off at the Tara Cross, where you take a left turn off the main road. The bus company also organises coach tours to Tara, check the website for info.

Trim

POP 8268

Dominated by its mighty castle and atmospheric ruins, the quiet town of Trim was an important settlement in medieval times. Five city gates surrounded a busy jumble of streets, and as many as seven monasteries were established in the immediate area.

It's hard to imagine nowadays, but a measure of Trim's importance was that Elizabeth I considered building Trinity College here.

Detour:
Loughcrew Cairns

With all the hoopla over Brú na Bóinne, the amazing Stone Age passage graves strewn about the Loughcrew Hills are often overlooked. There are 30-odd tombs here, but they're hard to reach and relatively few people ever bother, which means you can enjoy this moody and evocative place in peace.

Like Brú na Bóinne, the graves were all built around 3000 BC, but unlike their better-known and better-excavated peers, the Loughcrew tombs were used at least until 750 BC.

The cairns are west of Kells, along the R154, near Oldcastle.

CARNBANE EAST

Carnbane East has a cluster of sites. **Cairn T** (⊙10am-6pm Jun-Aug) **FREE** is the biggest at about 35m in diameter, with numerous carved stones. One of its outlying kerbstones is called the **Hag's Chair**, and is covered in gouged holes, circles and other markings. You need the gate key to enter the passageway and a torch to see anything in detail. It takes about half an hour to climb Carnbane East from the car park.

In summer, access to Cairn T is controlled by **Heritage Ireland** (www. heritageireland.ie), which provides guides. But locals are passionate about the place and at any time of the year you can arrange for guides who will not only show you Cairn T but take you to some of the other cairns as well. Enquire at Kells' tourist office, or pick up the key from the cafe at **Loughcrew Gardens** (☎049-854 1060; www.loughcrew.com; ⊙12.30pm-5pm Mar-Oct; 🛜🚹).

CARNBANE WEST

From the car park, it takes about an hour to reach the summit of Carnbane West, where Cairn D and L, both some 60m in diameter, are located. They're in poor condition, though you can enter the passage and chamber of Cairn L, where there are numerous carved stones and a curved basin stone in which human ashes were placed.

Cairn L is administered by **Heritage Ireland** (www.heritageireland.ie), which gives out the key only to those with an authentic research interest.

TOURS

Beyond the Blarney (☎087 151 1511; www.beyondtheblarney.ie) is a knowledgeable Oldcastle-based outfit offering day tours and workshops (from €60).

◉ Sights

Trim Castle   Castle
(King John's Castle; www.heritageireland.ie; adult/ child incl tour €4/2; ⊙10am-6pm Easter-Sep, to 5.30pm Oct-Nov, 10am-5pm Sat & Sun Feb-Easter; 🚹) This remarkably well-preserved edifice was Ireland's largest Anglo-Norman for-

tification and is proof of Trim's medieval importance. Hugh de Lacy founded Trim Castle in 1173, but Rory O'Connor, said to have been the last high king of Ireland, destroyed this motte and bailey within a year. The building that can be seen today was begun around 1200 and it has hardly been modified since.

The entertaining and informative tour includes climbing narrow, steep stairs so is not recommended for very young children or anyone with mobility problems. Self-guided tours are also available.

Sleeping

Trim Castle Hotel Hotel €€
(046-948 3000; www.trimcastlehotel.com; Castle St; d from €90; @ 🛜 🛗) This pleasant, modern hotel is popular for weddings with more than 150 taking place in 2012. Acres of glossy marble in the foyer set the scene for the stylish modern rooms. The spacious sun terrace overlooks the castle while the carvery restaurant pulls in the punters at weekends. Excellent online deals.

Eating & Drinking

Harvest Home Bakery Bakery, Cafe €
(Market St; snacks €3-5; 🕑9am-6pm Mon-Fri) This sweet little bakery sells delicious breads, cakes, pies and biscuits, as well as lightweight snacks, homemade soups and fit-to-bursting sandwiches. It has outside tables for al fresco dining. Sugar- and gluten-free cakes are also available.

James Griffin Pub
(www.jamesgriffinpub.ie; High St; 🕑4pm-late Mon-Fri, from noon Sat & Sun; 🛜) This award-winning historic pub dates from 1904 and offers traditional music sessions, live music and live sports, as well as top DJs on the weekends. The interior has retained its traditional Irish pub atmosphere and visitors are made to feel very welcome.

Getting There & Around

Bus Éireann runs a bus at least hourly between Dublin and Trim (€11.50, 70 minutes).

COUNTY LOUTH

....

Drogheda
POP 38,578

Just 48km north of Dublin, Drogheda is a historic fortified town straddling the River Boyne. A clutch of fine old buildings, a handsome cathedral and a riveting museum provide plenty of cultural interest, while its atmospheric pubs, fine restaurants, numerous sleeping options and good transport links make it an excellent base for exploring the region.

Sleeping

Scholars Townhouse Hotel Hotel €€
(041-983 5410; www.scholarshotel.com; King St; d from €89; 🛜) This former monastery dates from 1867 and has recently been revamped as a family-owned hotel and restaurant. Despite the rooms being on the small side, there is nothing monastic about the facilities which include power showers, wi-fi and a superb bar and restaurant. The central location is ideal for exploring the town. Breakfast included.

Eating

Kitchen Mediterranean €€
(041-983 4630; www.kitchenrestaurant.ie; 2 South Quay; mains €15-20; 🕑11am-10pm Wed-Sat, noon-9pm Sun; 🛜🛗) 🌿 Appropriately named after the shiny open-plan kitchen and with a soothing sage-and-cream colour scheme, organic local produce is used as far as possible. The chef is a well travelled Londoner and it shows in such worldly ingredients as fried haloumi from Cyprus and Spanish Serrano ham. Breads are made on the premises and there is an excellent choice of wines by the glass.

Getting There & Away

Bus
Bus Éireann regularly serves Drogheda from Dublin (€7, one hour, one to four hourly).

Drogheda to Dundalk is another busy route (€5.75, 30 minutes, hourly).

Matthews (☎042-937 8188; www.matthews. ie) also runs an hourly or better service to Dublin (€9) and Dundalk (€9).

Train

The train station (☎041-983 8749; www. irishrail.ie) is just off Dublin Rd. Drogheda is on the main Belfast–Dublin line (Dublin €13.50, 45 minutes; Belfast €27.50, 1½ hours). There are six express trains (and many slower ones) each way, with five on Sunday.

Around Drogheda

A number of historic sites lie close to Drogheda, but you'll need your own transport.

◉ Sights

Beaulieu House, Gardens & Car Museum
Historic Site

(☎041-983 8557; www.beaulieu.ie; admission house €8, garden €6, museum €6; ☉11am-5pm Mon-Fri May–mid-Sep, plus 1-5pm Sat & Sun Jul & Aug) Before Andrea Palladio and the ubiquitous Georgian style that changed Irish architecture in the early 18th century, there was the Anglo-Dutch style, a simpler, less ornate look that is equally handsome. **Beaulieu House** is a particularly good example. It was built between 1660 and 1666 on lands confiscated from Oliver Plunkett's family by Cromwell, and given to the marshal of the army in Ireland, Sir Henry Tichbourne. The red-brick mansion, with its distinctive steep roof and tall chimneys, has been owned by the same family ever since.

The interiors are stunning and house a superb art collection ranging from lesser Dutch masters to 20th-century Irish painters. There's also a beautiful formal garden and a classic racing and rally car museum.

Beaulieu is about 5km northeast of Drogheda on the Baltray road.

Old Mellifont Abbey
Ruin

(☎041-982 6459; www.heritageireland.ie; Tullyallen; adult/student €3/1; ☉visitor centre 10am-6pm Easter-Sep) In its Anglo-Norman prime, this abbey was the Cistercians' first and most magnificent centre in the country.

Old Mellifont Abbey

EOIN CLARKE/GETTY IMAGES ©

Detour:
Brook Lodge & Wells Spa

One of Wicklow's fanciest boltholes is the **Brook Lodge & Wells Spa** (📞0402-36444; www.brooklodge.com; Macreddin; r/ste from €260/310; 📶), 3km west of Rathdrum in the village of Macreddin. It has 86 beautifully appointed rooms spread about the main house and the annexes, ranging from standard bedroom to mezzanine suite that wouldn't seem out of place in a New York penthouse. The accommodation is pure luxury, but it's the outstanding spa that keeps guests coming back for more. Mud and flotation chambers, Finnish and aroma baths, hammam (Turkish bath) massages and a full range of Decléor and Carita treatments make this one of the top spas in the country. The **Strawberry Tree**, located at Brook Lodge, is one of the best restaurants in Wicklow.

An **organic market** (Macreddin; 🕙10am-5pm Sun, Apr-Oct) is also held in Macreddin on the first Sunday of each month during summer.

Although the ruins are highly evocative and well worth exploring, they still don't do real justice to the site's former splendour. Mellifont was eventually the mother house for 21 lesser monasteries; at one point as many as 400 monks lived here.

Mellifont's most recognisable building and one of the finest examples of Cistercian architecture in Ireland is the 13th-century *lavabo*, an octagonal washing room for the monks.

The visitor centre describes monastic life in detail. The ruins themselves are always open and there's good picnicking next to the rushing stream. The abbey is about 1.5km off the main Drogheda–Collon road (R168).

Monasterboice
Historic Site

(🕙sunrise-sunset) FREE Crowing ravens lend an eerie atmosphere to Monasterboice, an intriguing monastic site containing a cemetery, two ancient church ruins, one of the finest and tallest round towers in Ireland, and two of the best high crosses.

The high crosses of Monasterboice are superb examples of Celtic art. The crosses performed an important didactic use, bringing the gospels alive for the uneducated, and they were probably brightly painted originally, although all traces of colour have long disappeared.

The cross near the entrance is known as **Muirdach's Cross**, named after a 10th-century abbot. The western face relates more to the New Testament, and from the bottom depicts the arrest of Christ, Doubting Thomas, Christ giving a key to St Peter, the Crucifixion, and Moses praying with Aaron and Hur.

The **West Cross** is near the round tower and stands 6.5m high, which makes it one of the tallest high crosses in Ireland. It's much more weathered, especially at the base, and only a dozen or so of its 50 panels are still legible. The more distinguishable ones on the eastern face include David killing a lion and a bear.

The **round tower**, minus its cap, is over 30m tall, and stands in a corner of the complex. Records suggest the tower interior went up in flames in 1097, destroying many valuable manuscripts and other treasures. It's closed to the public.

Come early or late in the day to avoid the crowds. It's just off the M1 motorway, about 8km north of Drogheda.

Kilkenny & the Southeast

Counties Kilkenny, Wexford and Waterford are (along with the southern chunk of Tipperary) collectively referred to as the 'sunny southeast'. This being Ireland the term is, of course, relative. But due to the moderating effect of the Gulf Stream, it is the country's warmest, driest region.

County Kilkenny's namesake city is the urban star with a castle, cathedral, medieval lanes and superb pubs and restaurants. To the south, Wexford and Waterford are wreathed with wide, sandy beaches, along with thatched fishing villages, genteel seaside towns and remote, windswept peninsulas littered by wrecks – as well as a swashbuckling history of marauding Vikings, lighthouse-keeping monks and shadowy knights' sects.

River Nore, Kilkenny city (p140)
RICHARD CUMMINS/GETTY IMAGES ©

Kilkenny & the Southeast

OFFALY

GALWAY

Terryglass

Borrisokane

Cloughjordan

Roscrea

Borris-in-Ossory

Lough Derg

M7

M8

Dromineer

Portroe

Nenagh

Moneygall

CLARE

Arra Mountains

Toomyvara

Killaloe

Ballina

Templemore

Birdhill

R498

Urlingford

Slieveardag Hills

Silvermine Mountains

R503

Thurles

Limerick

Shannon Estuary

Ballingarry

TIPPERARY

Killenaule

LIMERICK

Dundrum

Dualla

Rock of Cashel

Cashel

Thomastown

Golden

Tipperary

Fethard

M8

Kilfrush Cross Roads

Slievenamuck Hills

Bansha

N24

N76

Newtown

Galtee Mountains

Cahir

Clonmel

River Suir

Fourmilewater

Comeragh Mountains

Rathgormuck

M8

Ardfinnan

Burncourt

Newcastle

Ballymacarbry

Knockanaffrin (753m)

Cloheen

Ballyporeen

Knockmealdown Mountains

Nire Valley

Monavullagh Mountains

Seefin (728m)

Vee Gap

Blackwater Valley

N25

Ballyduff

River Blackwater

Cappoquin

Clonea

Lismore

Dungarvan

WATERFORD

N72

Dungarvan Harbour

Tallowbridge

Villierstown

Newtown

Helvic Head

Pulla

Ring Peninsula

Ringville Head

CORK

Mine Head

Youghal

Ardmore Bay

Killeagh

Ardmore

1 Dungarvan

2 Rock of Cashel

3 Ardmore

4 Kilkenny city

5 National 1978 Rebellion Centre

Kilkenny & the Southeast's Highlights

Dungarvan

Dungarvan (p156) has a blossoming reputation as a foodie hub that is more than well deserved, but it's not putting it on for visitors or tourism. Dungarvan is a real town with lots going on – it just puts a high premium on good food. Waterford Festival of Food (p156)

Rock of Cashel

Surely a highlight of any trip to Ireland, the iconic and much-photographed Rock of Cashel (p161) is one of the country's most spectacular archaeological sites. For over a thousand years, the rock's sturdy walls have protected a fabulous castle, an atmospheric (if roofless) abbey, a perfectly preserved round tower and the country's finest example of a Romanesque chapel.

SEAN CAFFREY/GETTY IMAGES ©

TRAVEL INK/GETTY IMAGES ©

Ardmore

3

The somewhat secluded seaside village of Ardmore (p158) in County Waterford is best known for its wide, crescent beach and its collection of early Christian monuments, including a round tower. There are excellent cliff walks and one of the best hotels in the country to keep you occupied.

MAURICE SAVAGE/ALAMY ©

4

Kilkenny City

Forget Galway, ignore Cork and don't even bother with Dublin. Kilkenny (p140) can stake its claim as Ireland's best city because it combines a stunning medieval historical centre of winding streets and notable buildings with a rich heritage of arts and culture – best expressed in the myriad festivals it hosts – and a throbbing nightlife that draws them in from far afield. River Nore

5

National 1798 Rebellion Centre

Ireland's history is rich in drama, struggle and tragedy, expressed poignantly in the National 1798 Rebellion Centre (p150), located in Enniscorthy, County Wexford. Near Vinegar Hill, the site of the bloodiest battle of the 1798 Rebellion, this centre reconstructs the struggle for Irish independence in memorable, moving fashion.

Kilkenny & the Southeast's Best...

Beauty Spots

○ **Kilmore Quay** Small fishing village that's all atmosphere. (p145)

○ **Hook Head** Brave the winds for beauty. (p147)

○ **Ardmore Cliffs** Stunning views from the clifftop. (p159)

○ **Copper Coast** Beautiful stretch of south County Waterford. (p161)

○ **Rock of Cashel** Best viewed from just north of town. (p161)

Festivals

○ **Kilkenny Arts Festival** Second-largest festival of its kind in Ireland. (p144)

○ **Kilkenny Rhythm & Roots** Ireland's biggest music festival. (p144)

○ **Cat Laughs Comedy Festival** Acclaimed gathering of international comics. (p144)

○ **Kilmore Seafood Festival** Traditional music, dancing and lots of seafood (see opposite).

○ **Waterford Festival of Food** The best of the region's produce. (p156)

Historic Notables

○ **Kilkenny Castle** One of the country's most important heritage sites. (p140)

○ **Dunbrody Famine Ship** Full-scale replica of a 19th-century 'Famine ship'. (p148)

○ **Tintern Abbey** Evocative ruins of the 13th-century Cistercian abbey. (p149)

○ **Jerpoint Abbey** Fine Cistercian ruin. (p143)

○ **National 1798 Rebellion Centre & Vinegar Hill** A tale of rebellion and the hill it happened on. (p150)

Need to Know

Local Activities

○ **Sea angling** Off the coast of Kilmore Quay. (p145)

○ **St Declan's Way** Walk this cliff trail as far as the Rock of Cashel. (p159)

○ **Fly fishing** Try it in the Rivers Nire or Suir, County Waterford. (p151)

○ **Cooking course** Take a course with either of the region's top chefs.(p156)

ADVANCE PLANNING

○ **Five months before** Book hotels and tickets if you're attending any of the big festivals in Kilkenny or Wexford.

○ **One month before** Book your hotel and make a reservation if you want to take a cooking course.

○ **Two weeks before** Cram in a little bit of Irish history, especially about Ireland's monastic tradition and its long struggle against the English.

RESOURCES

○ **Heritage Ireland** (www. heritageireland.ie) Info on Office of Public Works (OPW) sites.

○ **Sailing Ireland** (www. sailingireland.ie) Details of sailing charters.

○ **Kilmore Seafood Festival** (www. kilmorequayseafood festival.com) Details of a superb foodie fest in July.

○ **Discover Ireland** (www.discoverireland.ie/ southeast) Official tourist website.

○ **Kilkenny Tourist** (www.kilkennytourist. com) What to see and do in Kilkenny and its environs.

GETTING AROUND

○ **Bus** Good bus networks cover most of the area, but it's a slow way of exploring.

○ **Train** The main towns are linked, but not necessarily to each other.

○ **Car** The region's beauty is off the beaten path; you'll need a car to get there.

BE FOREWARNED

○ **Crowds** Kilkenny gets slammed during the major festivals.

○ **Weather** Statistically speaking, the southeast is the warmest region of Ireland, which doesn't necessarily mean it's warm. Come prepared.

○ **Hurling** The sport of choice in the southeast, especially in Kilkenny, whose rivalry with Waterford and Wexford is passionate!

Left: Fishing boats, Kilmore Quay (p145);
Above: Nire Valley, County Waterford (p151)

(LEFT) RICHARD CUMMINS/GETTY IMAGES ©;
(ABOVE) RICHARD CUMMINS/GETTY IMAGES ©

Kilkenny & the Southeast Itineraries

Medieval treasures, a rich monastic heritage and some of the finest coastline in Ireland await you as you explore the southeast. The following itineraries will give you ample opportunity to sample all of it and more.

3 DAYS

KILKENNY CITY TO CASHEL

KILKENNY BUZZ

Between the city's imposing castle, the gorgeous medieval layout and its collection of world-class festivals, ❶**Kilkenny city** (p140) could keep you busy for months, never mind the three days you've allotted here. Still, to make the best of your time, make a beeline on day one to Kilkenny Castle, which has been central to the major developments of Irish history since its construction in 1192. The impressive Long Gallery is a good example of the kind of luxury the high and mighty afforded themselves. Be sure to look inside St Canice's Cathedral (which gave the city its name) and pay a visit to the National Craft Gallery & Kilkenny Design Centre,

where you'll find some of the best-made Irish handicrafts and designs in the country.

On day two, spread your wings and make for the antique shops of ❷**Thomastown** (p144) and the nearby ruins of ❸**Jerpoint Abbey** (p143).

On day three, make the trek across the border into County Tipperary and feast your eyes on the rock-top stronghold of ❹**Cashel** (p161). All the while, don't forget to sample Kilkenny's superb collection of great pubs!

5 DAYS

WEXFORD TO WATERFORD
SOUTHEASTERN COASTLINER

In five days you can explore the best of the coastline counties of Wexford and Waterford. Start in the town of ❶ **Enniscorthy** (p150), visiting the National 1798 Rebellion Centre and historic Vinegar Hill before turning south, on day two, towards the coast and the traditional fishing village of ❷ **Kilmore Quay** (p145), from which you can visit the bird sanctuary on the ❸ **Saltee Islands** (p146). On day three, continue westward around the Hook Peninsula, where you should take a peak at the atmospheric ruins of ❹ **Tintern Abbey** (p149). Cross the border into County Waterford and visit ❺ **Waterford city** (p151), making sure not to miss the excellent Waterford Museum of Treasures. On day four, keep going west and make for ❻ **Dungarvan** (p156) home to Paul Flynn's excellent Tannery Restaurant & Cookery School; or ❼ **Ardmore** (p158) on the border with County Cork. Here, you'll find some fine walks along the cliffs at the edge of town and the excellent Michelin-starred restaurant at the Cliff House Hotel.

Tintern Abbey (p149)
RICHARD CUMMINS/GETTY IMAGES ©

Discover Kilkenny & the Southeast

COUNTY KILKENNY

Kilkenny City

POP 24,423

Kilkenny (Cill Chainnigh) is the Ireland of many visitors' imaginations. Its majestic riverside castle, tangle of 17th-century passageways, rows of colourful, old-fashioned shopfronts and centuries-old pubs with traditional live music all have a timeless appeal, as does its splendid medieval cathedral. But Kilkenny is also famed for its contemporary restaurants and rich cultural life.

◎ Sights

Kilkenny Castle Castle
(www.kilkennycastle.ie; adult/child €6/2.50, audioguides €5, parkland admission free; ☉9.30am-5pm Mar-Sep, to 4.30pm Oct-Feb, parkland daylight hours) Rising above the Nore, Kilkenny Castle is one of Ireland's most visited heritage sites. The first structure on this strategic site was a wooden tower built in 1172 by Richard de Clare, the Anglo-Norman conqueror of Ireland better known as Strongbow. In 1192, Strongbow's son-in-law, William Marshall, erected a stone castle with four towers, three of which survive.

During the winter months (November to January) there are 40-minute guided tours which shift to self-guided tours from February to October. For most visitors the focal point of the visit is the **Long Gallery**, which showcases portraits of the Butler family members over the centuries and is an impressive hall with high ceilings vividly painted with Celtic and pre-Raphaelite motifs.

Kilkenny city
TRISH PUNCH/DESIGN PICS/GETTY IMAGES ©

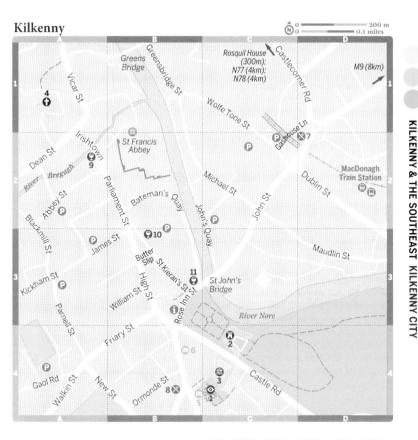

Kilkenny

The castle basement is also home to the **Butler Gallery** (www.butlergallery.com) FREE, featuring contemporary artwork in temporary exhibitions.

St Canice's Cathedral   Cathedral
(www.stcanicescathedral.ie; St Canice's Pl; adult/child €4/free; round tower €3/free; ⊙9am-6pm Mon-Sat, 2-6pm Sun, round tower Apr-Oct)
Soaring over the north end of the centre is Ireland's second-largest medieval cathedral (after St Patrick's in Dublin). This Gothic edifice with its iconic round tower has had a long and fascinating history. Legend has it that the first monastery was built here in the 6th century by St Canice, Kilkenny's patron saint. Records show that a wooden church on the site was burned down in 1087.

Outside the cathedral, a 30m-high **round tower** rises amid an odd array of ancient tombstones and is the oldest structure within the grounds.

National Craft Gallery & Kilkenny Design Centre   Gallery
(www.ccoi.ie; Castle Yard; ⊙10am-5.30pm Tue-Sat; ♿) Contemporary Irish crafts are showcased at these imaginative galleries in the former castle stables that also house the shops of the Kilkenny Design Centre. Behind the complex, look for the walkway that extends into the beautiful **Butler House gardens** with an unusual water feature constructed from remnants of the British-built Nelson Column, blown up by nationalists in Dublin around a century ago.

🛏 Sleeping

Rosquil House   Guesthouse €€
(📞056-772 1419; www.rosquilhouse.com; Castlecomer Rd; r from €70, 2-person apt from €60; 📶) Phil and Rhoda are the delightful hosts at this immaculately maintained guest house. Rooms are decorated with dark wood furniture and warm yellows with pretty paisley fabrics while the guest lounge is similarly tasteful with sink-into-sofas, brass framed mirrors and leafy plants. The breakfast is above average with homemade granola and fluffy omelettes with spinach and feta (and similar). The apartment is well equipped and comfortable (minimum three days stay).

Butler House   Boutique Hotel €€
(📞056-772 2828; www.butler.ie; 16 Patrick St; s/d from €77/135; @📶) You can't stay in Kilkenny Castle, but this historic mansion is surely the next best thing. Once the home of the earls of Ormonde, who built the castle, these days it houses a boutique hotel with aristocratic trappings including sweeping staircases, marble fireplaces, an art collection and impeccably trimmed gardens. The 13 generously sized rooms are individually decorated. Just to remind you you're staying in history, the floors creak.

Pembroke Hotel   Hotel €€€
(📞056-778 3500; www.pembrokekilkenny.com; Patrick St; r €109-160; @📶) Wake up

to castle views (from some of the 74 rooms) at this stylish, modern and central hotel. Deluxe rooms feature balconies, a rarity in Ireland, while the overall room decor is easy on the eye with a muted moss green and soft blue colourscheme. There's a leather sofa-filled bar on-site and the use of swimming and leisure facilities is just around the corner. Breakfast included.

🍴 Eating

Zuni   Cafe, Tapas €€
(www.zuni.ie; 26 Patrick St; dishes €7-15; ⊙9.30am-11pm; 📶) Dark leathers contrasting with lighter tables and walls at this one-time theatre provide a stylised backdrop for chef Maria Rafferty's inventive cooking. By day it's a swish cafe with a long breakfast and lunch menu, by night there's a varied tapas menu with some more hearty seafood options. Linger over small plates of tasty morsels like foie gras with chicken liver parfait and enjoy the fine wine selection.

Campagne   Modern Irish €€€
(📞056-777 2858; www.campagne.ie; 5 Gashouse Lane; lunch 2-/3-course set menu €24/29, dinner mains €25-30; ⊙12.30-2.30pm Fri-Sun, 6-10pm Tue-Sat) Chef Garrett Byrne has earned fame and a Michelin star for his bold, stylish restaurant in his native Kilkenny. A strong emphasis on local and artisan produce informs every dish, which have a French accent and are among the most memorable you'll enjoy in Ireland.

🍷 Drinking & Nightlife

Kyteler's Inn   Pub
(27 St Kieran's St; ⊙11am-midnight Sun-Thu, to 2am Fri & Sat, live music 6.30pm Mar-Oct) Dame Alice Kyteler's old house was built back in 1224 and has seen its share of history: the Dame had four husbands, all of whom died in suspicious circumstances, and she was charged with witchcraft in 1323. Today the rambling bar includes the original building, complete with vaulted ceiling and arches. There is a beer garden, courtyard and a

NICO TONDINI/GETTY IMAGES ©

⭐ Don't Miss
Jerpoint Abbey

One of Ireland's finest Cistercian ruins, Jerpoint Abbey is about 2.5km southwest of Thomastown on the M9. Established in the 12th century, it has been partially restored. The tower and cloister are late 14th or early 15th century. Look for the series of often amusing figures carved on the cloister pillars, including a knight. There are also stone carvings on the church walls and in the tombs of members of the Butler and Walshe families. Faint traces of a 15th- or 16th-century painting remain on the church's northern wall. This chancel area also contains a tomb thought to belong to hardheaded Felix O'Dulany, Jerpoint's first abbot and bishop of Ossory, who died in 1202.

NEED TO KNOW

☏ 056-772 4623; www.opw.ie; N9, Thomastown; adult/child €3/1; ⏱9am-5.30pm Mar-Oct, check hours Nov-Feb

large upstairs room for the live bands, ranging from trad to blues.

Tynan's Bridge House   Pub
(St John's Bridge; ⏱11am-late) This historic 1703 Georgian pub flaunting a brilliant blue facade is the best traditional bar in town with its horseshoe bar, original tile-work, regular clientele of crusty locals – and no TV! There is trad music on Monday to Thursday at 9pm

John Cleere's   Pub
(www.cleeres.com; 22 Parliament St; ⏱11.30am-11.30pm Mon-Thu, to 12.30am Fri & Sat, 1-11pm Sun) One of Kilkenny's finest venues for live music, theatre and comedy, this long bar has blues, jazz and rock, as well as trad music sessions on Monday and Wednesday. Recently introduced sandwiches and soups to the mix (five different soup choices daily).

If You Like...
Festivals

Kilkenny hosts several world-class events throughout the year that attract revellers in the thousands.

1 KILKENNY RHYTHM & ROOTS
(www.kilkennyroots.com) Over 30 pubs and other venues participate in hosting this major music festival during early May, with an emphasis on country and 'old-time' American roots music.

2 CAT LAUGHS COMEDY FESTIVAL
(www.thecatlaughs.com) Acclaimed gathering of world-class comedians in Kilkenny's hotels and pubs during early June.

3 KILKENNY ARTS FESTIVAL
(www.kilkennyarts.ie) The city comes alive with theatre, cinema, music, literature, visual arts, children's events and street spectacles for 10 action packed days in mid-August.

Information

Police (056-22222; Dominic St)

Tourist office (www.kilkennytourism.ie; Rose Inn St; 9.15am-5pm Mon-Sat) Stocks excellent guides and walking maps. Located in Shee Alms House, dating from 1582 and built in local stone by benefactor Sir Richard Shee to help the poor.

Getting There & Away

Bus

Bus Éireann (www.buseireann.ie) Operates from a shelter adjacent to the train station. Services: Carlow (€8.75, 35 minutes, three daily), Cork (€18.50, three hours, two daily), Dublin (€12, 2¼ hours, five daily) and Waterford (€10.50, one hour, two daily).

JJ Kavanagh & Sons (www.jjkavanagh.ie; stop at Ormonde Rd) Dublin airport (€13, three hours, six daily).

Train

Irish Rail (www.irishrail.ie) runs six times daily to/from Dublin's Heuston Station (from €10, 1¾ hours) and Waterford (from €10, 50 minutes) from the MacDonagh train station.

Central Kilkenny

THOMASTOWN

POP 1800

This small market town has a serenity it hasn't known in decades now that the M9 has diverted Dublin traffic away from the compact and attractive centre. Named after Welsh mercenary Thomas de Cantwell, Thomastown has some fragments of a medieval wall. Down by the bridge, **Mullin's Castle** is the sole survivor of the 14 castles once here.

Like the rest of Kilkenny, the area has a vibrant craft scene. Look out for **Clay Creations** (087 257 0735; Low St; 10am-5.30pm Tue-Sat) displaying the quixotic ceramics and sculptures of local artist Brid Lyons.

Just 4km southwest of Thomastown, high-fliers tee off at the Jack Nicklaus–blessed **Mount Juliet** (www.mountjuliet.ie; green fees from €100). Set over 600 wooded hectares, it also has its own equestrian centre, a gym and spa, two restaurants, wine master-classes, and luxurious rooms catering to every whim, right down to the pillow menu (accommodation from €130).

Eating

Sol Bistro   Modern Irish €€
(Low St; mains €12-25; noon-4pm, 6-10pm;) Kilkenny's modern Irish cafe has a branch in Thomastown's centre. It's a small cafe in a tidy old storefront and combines the best local ingredients for Irish classics with an innovative twist.

Getting There & Away

Trains on the Dublin to Waterford route via Kilkenny stop eight times daily in each direction in Thomastown. The station is 1km west of town.

INISTIOGE

POP 260

The little village of Inistioge (*in*-ish-teeg) is a picture. Its 18th-century, 10-arch **stone bridge** spans the River Nore and the central tranquil square is a delight. Somewhere so inviting could hardly hope to escape the attention of movie-location scouts: Inistioge's film credits include *Widow's Peak* (1993), *Circle of Friends* (1994) and *Where the Sun is King* (1996). After you have wandered through the tiny centre, take a **river walk** heading south from town.

Approximately 500m south, on Mt Alto, is the heavily forested **Woodstock Gardens** (www.woodstock.ie; parking in coins €4; ⊙ 9am-7pm Apr-Sep, 10am-4pm Oct-Mar), a beauty of a park with expansive 19th-century gardens, picnic areas and trails. The panorama of the valley and village below is spectacular. Coming from town, follow the signs for Woodstock Estate and enter the large gates then continue along the road for about 1km until you reach the car park. There are tearooms that open during the summer months.

GRAIGUENAMANAGH

POP 1300

Graiguenamanagh (greg-*na*-muh-na; known locally simply as Graigue) is the kind of place where you could easily find yourself staying longer than planned. Spanning the Barrow, an ancient six-arch stone bridge is illuminated at night and connects the village with the smaller township of Tinnahinch on the County Carlow side of the river (look for the darker stones on the Carlow side – a legacy from being blown up during the 1798 rebellion).

ℹ Getting There & Away

Graiguenamanagh is 23km southeast of Kilkenny city on the R703. Kilbride Coaches (www.kilbridecoaches.com) runs two buses Monday to Saturday to/from Kilkenny bus station (€6, 55 minutes).

COUNTY WEXFORD

....

Kilmore Quay

POP 417

Kilmore Quay is a small, working fishing village with thatched cottages and a harbour which is the jumping-off point for Ireland's largest bird sanctuary, the Saltee Islands. The cry of gulls and smell of the sea provide the appropriate atmosphere for sampling the local fish.

◎ Sights & Activities

Sandy beaches stretch northwest and northeast from Forlorn Point

Graiguenamanagh
IIC/GETTY IMAGES ©

Detour:
Saltee Islands

Once the haunt of privateers, smugglers and 'dyvars pyrates', the **Saltee Islands** (www.salteeislands.info; ⊙open for visits 11.30am-4pm) now have a peaceful existence as one of Europe's most important bird sanctuaries. Over 375 recorded species make their home here principally the gannet, guillemot, cormorant, kittiwake, puffin, aux and Manx shearwater. The best time to visit is the spring and early summer nesting season. The birds leave once the chicks can fly, and by early August it's eerily quiet.

The two islands are privately owned. The 90-hectare **Great Saltee** and the 40-hectare **Little Saltee** (closed to visits) were inhabited as long ago as 3500 to 2000 BC. From the 13th century until the dissolution of the monasteries, they were the property of Tintern Abbey, after which various owners were granted the land.

Boats make the trip from Kilmore Quay harbour, but docking depends on the wind direction and is often impossible. Book through **Declan Bates** (☑053-912 9684, 087 252 9736; day trip €25). Note that there are no facilities on the island, including toilets.

(Crossfarnoge). There are some signposted **walking trails** behind the peaceful dunes, circled by serenading skylarks.

Wrecks such as SS *Isolde* and SS *Ardmore,* both dating back to the 1940s, and extraordinary marine life keep divers enthralled. Contact **Wexford Sub Aqua Club** (www.divewexford.org) for info.

The local website, www.kilmorequay web.com, has links to local activities such as **fishing boat charters**.

Ballycross Apple Farm   Farm
(☑053-913 5160; www.ballycross.com; Bridgetown; walking trails adult/child €2/1.50; ⊙11am-6pm Sat & Sun mid-May–Sep; ⛨) About 9km north of Kilmore Quay, Ballycross sells its apples, apple juices, chutneys and jams direct to the public. There are also delicious home-made waffles and several signposted walking trails that run via riverbanks, woodland and orchards throughout the farm.

ⓘ Getting There & Away
Wexford Bus (www.wexfordbus.com) runs to/from Wexford up to four times daily (€7, 45 minutes).

Hook Peninsula & Around

The road shadowing the long, tapering finger of the Hook Peninsula is signposted as the **Ring of Hook coastal drive**. Around every other bend is a quiet beach, a crumbling fortress, a stately abbey or a seafood restaurant, and the world's oldest working lighthouse is flung out at its tip.

Strongbow (Robert FitzGilbert de Clare, Earl of Pembroke) landed here on his way to capture Waterford in 1170, reputedly instructing his men to land 'by Hook or by Crooke', the latter referring to the nearby settlement of Crooke in County Waterford across the harbour.

FETHARD-ON-SEA
POP 325
Fethard is one of the largest villages in the area. The short main drag has cafes, pubs and there are several B&Bs. The community run **tourist office** (☑051-397 502; www.hooktourism.com; Wheelhouse Cafe, Main St; ⊙10am-6pm May-Sep) covers the region.

◉ Sights & Activities

Fethard is home to the scant ruins of 9th-century **St Mogue's** and the unstable ruins of a 15th-century **castle**, which belonged to the bishop of Ferns. The small harbour is worth a visit for its views.

Southeast Ireland is popular with surfers and has many good dive sites, especially around Hook Head.

Freedom Surf School Surfing
(☏ 086 391 4908; www.freedomsurfschool.com; Carnivan Beach; surfboard hire €15, surf lessons from €35; ⊙ 9am-7pm Jun-Sep, 10am-4pm Oct-May; ♿) Located on the main surfing beach, this professionally run outfit has great facilities, including hot showers, changing rooms and complimentary tea and coffee.

Monkey's Rock Surf Shop Surfing
(☏ 087 647 2068; Main St; ⊙ 11am-5pm Sat & Sun Jun-Sep; ♿) Although only open on summer weekends, this shop has a good range of wetsuits, surfboards, bodyboards and boating accessories available for hire.

Hook Head Lighthouse

HOOK HEAD & AROUND

The journey from Fethard to Hook Head takes in a hypnotic stretch of horizon, with few houses between the flat, open fields on the tapering peninsula. Views extend across Waterford Harbour and, on a clear day, as far as the Comeragh and Galtee Mountains.

This is prime day-trip country from either Wexford or Waterford. Villages like **Slade**, where the most activity is in the swirl of seagulls above the ruined castle and harbour, beguile. Beaches include the wonderfully secluded **Dollar Bay** and **Booley Bay** just beyond Templetown en route to Duncannon.

◉ Sights

Hook Head Lighthouse Lighthouse
(www.hookheritage.ie; adult/child €6/3.50; ⊙ 9.30am-5pm; 📶 ♿) On its southern tip, Hook Head is capped by the world's oldest working lighthouse. It's said that monks first lit a beacon on the head during the 5th century and that the first Viking invaders were so happy to have a

DESIGN PICS/THE IRISH IMAGE COLLECTION/GETTY IMAGES ©

guiding light that they left them alone. In the early 13th century William Marshal erected a more permanent structure here, which is still standing today under its black and white exterior. Visitors can access the site by half-hour guided tour which includes a climb up the 115 steps for great views. The visitor centre has a small cafe while the grassy grounds and surrounding shore are popular for **picnics** and **walks**.

Loftus Hall   Haunted Tour

(📞051-397 728; www.loftushall.com; Hook Peninsula; adult/child €9/5; ⏰11am-6pm; 🚼) About 3.5km northeast of the Hook Head lighthouse, this ghostly manor house gazes across the estuary of The Three Sisters over to Dunmore East. Dating from the 1600s, Loftus Hall was re-built by the Marquis of Ely in the 1870s. Famed as being one of the most haunted houses in Ireland, it opened for tours at Halloween in 2012.

Activities

There are brilliant, blustery **walks** on both sides of Hook Head. Poke around the tide pools while watching for surprise showers from blowholes on the western side of the peninsula. The rocks around the shore are Carboniferous limestone, rich in **fossils**. Search carefully and you may find 350-million-year-old shells and tiny disc-like pieces of crinoids, a type of starfish. A good place to hunt is **Patrick's Bay**, on the southeast of the peninsula.

Eating

Templars Inn   Seafood €€

(Templetown; mains €10-22; ⏰noon-10pm) The inviting panoramic terrace at Templars Inn overlooks the ruins of a medieval church, fields of grazing cattle and the ocean beyond. Inside, the dark-timber interior resembles a wayfarers' tavern and is a cosy place for enjoying fresh seafood dishes.

New Ross

POP 4552

The big attraction at New Ross (Rhos Mhic Triúin) is the opportunity to board a 19th-century Famine ship.

Sights

Dunbrody Famine Ship   Museum

(📞051-425 239; www.dunbrody.com; The Quay; adult/child €8.50/5; ⏰10am-6pm Apr-Sep, to 5pm Oct-Mar; 🚼) Called 'coffin ships' due to the fatality rate of their passengers, the leaky, smelly boats that hauled a generation of Irish to America are recalled at this replica ship on the waterfront. The emigrants' sorrowful yet often-inspiring stories (they paid an average of £7 for the voyage) are brought to life by docents during 45-minute tours. A 10-minute **film** provides historical background about Ireland at the time. The Hall of Fame cafe recently opened serving snacks and meals.

Sleeping

Brandon House Hotel   Hotel €€

(📞051-421 703; www.brandonhousehotel.ie; New Ross; r from €80; @ 🛜 ♨ 🚼) This 1865-built red-brick manor certainly lives up to its reputation as family friendly, with kids happily bounding around the place. Winning elements include river views, open log fires, a library bar and large rooms, as well as a spa. It's up a steep driveway 2km south of New Ross.

Eating

Cafe Nutshell   Irish €€

(8 South St; mains €10-16; ⏰9am-5.30pm Tue-Sat; 🚼) It's a shame that Cafe Nutshell closes in the evening, as New Ross' town centre is short on places of this calibre. Scones, breads and buns are all baked on the premises, hot lunch specials utilise local produce and there's a great range of smoothies, juices and organic wines. Mains come with an array of fresh salads. The adjacent health food shop and deli are perfect for picnic provisions.

STEVE GEER/GETTY IMAGES ©

Don't Miss
Tintern Abbey

In better structural condition than its Welsh counterpart, from where its first monks hailed, Ireland's moody Tintern Abbey is secluded amid 40 hectares of woodland. William Marshal, Earl of Pembroke, founded the Cistercian abbey in the early 13th century after he nearly perished at sea and swore to establish a church if he made it ashore. You can still clearly see the cloister walls, nave crossing tower, chancel and south transept chapels.

The abbey sits amid trails, lined with the twisted trunks of bay trees like the work of some mad sculptor. There are lakes and streams as well as crumbling ruins, including a small single cell church. The highlight though is the beautiful 2.5 acre **Colclough Walled Garden** (www.colcloughwalledgarden.com; Tintern Abbey) which has recently been replanted and restored to its former glory.

The grounds are always open and the visitor's centre and gift shop will have been rebuilt by the time by the time you read this after a suspicious fire burned down the centre (along with the abbey's historic stables) in July 2012.

Tintern Abbey is signposted off the R734, around 5km north of Fethard.

NEED TO KNOW
Salt mills; adult/child €3/1; ☻10am-4pm

ⓘ Information

The tourist office (www.newrosstourism.com; The Quay; ☻9am-6pm Apr-Sep, to 5pm Oct-Mar) is located in the same building as the ticket office for the Dunbrody Famine Ship.

ⓘ Getting There & Away

Bus Éireann (www.buseireann.ie) From Dunbrody Inn on the Quay to Waterford (€7, 30 minutes, seven to 11 daily), Wexford (€8, 40 minutes, three to four daily) and Dublin (€16, three hours, four daily).

Detour:
Wexford & the Kennedys

In 1848 Patrick Kennedy left the horrible conditions in County Wexford aboard a boat like the Famine ship in New Ross. Hoping to find something better in America, he succeeded beyond his wildest dreams (a US president, senators and rum-runners are just some of his progeny). You can recall the family's Irish roots at two sites near New Ross.

Kennedy Homestead (☏051-388 264; www.kennedyhomestead.com; Dunganstown; adult/student €5/2.50; ☉10am-5pm Jul & Aug, 11.30am-4.30pm Mon-Fri May, Jun & Sep, by appointment rest of year) The birthplace of Patrick Kennedy, great-grandfather of John F Kennedy, is a farm that still looks – and smells – much as it must have 160 years ago. When JFK visited the farm in 1963 and hugged the current owner's grandmother, it was his first public display of affection, according to his sister Jean. The outbuildings have been turned into a museum that examines the Irish-American dynasty's history on both sides of the Atlantic, plus an informative visitor centre that opened in 2013. The homestead is located about 7km south of New Ross along a very narrow but beautifully overgrown road.

John F Kennedy Arboretum (www.heritageireland.ie; adult/child €3/1; ☉10am-8pm May-Aug, to 6.30pm Apr & Sep, to 5pm Oct-Mar; [⛽]) On a sunny day, this place is so nice for families that it could be called Camelot. The park, 2km southeast of the Kennedy Homestead, has a small visitor centre, tearooms and a picnic area; a miniature train tootles around in the summer months. It has 4500 species of trees and shrubs in 252 hectares of woodlands and gardens. **Slieve Coillte** (270m), opposite the park entrance, has a viewing point from where you can see the arboretum and six counties on a clear day.

....

Enniscorthy

POP 10,543

County Wexford's second-largest town, Enniscorthy (Inis Coirthaidh), has a warren of steep streets descending from Augustus Pugin's cathedral to the Norman castle and the River Slaney. Enniscorthy is inextricably linked to some of the fiercest fighting of the 1798 Rising, when rebels captured the town and set up camp at Vinegar Hill.

◎ Sights

National 1798
Rebellion Centre   Museum
(www.1798centre.ie; Mill Park Rd; adult/child €5.50/3; ☉10am-5pm Mon-Fri, noon-5pm Sat & Sun Apr-Sep, 9.30am-4pm Mon-Fri Oct-Mar; [⛽]) A visit here before climbing Vinegar Hill greatly enhances its impact. The centre's exhibits cover the French and American revolutions that sparked Wexford's abortive uprising against British rule in Ireland, before chronicling what was one of the most bloodthirsty battles of the 1798 Rebellion and a turning point in the struggle. Interactive displays include a giant chessboard with pieces representing key figures in the Rising, and a multiscreen recreation of the finale atop a virtual Vinegar Hill.

Vinegar Hill   Historic Site
To visit the scene of the 1798 events, get a map from the tourist office and look for signs. It's a 2km drive or about a 45-minute walk from Templeshannon on the eastern side of the river. At the summit there's a memorial to the uprising, explanatory signs and sweeping views across the county.

Sleeping

Woodbrook House
Guesthouse €€

(☏053-925 5114; www.woodbrookhouse.ie; Killanne; s/d from €95/150; ☺Easter-Sep; @ ☎ 🐾) 🖉 Damaged in the 1798 rebellion, this glorious country estate is now a three-room guesthouse. The entry features a gravity-defying spiral staircase that amazes now just as it did over 200 years ago. Green practices are used throughout and you can make arrangements for dinner (organic, of course). It is 13km west of Enniscorthy.

Eating

Cotton Tree Cafe
Cafe €

(☏053-923 4641; Slaney Place; mains €6-10; ☺8.30am-5pm Mon-Sat, 11am-5pm Sun; 🚼) A pleasantly informal cafe charmingly decorated with homey (and historic) decorations and artwork. The menu includes gourmet sandwiches with ingredients like roast Irish beef and hummus, as well as a choice of imaginative salads and a daily main.

Information

Tourist office (☏053-923 4699; www.knightsandrebels.ie; Castle Hill; ☺10am-5pm Mon-Fri, noon-5pm Sat & Sun Apr-Sep, 9.30am-4pm Mon-Fri Oct-Mar) Inside Enniscorthy Castle.

Getting There & Away

Bus
Bus Éireann (www.buseireann.ie) runs nine daily buses to Dublin (€15.75, 2½ hours), and eight to Rosslare Harbour (€11, one hour) via Wexford (€6.75, 25 minutes).

Train
The **train station** (Templeshannon) is on the eastern bank of the river. **Irish Rail** (www.irishrail.ie) runs to Dublin Connolly station (€10, 2¼ hours) and Wexford (€7, 25 minutes) three times daily.

COUNTY WATERFORD

Waterford City
POP 49,200

Waterford is Ireland's oldest city and celebrated its 1100th anniversary in 2014. A busy port, it lies on the tidal reach of the River Suir, 16km from the coast. Some parts of the city still feel almost medieval, with narrow alleyways leading off larger streets; an ongoing revitalisation campaign is polishing up one block after another. New and existing museums tell the story of Ireland's Middle Ages better than any other city in the country.

Sights & Activities

Waterford Museum of Treasures
Museum

(www.waterfordtreasures.com) This is the umbrella name for three excellent museums which cover 1000 years of local history. Note that the entrance price for the Bishop's Palace and Medieval Museum includes either an audio guide or guided tours by historically costumed guides (cum actors!).

Reginald's Tower
Historic Building

(The Quay; adult/child €3/1; ☺10am-5.30pm daily Easter-Oct, to 6pm Jun–mid-Sep, to 5pm Wed-Sun Nov-Easter; 🚼) The oldest complete building in Ireland and the first to use mortar, 12th-century Reginald's Tower is an outstanding example of medieval defences and was the city's key fortification. The Normans built its 3m- to 4m-thick walls on the site of a Viking wooden tower. Over the years, the building served as an arsenal, a prison and a mint. The exhibits relating to the latter role include medieval silver coins, a wooden 'tally stick' with notches indicating the amount owed, a 12th-century piggy bank (smashed) and a coin balance used to determine weight and bullion value. Architectural oddities include the toilet that drained halfway up the building.

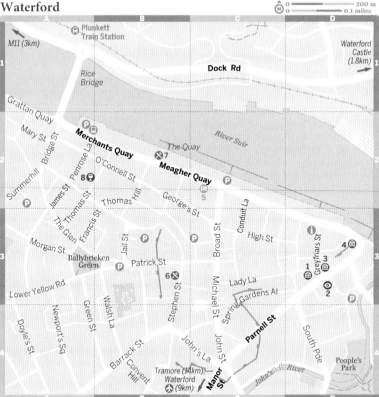

Waterford

⊙ Sights

🛏 Sleeping

⊗ Eating

🍷 Drinking & Nightlife

Medieval Museum   Museum

(Greyfriar's St; adult/child €5/3, combined with
Bishop's Palace €8/2; ⊙10am-5.30pm daily
Easter-Oct, to 6pm Jun–mid-Sep, to 5pm Wed-Sun
Nov-Easter; 👶) The latest museum of Wa-
terford's illustrious trio, the exhibits here

are expertly displayed with explanatory
plaques throughout and several extraordinary highlights, including the original
Great Parchment Book which documents in fascinating detail what medieval
life was like, including cases of petty
crime and the impact of the plague. There
is also an entertaining (and suitable for
kids) 12-minute audiovisual presentation
about the history of the vestments which
date from the 1450s and were discovered
hidden under Christ Church Cathedral.

Bishop's Palace   Museum

(The Mall, Bishop's Palace; adult/child €5/3,
combined with Medieval Museum €8/2; ⊙10am-
5.30pm daily Easter-Oct, to 6pm Jun–mid-Sep, to
5pm Wed-Sun Nov-Easter; 👶) This interactive museum detailing Waterford's long
history is in the aesthetically renovated
Bishop's Palace (1741). It has dazzling

displays covering Waterford's history from 1700 to 1970 and includes treasures from the city's collection, such as golden Viking brooches, jewel-encrusted Norman crosses and 18th-century church silver.

House of
Waterford Crystal   Crystal

(www.waterfordvisitorcentre.com; The Mall; adult/student €12/4; ☉9am-5pm) The city's famed Waterford Crystal is almost an icon in name only. The first Waterford glass factory was established at the western end of the riverside quays in 1783. Centuries later, after the boom of the 1980s and 1990s, the company fell on hard times and in 2009 was purchased by an American investment firm. Today around 60,000 pieces are made annually in Ireland, around 55%; the remaining is manufactured in Europe to strict Waterford standards.

The large modern centre on The Mall offers a tour showing how crystal is produced. A highlight is the blowing room where you can see the red-hot molten crystals take shape and seemingly miraculously transform into delicate glassware.

🛏 Sleeping

Granville Hotel   Hotel €€

(☑051-305 555; www.granville-hotel.ie; Meagher Quay; s/d from €80/100; 🛜) The floodlit 18th-century building overlooking the waterfront is the Granville, one of Ireland's oldest hotels. Brocaded bedrooms maintain a touch of Georgian elegance, as do the public areas with their showstopping stained glass, historic prints and antiques. The restaurant and bar are popular with locals for their reasonable prices and touch of old world luxury. Star turns at breakfast are the organic porridge with Baileys and a perfect eggs benedict.

Waterford Castle   Luxury Hotel €€€

(☑051-878 203; www.waterfordcastle.com; The Island, Ballinakill; r from €140, cottages from €130; @🛜) Getting away from it all is an understatement at this mid-19th-century turreted castle, which is located on its

Waterford–Wexford Ferry

If you're going to travel between Counties Waterford and Wexford along the coast, you can cut out a long detour around Waterford Harbour and the River Barrow by taking the five-minute **car ferry** (www.passageferry.ie; ☉7am-10pm Mon-Sat, 9.30am-10pm Sun Apr-Sep, 7am-8pm Mon-Sat, 9.30am-8pm Oct-Mar) between Passage East and Ballyhack in County Wexford. Single/return tickets for pedestrians or cyclists cost €2/3 and for cars €8/12.

own 124-hectare island roamed by deer. A free, private car ferry signposted just east of the Waterford Regional Hospital provides round-the-clock access. All 19 castle rooms have clawfoot baths, and some have poster beds. There are also 48 contemporary self-catering cottages on the island. Both guests and nonguests can dine on organic fare in chef Michael Quinn's sublime oak-panelled restaurant (menus from €28), or play a round of golf (green fees €20). Breakfast included.

🍴 Eating

Merchant's
Quay   Market, Restaurant €

(Merchants Quay; mains €8-12; ☉10am-5pm Sat & Sun, to 10pm Fri; 🚲) Opened in early 2013, this former grain store dating from 1759 has been transformed into a three floor space encompassing a farmers' market, casual dining space with brazier-style grill and a top floor venue for medieval-themed shows. Market stalls include an on-site bakery, organic produce, local ice cream, seafood, artisan cheeses and much more. Everything is sourced within a 50km radius. There are cookery demonstrations for children, as well as other activities planned.

If You Like…
Fine Food

If you like the fine food County Waterford has to offer at the likes of the Tannery (p157) in Dungarvan and the Cliff House (p159) in Ardmore, County Wexford has a few gourmet offerings of its own.

1 SILVER FOX SEAFOOD RESTAURANT
(www.thesilverfox.ie; Kilmore Quay; mains €16-32; ⊙noon-10pm May-Sep, reduced hours other times; 📶) The freshest local catch is on the menu at this popular Kilmore Quay spot.

2 GREENACRES
(www.greenacres.ie; 7 Selskar St; mains €20-30; ⊙deli 9am-6pm Mon-Sat, noon-6pm Sun; bistro 9am-10pm Mon-Sat, noon-8pm Sun; 📶) Wexford Town's most elegant food hall has a superb bistro featuring innovative Irish cuisine.

3 LA MARINE
(📞053-32114; Kelly's Resort Hotel; lunch mains €11-16, dinner mains €18-25; ⊙noon-10pm; 📶📶) A Gallic bistro bar at the popular Kelly's Resort in Rosslare Strand.

Harlequin   Italian €€
(37 Stephen St; lunch mains €8-12, dinner mains €10-14; ⊙8.30am-8.30pm Mon-Wed, 8.30am-10.30pm Thu-Sat; 📶) Italian run, this authentic little trattoria morphs throughout the day from a coffee and pastry stop to a busy dining spot to a candlelit wine bar. House speciality antipasti platters are laden with cheeses, marinated vegetables and/or finely sliced cured meats. No pizza.

🍷 Drinking & Nightlife

Henry Downes Bar   Pub
(Thomas St; ⊙5pm-late) For a change from stout, drop into Downes, which has been blending its No 9 Irish whiskey for over two centuries. Have a dram in its series of character-filled rooms, or buy a bottle to take away (€32). This place is a real one-off – they even have a squash court out back (€8 for 40 minutes).

ℹ Information
The large **tourist office** is the best source of info and help in counties Waterford and Wexford. Note that the office has future plans to move near Reginald's Tower but there was no definite date established at the time of research.

ℹ Getting There & Away
Air
Waterford Airport (WAT; 📞051-875 589; www.flywaterford.com) The airport is 9km south of the city centre at Killowen. Primarily has flights to London Luton, Manchester and Birmingham.

Bus
Bus Éireann (www.buseireann.ie; Merchant's Quay) Frequent services to Tramore (€3.25, 30 minutes), Dublin (€14.75 three hours) and Wexford (€10, one hour).

Train
Plunkett Train Station (www.irishrail.ie) North of the river. Up to eight services to/from Dublin's Heuston Station (from €20, two to 2½ hours) and Kilkenny (from €10, 40 minutes).

ℹ Getting Around
There is no public transport to the airport. A taxi (📞051-77710, 051-858 585) costs around €15.

Southeast County Waterford

This hidden corner of the county makes an easy day trip from Waterford city. The waters are tidal and shift and change throughout the day, adding to the atmosphere.

Less than 14km east of Waterford is the estuary village of **Passage East**, from where car ferries yo-yo to Ballyhack in County Wexford. It's a pretty little fishing village with thatched cottages around the harbour.

A little-travelled 11km-long **coast road** wiggles south between Passage East and Dunmore East. At times single-vehicle-width and steep, it offers mesmerising views of the ocean and undulating fields. On a bike it is a thrill.

ℹ️ Getting There & Away

Suirway (www.suirway.com; adult/child €4/2, 30 minutes) buses connect Waterford with Passage East seven to eight times daily.

....

Dunmore East

POP 1795

Some 19km southeast of Waterford, Dunmore East (Dún Mór) is strung out along a coastline of red sandstone cliffs full of screaming kittiwakes and concealed coves. In the 19th century, the town was a station for the steam packets that carried mail between England and the south of Ireland. Legacies left include picturesque thatched cottages lining the main street and an unusual Doric **lighthouse** (1825) overlooking the working harbour. Information on the area is available at www.discoverdunmore.com.

🛏️ Sleeping

Haven Hotel   Hotel **€€**
(📞 051-383 150; www.thehavenhotel.com; s/d from €45/90; hotel & restaurant open Mar-Oct; 📶) Built in the 1860s as a summer house for the Malcolmson family, whose coat of arms can still be seen on the fireplaces, the Haven is now run by the Kelly family and remains an elegant retreat with wood-panelled bathrooms and, in two rooms, four-poster beds. Local produce underpins dishes in the

casual **restaurant** (🕐 5.30-10pm Mon-Sat, 10am-3pm Sun; mains €12 to €20) and the low-lit crimson-toned bar.

⊗ Eating

Lemon Tree Cafe   Irish **€€**
(www.lemontreecatering.ie; mains €8-20; 🕐 10am-6pm Tue-Sun, 7-10pm Fri & Sat Jun-Aug; 👪) Come here for organic coffees, delectable baked goods and a deli counter (and freezer) with takeaway dishes ranging from nut and lentil loaf to seafood pie. There's plenty of seating, inside and out, and a menu of dishes with an emphasis on seafood. Play section for children.

ℹ️ Getting There & Away

Suirway (www.suirway.com; adult/child €4/2) buses connect Waterford with Dunmore East around eight times daily (€4, 30 minutes).

thatched cottages, Dunmore East
RICK PRICE/GETTY IMAGES ©

Dungarvan

POP 9427

Resembling a miniature version of Galway, pastel-shaded buildings ring Dungarvan's picturesque bay where the River Colligan meets the sea. Overlooking the bay are a dramatic ruined castle and an Augustinian abbey. Dungarvan is also renowned for its cuisine, with outstanding restaurants, a famous cooking school and the annual Waterford Festival of Food.

◉ Sights

Dungarvan Castle   Castle
(www.heritageireland.ie; ⊙10am-6pm Jun-Sep)
FREE Renovation is restoring this stone fortress to its former Norman glory. Once inhabited by King John's constable Thomas Fitz Anthony, the oldest part of the castle is the unusual 12th-century shell keep, built to defend the mouth of the river. The 18th-century British army barracks house a visitor centre with various exhibits. Admission is by guided tour only.

✪ Activities

**Tannery Cookery
School**   Cooking Course
(☏058-45420; www.tannery.ie; 10 Quay St; courses €75-150; ☎) Looking like a futuristic kitchen showroom, best-selling author and chef Paul Flynn's cookery school adjoins a fruit, vegetable and herb garden. Some courses include foraging for ingredients, while others cover market gardening, traditional Italian cuisine and the ever popular 'How To Cook Better' option.

✸ Festivals & Events

**Waterford
Festival of Food**   Food
(www.waterfordfestivaloffood.com; ⊙mid-Apr) The area's abundant fresh produce is celebrated at this hugely popular festival that features cooking workshops and demonstrations, talks by local producers and a food fair. A craft brew beer garden has suitably thirst-quenching appeal.

Dungarvan Castle gate

RICHARD CUMMINS/GETTY IMAGES ©

Sleeping

Tannery
Townhouse
Guesthouse €€

(☏058-45420; www.tannery.ie; Church St; s/d €65/110; ☺Feb-Dec; ☎) Just around the corner from the Tannery Restaurant is this boutique guesthouse, which spans two buildings in the town centre. Its 14 rooms are modern and stylish, and have fridges stacked with juices, fruit and muffins so you can enjoy a continental breakfast on your own schedule. An honour bar and snacks ease the transition from afternoon to evening.

Eating

Nude Food
Modern Irish €€

(www.nudefood.ie; 86 O'Connell St; mains €10-14; ☺9.15am-6pm Mon-Wed, to 9.30pm Thu-Sat; ☎⏏) The only thing bare naked here is the plates after diners finish. From carefully crafted coffees to a beautiful selection of deli items, this cafe stands out. Lunch and dinner menus feature top Waterford ingredients in sandwiches, salads, starters and hot mains that are hearty, honest and flavourful. Nude Food regularly hosts fringe events, like poetry readings.

Tannery
Modern Irish €€€

(☏058-45420; www.tannery.ie; 10 Quay St; mains €18-29; ☺12.30-2.30pm Fri & Sun, 6-9.30pm Tue-Sat, also Sun Jul & Aug) An old leather tannery houses this innovative and much-lauded restaurant, where Paul Flynn creates seasonally changing dishes that focus on just a few flavours and celebrates them through preparations that are at once comforting yet surprising. There's intimate seating downstairs or tables in the buzzing, loftlike room upstairs. Service is excellent. Book ahead.

ℹ Information

This helpful tourist office (☏058-41741; www.dungarvantourism.com; Courthouse Bldg, TF Meagher St; ☺9.30am-5pm Mon-Fri year-round, plus 10am-5pm Sat May-Sep) has stacks of informative brochures.

Local Knowledge

Dungarvan

BY PAUL FLYNN, HEAD CHEF AT TANNERY RESTAURANT & COOKERY SCHOOL

1 DUNGARVAN FARMERS MARKET
The Dungarvan Farmers Market helps engender a real sense of community as growers and customers come together to talk about produce, the weather and everything else! I love browsing the stalls – it is the best of what local growers have to offer.

2 WATERFORD FESTIVAL OF FOOD
The Waterford Festival of Food (p156) has a terrific food fair, a host of cooking workshops and demonstrations, and plenty of talks by local producers at their farms, which is about as close to the source as you can get.

3 NUDE FOOD
Nude Food is the antithesis of what I call 'chefiness', which is all about drips, splodges and towers. Here you get big bowls of great food – impeccably sourced and put together in a wonderful way. As I often say to students, I spent 15 years trying to be a chef, and then the next 10 learning how to be a cook.

4 CLIFF HOUSE HOTEL
OK, so it's not technically in Dungarvan, but Ardmore isn't too far away and the Cliff House Hotel (p159) should be in any list of top picks for the southeast. It's a great restaurant in a wonderful and elegant boutique hotel that has managed to make the most of the views and location.

5 TANNERY RESTAURANT & COOKERY SCHOOL
The secret to my success is in my garden. Having the garden attached to the cooking school gives it soul. The economic downturn means that more people want to grow their own produce; we also help local special-needs schools set up gardens.

If You Like…
Memorable Accommodation

The Southeast's reputation for good hospitality is ably represented by fine hotels like the Cliff House in Ardmore. Other marvelous overnights can be enjoyed at the following.

1 GLENDINE COUNTRY HOUSE
(☑051-389 500; www.glendinehouse.com; Arthurstown; s/d from €45/90; 🖥) Vine-covered 1830s-built former dower house with individually appointed rooms.

2 HANORA'S COTTAGE
(☑052-36134; www.hanorascottage.com; Nire Valley, Ballymacarbry; full-board per person from €75, B&B s/d from €65/120; 🕐dinner Mon-Sat; 🖥) Nineteenth-century ancestral home beautifully located between a bubbling river and a picturesque church.

3 LAWCUS FARM
(www.lawcusfarmguesthouse.com; Kells; r from €80; 🖥) A carefully restored thatched home dating from the 1700s is now a working farm.

🛈 Getting There & Away

Bus Éireann (www.buseireann.ie) buses pick up and drop off on Davitt's Quay on the way to and from Waterford (€12, one hour, 12 daily) and Cork (€16, 1½ hours, 12 daily).

Ring Peninsula
POP 1689

Just 15 minutes' drive from Dungarvan, the Ring Peninsula (An Rinn, meaning 'the headland') is one of Ireland's best-known Gaeltacht (Irish speaking) areas. En route, views of the Comeragh Mountains, Dungarvan Bay and the Copper Coast drift away to the northeast. You can easily spend a day exploring quiet country lanes here, with the promise of a hidden beach or fine old trad pub around the next bend in the road.

Ex-Waterford Crystal worker Eamonn Terry returned home to the peninsula to set up his own workshop, **Criostal na Rinne** (☑058-46174; www.criostal.com; 🕐by appointment), where you can buy deep-prismatic-cut, full-lead crystal vases, bowls, clocks, jewellery and even chandeliers.

🛈 Getting There & Around

Pubs, accommodation and shops are scattered along the peninsula; you will need your own wheels to get around.

Bus Éireann (www.buseireann.ie) stops in Ring en route between Ardmore (30 minutes) and Waterford (1¼ hours) via Dungarvan. But frequency is seldom: once daily in summer, far less other times.

Ardmore
POP 410

The enticing seaside village of Ardmore may look quiet these days, but it's claimed that St Declan set up shop here between 350 and 420. This brought Christianity to southeast Ireland long before St Patrick arrived from Britain. Today's visitors come for its beautiful strand, water sports, ancient buildings and reliably good places to eat and sleep.

◉ Sights & Activities

Plan on spending a day strolling about the town, ancient sites, coast and countryside.

St Declan's Church   Ruin
In a striking position on a hill above town, the ruins of St Declan's Church stand on the site of St Declan's original monastery alongside an impressive cone-roofed, 29m-high, 12th-century **round tower**, one of the best examples of these structures in Ireland.

Ballyquin Beach   Beach
Tide pools, fascinating rocks and sheltered sand are just some of the appeals of this beautiful beach. It's 1km off the R673, 4km northeast of Ardmore. Look for the small sign.

Ardmore Pottery
Ceramics

(www.ardmorepottery.com; ⏰10am-6pm Mon-Sat, 2-6pm Sun May-Oct) Near the start of the cliff walk, this cosy little house sells beautiful pottery, many in lovely shades of blue and cream. Other locally produced goods include warm hand-knitted socks. This is a good source of tourist information for the area.

Walks
Walking

A 5km, cobweb-banishing **cliff walk** leads from St Declan's Well. On the one-hour round trip you'll pass the wreck of a crane ship that was blown ashore in 1987 on its way from Liverpool to Malta. The 94km **St Declan's Way** mostly traces an old pilgrimage route from Ardmore to the Rock of Cashel (County Tipperary) via Lismore. Catholic pilgrims walk along it on St Declan's Day (24 July).

Sleeping

Cliff House Hotel
Luxury Hotel €€€

(☎024-87800; www.thecliffhousehotel.com; r €225-450; @ 🛜 ≋) Built into the cliff-face, all guest rooms at this cutting-edge edifice overlook the bay, and most have balconies or terraces. Some suites even have two-person floor-to-ceiling glass showers (strategically frosted in places) so you don't miss those sea views. There are also sea views from the indoor swimming pool, outdoor Jacuzzi and spa, the bar and the much-lauded modern Irish restaurant (menu from €68), which has a Michelin star to its name.

✖ Eating

White Horses
Seafood €€

(☎024-94040; Main St; lunch mains €8-13, dinner mains €22-33; ⏰11am-11pm Tue-Sun May-Sep, Fri-Sun Oct-Apr) Energetically run by three sisters, this bistro concentrates on fresh seafood. Push the boat out and try the Dublin Bay King prawns (€33) on plates handmade in the village. Enjoy a drink on the bench out front or a meal at a sunny lawn table out back.

ℹ Getting There & Away

Bus Éireann (www.buseireann.ie) operates one to three buses daily west to Cork (€15, 1¾ hours); connections east to Dungarvan and beyond range from one daily in summer to seldom other times.

Cemetery, St Declan's Church

M TIMOTHY O'KEEFE/GETTY IMAGES ©

Lismore

POP 1370

Lismore's enormous 19th-century castle seems out of proportion to this quiet, elegant town on the River Blackwater where most of the existing buildings date from the early 19th century. Over the centuries, statesmen and luminaries streamed through the town, the location of a great monastic university founded in the 7th century on the site of the current castle.

Sights

Lismore Castle Castle

(www.lismorecastlearts.ie; gardens adult/child €8/4; 11am-4.45pm mid-Mar–Sep;) From the Cappoquin road there are stunning glimpses of the riverside 'castle'. The original castle was erected by Prince John, lord of Ireland, in 1185, although most of what you see now is from the early 19th century. While you can't get inside the four impressive walls of the main, crenulated building, you can visit the 3 hectares of ornate and manicured **gardens**. Thought to be the oldest in Ireland, they are divided into the walled Jacobean upper garden and less formal lower garden. There are brilliant herbaceous borders, magnolias and camellias, and a splendid **yew walk** where Edmund Spenser is said to have written *The Faerie Queen*. There are modern sculptures in the gardens and a contemporary **art gallery** in the west wing of the castle.

St Carthage's Cathedral Cathedral

(varies) FREE 'One of the neatest and prettiest edifices I have seen', commented William Thackeray in 1842 about the striking 1679 cathedral. And that was before the addition of the Edward Burne-Jones **stained-glass window**, which features all the Pre-Raphaelite hallmarks: an effeminate knight and a pensive maiden against a sensuous background of deep-blue velvet and intertwining flowers. Justice, with sword and scales, and Humility, holding a lamb, honour Francis Currey, who helped to relieve the suffering of the poor during the Famine. There are some noteworthy 16th-century **tombs**, including the elaborately carved MacGrath family crypt dating from 1557.

Sleeping

Lismore House Hotel Hotel €€

(058-72966; www.lismorehouse-hotel.com; Main St; s/d from €55/120;) Directly opposite the Heritage Centre, Ireland's oldest purpose-built hotel was built in 1797 by the Duke of Devonshire. He'd still recognise the exterior, but rooms within have had a contemporary makeover with sleek dark timber furniture and cream-and-gold fabrics. Book online for deals.

Lismore Castle

RICHARD CUMMINS/GETTY IMAGES ©

Detour:
The Copper Coast

Cerulean skies, azure waters, impossibly green hills and ebony cliff faces provide a vibrant palette of colour on the beautiful **Copper Coast** drive west of Tramore to Dungarvan. The R675 winds its way from one stunning vista to another.

Annestown has a couple of welcoming cafes and is a good place to stop after the boisterous charms of Tramore. At **Dunabrattin Head** watch for a small **cove beach** just west. It's wide and inviting with virtually no development.

At 25km west of Tramore, the rugged coastline of the **Copper Coast European Geopark** (www.coppercoastgeopark.com; ⊙park office 9.30am-5pm Mon-Fri) takes its name from the 19th-century copper mines outside Bunmahon. Among the area's scalloped coves and beaches are geological formations dating back 460 million years, including quartz blocks, fossils and former volcanoes. Free one-hour guided **walks** are available in summer or download a walking guide from the website.

To explore the Copper Coast's caves, coves and cliffs in sea kayaks, contact **Sea Paddling** (☏051-393 314; www.seapaddling.com; tours from €35; ♦). Tours last from a few hours to a few days and cover various parts of Waterford's coast. Also geared for children from 13 years.

Before you reach Dungarvan, on the north side of the harbour near Ballynacourty, is **Clonea Strand**, a beautiful stretch of pristine sand.

Eating

Lismore Farmers Market
Market €

(Castle Ave; ⊙10am-4pm Sun) The upscale surrounds attract a fab collection of vendors including Dungarvan's Naked Lunch, whose tasty sandwiches you can enjoy in the park or at tables set up on the gravel path.

Information

Tourist Office (www.discoverlismore.com; Main St; ⊙9.30am-5.30pm Mon-Fri, 10am-5.30pm Sat, noon-5.30pm Sun mid-Mar–Christmas) Inside the Lismore Heritage Centre; pick up the info-packed *Lismore Walking Tour Guide* (€3).

Getting There & Around

Bus Éireann (www.buseireann.ie) serves Cappoquin (€3.75,10 minutes) and Dungarvan (€6, 20 minutes) on Sunday only.

COUNTY TIPPERARY

Cashel
POP 2276

It's no wonder that Cashel (Caiseal Mumhan) is popular with visitors (the Queen included it on her historic visit in 2011). The iconic Rock of Cashel and historical religious buildings that crown its breezy summit seem like a magical extension of the rocky landscape itself, and Cashel maintains a certain charm as a smallish market town.

Sights

Rock of Cashel
Historic Site

(www.heritageireland.com; adult/child €6/2; ⊙9am-5.30pm mid-Mar–mid-Oct, to 7pm mid-Jun–Aug, to 4.30pm mid-Oct–mid-Mar) The Rock of Cashel is one of Ireland's most spectacular archaeological sites. The 'Rock' is a prominent green hill, banded with limestone outcrops. It rises from a

Right: Cormac's Chapel, Rock of Cashel (p161);
Below: Hall of the Vicar's Choral, Rock of Cashel (p161)
(RIGHT) STEPHEN SAKS/GETTY IMAGES ©; (BELOW) JOHN ELK III/GETTY IMAGES ©

grassy plain on the edge of the town and bristles with ancient fortifications – the word 'cashel' is an anglicised version of the Irish word *caiseal,* meaning 'fortress'. Sturdy walls circle an enclosure that contains a complete round tower, a 13th-century Gothic cathedral and the finest 12th-century Romanesque chapel in Ireland.

In the 4th century the Rock of Cashel was chosen as a base by the Eóghanachta clan from Wales, who went on to conquer much of Munster and become kings of the region. For some 400 years it rivalled Tara as a centre of power in Ireland. The clan was associated with St Patrick, hence the Rock's alternative name of St Patrick's Rock. In the 10th century, the Eóghanachta lost possession of the rock to the O'Brien (or Dál gCais) tribe under Brian Ború's leadership. In 1101, King

Muircheartach O'Brien presented the Rock to the Church to curry favour with the powerful bishops and to end secular rivalry over possession of the Rock with the Eóghanachta, by now known as the MacCarthys.

Numerous buildings must have occupied the Rock over the years, but it is the ecclesiastical relics that have survived even the depredations of the Cromwellian army in 1647. The cathedral was used for worship until the mid-1700s.

Among the graves are a 19th-century high cross and mausoleum for local landowners the Scully family; the top of the Scully Cross was razed by lightning in 1976.

It's a five-minute stroll from the town centre up to the Rock. You can take some pretty paths including the **Bishop's Walk** from the gardens of the Cashel Palace Hotel. Sheep grudgingly allow you to

bass. The scaffolding moves from place to place each year as part of the never-ending struggle to keep the Rock caulked.

Call ahead for details of guided tours.

Sleeping

Cashel Palace Hotel
Historic Hotel €€

(📞062-62707; www.cashel-palace.ie; Main St; s/d from €95/134; @ 📶) This handsome red-brick, late-Queen Anne archbishop's residence is a local landmark. whose gardens contain the progenies of the original hop plants used to brew the first Guinness. Fully restored, it has 23 antique-furnished rooms in the gracious main building or quaint mews, with direct access through the grounds to the base of the Rock of Cashel. Some rooms have soaking tubs you'll leave only after you're totally pruni-fied. The **bar** is the place to talk about your upcoming hunt before dining at the vaulted-ceilinged **Bishops Buttery Restau-rant** (mains €10-21; ⏱7.30-9.30pm).

Eating

Cafe Hans
Cafe €€

(📞062-63660; Dominic St; mains €13-18; ⏱noon-5.30pm Tue-Sat; 👶) Competition for the 32 seats is fierce at this gourmet cafe run by the same family as Chez Hans next door. There's a fantastic selection of salads, open sandwiches (including succulent prawns with tangy Marie Rose sauce) and filling fish, shell-fish, lamb and vegetarian dishes, with a discerning wine selection and mouth-watering desserts such as homemade caramel ice cream with butterscotch sauce. Arrive before or after the lunch-time rush or plan on queuing.

Information

The helpful tourist office (📞062-62511; www.cashel.ie; Main St, Town Hall; ⏱9.30am-5.30pm Mon-Sat mid-Mar–mid-Oct, 9.30am-5.30pm Mon-Fri mid-Oct–mid-Mar) has reams of info on the area.

Rock of Cashel

For more than 1000 years the Rock of Cashel was a symbol of power and the seat of kings and churchmen who ruled over the region. Exploring this monumental complex offers a fascinating insight into Ireland's past.

Enter via the 15th-century **Hall of the Vicars Choral** ❶, built to house the male choristers who sang in the cathedral. Exhibits in its undercroft include rare silverware, stone reliefs and the original St Patrick's Cross. In the courtyard you'll see the replica of **St Patrick's Cross** ❷. A small porch leads into the 13th-century Gothic **Cathedral** ❸. To the west of the nave are the remains of the **Archbishop's Residence** ❹. From the cathedral's north transept on the northeastern corner is the Rock's earliest building, an 11th- or 12th-century **Round Tower** ❺. The south transept leads to the compelling **Cormac's Chapel** ❻, probably the first Romanesque church in Ireland. It dates from 1127 and the medieval integrity of its trans-European architecture survives. Inside the main door on the left is the sarcophagus said to house King Cormac, dating from between 1125 and 1150. Before leaving, take time for a close-up look at the Rock's **enclosing walls and corner tower** ❼.

Hall of the Vicars Choral

Head upstairs from the ticket office to see the choristers' restored kitchen and dining hall, complete with period furniture, tapestries and paintings beneath a fine carved-oak roof and gallery.

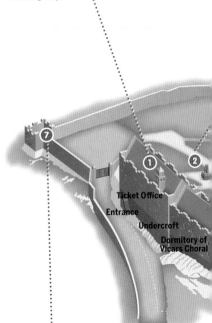

Ticket Office
Entrance
Undercroft
Dormitory of Vicars Choral

TOP TIPS

» Good photographic vantage points for framing the mighty Rock are on the road into Cashel from the Dublin Rd roundabout or from the little roads just west of the centre.

» The best photo opportunities, however, are from inside the atmospheric ruins of Hore Abbey, 1km to the north.

Enclosing Walls & Corner Tower

Constructed from lime mortar around the 15th century, and originally incorporating five gates, stone walls enclose the entire site. It's thought the surviving corner tower was used as a watchtower.

St Patrick's Cross
In the castle courtyard, this cross replicates the eroded Hall of the Vicars Choral original – an impressive 12th-century crutched cross depicting a crucifixion scene on one face and animals on the other.

Archbishop's Residence
The west side of the cathedral is taken up by the Archbishop's Residence, a 15th-century, four-storey castle, which had its great hall built over the nave, reducing its length. It was last inhabited in the mid-1700s.

Cathedral
A huge square tower with a turret on the southwestern corner soars above the cathedral. Scattered throughout are monuments, a 16th-century altar tomb, coats of arms panels, and stone heads on capitals and corbels.

Turret

④

③

⑤

⑥

Choir

Scully Cross

Cormac's Chapel
Look closely at the exquisite doorway arches, the grand chancel arch and ribbed barrel vault, and carved vignettes, including a trefoil-tailed grotesque and a Norman-helmeted centaur firing an arrow at a rampaging lion.

Round Tower
Standing 28m tall, the doorway to this ancient edifice is 3.5m above the ground – perhaps for structural rather than defensive reasons. Its exact age is unknown but may be as early as 1101.

Detour:
Holy Cross Abbey

Beside the River Suir, 15km north of Cashel and 6km southwest of Thurles, the magnificently restored **Holy Cross Abbey** (holycrossabbeytours@gmail.com; admission by donation; ⊙9am-8pm) proudly displays two relics of the True Cross. Although the Cistercian abbey was founded in 1168, the large buildings that survive today date from the 15th century. Look for the ornately carved sedilia near the altar and pause to appreciate the early form of 'stadium seating'. Guided tours take place three times a week in spring and summer. A bookshop is open irregular hours.

ℹ Getting There & Away

Bus Éireann (www.buseireann.ie) runs eight buses daily between Cashel and Cork (€14.50, 1½ hours) via Cahir (€5.50, 20 minutes, six to eight daily). The bus stop for Cork is outside the Bake House on Main St. The Dublin stop (€11.70, three hours, six daily) is opposite.

Ring a Link (✆1890 424 141; www.ringalink. ie) A not-for-profit service for rural residents that's also available to tourists, has a service to Tipperary (€3, 50 minutes).

Around Cashel

The atmospheric – and, at dusk, delightfully creepy – ruins of **Athassel Priory** sit in the shallow and verdant River Suir Valley, 7km southwest of Cashel. The original buildings date from 1205, and Athassel was once one of the richest and most important monasteries in Ireland. What survives is substantial: the gatehouse and portcullis gateway, the cloister and stretches of walled enclosure, as well as some medieval tomb effigies. To get here, take the N74 to the village of **Golden**, then head 2km south along the narrow road signed Athassel Abbey. Roadside parking is limited and *very* tight; you're best off leaving your car in Golden. The Priory is reached across often-muddy fields. The welter of back lanes is good for cycling.

Cahir
POP 1150

At the eastern tip of the Galtee Mountains 15km south of Cashel, Cahir (An Cathair; pronounced 'care') is a compact and attractive town that encircles its namesake castle, which does a good job of looking like every castle you ever tried building at the beach, with towers, a moat and battlements. Walking paths follow the banks of the **River Suir** – you can easily spend a couple of hours wandering about.

◉ Sights

Cahir Castle   Historic Site
(✆052-744 1011; www.heritageireland.ie; Castle St; adult/child €3/1; ⊙9am-6.30pm mid-Jun–Aug, 9.30am-5.30pm mid-Mar–mid-Jun & Sep–mid-Oct, to 4.30pm mid-Oct–mid-Mar) Cahir's awesome castle is feudal fantasy in a big way, with a river-island site with moat, rocky foundations, massive walls, turrets and towers, defences and dungeons. Founded by Conor O'Brien in 1142, this castle is one of Ireland's largest. It was passed to the Butler family in 1375. In 1599 it lost the arms race of its day when the Earl of Essex used cannons to shatter the walls, an event explained with a huge model.

The castle was surrendered to Cromwell in 1650 without a struggle; its future usefulness may have discouraged the usual Cromwellian 'deconstruction' – it is largely intact and still formidable. It was restored in the 1840s and again in the 1960s when it came under state ownership.

A 15-minute audiovisual presentation puts Cahir in context with other Irish castles. The buildings within the castle are sparsely furnished, although there are good displays. The real rewards come from simply wandering through this remarkable survivor of Ireland's medieval past. There are frequent guided tours.

Sleeping

Tinsley House B&B €
(☏052-744 1947; www.tinsleyhouse.com; The Square; d from €55; ☾Apr-Sep; ☏) This mannered house has a great location, four period-furnished rooms and a roof garden. The owner, Liam Roche, is an expert on local history and can recommend walks and other activities.

Information

Post office (Church St) North of the Square.

Tourist office (☏052-744 1453; www. discoverireland.ie/tipperary; Cahir Castle car park; ☾9.30am-5.30pm Mon-Sat Easter-Oct) Has information about the town and region.

Getting There & Away

Bus

Cahir is a hub for several Bus Éireann routes, including Dublin–Cork, Limerick–Waterford, Galway–Waterford, Kilkenny–Cork and Cork–Athlone. There are eight buses per day Monday to Saturday (six buses on Sunday) to Cashel (€5.50, 20 minutes). Buses stop in the car park beside the tourist office.

Train

From Monday to Saturday, the Limerick Junction–Waterford train stops three times daily in each direction.

Cork & the Ring of Kerry

The southwest corner of Ireland – encompassing the counties of Cork and Kerry – epitomises romantic, rustic and rural Ireland. While it may groan under the weight of tourist numbers, the southwest never fails to astonish and beguile those who drive, cycle, walk and amble through the twists, turns and inlets of the eroded coasts and the endless fields of green criss-crossed by stone walls and ancient monuments.

Yet the southwest is not just about amazing views and wondrous rambles. It's about food – Cork City and the surrounding county have deservedly earned a reputation as the gourmet heart of Ireland. It's about history – from the monuments of the Beara Peninsula to the monastic ruins on unforgiving Skellig Michael and the extraordinary collection of Celtic ruins and stones around Dingle. If you were forced to visit only one corner of the Emerald Isle, the southwest would leave you feeling like you didn't miss a thing.

Ring of Kerry (p196)

DON KLUMPP/GETTY IMAGES ©

Cork & the Ring of Kerry

CLARE

ATLANTIC
OCEAN

Shannon Estuary
Carrig
Loop Head
Ballylongford • Tarbert
Glin
Mouth of the Shannon
Ballybunion
Cashen Bay
Ballyduff •
Listowel •
River Feale
Ath
Kerry Head
Ballyheigue
Abbeyfeale •
N69
Maharees Islands
Ballyheigue Bay
Banna
Banna Strand
Brandon Point
Fahamore •
Kilshannig
Ardfert
Ballydavid
Brandon •
Brandon Head
Cloghane
Brandon Bay
Tralee Bay
Fenit
Tralee
N21
Brandon •
Castlegregory
Blennerville
Castleisland
Brandon Creek
Connor Pass) (
Kilcummin
Slieve Mish Mountains
Dingle Peninsula
Camp
Sybil Point
Annascaul
Lougher
Castlemaine
Farranfore
Clogher •
N86
Inch •
Castlemaine Harbour
Annagh Bog
Inishtooskert
Dingle
Lispole
Killorglin
KERRY
Innisfallen Island
Blasket Sound
Dunmore Head
Slea Head
Glenbeigh
Lough Caragh
Gap of Dunloe
Lough Leane
Killarney
Blasket Islands
Dingle Bay
N70
MACGILLYCUDDY'S REEKS) (
Derrynasaggart Mountains
Inishvickillane
Doulus Head
Kells
Ring of Kerry
Killarney National Park
Caherciveen
Iveragh Peninsula
Valentia Island
Beginish
Knightstown
Chapeltown
Deriana Lough
Kenmare
Portmagee
N70
Sneem
Tahilla
Puffin Island
Ballinskelligs •
Waterville
Parknasilla
N71
Skellig Islands
Saint Finan's Bay
Ballinskelligs Bay
Lough Currane
Caherdaniel
Tuosist •
Beara Peninsula
Knockboy (706m)
Bolus Head
Derrynane Bay
Lamb's Head
Kenmare River
Lauragh
Caha Mountains
Glengarriff
Kealkill
Scariff
Ardgroom •
Beara Way
Ballylickey
Coulagh Bay
Hungry Hill (685m)
Eyeries •
Adrigole
Whiddy Island
Bantry
Cod's Head
Allihies •
Castletownbere
Bantry Bay
Drimoleagu
Dursey Head
R572
Bere Island
Mt Seefin (491m)
Ahakista
Durrus
Sheep's Head
Kilcrohane
Mt Gabriel (407m)
Ballydehob
Dunmanus Bay
Mizen Head Peninsula
Schull
Skibberee
Goleen •
Roaringwater Bay
Baltimore •
Barleycove •
Crookhaven
Sherkin Island
Brow Head

Cork & the Ring of Kerry's Highlights

Skellig Michael

This desolate, storm-lashed rocky outcrop off the Kerry coast was the ideal spot for a group of foolhardy monks to set up shop in ancient times, and today the Unesco World Heritage si of Skellig Michael (p198) reminds us not just of the extraordinary efforts they went to for a little solitude but of how magnificent untrammelled nature can truly be.

Killarney National Park

Nowhere else in Ireland will you find a forest of ancient oaks, two glacial lakes, the island's only herd of native red deer and a couple of stunning buildings. But Killarney National Park (p191) is far, far bigger than the sum of its individual parts: it affords some of the best views in the country and is the gateway to one of Ireland's most scenic drives.

Rhododendrons

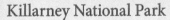

DAVID TIPLING/GETTY IMAGES ©

PETER ZOELLER/DESIGN PICS/GETTY IMAGES ©

Cork City

3

The Republic's second city (p178) is big enough to keep you entertained but compact enough to ensure that everything is within virtual arm's reach of each other, especially the city's collection of superb restaurants, fine pubs and, in the English Market (p179), the country's best food hall. English Market

ILO/AXIOM/GETTY IMAGES ©

4

Ring of Kerry

Ireland's most famous circular route (p196) is where you'll find all the scenes that keep the Irish postcard industry buoyant. The vistas unfold one after another: a mountain rising from the edges of a dark shimmering lake gives way to a golden beach framed by sand dunes and stone-wall fields.

5

Kinsale

History, scenery and great food conspire to make Kinsale one of Ireland's top destinations, a picture-postcard idyll at the head of a sheltered bay. After walking around the bay to explore the vast Charles Fort, recharge your batteries with a memorable seafood platter at Fishy Fishy Cafe (p184).

Cork & the Ring of Kerry's Best...

Beauty Spots

○ **Kinsale** The perfect southern town. (p184)

○ **Ladies' View** Queen Victoria and her ladies loved the scenery. (p195)

○ **Gap of Dunloe** Awe-inspiring mountain pass. (p194)

○ **Connor Pass** Ireland's highest pass has stunning views. (p207)

○ **Bantry Bay** Watery perfection. (p187)

Local Activities

○ Sampling the local **produce**, from black pudding to seafood.

○ Trout or salmon **fishing** in the rivers around Killarney. (p188)

○ **Bird-watching** on the Skellig Islands. (p199)

○ Improving your cooking at **Ballymaloe House**. (p186)

Historic Notables

○ **Skellig Michael** One of the most impressive monastic sites in the world. (p198)

○ **Kerry Bog Village Museum** A typical 19th-century bog village. (p197)

○ **Slea Head** Packed with Stone Age monuments. (p206)

○ **Charles Fort** Best-preserved 17th-century fort in the region. (p184)

Need to Know

Memorable Drives

○ The **Ring of Kerry**, especially the stretch between Kenmare and Killarney. (p196)

○ The R575 coastal road between Allihies and Lauragh on the north side of the **Beara Peninsula**. (p199)

○ The **Healy Pass**, between Cork and Kerry. (p199)

○ The scenic detour off the N71 to **Brandon's Cottage** along the R568. (p194)

ADVANCE PLANNING

○ **Two months before** Book hotels, especially in popular areas such as Killarney, the Dingle Peninsula and West Cork.

○ **One month before** Book now if you want a place in a cooking course at the likes of Ballymaloe.

○ **Two weeks before** Make a list of sweater sizes for friends and family not travelling with you.

RESOURCES

○ **People's Republic of Cork** (www.peoples republicofcork.com) Picking up on the popular nickname for this liberal-leaning city, this indie website has excellent info.

○ **Discover Ireland** (www.discoverireland.ie/ southwest) Official tourist website.

○ **Killarney** (www.killarney.ie) The official site for the town, with lots of tourism links.

○ **GAA** (www.gaa.ie) For all things related to Gaelic sports.

GETTING AROUND

○ **Bus** Good bus networks cover most of the area, but it's a slow way of exploring.

○ **Train** The main towns are linked, but not necessarily to each other.

○ **Car** The region's beauty is off the beaten path; you'll need a car to get there.

BE FOREWARNED

○ **Crowds** Summer crowds and traffic jams – especially on the Ring of Kerry – are a mainstay of the peak tourist season.

○ **Weather** The southwest has a microclimate, which allows for warm summers and the growth of palm trees, but the weather can be very unpredictable.

○ **Gaelic football** It's a *religion* in Kerry; Cork are very good at both football and hurling.

Left: Gap of Dunloe (p194);
Above: Kittiwakes, Skellig Islands (p199)

(LEFT) MARK DAFFEY/GETTY IMAGES ©; (ABOVE) DESIGN PICS/
THE IRISH IMAGE COLLECTION/GETTY IMAGES ©

Cork & the Ring of Kerry Itineraries

If you don't have a month or more to spend in the southwest, these itineraries will allow you to explore stunning landscapes and dip into the region's outstanding culinary reputation in a limited amount of time.

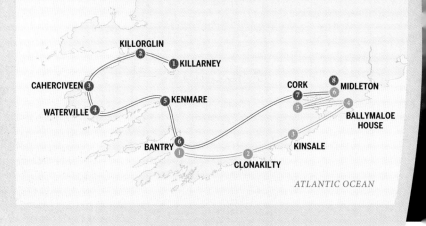

KILLORGLIN
② ① KILLARNEY
CAHERCIVEEN ③ CORK ⑧ MIDLETON
⑦
⑤ KENMARE ⑥
WATERVILLE ④ ④
⑤ BALLYMALOE
HOUSE
③
BANTRY ⑥ KINSALE
① ②
CLONAKILTY
ATLANTIC OCEAN

KILLARNEY TO MIDLETON
SOUTHWEST BLITZ

Start in the region's most popular tourist town, ❶**Killarney** (p188), visiting magnificent Killarney National Park – Muckross House is well worth the visit – before embarking on the perennially popular Ring of Kerry, taking in towns like ❷**Killorglin** (p196), ❸**Caherciveen** (p197), ❹**Waterville** (p200), where you can play some fabulous golf, and ❺**Kenmare** (p202). This is an ideal stopover town as it has some fine B&Bs, welcoming pubs and excellent restaurants. On day two, cross over to historic ❻**Bantry** (p187) before heading east to ❼**Cork City** (p178). Spend the day discovering the city, visiting the excellent Crawford Municipal

Gallery and the unmissable English Market, where you can sample some of the finest produce from the region – this is unquestionably Ireland's best covered market. With the taste of Cork's gourmet genius now firmly on the palate, head east to ❽**Midleton** (p190), visit the distillery museum (and purchase some fine Irish whiskey) and wrap up your lightning tour with a meal in the sublime Farmgate Restaurant.

5 DAYS

BANTRY TO MIDLETON
THE SOUTHERN PANTRY

County Cork has earned itself a justifiable reputation as the gourmet capital of Ireland. Start in West Cork, where gourmet cuisine is taken for granted. In ① **Bantry** (p187), unassuming Manning's Emporium will give you a sense of what's in store. If you're looking for the best black pudding, head to ② **Clonakilty** (the town is famous for it; p185) and try Edward Twomey, which has followed the same recipe for over a century. Further east, ③ **Kinsale** (p184) is just full of top nosh, including Fishy Fishy Cafe and John Edwards – although it looks like an ordinary pub, it's anything but. Over the weekend, enrol in a cooking course at

the world-famous ④ **Ballymaloe House** (p186), south of Cork City. Back in ⑤ **Cork city** (p178), stock up at the daily English Market, which wowed Queen Elizabeth during her 2011 visit. Baskets full, head east to ⑥ **Midleton** (p190) for the Farmgate Restaurant, one of Ireland's very best – make a visit to the classic Old Jameson Distillery while you're in town. Midleton's farmers market is better than the one in Cork City, but it's only a weekly affair.

Jameson Experience (p190), Midleton
GEORGE MUNDAY/ALAMY ©

Discover Cork & the Ring of Kerry

COUNTY CORK

Cork City

POP 120,000

Ireland's second city is first in every important respect, at least according to the locals, who cheerfully refer to it as the 'real capital of Ireland'. The compact city centre is surrounded by interesting waterways and is chock full of great restaurants fed by arguably the best foodie scene in the country.

◉ Sights

Crawford Municipal Art Gallery
Gallery

(☎021-480 5042; www.crawfordartgallery. ie; Emmet Pl; ⏱10am-5pm Mon-Wed, Fri & Sat, 10am-8pm Thu) FREE Cork's public gallery houses a small but excellent permanent collection covering the 17th century to the modern day. Highlights include works by Sir John Lavery, Jack B Yeats, Nathaniel Hone and a room devoted to Irish women artists from 1886 to 1978 – don't miss the works by Mainie Jellet and Evie Hone.

🛏 Sleeping

CITY CENTRE

Imperial Hotel
Hotel €€

(☎021-427 4040; www.flynnhotels.com; South Mall; d/ste from €109/450; @ 🛜)
Recently celebrating its bicentenary, the Imperial knows how to age gracefully. Public spaces resonate with opulent period detail such as marble floors, elaborate floral bouquets and more. The 130 rooms are of four-star hotel standard: and include writing

Crawford Municipal Art Gallery
TRISH PUNCH/GETTY IMAGES ©

TRISH PUNCH/GETTY IMAGES ©

⭐ Don't Miss
The English Market

It could just as easily be called the Victorian Market for its ornate vaulted ceilings and columns, but the English Market is a true gem, no matter what you name it. Scores of vendors sell some of the very best local produce, meats, cheeses and takeaway food in the region. On decent days, take your lunch to nearby Bishop Lucey Park, a popular al fresco eating spot.

Looking down over the market from a mezzanine, **Farmgate Cafe** (www.farmgate.ie; dishes €4.50-15; ⊘8.30am-5pm Mon-Sat) is an unmissable experience. Like its sister restaurant in Midleton, this cafe has mastered the magic art of producing delicious meals without fuss or faddism. The food, from rock oysters to the lamb for Irish stew, is sourced from the market below. There are tables but the best seats are at the balcony counter, where you can ponder the passing parade of shoppers.

NEED TO KNOW
www.englishmarket.ie; Princes St; ⊘9am-5.30pm Mon-Sat

desks, restrained decor and modern touches including the Aveda spa and a digital music library – something unheard of when Charles Dickens stayed. Irish Free State commander-in-chief Michael Collins spent his final night here; you can check into his suite.

WESTERN ROAD & AROUND

Garnish House   B&B €€
(☏021-427 5111; www.garnish.ie; Western Rd; s/d from €75/89; 🛜) Every attention is lavished upon guests at this award-winning B&B. The legendary breakfast menu (30 choices!) includes fresh fish and French

Cork

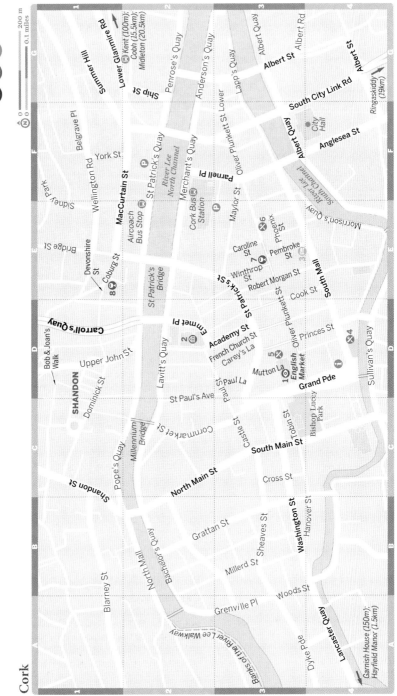

Cork

toast. Typical of the touches here is the freshly cooked porridge, which comes with creamed honey and your choice of whiskey or Baileys. Enjoy it out on the garden terrace. The 14 rooms are very comfortable; reception is open 24 hours.

Hayfield Manor　　Hotel €€€
(☎021-484 5900; www.hayfieldmanor.ie; Perrott Ave, College Rd; d €195-310; @ 🛜 🏊) Roll out the red carpet and pour yourself a sherry for *you have arrived*. Just 1.5km south-west of the city centre but with all the ambience of a country house, Hayfield combines the luxury and facilities of a big hotel with the informality and welcome of a small one. The 88 beautiful bedrooms (choose from traditional or contemporary styling) enjoy 24-hour room service, although you may want to idle the hours away in the library, luxurious spa and leisure centre or gourmet restaurants.

✖ Eating

Electric　　Modern Irish €€
(www.electriccork.com; 41 South Mall; mains €15-27; ⊙noon-10pm; 🛜) The market-sourced menu at this this transformed art deco bank includes broccoli risotto with pear, blue cheese and walnut dressing and succulent steaks. From Thursday to Saturday it also has a rustic Mediterranean-style fish bar. But it's the big riverside deck and upstairs restaurant balcony with knockout cathedral views that amps up the

crowds – along with wines by the glass, and over two dozen beers.

**Jacques
Restaurant**　　Modern Irish €€€
(☎021-427 7387; www.jacquesrestaurant.ie; 23 Oliver Plunkett St; mains €20-28; ⊙10am-4pm Mon, to 10pm Tue-Sat) Now in sleek new premises, Jacqueline and Eithne Barry continue to draw on the terrific network of local suppliers they've built up over nearly three decades to help them realise their culinary ambitions – the freshest Cork food cooked simply. The menu changes daily: quail with jewelled couscous, perhaps, or Castletownbere scallops with pomegranate, raisin and caper salsa.

🍷 Drinking & Nightlife

Sin É　　Pub
(8 Coburg St) You could easily while away an entire day at this great old place, which is every thing a craic-filled pub should be – long on atmosphere and short on pretension. There's music most nights, much of it traditional, but with the odd surprise.

Long Valley　　Pub
(10 Winthrop St) A Cork institution that dates from the mid-19th century and is still going strong. Some of the furnishings hail from White Star Line ocean liners that used to call at Cobh.

❶ Information

The **Cork City Tourist Office** (☎021-425 5100; www.corkcity.ie; Grand Pde; ⊙9am-6pm Mon-Sat, 10am-5pm Sun Jul & Aug, 9.15am-5pm Mon-Sat Sep-Jun) has a souvenir shop and information desk. It also sells Ordnance Survey maps; **Stena Line** ferries has a desk here.

❶ Getting There & Away

Air

Cork Airport (☎021-431 3131; www.cork-airport.com) is 8km south of the city on the N27. Facilities include ATMs and car-hire desks for all the main companies. Airlines servicing the airport include Aer Lingus, Ryanair and Jet2.com. There are flights to Dublin, London (Heathrow, Gatwick and Stansted) and a few other cities in Britain and across Europe.

Boat

Brittany Ferries (📞021-427 7801; www.brittanyferries.ie; 42 Grand Pde) sails to Roscoff (France) weekly from the end of March to October. The crossing takes 14 hours; fares vary widely. The ferry terminal is at Ringaskiddy,15 minutes by car southeast of the city centre along the N28. Taxis cost €28 to €35. Bus Éireann runs a service from Cork's bus station to link up with departures (adult/child €7.90/5.60, 40 minutes); confirm times. There's also a service to Rosslare Harbour (adult/child €26/17.50, four to five hours).

Bus

Aircoach (📞01-844 7118; www.aircoach.ie) Serves Dublin Airport and Dublin city centre from St Patrick's Quay (€15; 4¼ hours; every two hours 1am to 11pm).

Bus Éireann (📞021-450 8188; www.buseireann.ie) Operates from the bus station (cnr Merchants Quay & Parnell Pl). You can get to most places in Ireland from Cork, including Dublin (€14.50, three hours, six daily), Killarney (€15.30, 1¾ hours, 14 daily), Kilkenny (€19, three hours, two daily) and Waterford (€21.20, 2¼ hours, 13 daily).

Citylink (📞091-564 164; www.citylink.ie; 📶) Operates services to Galway (three hours) and Limerick (1½ hours). Buses are frequent and fares are as low as €10.

GoBus (📞091-564 600; www.gobus.ie; 📶) Links Cork's bus station with Dublin (€12, three hours, nine daily).

Train

Kent Train Station (📞021-450 4777) is north of the River Lee on Lower Glanmire Rd. Buses run into the centre (€1.80); a taxi costs from €9 to €10.

ℹ️ Getting Around

To/From the Airport

Bus Éireann has frequent services between the bus station and Cork Airport between 6am and 11pm (€5, 30 minutes).

A taxi to/from town costs €20 to €25.

Bus

Most places are within easy walking distance of the centre. Single bus tickets costs €1.80 each; a day pass is €4.80. Buy all tickets on the bus.

Left: Cork city; **Below:** Blarney Castle
(LEFT) TRISH PUNCH/GETTY IMAGES ©; (BELOW) DANITA DELIMONT/GETTY IMAGES ©

Car

Streetside parking requires scratch-card parking discs (€2 per hour), obtained from the tourist office and some newsagencies. Be warned – the traffic wardens are ferociously efficient and the cost of retrieving your vehicle is hefty. There are several signposted car parks around the central area, with charges of €2 per hour and €12 overnight.

Taxi

For taxi hire try Cork Taxi Co-op (☏ 021-427 2222; www.corktaxi.ie) or Shandon Cabs (☏ 021-450 2255).

....

Around Cork City

BLARNEY CASTLE

If you need proof of the power of a good yarn, then join the queue to get into this 15th-century **castle** (☏ 021-438 5252; www.blarneycastle.ie; adult/child €12/5; ⊙ 9am-7pm Mon-Sat, to 6pm Sun Jun-Aug, 9am-6.30pm Mon-Sat, to 6pm Sun May & Sep, 9am-6pm Mon-Sat, to 5pm Sun Oct-Apr), one of Ireland's most inexplicably popular tourist attractions.

People are here, of course, to plant their lips on the **Blarney Stone**, a cliché that has entered every lexicon and tour route. The object of their affections is perched at the top of a steep climb up slippery, spiral staircases. On the battlements, you bend backwards over a long, long drop (with safety grill and attendant to prevent tragedy) to kiss the stone; as your shirt rides up, coach loads of onlookers stare up your nose. Try not to think of the local lore about the fluids other than saliva that drench the stone. Better yet, just don't do it.

Blarney is 8km northwest of Cork. The castle itself is poorly signed – follow the signs for the Blarney Woollen Mills gift emporium and hotel complex. Buses run frequently from Cork bus station (adult/child €3.80/2, 30 minutes).

183

Kinsale & West Cork

KINSALE

POP 2200

Narrow, winding streets lined with artsy little shops, lively bars and superb restaurants, and a handsome harbour full of bobbing fishing boats and pleasure yachts make Kinsale (Cionn tSáile) one of Ireland's favourite midsized towns. Its sheltered bay is guarded by a huge and engrossing fort.

◎ Sights

Charles Fort   Fort

(☎021-477 2263; www.heritageireland.ie; adult/child €4/2; ◷10am-6pm mid-Mar–Oct, 10am-5pm Nov–mid-Dec, 10am-5pm Tue-Sun mid-Dec–mid-Mar) One of the best-preserved, 17th-century, star-shaped forts in Europe, this wonderful fort 3km east of Kinsale would be worth a visit for its spectacular views alone. But there's much more here: ruins inside the vast site date from the 18th and 19th centuries and make for some fascinating wandering. Displays explain the typically tough lives led by the soldiers who served here and the comparatively comfortable lives of the officers. Built in the 1670s to guard Kinsale Harbour, the fort was in use until 1921, when much of it was destroyed as the British withdrew. It's a lovely walk around the bay.

The Best Black Pudding

Clonakilty's most treasured export is its black pudding, the blood sausage that features on most local restaurant menus. The best place to buy it is from butcher **Edward Twomey** (☎023-883 3733; www. clonakiltyblackpudding.ie; 16 Pearse St; puddings from €2.75; ◷9am-6pm Mon-Sat), selling different varieties based on the original recipe, formulated in the 1880s.

◻ Sleeping

Old Presbytery   B&B €€

(☎021-477 2027; www.oldpres.com; Cork St; d €125-160; ◷closed Jan–mid-Feb; ⊚) ⊘ The Old Presbytery has gracefully moved into the 21st century with a careful refurbishment that maintains its character and incorporates solar heating. Stay in room 6 only if you have plans to see nothing of Kinsale: with its sunroom and balcony, you'll never want to leave. The organic breakfasts, cooked by landlord and former chef Phillip, are the stuff of legend.

✗ Eating

Finn's Table   Modern Irish €€€

(☎021-470 9636; www.finnstable.com; 6 Main St; mains €24.50-33; ◷from 5.30pm Thu-Mon) ⊘ Opening a gourmet restaurant in Kinsale means plenty of competition but John and Julie Finn's new venture is more than up to the challenge. It pushes the culinary envelope with dishes such as fillet steak and tobacco, and salt and pepper squid served with curried crab mayonnaise and herb oil. Seafood (including lobster in season) is from West Cork, while meat is from the Finn family's butchers.

Fishy Fishy Cafe   Seafood €€€

(☎021-470 0415; www.fishyfishy.ie; Crowley's Quay; mains €19-34.50; ◷noon-9pm Mar-Oct, to 4pm Sun-Wed & to 9pm Thu-Sat Nov-Feb) One of the most famous seafood restaurants in the country, Fishy Fishy has a wonderful setting, with stark white walls splashed with bright artwork and a terrific decked terrace at the front. It's pricey but all the fish is caught locally. Have the cold seafood platter – a concert of what's fresh.

❶ Information

Pearse St has a post office and banks with ATMs. Tourist office (☎021-477 2234; www.kinsale.ie; cnr Pier Rd & Emmet Pl; ◷9.15am-5pm Tue-Sat Nov-Mar, Mon Apr-Jun, Sep & Oct, 10am-5pm Sun Jul & Aug) Has a good map detailing walks in and around Kinsale.

Kinsale

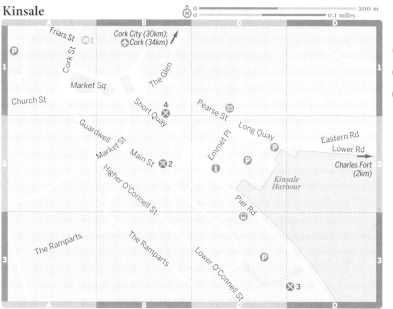

Kinsale

Getting There & Around

Bus Éireann (021-450 8188) services connect Kinsale with Cork (€8.50, 50 minutes, 14 daily Monday to Friday, 11 Saturday and four Sunday) via Cork airport. The **bus stop** is on Pier Rd, near the tourist office.

Kinsale Cabs (021-477 2642; www. kinsalecabs.com) also arranges golfing tours of West Cork.

CLONAKILTY

POP 4000

Cheerful, brightly coloured Clonakilty is a bustling market town that serves as a hub for the scores of beguiling little coastal towns that surround it.

Clonakilty is famous for two things: it's the birthplace of Irish Free State commander-in-chief Michael Collins, embodied in a large **statue** on the corner of Emmet Sq; and it's the home of the most famous black pudding in the country.

Sights & Activities

For an insight into a pivotal chapter of Irish history, **Michael Collins Centre** (023-884 6107; www.michaelcollinscentre. com; adult/child €5/3; 10.30am-5pm mid-Jun–Sep), 6km northeast of Clonakilty, is a must.

Wandering the centre is good for a couple of hours; Georgian **Emmet Square** attests to the area's traditional wealth. **Spillers Lane** has nifty little shops.

Sleeping

Inchydoney Island Lodge & Spa Resort Hotel €€€
(023-883 3143; www.inchydoneyisland.com; s midweek/weekend €145/175, d €190/250, @ 🛱 🛋 🛗) A superb sea water spa is at the heart of this sprawling resort 5km

Detour:
The Gourmet Heartland of Ballymaloe

Drawing up at wisteria-clad **Ballymaloe House** (☑021-465 2531; www.ballymaloe.ie; Shanagarry; s/d from €135/230, lunch mains €13-24, 4-course dinner menu €70; ☺restaurant 8-10.30am, 1-3pm & 7-9.30pm; 🕾👪) you know you've arrived somewhere special. The Allen family bought the property in 1948 and has been running this superb hotel and restaurant in the old family home for decades. Myrtle Allen is a living legend, acclaimed internationally for her near single-handed creation of fine Irish cooking. Rooms are individually decorated with period furnishings and are a pleasing mass of different shapes and sizes. Amid the beautiful grounds, amenities, include a tennis court, a swimming pool, a shop and a cafe.

The menu at Ballymaloe House's celebrated **restaurant** changes daily to reflect the availability of produce from its extensive farms and other local sources, but might include local Ballycotton scallops and artichoke purée with garden herb relish, or spiced braised lamb with garden swede turnips. The hotel also runs wine and gardening weekends.

Just over 3km east on the R628, Myrtle's daughter-in-law, TV personality Darina Allen, runs Ballymaloe's famous **cookery school** (☑021-464 6785; www. cookingisfun.ie). Darina's own daughter-in-law, Rachel Allen, is also a high-profile TV chef and author who regularly teaches at the school. Demonstrations cost €70; lessons, from half-day sessions (€95 to €125) to 12-week certificate courses (€10,695), are often booked well in advance. There are pretty cottages amid the 100 acres of grounds for overnight students.

---

south of Clonakilty, where the service is outstanding and recently redesigned rooms overlook the ocean from private balconies and terraces. The food at the French-inspired **restaurant** (☺6.30-9.45pm daily & 1-3pm Sun; mains €18.50-34.50) is delicious.

Eating

An Súgán
Modern Irish €€
(☑023-883 3719; www.ansugan.com; 41 Wolfe Tone St; mains €12-22; ☺noon-10pm) A traditional bar with a national reputation for excellent seafood. You dine in a room crammed with knick-knacks – jugs dangle from the ceiling, patrons' business cards are stuffed beneath the rafters, and lanterns and even ancient fire-extinguishers dot the walls. But there's nothing idiosyncratic about the food – the seafood chowder and crab cakes are great, and there's a choice of around 10 different kinds of fish, depending on the daily catch.

Drinking & Nightlife

De Barra's
Pub
(www.debarra.ie; 55 Pearse St) A marvellous atmosphere, walls splattered with photos, press cuttings, masks and musical instruments, plus the cream of live music, particularly folk, from around 9.30pm make this a busy pub.

Information

Tourist office (☑023-883 3226; www.clonakilty. ie; Ashe St; ☺9.15am-5pm Mon-Sat)

Getting There & Away

There are seven daily buses to Cork (€14.20, 65 minutes) and Skibbereen (€9.80, 40 minutes). The **bus stop** is across from Harte's Spar shop on the bypass to Cork.

Note that the alternative route to Kinsale is on the R600.

Mizen Head Peninsula

BANTRY

POP 3300

Framed by the craggy Caha Mountains, vast, magnificent Bantry Bay is one of the country's most attractive inlets and a worthwhile stop on any West Cork itinerary. Pride of place goes to Bantry House, the former home of one Richard White, who earned his place in history when in 1798 he warned authorities of the imminent landing of patriot Wolfe Tone and his French fleet in their effort to join the countrywide rebellion of the United Irishmen.

Bantry struggled through the 19th century due to famine, poverty and mass emigration but today its industry derives from the bay: you'll see Bantry oysters and mussels on menus throughout County Cork.

Sights

Bantry House Historic Building
(☎ 027-50047; www.bantryhouse.com; Bantry Bay; adult/child €11/3; ☺10am-5pm Apr-Oct)
The house has belonged to the White

family since 1729 and every room brims with treasures brought back from each generation's travels since then. Upstairs, worn bedrooms look out wanly over an astounding view of the bay – the 18th-century Whites had ringside seats to the French armada. Experienced pianists are invited to tinkle the ivories of the ancient piano in the library. It's possible to stay in the wings.

Bantry House is 1km southwest of the town centre on the N71.

Sleeping

Bantry House Manor House €€€
(☎027-50047; www.bantryhouse.com; Bantry Bay; d from €169; ☺Apr-Oct; ☎) Bantry House's guest rooms, decorated in pale hues and a mixture of antiques and contemporary furnishings, are luxurious places to while away the hours – when you're not playing croquet, lawn tennis or billiards and lounging in the house's library once the doors are shut to the public (guests also receive free access to the house). Rooms 22 and 25 are double winners, with views of both the garden and the bay.

Bantry House

JOHN ELK/GETTY IMAGES ©

If You Like...
Food Festivals

Whet your appetite at these culinary celebrations:

1 GOURMET FESTIVAL
(www.kinsalerestaurants.com) Tastings, meals and harbour cruises add to the town's foodie reputation come early October.

2 SEAFOOD FESTIVAL
(www.baltimore.ie) Jazz bands perform and pubs bring out the mussels and prawns, and there's a wooden boat parade, too.

3 TASTE OF WEST CORK FOOD FESTIVAL
(www.atasteofwestcork.com) If you're in town in mid-September, don't miss this festival which has a lively market and events at local restaurants.

4 DINGLE FOOD & WINE FESTIVAL
(www.dinglefood.com) Fabulous foodie fest in early October featuring a 'taste trail' with cheap-as-chips sampling at over 40 locations around town, plus a market, cooking demonstrations, workshops and a foraging walk.

 Eating

Manning's Emporium   Cafe, Deli €
(www.manningsemporium.ie; Ballylickey; tasting plates €8; ⊙9am-6pm Mon-Sat, 9am-5pm Sun)
🍃 It looks like a garden centre from the outside, with a profusion of pot plants and hanging baskets, but inside it's an Aladdin's cave of West Cork's best produce. Tasting plates are the best way to sample the local artisan produce and farmhouse cheeses on offer. Foodie events take place regularly. It's on the N71 in Ballylickey (on your right as you're coming from Bantry).

ℹ **Information**

The **tourist office** (☎027-50229; Wolfe Tone Sq; ⊙9.15am-1pm & 2-5pm Mon-Sat Apr-Oct) is located in the old courthouse.

ℹ **Getting There & Away**

Bus Éireann (www.buseireann.ie) has seven buses daily Monday to Saturday (four on Sunday) between Bantry and Cork (€19, two hours). There's five daily to Glengarriff (€4.70, 25 minutes). Heading north by bus to the Ring of Beara, Kenmare and Killarney requires backtracking through Cork.

Bantry Rural Transport (☎027-52727; www.ruraltransport.ie; 5 Main St) runs a useful series of circular routes to Dunmanway, Durrus, Goleen, Schull, Skibbereen and outlying villages. There's a set price of €4/6 one-way/return. Service is not frequent; check the website for details.

COUNTY KERRY

Killarney

POP 12,750

In a town that's been practising the tourism game for over 250 years, Killarney is a well-oiled machine in the middle of the sublime scenery of its namesake national park. Beyond the obvious proximity to lakes, waterfalls, woodland and moors dwarfed by 1000m-plus peaks, it has many charms of its own. Competition keeps standards high, and no matter your budget, you can expect to find good restaurants, fine pubs and plenty of accommodation.

Mobbed in summer, Killarney is perhaps at its best in the late spring and early autumn when you can enjoy its outdoor pursuits and the crowds are manageable.

◎ **Sights & Activities**

Killarney's biggest attraction, in every sense, is Killarney National Park (p193). The town itself can easily be explored on foot in an hour or two.

🛏 **Sleeping**

Crystal Springs   B&B €€
(☎064-663 3272; www.crystalspringsbb.com; Ballycasheen Cross; s/d from €45/70;)

Killarney

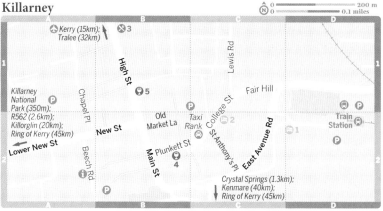

You can cast a line from the timber deck of this wonderfully relaxing riverside B&B or just laze about on the adjacent lawn. Rooms are richly furnished with patterned wallpapers and walnut timber; private bathrooms (most with spa baths) are huge. The glass-enclosed breakfast room also overlooks the rushing River Flesk. It's about a 15-minute stroll to town.

Murphy's of Killarney
Inn €€

(☑064-663 1294; www.murphysofkillarney.com; College St; d from €85; 🛜) A great midrange option close to the action, Murphy's 20 rooms have been stylishly refurbished – ask for one overlooking the street. If it's lashing rain, you won't have to leave as there's a highly respected restaurant and pub on-site.

Malton
Hotel €€€

(☑064-663 8000; www.themalton.com; s/d from €120-180; @🛜≋👪) So commanding it doesn't need an address, the pillared, ivy-covered Malton in the centre of town is a throwback to Victorian elegance – at least from the outside. Inside it's had a thorough strip-and-refit; of the 172 rooms, the pick are those in the 1852 wing, which have retained their period opulence. There are several stunning restaurants and a spa and leisure centre with a 17m swimming pool, gym and two tennis courts.

🍴 Eating

Smoke House
Bistro €€

(☑064-662 0801; www.thesmokehouse.ie; High St; lunch mains €7-14, dinner mains €15-28; ⏰9am-late; 🍴) One of Killarney's busiest ventures since it opened a couple of years ago, this tiled bistro was the first establishment in Ireland to cook with a Josper (Spanish charcoal oven). Stylish salads include Norwegian king crab; its Kerry surf 'n' turf burger – with prawns and house-made barbecue sauce – has a local following.

Gaby's Seafood Restaurant
Seafood €€€

(☑064-663 2519; www.gabysireland.com; 27 High St; mains €28-50; ⏰6-10pm Mon-Sat) Gaby's is a refined dining experience serving superb seafood served in a traditional manner. Peruse the menu by the

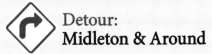

Detour:
Midleton & Around

Aficionados of a particularly fine Irish whiskey will recognise the name, and the main reason to linger in this bustling market town is to tour the restored 200-year-old building housing the **Jameson Experience** (☑021-461 3594; www. jamesonwhiskey.com; Old Distillery Walk; tours adult/child €13/7.70, restaurant mains €9-11; ⏰shop 10am-6.30pm, tour times vary, restaurant noon-3pm). Exhibits and tours explain the process of taking barley and creating whiskey (Jameson is today made in a modern factory in Cork). There's a well-stocked gift shop; the **Malt House Restaurant** has live music on Sundays.

Highly recommended is the **Farmgate Restaurant** (☑021-463 2771; www. farmgate.ie; The Coolbawn, off Broderick St; lunch mains €12-15, dinner mains €18-30; ⏰coffee & snacks 9am-5.30pm, lunch noon-3.30pm Tue-Sat, dinner 6.30-9.30pm Thu-Sat), the original and sister establishment to Cork city's Farmgate Cafe, which offers the same superb blend of traditional and modern Irish in its approach to cooking. Squeeze through its deli selling amazing baked goods and local produce, including organic fruit and vegetables, cheeses and preserves to the farmhouse-style cafe-restaurant, where you'll eat as well as anywhere in Ireland.

Midleton is 20km east of Cork. The **train station** (5 McSweeney Terrace) is 1.5km north of the Jameson Experience. From Monday to Friday, there are 21 services to Cork, with 17 on Saturday and nine on Sunday (€2.20, 20 minutes). Change in Glounthaune for Cobh.

There are less frequent buses to Cork bus station (€7.10, 25 minutes). You'll need a car to explore the surrounding area.

---

fire before drifting past the wine cellar to the low-lit dining room to savour exquisite Gallic dishes such as lobster in cognac and cream. The wine list is long and the advice unerring.

🍷 Drinking & Nightlife

O'Connor's
Pub

(High St) This tiny traditional pub with leaded glass doors is one of Killarney's most popular haunts. Live music plays every night; good bar food is served daily in summer. In warmer weather, the crowds spill out into the adjacent laneway.

Courtney's
Pub

(www.courtneysbar.com; Plunkett St) Inconspicuous on the outside, inside this timeless pub bursts at the seams with

traditional music sessions many nights year-round. This is where locals come to see their old mates perform and to kick off a night on the town.

ℹ️ Information

The tourist office (☑064-663 1633; www. killarney.ie; Beech Rd; ⏰9am-6pm Mon-Sat, to 5pm Sun Jun-Aug, 9am-6pm Mon-Sat Sep-May) can handle almost any query, especially dealing with transport intricacies.

ℹ️ Getting There & Away

Air

Kerry Airport (KIR; ☑066-976 4644; www. kerryairport.ie; Farranfore) is at Farranfore, about 15km north of Killarney along the N22, then a further 1.5km along the N23.

Ryanair (www.ryanair.com) rules the roost with daily flights to Dublin and London's Luton and Stansted airports, and less frequent services to Hahn, Germany; Faro, Portugal; and Alicante, Spain.

The small airport has a restaurant, bar, bureau de change and ATM. Virtually all the major car-hire firms have desks at the airport.

Bus

Bus Éireann (☎ 064-663 0011; www. buseireann.ie) operates from the east end of the Killarney Outlet Centre, offering regular links to destinations including Cork (€19, two hours, 15 daily); Dublin (€28, six hours, six daily); Galway (€26, seven hours, seven daily) via Limerick (€20.20, 2¼ hours); Tralee (€8.70, 40 minutes, hourly); and Waterford (€26, 4½ hours, hourly).

Train

Killarney's train station is behind the Malton Hotel, just east of the centre.

Irish Rail (☎ 064-6631067; www.irishrail. ie) has up to nine direct trains a day to Tralee (€10.80, 45 minutes) and three trains a day via Mallow to Cork (€26.80, 1½ hours). There's one direct train daily to Dublin (from €33, 3½ hours), otherwise you'll have to change at Mallow.

🛈 Getting Around

To/From the Airport

Bus Éireann has six to seven services daily between Killarney and Kerry Airport (€5, 20 minutes); frustratingly, they're not coordinated with flight times.

Tralee–Killarney trains stop at Farranfore station, a 10-minute walk (at minimum) from the airport.

A taxi to Killarney costs about €35.

Bicycle

Bicycles are ideal for exploring the scattered sights of the Killarney area, many of which are accessible only by bike or on foot.

O'Sullivan's Bike Hire (www.killarney rentabike.com; per day/week €15/85) has branches on New St, opposite the cathedral, and on Beech Rd, opposite the tourist office. Road, mountain and children's bikes are available.

Jaunting Car

Killarney's traditional transport is the horse-drawn jaunting car (☎ 064-663 3358; www.killarneyjauntingcars.ie), also known as a

Local Knowledge

Killarney's Don't Miss List

BY ALOYSIUS 'WEESHIE' FOGARTY, RADIO PRESENTER AND EX-KERRY FOOTBALLER

1 KILLARNEY TOWN
Killarney is one of the top tourist attractions in the world, absolutely buzzing in summer and very cosmopolitan too. It's so busy that every time you step off the sidewalk, you're likely to meet a person from anywhere in the world.

2 KILLARNEY NATIONAL PARK
There's nowhere more special to me than Killarney National Park (p193), which is part of Killarney Town but in a world of its own. The lakes, mountains and stunning views are as beautiful as any I've seen in all my years of travelling. Thank God they're on my doorstep!

3 JIMMY O'BRIEN'S
It is said that the secret to Ireland is to go into a pub and meet a local. Killarney's pubs are fine pubs indeed, but the best of them is unquestionably Jimmy O'Brien's. It's old, unique and full of wonderful characters.

4 RING OF KERRY
Killarney is the doorway to the Ring of Kerry, a circular drive of such stunning beauty that you'd have to travel to Slea Head at the tip of the Dingle Peninsula to see its equal. You haven't seen Ireland until you've seen the Ring.

5 THE CHANGING SEASONS
Killarney is a year-round destination and each season is special. There's the green haze of summer, the rich bloom of spring and the bare frost of winter, when the whole place might be enveloped in snow.

TRAVEL INK/GETTY IMAGES ©

⭐ Don't Miss
Muckross Estate

The core of Killarney National Park is the Muckross Estate, donated to the state by Arthur Bourn Vincent in 1932. **Muckross House** (☎064-667 0144; www.muckross-house.ie; adult/child €7.50/4, combined ticket with farms €12.50/7; ☻9am-7pm Jul & Aug, to 5.30pm Sep-Jun) is a 19th-century mansion, restored to its former glory and packed with contemporaneous fittings. Entrance is by guided tour.

Immediately east of Muckross House are the **Muckross Traditional Farms** (☎064-663 1440; adult/child €7.50/4, combined ticket with Muckross House €12.50/7; ☻10am-6pm Jun-Aug, 1-6pm May & Sep, 1-6pm Sat, Sun & public holidays Apr & Oct). These reproductions of 1930s Kerry farms, complete with chickens, pigs, cattle and horses, show farming and living conditions when people had to live off the land.

Muckross House is 5km south of town, signposted from the N71. If you're walking or cycling, there's a cycle track alongside the Kenmare road for most of the first 2km. A path then turns right into Killarney National Park. Following this path, after 1km you'll come to **Muckross Abbey**, which was founded in 1448 and burned by Cromwell's troops in 1652. William Thackeray called it 'the prettiest little bijou of a ruined abbey ever seen'. Muckross House is another 1.5km from the abbey ruins.

trap, which comes with a driver known as a jarvey. The **pick-up point**, nicknamed 'the Ha Ha' or 'the Block', is on Kenmare Pl. Trips around town cost €30 to €70, depending on distance; traps officially carry four people. Jaunting cars also congregate in the N71 car park for Muckross House and Abbey, and at the Gap of Dunloe.

Around Killarney

Castles, gardens and lake adventures are among the highlights of a visit to Killarney National Park, immediately south of the city. Just beyond, there's rugged scenery including the too-gorgeous-for-words Gap of Dunloe, with its rocky terrain, babbling brooks and alpine lakes.

KILLARNEY NATIONAL PARK

You can escape Killarney for the surrounding wilderness surprisingly quickly. Buses rumble up to Ross Castle and Muckross House, but it's possible to find your own refuge in the 10,236 hectares of **Killarney National Park** (www.killarney-nationalpark.ie) among Ireland's only wild herd of native red deer, the country's largest area of ancient oak woods and views of most of its major mountains.

Glacial **Lough Leane** (the Lower Lake or 'Lake of Learning'), **Muckross Lake** and the **Upper Lake** make up about a quarter of the park. Their peaty waters are as rich in **wildlife** as the surrounding soil: cormorants skim across the surface, deer swim out to graze on the islands, and salmon, trout and perch prosper in a pike-free environment. Lough Leane has vistas of reeds and swans.

The park was designated a Unesco Biosphere Reserve in 1982.

Other **wildlife** found in the park includes reintroduced white-tail eagles; in 2013, the first white-tail eagle chicks hatched in Ireland in over a hundred years.

Pedestrian entrances are located opposite St Mary's Cathedral in Killarney; there are other entrances for drivers off the N71.

ROSS CASTLE

Restored by Dúchas, lakeside **Ross Castle** (☎ 064-663 5851; www.heritageire-land.ie; Ross Rd; adult/child €4/2; ⊘ 9am-5.45pm Mar-Oct) dates back to the 15th century, when it was a residence of the O'Donoghues. It was the last place in Munster to succumb to Cromwell's forces, thanks partly to its cunning spiral staircase, every step of which is a different height in order to break an attacker's stride.

The castle is a lovely 3km walk from the St Mary's Cathedral pedestrian park entrance; you may well see deer. If you're driving from Killarney, turn right opposite the petrol station at the start of Muckross Rd. Access is by guided tour only.

INISFALLEN ISLAND

The first monastery on Inisfallen Island (at 22 acres, the largest of the national park's 26 islands) is said to have been founded by St Finian the Leper in the 7th century. The island's fame dates

Pub front, Killarney
EOIN CLARKE/GETTY IMAGES ©

Around Killarney

from the early 13th century when the Annals of Inisfallen were written here. Now in the Bodleian Library at Oxford, they remain a vital source of information on early Munster history. On Inisfallen are the ruins of a 12th-century **oratory** with a carved Romanesque doorway and a **monastery** on the site of St Finian's original.

You can hire boats (around €5) from Ross Castle to row to the island.

GAP OF DUNLOE

Geographically, the Gap of Dunloe is outside the Killarney National Park, but most people include it in their visit to the park. The land is ruggedly beautiful, and

fast-changing weather conditions add drama.

In the winter, it's an awe-inspiring mountain pass, overshadowed by Purple Mountain and Macgillycuddy's Reeks. In high summer, though, it's a bottleneck for the tourist trade, with buses ferrying countless visitors for horse-and-trap rides through the Gap.

In the south, surrounded by lush, green pastures, **Brandon's Cottage** (dishes €3-6; ☺ breakfast & lunch Apr-Oct) is a simple old 19th-century hunting lodge with an open-air cafe and a dock for boats crossing the Upper Lake.

From here a narrow road weaves up the hill to the Gap. Heading down towards the north the scenery is a

Tours

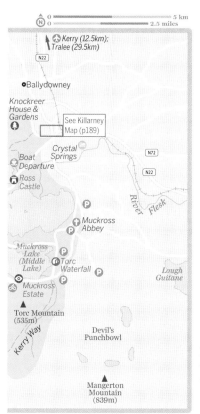

Killarney
Guided Walks
Walking Tour

(☎087 639 4362; www.killarneyguidedwalks.
com; adult/child €9/5) Guided two-hour
national park walks leave at 11am daily
from opposite St Mary's Cathedral at the
western end of New St. The tours me-
ander through Knockreer gardens, then
head to spots where Charles de Gaulle
holidayed, David Lean filmed *Ryan's
Daughter* and Brother Cudda slept for
200 years. Trips are available at other
times on request.

Ross Castle
Open Boats
Boat Tour

(☎087 689 9241) The open boats you
can charter at Ross Castle offer appealing trips with boatmen who define
'character'. It normally costs €10 from
Ross Castle to the Muckross (Middle)
Lake and back; €15 for a tour of all three
lakes.

KILLARNEY TO KENMARE

The vista-crazy N71 to Kenmare (32km)
winds between rock and lake, with plenty
of lay-bys to stop and admire the views
(and recover from the switchback bends).
Watch out for the buses squeezing along
the road.

About 2km south of the entrance to
Muckross House, a path leads 200m to
the pretty **Torc Waterfall**. After another
8km on the N71 you come to **Ladies'
View**, where the fine views along Upper
Lake were enjoyed by Queen Victoria's
ladies-in-waiting.

A further 5km on, **Moll's Gap** is worth
a stop for great views and food – and
not necessarily in that order. **Avoca Cafe**
(☎064-663 4720; www.avoca.ie; mains €7.50-
13.50; ⊙9.30am-5pm Mon-Fri, 10am-6pm Sat
& Sun) has awesome panoramas and
delicious fare such as smoked salmon
salad, pistachio-studded pork terrine and
decadent cakes.

fantasy of rocky bridges over clear
mountain streams and lakes.

At the northern end of the Gap of
Dunloe is the 19th-century pub **Kate
Kearney's Cottage** (☎064-664 4146; www.
katekearneyscottage.com; mains €7.50-19.50;
⊙10am-11.30pm Mon-Thu, to 12.30am Sat, to
11pm Sun; ⊡), where many drivers park in
order to walk up to the Gap. You can also
rent ponies and jaunting cars here (bring
cash).

Continuing north to the N72, you'll
reach a charming 1851 stone pub housing
the **Beaufort Bar & Restaurant** (☎064-
664 4032; www.beaufortbar.com; Beaufort; mains
€13-20; ⊙6.30-9.30pm Fri & Sat, 12.30-2.30pm
Sun). Its gleaming timber dining room is
refined, intimate and relaxed.

Ring of Kerry

The Ring of Kerry is the longest and the most diverse of Ireland's big circle drives, combining jaw-dropping coastal scenery with emerald pastures and villages.

The 179km circuit winds past pristine beaches, the island-dotted Atlantic, medieval ruins, mountains and loughs (lakes). The coastline is at its most rugged between Waterville and Caherdaniel in the southwest of the peninsula. It can get busy in summer, but even then, the remote Skellig Ring can be uncrowded and serene – and starkly beautiful.

The Ring of Kerry can easily be done as a day trip, but if you want to stretch it out, places to stay are scattered along the route. Killorglin and Kenmare have the best concentration of dining options; elsewhere, with a couple of notable exceptions, basic pub fare is the norm.

ⓘ Getting Around

Tour buses travel the Ring in an anticlockwise direction. Getting stuck behind one is tedious, so consider driving clockwise; just watch out on blind corners. The road is extremely narrow and twisty in places, but surface upgrades are under way. There's little traffic on the **Ballaghbeama Gap**, which cuts across the peninsula's central highlands with some spectacular views: it's perfect for a shortcut by car or a long cycle, as is the longer **Ballaghisheen Pass** to Waterville.

Between late June and late August, Bus Éireann (☏ 064-663 0011; www.buseireann.ie) circumnavigates the Ring of Kerry daily (Killarney to Killarney €28.50, seven hours). Stops include Killorglin, Glenbeigh, Caherciveen, Waterville and Caherdaniel. Outside summer, transport on the Ring is not good.

KILLORGLIN

POP 4150

Travelling anticlockwise from Killarney, the first town on the Ring is Killorglin (Cill Orglan), 23km northwest. For most of the year, the town is quieter than the waters of the River Laune that lap against the1885-built eight-arched bridge. In August, however, there's an explosion of time-honoured ceremonies at the famous pagan festival, the Puck Fair.

Ring of Kerry

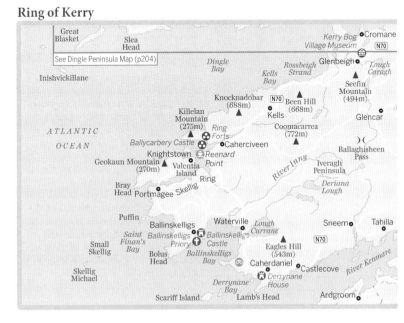

✿ Festivals & Events

Puck Fair Festival Historic

(Aonach an Phuic; www.puckfair.ie) First recorded in 1603, with hazy origins, this lively festival held mid-August is based around the custom of installing a billy goat (a poc, or puck), the symbol of mountainous Kerry, on a pedestal in the town, its horns festooned with ribbons. Other entertainment ranges from a horse fair and bonny baby competition to street theatre, concerts and fireworks; the pubs stay open until 3am.

🛏 Sleeping & Eating

Bianconi Inn €€

(☎066-976 1146; www.bianconi.ie; Bridge St; s/d from €70/110; mains €8.50-25.50; ☉restaurant 8am-11.30pm Mon-Thu, 8-12.30am Fri & Sat, 6-11pm Sun; 🛜) Bang in the centre of town, this low-lit inn has a classy ambience and Modern Irish fare such as sage-stuffed roast chicken with cranberry sauce. Its spectacular salads, such as Cashel blue cheese, apple, toasted almonds and chorizo, are a meal in themselves. Upstairs, newly refurbished guest rooms have olive and truffle tones and luxurious bathrooms (try for a rolltop tub).

ℹ️ Information

The **tourist office** (☎066-976 1451; Library Pl; ☉10am-4pm) sells maps, walking guides, fishing licences and souvenirs. Opening times vary.

KERRY BOG VILLAGE MUSEUM

On the N70 between Killorglin and Glenbeigh, the **Kerry Bog Village Museum** (www.kerrybogvillage.ie; admission €5; ☉8.30am-6pm) recreates a 19th-century bog village, typical of the small communities that carved out a precarious living in the harsh environment of Ireland's ubiquitous peat bogs. You'll see the thatched homes of the turfcutter, blacksmith, thatcher and labourer, as well as a dairy, and meet rare Kerry Bog ponies. The museum adjoins the sprawling **Red Fox** pub, which remains popular with locals for a sociable pint.

CAHERCIVEEN

POP 1200

Caherciveen's population, over 30,000 in 1841, was decimated by the Great Famine and emigration to the New World. A sleepy outpost remains, overshadowed by the 688m peak of **Knocknadobar**. It's rather dour compared with the peninsula's other settlements, but in many ways this village does more to recall the tough 1930s in Ireland than any other you'll see in Kerry. Lately the community has undertaken a big spruce-up, dressing empty shop windows and cleaning, painting and gardening along the main streets to give the town a fresh lease of life.

◉ Sights

Ballycarbery Castle & Ring Forts Castle, Fort

The atmospheric remains of 16th-century Ballycarbery Castle, 2.4km along the road to White Strand Beach from the barracks,

PAULGMCCABE/GETTY IMAGES ©

⭐ Don't Miss
Skellig Michael

The jagged, 217m-high rock of **Skellig Michael** (Archangel Michael's Rock; www.heritageireland.
ie) – like St Michael's Mount in Cornwall and Mont Saint Michel in Normandy – is
the larger of the two islands and a Unesco World Heritage site. It looks like the last
place on earth where anyone would try to land, let alone establish a community, yet
Christian monks survived here from the 6th until the 12th or 13th century. Influenced
by the Coptic Church (founded by St Anthony in the deserts of Egypt and Libya), their
determined quest for ultimate solitude led them to this remote edge of Europe.

The **monastic buildings** perch on a saddle in the rock, some 150m above sea
level, reached by 600 steep steps cut into the rock face. The astounding 6th-century
oratories and beehive cells vary in size; the largest cell has a floor space of 4.5m
by 3.6m. You can see the monks' south-facing vegetable garden and their cistern
for collecting rainwater. The most impressive structural achievements are the
settlement's foundations – platforms built on the steep slope using nothing more
than earth and drystone walls.

Not much is known about the life of the monastery, but there are records
of Viking raids in AD 812 and 823. Monks were kidnapped or killed, but the
community recovered and carried on. In the 11th century a rectangular oratory
was added to the site, but although it was expanded in the 12th century, the monks
abandoned the rock around this time.

After the introduction of the Gregorian calendar in 1582, Skellig Michael
became a popular spot for weddings. Marriages were forbidden during Lent,
but since Skellig used the old Julian calendar, a trip to the islands allowed those
unable to wait for Easter to tie the knot.

In the 1820s two **lighthouses** were built on Skellig Michael, together with the
road that runs around the base.

Detour:
Beara Peninsula (Ring of Beara)

After Kerry and Dingle, the Beara Peninsula is the third major 'ring' (circular road around a peninsula) in the west. The entire north side is the scenic highlight of the Beara Peninsula. A series of roads, some of them single-lane tracks, snake around the ins and outs of the weathered, rugged coast. Boulder-strewn fields tumble dramatically towards the ocean and it's blissfully remote – your only company along some stretches are flocks of sheep and the odd sheepdog.

You can easily drive the 137km around the coast in one day, but you would miss the spectacular **Healy Pass Road** (R574), which cuts across the peninsula from Cork to Kerry. In fact, if pressed for time, skip the rest and do the pass.

are surrounded by green pastures inhabited by cows who like to get in the pictures.

Along the same road are two stone ring forts. **Cahergall**, the larger one, dates from the 10th century and has stairways on the inside walls, a *clochán* (beehive hut), and the remains of a house. The smaller, 9th-century **Leacanabuile** has the entrance to an underground passage. Their inner walls and chambers give a strong sense of what life was like in a ring fort. Leave your car in the parking area next to a stone wall and walk up the footpaths.

SKELLIG ISLANDS

GANNET POP 50,000

The Skellig Islands (Oileáin na Scealaga) are impervious to the ever-pounding Atlantic. George Bernard Shaw said Skellig Michael was 'the most fantastic and impossible rock in the world'.

You'll need to do your best grisly sea-dog impression ('argh!') on the 12km crossing, which can be rough. There are no toilets or shelter on Skellig Michael, the only island that visitors are permitted to land on.

Bring something to eat and drink and wear stout shoes and weatherproof clothing. Due to the steep (and often slippery) terrain and sudden wind gusts, it's not suitable for young children or people with limited mobility.

The Skelligs are a **birdwatching** paradise. During the boat trip you may spot diminutive storm petrels (also known as Mother Carey's chickens) darting above the water like swallows. Gannets are unmistakable with their savage beaks, imperious eyes, yellow caps and 100cm-plus wing spans. Kittiwakes – small, dainty seabirds with black-tipped wings – are easy to see and hear around Skellig Michael's covered walkway as you step off the boat. They winter at sea then land in their thousands to breed between March and August.

Small Skellig

While Skellig Michael looks like two triangles linked by a spur, Small Skellig is longer, lower and much craggier. From a distance it looks as if someone battered it with a feather pillow that burst. Close up you realise you're looking at a colony of over 20,000 pairs of breeding gannets, the second-largest breeding colony in the world. Most boats circle the island so you can see the gannets and you may see basking seals as well. Small Skellig is a bird sanctuary; no landing is permitted.

ⓘ Getting There & Away

Skellig Michael's fragility places limits on the number of daily visitors. The 15 boats are licensed to carry no more than 12 passengers each, for a maximum of 180 people at any one time. It's wise to book ahead in July and August, bearing in mind

that if the weather's bad the boats may not sail (about two days out of seven). Trips usually run from Easter until September, depending, again, on weather.

Boats leave around 10am and return at 3pm, and cost about €60 per person. You can depart from Portmagee, Ballinskelligs or Derrynane (and sometimes Knightstown). Boat owners generally restrict you to two hours on the island, which is the bare minimum to see the monastery, look at the birds and have a picnic. The crossing takes about 1½ hours from Portmagee, 35 minutes to one hour from Ballinskelligs and 1¾ hours from Derrynane.

If you just want to see the islands up close and avoid actually having to clamber out of the boat, consider a cruise with Skellig Experience on Valentia Island.

The Skellig Experience heritage centre, local pubs and B&Bs will point you in the direction of boat operators, including the following:

Ballinskelligs Boats (☏086 417 6612; http://bestskelligtrips.com; Ballinskelligs)

Casey's (☏066-947 2437; www.skelligislands.com; Portmagee)

John O'Shea (☏087 689 8431; www.skelligtours.com; Derrynane)

Seanie Murphy (☏066-947 6214; www.skelligsrock.com; Reenard Point, Valentia Island)

WATERVILLE

POP 550

Waterville consists of a line of colourful houses strung on the N72 between Lough Currane and Ballinskelligs Bay. A statue of its most famous guest, Charlie Chaplin, beams out from the seafront. The **Charlie Chaplin Comedy Film Festival** (charliechaplincomedyfilmfestival.com) takes place in late August.

CAHERDANIEL

POP 350

Hiding between Derrynane Bay and the foothills of Eagles Hill, Caherdaniel barely qualifies as a tiny hamlet. Businesses are scattered about the undergrowth like smugglers, fitting since this was once a haven for the same.

Left: Atlantic puffins, Skellig Michael (p198);
Below: Climbing steps, Skellig Michael (p198)
(LEFT) DREAMPICTURES/GETTY IMAGES ©; (BELOW) GARETH MCCORMACK/GETTY IMAGES ©

This is the ancestral home of Daniel O'Connell, 'the Liberator', whose family made money smuggling from their base by the dunes. The area boasts a blue flag beach, plenty of activities, good hikes and some pubs where you may be tempted to break into pirate talk. Lines of wind-gnarled trees add to the wild air.

◉ Sights

Derrynane National Historic Park
Historic Site

(☎ 066-947 5113; www.heritageireland.ie; Derrynane; adult/child €3/1; ☺ 10.30am-6pm May-Sep, 10.30am-5pm Wed-Sun Oct-late Nov)
Derrynane House is the family home of Daniel O'Connell, the campaigner for Catholic emancipation. His ancestors bought the house and surrounding parkland, having grown rich on smuggling with France and Spain. It's largely furnished with O'Connell memorabilia, including the restored triumphal chariot in which he lapped Dublin after his release from prison in 1844.

The **gardens**, warmed by the Gulf Stream, hold palms, 4m-high tree ferns, gunnera ('giant rhubarb') and other South American species. A walking track leads to wetlands, beaches and clifftops. You can spot wild pheasants and other birds, whose musical calls add a note of contrast to the dull roar of the surf. The **chapel**, which O'Connell added to Derrynane House in 1844, is a copy of the ruined one on **Abbey Island**, which can usually be reached on foot across the sand.

Look out for the **Ogham stone** on the left of the road to the house. With its carved notches representing the simple Ogham alphabet of the ancient Irish, the stone has several missing letters, but is thought to represent the name of a local chieftain.

If You Like...
Great Irish Food

If restaurants such as Fishy Fishy Cafe (p184) in Kinsale make your mouth water, you should also sample the menus at the following gourmet spots.

1 JIM EDWARDS

(☎021-477 2541; www.jimedwardskinsale.com; Market Quay, Kinsale; bar mains €13-19, restaurant mains €16-30; ⊗bar food noon-10pm, restaurant 5.30-10pm) A very traditional ambience belies the high quality of the menu at this Kinsale pub, which specialises in all kinds of locally caught fish.

2 JOSIE'S LAKEVIEW HOUSE

(☎064-83155; www.josiesrestaurant.ie; Glanmore Lake; lunch mains €7-14, dinner mains €11-25, d €70; ⊗food from 10.30am) Captivating lake views accompany scrumptious, home-cooked food at Josie's, set on a hill overlooking forest-shrouded Glanmore Lake.

3 GLANDORE INN

(☎028-33468; www.theglandoreinn.com; Main St, Glandore; mains €10-16; ⊗from 10am summer, from noon winter; 🛜) Front-row views over the harbour and a superlative menu, featuring exquisite seafood, make this one of Cork's finest places to dine.

SNEEM

Halfway between Caherdaniel and Kenmare, Sneem (An tSnaidhm) is a good place to pause, especially if you're travelling anticlockwise, as for the remaining 27km to Kenmare the N70 drifts away from the water and coasts along under a canopy of trees.

KENMARE

POP 2900

The copper-covered limestone spire of Holy Cross Church, drawing the eye to the wooded hills above town, may make you forget for a split second that Kenmare (pronounced 'ken-*mair*') is a seaside town. But with rivers named Finnihy, Roughty and Sheen emptying into Kenmare Bay, you couldn't be anywhere other than southwest Ireland.

Sleeping

Virginia's Guesthouse B&B €€
(☎064-664 1021; www.virginias-kenmare.com; Henry St; s/d €60/90; 🛜👪) You can't get more central than this award-winning B&B, whose creative breakfasts celebrate organic local produce (rhubarb and blueberries in season, for example, as well as fresh-squeezed OJ and porridge with whiskey). Its eight rooms are super comfy without being fussy.

Sheen Falls Lodge Boutique Hotel €€€
(☎064-664 1600; www.sheenfallslodge.ie; s/d from €160/220; restaurant 3-/4-course menu €45/65; ⊗Feb-Dec; @🛜) The Marquis of Landsdowne's former summer residence still feels like an aristocrats' playground, with a fine-dining French restaurant, bar, a spa and 66 rooms with DVD players and Italian marble bathrooms, and views of the falls and across Kenmare Bay to Carrantuohil. Amenities are many (clay-pigeon shooting, anyone?).

Eating

Tom Crean Fish & Wine Irish €€
(☎064-664 1589; www.tomcrean.ie; Main St; mains €17-25.50; ⊗5-9.30pm; 🛜👪) ✔ Formerly known as D'Arcy's, this venerable restaurant has been renamed in honour of owner/chef Aileen d'Arcy's grandfather, Kerry's pioneering Antarctic explorer Tom Crean. Local purveyors supply the best in organic produce, cheeses and fresh seafood, all served in modern, low-key surrounds. The raw oysters capture the scent of the bay; the homemade ravioli of prawn mousse and sesame seed-crusted Atlantic salmon with lime and coriander are divine. Breakfast isn't included in room rates, but guests staying in its **townhouse** (d €60) get discounted evening meals.

DINGLE BREWING COMPANY ©

★ Don't Miss
Dingle Brewing Company

On the site of a 19th-century creamery, this terrific craft brewery launched in 2011 on 20 July – not coincidently Tom Crean's birthday (its single brew, a crisp, hoppy lager, is named after the local Antarctic explorer). Admission includes a self-guided or guided brewery tour as well as a pint. If you're not doing the tour you can't stop in for a drink here, but you'll find it in bottled and draught form at numerous pubs throughout the peninsula and beyond.

NEED TO KNOW

☑066-915 0743; www.dinglebrewingcompany.com; Spa Rd; admission €7; ⊙tours by reservation

ⓘ Getting There & Away

The twisting, 32km-long drive on the N71 from Killarney is surprisingly dramatic with tunnels and stark mountain vistas. (Heading south, it's 27km along the N71 and Beara Peninsula to Glengarriff in County Cork.)

Twice-daily buses serve Killarney (€10.90, 50 minutes), with additional services in summer. Buses stop outside Roughty Bar (Main St).

Finnegan's Coach & Cab (☑064-664 1491; www.kenmarecoachandcab.com) Runs a variety of tours including the Ring of Kerry.

Dingle Peninsula

Unlike the Ring of Kerry, where the cliffs tend to dominate the ocean, it's the ocean that dominates the smaller Dingle Peninsula. The opal-blue waters surrounding the promontory's green hills and golden sands give rise to aquatic adventures and to fishing trawlers that haul in impossibly fresh seafood that appears on the menus of some of the county's finest restaurants.

Centred on charming Dingle town, there's an alternative way of life here, lived by artisans and idiosyncratic

Dingle Peninsula

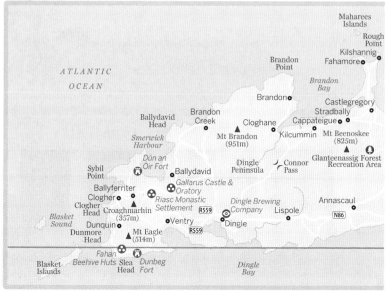

characters and found at trad sessions and folkloric festivals across Dingle's tiny settlements.

The classic loop drive around Slea Head from Dingle town is 50km, but allow a day to take it all in. The main road to Dingle town is the N86 via Tralee but the coast road is far more beautiful and shouldn't be missed.

DINGLE TOWN

POP 1500

Framed by its fishing port, the peninsula's charming little 'capital' is quaint without even trying. Dingle is one of Ireland's largest Gaeltacht towns; many pubs double as shops, so you can enjoy Guinness and a singalong among screws and nails, wellies and horseshoes. It has long drawn runaways from across the world, making it a cosmopolitan, creative place. In summer its hilly streets can be clogged with visitors; in other seasons its authentic charms are yours for the savouring.

Activities

In 1983 a bottlenose dolphin swam into Dingle Bay and local tourism hasn't been the same since. Showing an unnatural affinity for humans, he swam around with the local fishing fleet. Eventually somebody got the idea of charging tourists to go out on boats and see the friendly dolphin (nicknamed Fungie). Today up to 12 boats at a time and over 1000 tourists a day ply the waters with Dingle's mascot, the cornerstone of the local economy.

Fungie the Dolphin   Boat Tour
(066-915 2626; www.dingledolphin.com; The Pier; adult/child €16/8) Boats run by the Dingle Boatmen's Association cooperative leave the pier daily for one-hour dolphin-spotting trips of Dingle's most famous resident, Fungie. It's free if Fungie doesn't show, but he usually does.

Eating

Out of the Blue Seafood €€€

(☏066-915 0811; www.outoftheblue.ie; The Wood; lunch €10-20, mains €22.50-29; ⊙5.30-9.30pm Mon-Sat, 12.30-3pm & 5.30-9.30pm Sun) 'No chips', reads the menu of this funky blue-and-yellow, fishing-shack-style restaurant on the waterfront. Despite its rustic surrounds, this is Dingle's best restaurant, with an intense devotion to fresh local seafood (and only seafood); if they don't like the catch, they don't open. Creative dishes change daily, but might include steamed crab claws in garlic butter or pan-seared scallops flambéed in Calvados. Who needs chips?

Drinking & Nightlife

John Benny's Pub

(www.johnbennyspub.com; Strand St; ⊙bar food noon-9.30pm) A toasty cast iron woodstove, stone slab floor, memorabilia on the walls, great staff and no intrusive TV make this one of Dingle's most enjoyable traditional pubs. Local musos pour in most nights for rockin' trad sessions. Mains cost €12 to €22.50.

Getting There & Away

Bus Éireann (www.buseireann.ie) buses stop outside the car park behind the supermarket. Up to six buses a day serve Killarney (€16, 80 minutes) via Tralee (€13, 45 minutes).

WEST OF DINGLE

At the tip of the peninsula is the Slea Head drive along the R559. It has the greatest concentration of ancient sites in Kerry, if not the whole of Ireland.

The landscape is dramatic, especially in shifting mist, although full-on sea fog obliterates everything. For the best views, follow the Slea Head drive in a clockwise direction. Although a mere 50km in length, doing this drive justice requires a full day, at least.

In the warmer months, the association also runs a daily two-hour boat trip when you can **swim with Fungie** (☏066-915 1146; per person €25, plus wetsuit hire €20; ⊙8am or 9am Apr–mid-Sep). Advance bookings are essential.

Sleeping

Dingle Harbour Lodge Hotel €€

(☏066-915 1577; www.dingleharbourlodge.com; The Wood; s/d from €50/75; 🛜🛗) Recently transformed with an airy, timber-floored lobby filled with fresh flowers, neat rooms equipped with flat-screen TVs and ultra-efficient new managers, Dingle Harbour Lodge fills a niche for inexpensive contemporary accommodation. Although just five minutes' walk from the centre, its position above the harbour means no street noise and stunning views from upper-level rooms.

Blasket Islands

The Blasket Islands (Na Blascaodaí), 5km out into the Atlantic, are the most westerly islands in the country. At 6km by 1.2km, **Great Blasket** (An Blascaod Mór) is the largest and most visited, and mountainous enough for strenuous **walks**. All of the Blaskets were inhabited at one time or another; there is evidence of Great Blasket being inhabited during the Iron Age and early Christian times. The last islanders left for the mainland in 1953 after they and the government agreed that it was no longer feasible to live in such isolated and harsh conditions, although today a few people make their home out here for part of the year.

There are no camping facilities on the islands.

Boats trips generally run from Easter to September, but even then weather can cause boat cancellations – call for seasonal sailing times.

Blasket Island Ferries (☎ 066-915 1344, 066-915 6422; www.blasketisland.com; adult/child €20/10) Boats depart from Dunquin Harbour and take 20 minutes.

Blasket Islands Eco Marine Tours (☎ 087 231 6131; www.marinetours.ie; morning/afternoon/day tour €25/40/50) Eco-oriented tours departing from Ventry Harbour.

Dingle Marine & Leisure (☎ 066-915 1344, 087 672 6100; www.dinglebaycharters.com; ferry adult/child return €30/15, 3hr island tour €40/15) Ferries take 45 minutes from Dingle town's marina. Fishing trips (from €25/15 for two hours) are also available.

Slea Head & Dunmore Head

Overlooking the mouth of Dingle Bay, Mt Eagle and the Blasket Islands, Slea Head has fine **beaches**, good walks and superbly preserved structures from Dingle's ancient past including **beehive huts**, forts, inscribed stones and church sites. Dunmore Head is the westernmost point on the Irish mainland and the site of the wreckage in 1588 of two Spanish Armada ships.

Riasc Monastery Settlement

The remains of the 5th- or 6th-century **Riasc Monastic Settlement** are one of the peninsula's more impressive and haunting sites, particularly the pillar with beautiful Celtic designs. Excavations have also revealed the foundations of an oratory first built with wood and later stone, a kiln for drying corn and a cemetery. The ruins are signposted as 'Mainistir Riaisc' along a narrow lane off the R559, about 2km east of Ballyferriter.

Gallarus Castle & Oratory

One of the Dingle Peninsula's few surviving castles, **Gallarus Castle** (www.heritageireland.ie) was built by the FitzGeralds around the 15th century. Although it's closed indefinitely to the public for safety reasons, you can walk around the exterior. Note that there's no parking next to the castle.

The dry-stone **Gallarus Oratory** (☎ 066-915 6444; www.heritageireland.ie; ⊙10am-6pm May-Aug) FREE is quite a sight, standing in its lonely spot beneath the brown hills as it has done for some 1200 years. It has withstood the elements perfectly, apart from a slight sagging in the roof. Traces of mortar suggest that the interior and exterior walls may have been plastered. Shaped like an upturned boat, it has a doorway on the western side and a round-headed window on the eastern side. Inside the doorway are two projecting stones with holes that once supported the door.

The castle and oratory are signposted off the R559, about 2km further on from the Riasc Monastic Settlement turn-off.

CONNOR PASS

At 456m, the Connor (or Conor) Pass is Ireland's highest mountain pass. On a foggy day you'll see nothing but the road just in front of you, but in fine weather it offers phenomenal views of Dingle Harbour to the south and Mt Brandon to the north. The road is in good shape, despite being very narrow and *very* steep (large signs portend doom for buses and trucks).

Next to a waterfall, the summit car park yields views down to two lakes in the rock-strewn valley below plus the remains of walls and huts where people once lived impossibly hard lives. When visibility is good, it's well worth the 10-minute climb to the summit to reach hidden **Peddlers Lake** and the kind of vistas that inspire mountain-climbers.

Galway, Clare & the West

In the heart of the west, Galway City is a swirl of enticing old pubs that hum with trad music sessions throughout the year.

To the north, the Connemara Peninsula matches the beauty of the other Atlantic outcrops to the south: tiny roads wander along a coastline studded with islands, surprisingly white beaches and intriguing old villages with views over it all. This is the place to don the hiking boots and take to the well-marked network of trails that wander through lonely valleys and past hidden lakes before ending at sprays of surf at the Atlantic. Beyond it, the rugged beauty stretches in County Mayo, home to Ireland's most sacred pilgrimage site, Croagh Patrick, which rewards the penitent with stunning views of the surrounding countryside.

South of Galway, Clare combines the stunning natural beauty of its long and meandering coastline with unique windswept landscapes and a year's worth of dollops of Irish culture.

Clifden (p227)
MARTIN SIEPMANN/GETTY IMAGES ©

Galway, Clare & the West

Kilcummin
Drom
Wes
Ballycastle
Killala
Bay
Killala
River Owenmore
Ballinaboy
Mullet
Peninsula
Bangor
Erris
Ballina
N59
Blacksod
Bay
Castlehill
Lough
Conn
Aghleam
Blacksod
Point
Ballycroy
National
Park
Dugort
Ballycroy
Nephin Beg
(628m)
Mt Nephin
(806m)
Foxford
Achill
Head
Achill Island
Keel
Achill
Sound
Pontoon
Swinford
Straide
Curraun
Peninsula
Mulranny
Newport
MAYO
Clare
Island
Clew
Bay
Turlough
Castlebar
Roonagh
Quay
Louisburgh
Murrisk
Westport
Balla
Inishturk
Murrisk
Croagh
Patrick
(765m)
Doolough
Valley
Partry
Claremorris
Killadoon
Cregganbaun
Sheeffry
Hills
N59
Partry
Mountains
Lough
Mask
Ballinrobe
Inishshark
Delphi
Tully
Killary
Harbour
Leenane
Joyce's
Country
Renvyle
Cleggan
Letterfrack
Clonbur
Cong
Claddaghduff
Omey
Island
Kingston
Twelve Bens
Headford
Clifden
Connemara
N59
Recess
Maumturk
Mountains
N59
Maam
Cross
Lough
Corrib
Ballinaboy
Toombeola
Ballyconneely
Roundstone
Cashel
Gortmore
Oughterard
Screeb
Moyrus
Glinsk
Rosmuc
Iar Connaught
N59
Moycullen
Carna
Killeieran
Bay
Galway
Carnm
Carraroe
Gorumna
Island
Costello
Rossaveal
Salthill
Oranm
R336
Barna
Inverin
Kinva
Bay
North
Sound
Finavarra
Point
Burren Village
Kinv
Inishmór
Kilronan
Galway
Bay
Fanore
Ballyvaughan
The Burren
Oughtm
Valle
Aran
Islands
Inishmaan
Doolin
Point
Lisdoonvarna
Carron
Inisheer
Doolin
Kilfenora
Kilnaboy
Cliffs of
Moher
Liscannor
Ennistymon
Corofir
ATLANTIC
OCEAN
Hag's
Head
Lahinch
R460
CLARE
Liscannor
Bay
Inagh
Miltown Malbay
Ennis
Mutton
Island
Quilty
Clarecastle
Doonbeg
Bay
Fergus
Bay
Donegal
Point
Doonbeg
N68
Shann
Kilkee
Moyasta
Knockalough
Kilrush
Labasheeda
Carrigaholt
Shannon
Estuary
Killimer
Loop
Head
Kilbaha
KERRY

0 ——— 50 km
0 ——— 25 miles

① Trad music sessions,
   County Clare
② Connemara
③ Cliffs of Moher
④ Galway city
⑤ Clonmacnoise

Galway, Clare & the West's Highlights

Trad Sessions in Clare

Other counties have their distinctive musical styles, but County Clare (p232) is the heartland of traditional music: nowhere else will you find such a concentration of talented musicians, singers and dancers. There are organised sessions throughout the county, the best of which are often in a village pub, where musicians play as much for their own pleasure as the punters' entertainment.

Connemara

Connemara (p225) is the 'real Ireland' and one of the few places where you'll hear Irish spoken in the local pubs. Peat bogs are still being cut and dried by farmers and local fishermen can be seen using *currachs* (rowing boats) on the Killary Fjord.

MECKY/GETTY IMAGES ©

Cliffs of Moher

DAVID CLAPP/GETTY IMAGES ©

3

Rising to a height of 203m from the constantly churning Atlantic, the Cliffs of Moher (p238) are one of Ireland's most visited natural attractions. Yet, unlike so many hugely popular wonders, the hype is spot on, especially if you wend your way past the open-mouthed crowds and venture south beyond the viewing areas to observe the entirely vertical cliffs as nature intended them.

HOLGER LEUE/GETTY IMAGES ©

4

Galway City

Galway (p218) is one of Ireland's loveliest burgs, a thriving centre that has retained much of its easygoing charm. The real treat is enjoying its wonderful pubs, not least Séhán Ua Neáchtain (p220), a contender for finest watering hole in Ireland. July and early August is the festival season, with a superb film festival, the country's biggest arts festival and Galway Race week.

5

Clonmacnoise

Ireland's most important ecclesiastical site, Clonmacnoise (p230) is one of the main reasons Ireland was known as the 'land of saints and scholars'. Scholars and monks from all over Europe came to what was then a thriving city to study, and while it's quieter these days, the ruined temples and cathedral, as well as the superb collection of high crosses, is still very impressive. Cross of the Scriptures (King Flann's Cross)

Galway, Clare & the West's Best...

Music Houses

o **Matt Molloy's** Owner Matt Molloy plays fife in The Chieftains. (p247)

o **O'Friel's Bar** In the traditional heartland. (p237)

o **MacDiarmada's** The definition of great craic. (p242)

Beauty Spots

o **Oughterard** William Thackeray's idea of heaven. (p225)

o **Roundstone** Stunning harbour village. (p226)

o **Croagh Patrick** The perfect summit. (p246)

o **Inishmaan** Traditional island living. (p224)

o **Cliffs of Moher** Hardly a surprise, but always capable of springing one. (p238)

Scenic Drives

o **Sky Road** A spectacular loop from Clifden to Kingston. (p227)

o **Lough Inagh Valley** Cut through Connemara in the shadow of the brooding Twelve Bens. (p232)

o **Killary Harbour** A drive along Ireland's only fjord. (p229)

o **The Burren** Cut through this bizarre landscape from Ballyvaughan to Ennistymon. (p239)

o **Clare Coast** Scenic coastal route from the Cliffs of Moher to Ballyvaughan. (p238)

Need to Know

Unlikely Activities

- **Patrician Pilgrimage** You don't have to be a believer to be struck by the spirituality of the climb. (p246)

- **Get adventurous** Try kayaking, rock climbing or spelunking... (p229)

- **Go underground** Explore the ancient Aillwee Caves. (p243)

- **Clonmacnoise cruise** Travel the Shannon to the monastic site. (p230)

- **Walk the Burren** A beautiful but bizarre landscape that makes for excellent walks. (p239)

ADVANCE PLANNING

- **Two months before** Book hotels, especially in popular areas such as Galway City, Connemara and the music towns of County Clare if there's a festival on.

- **One month before** Book your flight to the Aran Islands if you don't fancy a stormy crossing.

- **Two weeks before** Check out the weather forecast for the likes of an Aran Island crossing, then ignore it – the weather changes every 20 minutes.

RESOURCES

- **Discover Ireland** (www.discoverireland.ie/west) Ireland's tourist authority.

- **Galway.Net** (www.galway.net) Unofficial tourist site.

- **Visit Mayo** (www.mayo.ie) Attractions, restaurants, pubs and clubs.

- **Surf Mayo** (www.surfmayo.com) Beaches, breaks and other surf info.

- **Visit Clare** (www.visitclare.net) Official East Clare Tourism Authority.

GETTING AROUND

- **Bus** Good bus networks cover most of the region, but it's a slow way of exploring.

- **Train** Only the major towns are served by train – Galway, Ennis and Westport.

- **Car** You'll need your own car to really explore the Burren and Connemara.

- **Boat** The most straightforward way of getting to the Aran Islands.

BE FOREWARNED

- **Crowds** Summer festival season sees throngs flooding into Clare.

- **Weather** The Aran Islands can be weather-bound, making crossings impossible.

- **Reek Sunday** 20,000-plus people will climb Croagh Patrick on the third Sunday in July. You've been warned!

Left: Musicians at Matt Molloy's (p247), Westport; **Above:** Roundstone (p226)

(LEFT) VINCENT MACNAMARA/ALAMY © GETTY IMAGES ©; (ABOVE) JOHN ELK/GETTY IMAGES ©

Galway, Clare & the West Itineraries

Follow these itineraries to experience the west's three distinct but interwoven characters – the exciting urban feel of Galway, the rich musical heritage of County Clare and the jaw-dropping beauty of the landscape.

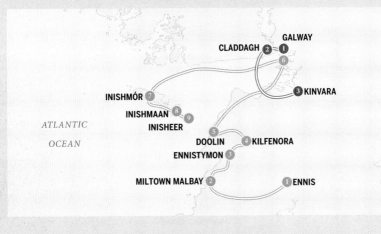

GALWAY CITY TO KINVARA
GALWAY & AROUND

3 DAYS

You could spend a week in **❶ Galway city** (p218) and not get bored, such is the variety of things to enjoy in the west's largest city. Explore the old city, including the Spanish Arch and medieval walls, and if you're in town between May and June, make your way up to the salmon weir to see the fish pass down on their final descent to the sea. Visit the house where James Joyce courted the love of his life, Nora Barnacle. Then indulge the local culture with a pint (or more) in one of Ireland's great bars, Séhán Ua Neáchtain – there's a good chance you'll have musical accompaniment of the traditional kind as you quench your thirst. If you

can tear yourself away, get out of town and visit the small fishing village of **❷ Claddagh** before heading to pretty **❸ Kinvara**, which is the doorway to the Burren and County Clare.

 ENNIS TO THE ARAN ISLANDS
A MUSICAL LANDSCAPE

This five-day route takes in the traditional charms of the region, both musical and otherwise. Begin in central Clare in ❶ **Ennis** (p232), from which you can reach any part of the county in under two hours. Head west to ❷ **Miltown Malbay** (p237) and begin your exploration of the area's rich musical heritage by attending a formal (or informal) pub 'session' – unless you're a player with any kind of pedigree, you won't be encouraged to join in with more than a toe-tap or hand-clap!

Continue your explorations in ❸ **Ennistymon** (p242) and ❹ **Kilfenora** (p242) before crossing the heart of the

Burren, making a pit stop in ❺ **Doolin** (p241) before heading towards ❻ **Galway city** (p218). From here, take the boat (or plane from Minna, about 35km west of the city) and make the short hop across the choppy waters to ❼ **Inishmór** (p222) and get to grips with a traditional life that has changed little for centuries. You could easily spend a couple of days here, or use the time to visit the other two islands, ❽ **Inishmaan** (p224) and ❾ **Inisheer** (p224), where life really is untroubled by the demands of the modern age.

Musicians playing in O'Connor's (p242), Doolin
DOUG MCKINLAY/GETTY IMAGES ©

Discover Galway, Clare & the West

At a Glance

○ **Galway city** (p218) The West's hippest town.

○ **Connemara** (p225) Stunning landscapes and filigreed coastlines.

○ **Aran Islands** (p222) Wild, ancient and beguiling.

○ **County Clare** (p232) Traditional music to match the unique landscapes.

○ **County Mayo** (p244) In the shadow of Ireland's holiest mountain.

Waterfront, Galway Bay
JOHN ELK/GETTY IMAGES ©

GALWAY COUNTY

Galway City

POP 75,600

Arty, bohemian Galway (Gaillimh) is renowned for its pleasures. Brightly painted pubs heave with live music, while cafes offer front-row seats for observing street performers, weekend parties run amuck, lovers entwined and more.

◉ Sights & Activities

Spanish Arch   Historic Site

Framing the river east of Wolfe Tone Bridge, the Spanish Arch is thought to be an extension of Galway's medieval walls. The arch appears to have been designed as a passageway through which ships entered the city to unload goods, such as wine and brandy from Spain.

Today it reverberates to the beat of bongo drums, and the lawns and riverside form a gathering place for locals and visitors on any sunny day. Many watch kayakers manoeuvre over the minor rapids of the River Corrib.

**Hall of the
Red Earl**   Archaeological Site

(www.galwaycivictrust.ie; Druid Lane; ⊙9.30am-4.45pm Mon-Fri, 10am-1pm Sat) **FREE** Back in the 13th century when the de Burgo family ran the show in Galway, Richard – the Red Earl – had a large hall built as a seat of power. Here locals would come looking for favours or to do a little grovelling as a sign of future fealty. After the 14 tribes took over, the hall fell into ruin and was lost. Lost that is until 1997 when expansion of the city's Custom

House uncovered its foundations. The Custom House was built on stilts overhead, leaving the old foundations open. Artefacts and a plethora of fascinating displays give a sense of Galway life some 900 years ago.

Collegiate Church of St Nicholas of Myra
Church

(Market St; admission by donation; ☺9am-5.45pm Mon-Sat, 1-5pm Sun Apr-Sep, 10am-4pm Mon-Sat, 1-5pm Sun Oct-Mar) Crowned by a pyramidal spire, the Collegiate Church of St Nicholas of Myra is Ireland's largest medieval parish church still in use. Dating from 1320, the church has been rebuilt and enlarged over the centuries, though much of the original form has been retained.

Salmon Weir
Landmark

Upstream from Salmon Weir Bridge, which crosses the River Corrib just east of Galway Cathedral, the river cascades down the great weir, one of its final descents before reaching Galway Bay. The weir controls the water levels above it, and when the salmon are running you can often see shoals of them waiting in the clear waters before rushing upriver to spawn.

The salmon and sea-trout seasons usually span February to September, but most fish pass through the weir during May and June.

Sleeping

Heron's Rest
B&B €€

(☏091-539 574; www.theheronsrest.com; 16A Longwalk; s/d from €70/140; ☏) Ideally located on the banks of the Corrib, the endlessly thoughtful hosts here will give you deck chairs so you can sit outside and enjoy the scene. Other touches include holiday-friendly breakfast times (8am to 11am), decanters of port etc. Rooms, all with water views, are small and cute.

House Hotel
Hotel €€€

(☏091-538 900; www.thehousehotel.ie; Spanish Pde; r €100-220; ☏) It's a design odyssey at this boutique hotel. Public spaces contrast modern art with trad details and

Claddagh Rings

The fishing village of Claddagh has long been subsumed into Galway's city centre, but its namesake rings survive as both a timeless reminder and a timeless source of profits.

Popular with people of real or imagined Irish descent everywhere, the rings depict a heart (symbolising love) between two outstretched hands (friendship), topped by a crown (loyalty). Rings are handcrafted at jewellers around Galway, and start from about €20 for a simple band to well over €1000 for a blinged-up diamond-covered version.

Jewellers include Ireland's oldest jewellery shop, **Thomas Dillon's Claddagh Gold** (www.claddaghring.ie; 1 Quay St; ☺10am-6pm), which was established in 1750 and is adorned with Claddagh history placards.

bold accents. Cat motifs abound. The 40 rooms are plush, with beds having conveniently padded headboards and a range of colour schemes. Bathrooms are commodious and ooze comfort.

Eating

Oscar's
Seafood €€

(☏091-582 180; www.oscarsbistro.ie; Upper Dominick St; mains €13-25; ☺6-9.30pm Mon-Sat) Galway's best seafood restaurant is just west of the tourist bustle. The long and ever-changing menu has a huge range of local specialties, from shellfish to white fish (which make some superb fish and chips). The flavours are bold, not unlike the bright red accents inside and out.

Aniar
Modern Irish €€€

(☏091-535 947; www.aniarrestaurant.ie; 53 Lower Dominick St; mains from €30; ☺6-10pm Tue-Sat) Deeply committed to the flavours and food producers of Galway and West Ireland, Aniar wears its Michelin

219

star with pride. There's no fuss here, however. The casual spring-green dining area is a relaxed place to taste from the nightly menu. The wine list favours small producers.

 Drinking & Nightlife

Séhán Ua Neáchtain Pub
(17 Upper Cross St) Painted a bright corn-flower blue, this 19th-century pub, known simply as Neáchtain's (*nock*-tans) or

Galway

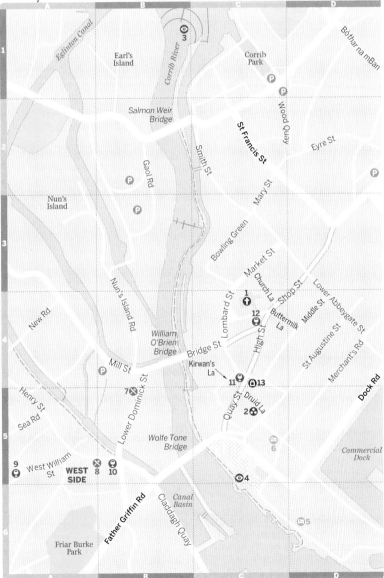

Naughtons, has a wraparound string of tables outside, many shaded by a large tree. It's a place where a polyglot mix of locals plop down and let the world pass them by – or stop and join them for a pint. Good lunches.

Crane Bar
Pub

(www.thecranebar.com; 2 Sea Rd) An atmospheric old pub west of the Corrib, the Crane is the best spot in Galway to catch an informal *céilidh* (session of trad music and dancing) most nights. Talented bands play its rowdy, good-natured upstairs bar.

ℹ Information

The large, efficient regional information centre (www.discoverireland.ie; Forster St; ⊙9am-5.45pm daily Easter-Sep, closed Sun Oct-Easter) can help arrange local accommodation and tours.

ℹ Getting There & Away

Bus

Several private bus companies are based at the modern Galway Coach Station (New Coach Station; Bothar St), which is located near the tourist office.

Bus Éireann (www.buseireann.ie; Station Rd, Cara Bus Station) Services to all major cities in the Republic and the North from just off Eyre Square, near the train station. Dublin (€14, three to 3¾ hours) has hourly service. Other services fan out across the region.

Citylink (www.citylink.ie; ticket office Forster St; ⊙office 9am-6pm; 🛜) Services depart from

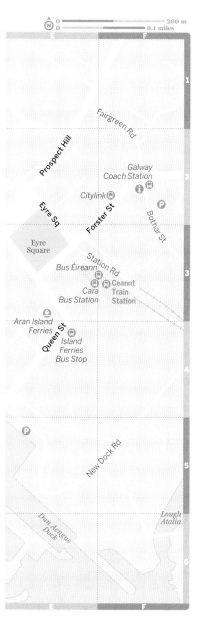

Galway

◎ Sights
1 Collegiate Church of St Nicholas of Myra C4
2 Hall of the Red Earl C5
3 Salmon Weir B1
4 Spanish Arch C5

⌂ Sleeping
5 Heron's Rest D6
6 House Hotel C5

⊗ Eating
7 Aniar B5
8 Oscar's A5

◉ Drinking & Nightlife
9 Crane Bar A5
10 Monroe's Tavern B5
11 Séhán Ua Neáchtain C4
12 Tig Cóilí C4

◉ Shopping
13 Thomas Dillon's Claddagh Gold......... C4

221

Galway Coach Station for Dublin (from €11, 2½ hours, hourly), Dublin Airport (from €17, 2½ hours, hourly), Cork, Limerick and Connemara. Departures are frequent and fares are as low as €10.

Train

From the **train station** (☎091-564 222; www. irishrail.ie), just off Eyre Square, there are up to eight fast, comfortable trains daily to/from Dublin's Heuston Station (one-way from €34, 2¼ hours). Connections with other train routes can be made at Athlone (one hour). The line to Ennis is scenic (€19, 1¾ hours, five daily).

Aran Islands

Easily visible from large swaths of coastal Galway and Clare Counties, the Aran Islands sing their own siren song to thousands of travellers each year who find their desolate beauty beguiling. Day trippers shuttle through in a daze of rocky magnificence, while those who stay longer find places that, in many ways, seem further removed from the Irish mainland than a 45-minute ferry ride or 10-minute flight.

Bridging the Quiet Man

Whenever an American cable TV station needs a ratings boost with older viewers (and they've already just shown *Gone With the Wind*), they trot out the iconic 1952 film *The Quiet Man*. Director John Ford returned to his Irish roots and filmed the movie almost entirely on location in Connemara and the little village of Cong (the beach horse-racing sequences were shot at Lettergesh), just over the border in County Mayo. One of the most photogenic spots from the film, the eponymous **Quiet Man Bridge**, is just 3km west of Oughterard off the N59.

ℹ️ Getting There & Away

Air

All three islands have landing strips. The mainland departure point is Connemara regional airport at Minna, near Inverin (Indreabhán), about 35km west of Galway. **Aer Arann Islands** (☎091-593 034; www.aerarannislands.ie) offers return flights to each of the islands several times daily (hourly in summer) for adult/child €45/25; the flights take about 10 minutes, and groups of four or more can get group rates.

Boat

Island Ferries (www.aranislandferries.com; Merchant's Rd, Galway Ticket Office; adult/child return fare from €25/13; ⏰8am-5pm) serves all three islands and also links Inishmaan and Inisheer. Schedules peak in July and August, with several boats a day. The crossing can take up to one hour and is subject to cancellation in high seas. Boats leave from Rossaveal, 40km west of Galway City on the R336. Buses from Galway (adult/child €7/4) connect with the sailings; ask when you book.

Ferries to the Arans (primarily Inisheer) also operate from Doolin.

INISHMÓR

POP 830

Most visitors who venture out to the islands don't make it beyond Inishmór (Árainn) and its main attraction, Dún Aengus, the stunning stone fort perched perilously on the island's towering cliffs. The arid landscape west of Kilronan (Cill Rónáin), Inishmór's main settlement, is dominated by stone walls, boulders, scattered buildings and the odd patch of deep-green grass and potato plants.

🛏️ Sleeping

Kilmurvey House   B&B €€

(☎099-61218; www.kilmurveyhouse.com; Kilmurvey; s/d from €55/90; ⏰Apr-Sep) On the path leading to Dún Aengus is this grand 18th-century stone mansion. It's a beautiful setting and the 12 rooms are well maintained. Hearty meals (dinner €30) incorporate vegetables from the garden, and local fish and meats. You can swim at a pretty beach that's a short walk from the house.

ROBIN BUSH/GETTY IMAGES ©

⭐ Don't Miss
Dún Aengus

Three spectacular forts stand guard over Inishmór, each believed to be around 2000 years old. Chief among them is Dún Aengus, which has three nonconcentric walls that run right up to sheer drops to the ocean below. It is protected by remarkable chevaux de frise, fearsome and densely packed defensive stone spikes that surely helped deter ancient armies from invading the site.

Powerful swells pound the 60m-high cliff face. A complete lack of rails or other modern additions that would spoil this amazing ancient site means that you can not only go right up to the cliff's edge but also potentially fall to your doom below quite easily. When it's uncrowded, you can't help but feel the extraordinary energy that must have been harnessed to build this vast site.

A small visitor centre has displays that put everything in context. A slightly strenuous 900m walkway wanders uphill to the fort, through a rocky landscape lined with hardy plants.

NEED TO KNOW

Dún Aonghasa; www.heritageireland.ie; adult/child €3/1; ☻9.45am-6pm Apr-Oct, 9.30am-4pm Nov-Mar, closed Mon & Tue Jan & Feb

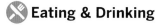 Eating & Drinking

Joe Watty's Bar Pub
(www.joewattys.com; Kilronan; mains €8-20; ☻kitchen 12.30-9pm) The best local pub, with trad sessions most summer nights and weekends other times. Posh pub food ranges from fish and chips to steaks. Peat fires warm the air on the 50 weeks a year when this is needed. Book ahead for dinner in summer.

Festivals of Fun

Galway's packed calendar of festivals turns the city and surrounding communities into what feels like one nonstop party – streets overflow with revellers, and pubs and restaurants often extend their opening hours. Highlights include:

Galway Food Festival (www.galwayfoodfestival.com) Galway's lively food scene is celebrated late March.

Cúirt International Festival of Literature (www.cuirt.ie) Top-name authors converge on Galway in April for one of Ireland's premier literary festivals, featuring poetry slams, theatrical performances and readings.

Galway Arts Festival (www.galwayartsfestival.ie) A two-week extravaganza of theatre, music, art and comedy around mid-July.

Galway Film Fleadh (www.galwayfilmfleadh.com) One of Ireland's biggest film festivals, held early July, right before the arts festival.

Galway Race Week (www.galwayraces.com; ⏱late Jul or early Aug) Horse races in Ballybrit, 3km east of the city, are the centrepiece of Galway's biggest, most boisterous festival of all. Thursday is a real knees-up: by night the swells have muddy knees on their tuxes and are missing random high heels.

Galway International Oyster Festival (www.galwayoysterfest.com) Oysters are washed down with plenty of pints in the last week in September.

ℹ Information

The useful **tourist office** (📞099-61263; Kilronan; ⏱10am-5pm May & Jun, 10am-5.45pm Jul & Aug, 11am-5pm Sep-Apr) can be found on the waterfront west of the ferry pier in Kilronan.

ℹ Getting Around

The airstrip is 2km southeast of town; a shuttle to Kilronan costs €5 return (be sure to carefully reconfirm return pickups for flights lest you be forgotten).

Year-round, numerous **minibuses** greet each ferry and also prowl the centre of Kilronan. All offer 2½-hour tours of the island (€10) to ad hoc groups. The drive – which comes with commentary – between Kilronan and Dún Aengustakes is about 45 minutes each way. You can also negotiate for private and customised tours.

To see the island at a gentler pace, **pony traps** with a driver are available for trips between Kilronan and Dún Aengus; the return journey costs between €60 and €100 for up to four people.

INISHMAAN

POP 150

The least-visited of the islands, with the smallest population, Inishmaan (Inis Meáin) is a rocky respite. Inishmaan's scenery is breathtaking, with a jagged coastline of startling cliffs, empty beaches and fields where the main crop seems to be stone.

INISHEER

POP 200

Inisheer (Inis Oírr), the smallest of the Aran Islands, has a palpable sense of enchantment, enhanced by the island's deep-rooted mythology, its devotion to traditional culture and ethereal landscapes.

Connemara

The filigreed coast of the Connemara Peninsula is endlessly pleasing, with pockets of sheer delight awaiting discovery. Connemara's interior is a kaleidoscope of rusty bogs, lonely valleys and shimmering black lakes. At its heart are the Maumturk Mountains and the pewter-tinged quartzite peaks of the Twelve Bens mountain range, with a network of scenic hiking and biking trails.

ℹ Information

Galway's tourist office has lots of information on the area. Online, Connemara Tourism (www.connemara.ie) and Go Connemara (www.goconnemara.com) have region-wide info and links.

ℹ Getting There & Around

Bus

Organised bus tours from Galway are many and offer a good overview of the region, though ideally you'll want more than one day to absorb the area's charms, plus you'll want the freedom to make your own discoveries.

Bus Éireann (☎ 091-562 000; www.buseireann.ie) Serves most of Connemara. Services can be sporadic, and many buses operate May to September only, or July and August only. Some drivers will stop in between towns.

Citylink (www.citylink.ie) Has several buses a day linking Galway city with Clifden, with stops in Moycullen, Oughterard, Maam Cross, and Recess, and on to Cleggan and Letterfrack. If you're going somewhere between towns, you might be able to arrange a drop-off with the driver.

Car

Your own wheels are the best way to get off this scenic region's beaten track – though watch out for the narrow roads' stone walls.

OUGHTERARD & AROUND
POP 1400

The workaday village of Oughterard (Uachtar Árd) is one of Ireland's principal angling centres. Immediately west, the countryside opens up to sweeping panoramas of lakes, mountains and bogs, which get more spectacular the further west you travel.

Oughterard

ANNIE JAPAUD/GETTY IMAGES ©

Connemara

◉ Sights

Aughnanure Castle
Castle

(www.heritageireland.com; off N59; adult/child €3/1; ☾9.30am-6pm Apr–mid-Oct) Built around 1500, this bleak fortress was home to the 'Fighting O'Flahertys', who controlled the region for hundreds of years after they fought off the Normans. The six-storey tower house stands on a rocky outcrop overlooking Lough Corrib and has been extensively restored.

Aughnanure Castle is situated 3km east of Oughterard.

ℹ Getting There & Away

Bus Éireann (www.buseireann.ie) and Citylink (www.citylink.ie) have regular buses from Galway to Oughterard.

ROUNDSTONE
POP 250

Clustered around a boat-filled harbour, Roundstone (Cloch na Rón) is the kind of Irish village you hoped to find. Colourful terrace houses and inviting pubs overlook the shimmering recess of Bertraghboy Bay, which is home to dramatic tidal flows, lobster trawlers and traditional *currachs* with tarred canvas bottoms stretched over wicker frames.

⊟ Sleeping & Eating

Wits End B&B
B&B €

(☏091-35813; www.roundstoneaccommodation.com; Main St; s/d from €30/50; ☾Mar-Nov; ☎) Right in the centre of town, this pink palace (well, modest pink house) has

CLIFDEN & AROUND

POP 2100

Connemara's 'capital', Clifden (An Clochán), is an appealing Victorian-era country town with a vaguely-harp-shaped oval of streets offering evocative strolls. It presides over the head of the narrow bay where the River Owenglin tumbles into the sea. The surrounding countryside beckons you to walk through woods and above the shoreline.

◉ Sights & Activities

Sky Road   Scenic Route

This 12km route traces a spectacular loop out to the township of Kingston and then back to Clifden, taking in some rugged, stunningly beautiful coastal scenery en route. The round trip is about 12km long and can be easily walked or cycled. Head directly west from Clifden's Market Square.

🛏 Sleeping & Eating

Quay House   Hotel €€

(☏095-21369; www.thequayhouse.com; Beach Rd; s/d from €90/150; ⊙mid-Mar–mid-Nov; ⊚) Down by the harbour, a 10-minute walk from town, this rambling 1820 house has 14 rooms filled with antiques and manages an unfussy style that seems contemporary. Run by an offshoot of the Foyle family of hoteliers, it has pleasures unheard of during past careers as a convent and monastery.

rooms which look over the road to the water. The accommodation is basic but comfortable and is a mere stumble from the fine pubs.

O'Dowd's   Seafood €€

(☏091-35809; www.odowdsseafoodbar.com; Main St; mains €13-22; ⊙restaurant 10am-9.30pm Jun-Sep, to 9pm Oct-May) This well-worn, comfortable old pub hasn't lost any of its authenticity since it starred in the 1997 Hollywood flick *The Matchmaker*. Specialities at its adjoining restaurant include seafood sourced off the old stone dock right across the street. Produce comes from their own garden. There's a good list of Irish microbrews and you can get breakfast before noon.

Mitchell's   Seafood €€

(☏095-21867; Market St; lunch mains €8-12, dinner mains €15-25; ⊙noon-10pm Mar-Oct) Seafood takes centre stage at this elegant spot. From a velvety chowder right through a long list of ever-changing and inventive specials, the produce of the surrounding waters is honoured. The wine list does the food justice. Book for dinner. (Lunch includes sandwiches and casual fare.)

LETTERFRACK & AROUND

POP 200

Founded by Quakers in the mid-19th century, Letterfrack (Leitir Fraic) is a crossroads with a few pubs and B&Bs. But the forested setting and nearby coast are a magnet for outdoors adventure seekers. A 4km walk to the peak of **Tully Mountain** takes 40 minutes and affords wonderful ocean views.

◉ Sights

Connemara National Park   National Park

(www.connemaranationalpark.ie; off N59; admission free; ⊙always open) Immediately southeast of Letterfrack, Connemara National Park spans 2000 dramatic hectares of bog, mountain and heath. The **visitor centre** (www.connemaranationalpark.ie; Letterfrack; ⊙9am-6.30pm Jun-Aug, to 5.30pm Mon-Sat Mar-May & Sep-Oct) **FREE** is in a beautiful setting off a parking area 300m south of the Letterfrack crossroads. The park encloses a number of the **Twelve Bens**, including Bencullagh, Benbrack and Benbaun. The heart of the park is **Gleann Mór** (Big Glen), through which the River Polladirk

flows. There's fine walking up the glen and over the surrounding mountains, as well as short, self-guided walks. If the Bens look too daunting, you can hike up **Diamond Hill** nearby.

Kylemore Abbey   Historic Building

(www.kylemoreabbeytourism.ie; off N59; adult/child €12.50/free; ⊙9am-6.30pm Apr-Sep, 10am-4.30pm Oct-Mar) Magnificently situated on the shores of a lake, this crenulated 19th-century neo-Gothic fantasy was built for a wealthy English businessman, Mitchell Henry, who spent his honeymoon in Connemara. His wife died tragically young.

Admission also covers the abbey's **Victorian walled gardens**. Kylemore's tranquillity is shattered in high summer with the arrival of dozens of tour coaches per day, each one followed in by an average of 50 cars (yes, over 2500 cars a day). It's 4.5km east of Letterfrack.

❶ Getting There & Away

Bus Éireann (www.buseireann.ie) and Citylink (www.citylink.ie) buses continue to Letterfrack at least once a day from Clifden, 15km southwest on the N59.

Connemara National Park

MICHELLE MCCARRON/GETTY IMAGES ©

LEENANE & KILLARY HARBOUR

The small village of Leenane (also spelled Leenaun) drowses on the shore of dramatic Killary Harbour. Dotted with mussel rafts, the long, narrow harbour is Ireland's only fjord – maybe. Slicing 16km inland and more than 45m deep in the centre, it certainly looks like a fjord, although some scientific studies suggest it may not actually have been glaciated. **Mt Mweelrea** (819m) towers to its north.

🏃 Activities

Killary Cruises
Boat Cruise

(www.killarycruises.com; N59; adult/child €21/10; ⏷Apr-Oct) From Nancy's Point, about 2km west of Leenane, Killary Cruises offers 1½-hour cruises of Killary Harbour. Dolphins leap around the boat, which passes by a mussel farm and stops at a salmon farm. There are four cruises daily in summer.

Killary Adventure Centre
Adventure Sports

(📞095-43411; www.killaryadventure.com; off N59; activity rates from €46/31; ⏷10am-5pm) Canoeing, sea kayaking, sailing, rock climbing, windsurfing and day hikes are but a few of the activities on offer at this adventure centre about 3km west of Leenane.

🛏 Sleeping

Delphi Lodge
Lodge €€€

(📞095-42222; www.delphilodge.ie; off R335; s/d from €125/290; @ 📶) You'll wish the dreamy views at this gorgeous country estate could follow you into your dreams. Set among truly stunning mountain and lake vistas, this isolated country house has 12 posh bedrooms and a bevy of common areas including a library and billiards room. The cooking is modern Irish, sourced locally. Meals (dinner €55) are taken at a vast communal table. Walks, fishing and much more await outside. The lodge is 13km northwest of Leenane.

Local Knowledge

Connemara Don't Miss List

BY STEVE WHITFIELD,
OUTDOOR INSTRUCTOR, KILLARY ADVENTURE CENTRE

1 KAYAKING THE KILLARY FJORD
As you paddle your way through this mountainous region, often with seals, dolphins and sea otters for company, you can follow the old famine track used during the Great Famine of 1845–9, along the shoreline, all the way to the Atlantic.

2 HIKE THE TWELVE BENS
Although dedicated fell runners have been known to race up all 12 peaks in a single day, just climbing one is an unforgettable experience – the views from the top are spectacular, whether you're looking out on to the coastline or inland to the brooding expanse of Connemara itself.

3 KYLEMORE ABBEY
Kylemore Abbey (left) looks like a fairytale castle shimmering in the lake. It was a castle, but then in 1920, it was handed over to the Benedictines; today it's a girls' school. And while you might just photograph it and move on, you should spend a couple of hours wandering about the castle or the gorgeous gardens.

4 ROUNDSTONE
The road into Roundstone is one of the most spectacular coastal drives in the country, and the village itself is just as beautiful. The lovely coloured terraces are home to some great seafood restaurants and craft shops, the beach is always busy with lobster trawlers and *currachs* (rowing boats), and there are some fine beaches nearby.

5 KILLARY ADVENTURE CENTRE
This place (p229) has a huge range of activities – from rock climbing and gorge walking to kayaking and bungee jumps, speed boating and sailing.

If You Like…
Music Pubs

If you like authentic traditional sessions like Crane Bar (p221) in Galway city, darken the door of these other County Galway bars for more of the same.

1 TIG CÓILÍ

(Mainguard St) Two live *céilidh* (traditional music and dancing) a day draw the crowds to this authentic fire-engine-red pub. This is where musicians go to hear other musicians.

2 MONROE'S TAVERN

(www.monroes.ie; Upper Dominick St) Often photographed for its classic, world-weary facade, Monroe's delivers traditional music and ballads, plus it remains the only pub in the city with regular Irish dancing.

3 TÍ JOE MAC'S

(Kilronan) Informal music sessions, peat fires and a broad terrace with harbour views make Tí Joe Mac's a local favourite. Food is limited to a few sandwiches slapped together between pints.

CLONMACNOISE

Gloriously placed overlooking the River Shannon, **Clonmacnoise** (www.heritageireland.ie; adult/child €6/2; ⊙9am-7pm mid-May–mid-Sep, 10am-5.30pm mid-Sep–mid-May, last admission 45min before closing) is one of Ireland's most important ancient monastic cities. The site is enclosed in a walled field and contains several early churches, high crosses, round towers and graves in astonishingly good condition. The surrounding marshy area is known as the **Shannon Callows**, home to many wild plants and one of the last refuges of the seriously endangered corncrake (a pastel-coloured relative of the coot).

History

When St Ciarán founded a monastery here, in AD 548, it was the most important crossroads in the country, the intersection of the north–south River Shannon, and the east–west Esker Riada (Highway of the Kings).

The giant ecclesiastical city had a humble beginning and Ciarán died just seven months after building his first church. Over the years, however, Clonmacnoise grew to become an unrivalled bastion of Irish religion, literature and art and attracted a large lay population. Between the 7th and 12th centuries, monks from all over Europe came to study and pray here, helping to earn Ireland the title of the 'land of saints and scholars'.

Most of what you can see today dates from the 10th to 12th centuries. The monks would have lived in small huts surrounding the monastery. The site was burned and pillaged on numerous occasions by both the Vikings and the Irish. After the 12th century it fell into decline, and by the 15th century was home solely to an impoverished bishop. In 1552 the English garrison from Athlone reduced the site to a ruin.

◉ Sights

Museum   Museum
(www.heritageireland.ie; ⊙9am-7pm mid-May–mid-Sep, 10am-5.30pm mid-Sep–mid-May, last admission 45min before closing) Three connected conical huts, echoing the design of early monastic dwellings, house the museum. The centre's 20-minute audiovisual show provides an excellent introduction to the site.

The exhibition area contains the original high crosses (replicas have been put in their former locations outside), and various artefacts uncovered during excavation, including silver pins, beaded glass and an Ogham stone. It also contains the largest collection of early Christian grave slabs in Europe. Many with inscriptions clearly visible, often starting with *oroit do* or *ar* (a prayer for).

There's a real sense of drama as you descend to the foot of the imposing **Cross of the Scriptures (King Flann's Cross)**, one of Ireland's finest. It's very

Clonmacnoise

distinctive, with unique upward-tilting arms and richly decorated panels depicting the Crucifixion, the Last Judgement, the arrest of Jesus, and Christ in the tomb.

Only the shaft of the **North Cross**, which dates from around AD 800, remains. It is adorned by lions, convoluted spirals and a single figure, thought to be the Celtic god Cernunnos. The richly decorated **South Cross** has mostly abstract carvings – swirls, spirals and fretwork – and, on the western face, the Crucifixion plus a few odd cavorting creatures.

Cathedral   Ruin

The largest building at Clonmacnoise, the cathedral was originally built in AD 909, but was significantly altered and remodelled over the centuries. Its most interesting feature is the intricate 15th-century Gothic doorway with carvings of Sts Francis, Patrick and Dominic. A whisper carries from one side of the door to the other, and this feature was supposedly used by lepers to confess their sins without infecting the priests.

The last High Kings of Tara – Turlough Mór O'Connor (died 1156) and his son Ruairí (Rory; died 1198) – are said to be buried near the altar.

Temples   Churches

The small churches are called temples, a derivation of the Irish word *teampall*

Cross, Clonmacnoise
HOLGER LEUE/GETTY IMAGES ©

Detour:
Lough Inagh Valley

This stark brown landscape beguiles by its very simplicity.

The R344 enters the valley from the south, just west of playfully named Recess. The moody waters of Loughs Derryclare and Inagh reflect the colours of the moment. On the western side is the brooding **Twelve Bens** mountain range. At the north end of the valley, the R344 meets the N59, which loops around Connemara to Leenane.

Towards the northern end of the valley, a track leads west off the road up a blind valley, which is well worth exploring.

(church). The little, roofed church is **Temple Conner**, still used by Church of Ireland parishioners on the last Sunday of the summer months. Walking towards the cathedral, you'll pass the scant foundations of **Temple Kelly** (1167) before reaching tiny **Temple Ciaran**, reputed to be the burial place of St Ciarán, the site's founder.

The floor level in Temple Ciaran is lower than outside because local farmers have been taking clay from the church for centuries to protect their crops and cattle. The floor has been covered in slabs, but handfuls of clay are still removed from outside the church in the early spring.

Near the temple's southwestern corner is a **bullaun** (ancient grinding stone) supposedly used for making medicines for the monastery's hospital. Today the rainwater that collects in it is said to cure warts.

Continuing round the compound you come to the 12th-century **Temple Melaghlin**, with its attractive windows,

and the twin structures of **Temple Hurpan** and **Temple Doolin**.

Round Towers   Historic Buildings
Overlooking the River Shannon is the 20m-high **O'Rourke's Tower**. Lightning blasted the top off the tower in 1135, but the remaining structure was used for another 400 years.

Temple Finghin and its round tower are on the northern boundary of the site, also overlooking the Shannon. The building dates from around 1160 and has some fine Romanesque carvings. The herringbone-patterned tower roof is the only one in Ireland that has never been altered.

Other Remains   Historic Buildings
Beyond the site's boundary wall, about 500m east through the modern grave-yard, is the secluded **Nun's Church** with wonderful Romanesque arches and minute carvings; one has been inter-preted as Ireland's earliest sheila-na-gig (carved female figure), in an acrobatic pose with feet tucked behind the ears.

To the west of the site, on the ridge near the car park, is a motte with the oddly shaped ruins of a 13th-century **castle**, built by John de Grey, bishop of Norwich, to watch over the Shannon.

Getting There & Away
By car Clonmacnoise is 7km northeast of Shannonbridge on the R444.

COUNTY CLARE

Ennis
POP 20,200

Ennis (Inis) is the busy commercial centre of Clare. It lies on the banks of the small-ish River Fergus, which runs east, then south into the Shannon Estuary.

It's short on sights but the place to stay if you want a bit of urban flair; from Ennis, you can reach any part of Clare in under two hours.

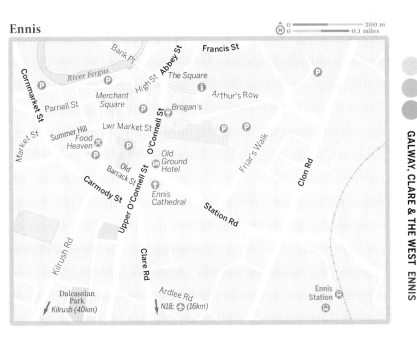

Ennis

Sleeping & Eating

Old Ground Hotel   Hotel €€
(☏065-682 8127; www.flynnhotels.com;
O'Connell St; s/d from €90/120; @ 🛜) The
lobby at this local institution is always a
scene: old friends sprawl on the sofas,
deals are cut at the tables, and ladies
from the neighbouring church's altar
society exchange gossip over tea. Parts
of this rambling landmark date back to
the 1800s. The 83 rooms vary greatly in
size and decor – don't hesitate to inspect
a few. On balmy days, retire to tables on
the lawn.

Food Heaven   Cafe €
(www.foodheaven.eu; 21 Market St; mains €6-10;
🕗8.30am-6pm Mon-Sat) One of several fine
choices in the Market St area, this small
cafe-deli lives up to its ethereal name with
creative and fresh fare. Sandwiches come
on renowned brown bread, while soups
and salads change daily. Hot specials are
just that. Be ready to queue at lunch.

Drinking & Nightlife

Brogan's   Pub
(24 O'Connell St) On the corner of Cooke's
Lane, Brogan's sees a fine bunch of
musicians rattling even the stone floors
from about 9pm Monday to Thursday,
plus even more nights in summer. It's a
big pub that rambles from one room to
the next.

Entertainment

Cois na hAbhna   Traditional Music
(☏065-682 0996; www.coisnahabhna.ie; Gort
Rd; 🕗shop 9am-5pm, trad sessions 9pm Tue)
This important point for traditional music
and culture is 1.5km north of town along
the N18. It has performances (plus weekly
trad sessions) and a full range of classes
in dance and music. The archive covers
Irish traditional music, song, dance and
folklore relating mainly to County Clare;
books and recordings are on sale.

ⓘ Information

The tourist office (☎065-682 8366; www.
visitennis.ie; Arthur's Row; ⏰9.30am-1pm &
2-5.30pm Tue-Fri) is very helpful and efficient. Can
book accommodation for a €4 fee.

ⓘ Getting There & Away

The M18 bypass east of the city lets traffic
between Limerick and Galway whiz right past,
although trips to the coast still take you through
the centre.

Bus

Bus Éireann (☎065-682 4177; www.buseireann.
ie) services operate from the bus station beside
the train station.

Buses run from Ennis to Cork (€16, three
hours, 11 daily); Doolin (€12, 1½ hours, two daily)
via Corofin, Ennistymon, Lahinch and Liscannor;
Galway (€10, 1½ hours, hourly) via Gort; Limerick
(€9, 40 minutes, hourly) via Bunratty; and
Shannon Airport (€8, 50 minutes, hourly).

To reach Dublin (€20), connect through
Limerick.

Train

Irish Rail (www.irishrail.ie) trains from Ennis
station (☎065-684 0444; Station Rd) serve
Limerick (€10, 40 minutes, nine daily), where you
can connect to trains to places further afield like
Dublin. The line to Galway (€19, 1¾ hours, five
daily) features good Burren scenery.

Bunratty

Conveniently located beside the N18
motorway and with plenty of bus-sized
parking, Bunratty (Bun Raite) – home
to government schemes for hawking
tourism hard – draws more tourists than
any other place in the region. A theme
park recreates a clichéd Irish village of old
(where's the horseshit, lash and disease
we ask?) and each year more and more
shops crowd the access roads – many
selling authentic Irish goods just out of
the container from China.

Groups lay siege to Bunratty from April
to October.

Left: Bunratty Folk Park; **Below:** Ennis (p232)

(LEFT) GLOWIMAGES/GETTY IMAGES ©; (BELOW) RICHARD CUMMINS/GETTY IMAGES ©

◉ Sights

Bunratty Castle & Folk Park
Castle

(www.shannonheritage.com; adult/child €15/1; ⊙9am-5.30pm, last admission 4.15pm; 👪) Square and hulking Bunratty Castle is only the latest of several constructions to occupy its location beside the River Ratty. Vikings founded a settlement here in the 10th century, and other occupants included the Norman Thomas de Clare in the 1270s. The present structure was put up in the early 1400s by the energetic MacNamara family, falling shortly thereafter to the O'Briens, in whose possession it remained until the 17th century. Fully restored, the castle is loaded with 14th- to 17th-century furniture, paintings and wall hangings.

Adjoining the castle, the folk park is a reconstructed traditional Irish village with cottages, a forge and working blacksmith, weavers, post office, pub and small cafe. There's a pervading theme-park artificiality (without the rides).

✦ Activities

Traditional Irish Night
Banquet

(📞061-360 788; adult/child €40/20; ⊙7-9.30pm Apr-Oct) Traditional Irish nights are held in a corn barn in the folk park. Lots of red-haired (real or fake, it's clearly a big help in securing employment) servers dish up trad chow plus music and dancing. There's nontraditional wine as well, which may put you in the mood for the singalong.

Medieval Banquet
Banquet

(📞061-360 788; adult/child €50/25; ⊙5.30pm & 8.45pm Apr-Oct, schedule varies Nov-Mar) If you skip the high-jinks in the corn barn, you may opt for a medieval banquet, replete with harp-playing maidens, court jesters and food with a medieval motif (lots of meaty items, but somehow we think the real stuff would empty the place right out). It's all washed down with mead – a kind of honey wine. The banquets are popular with

235

Detour:
Athlone Castle

The nearest town to Clonmacnoise is Athlone, 22km to the north, and a useful stop if you're driving across country between Galway and Dublin. **Athlone Castle** (www.athloneartandheritage.ie; adult/child €8/4; ⏱11am-5pm Tue-Sat, 12pm-5pm Sun; ♿) has existed in some form since the early 13th century, and in February 2013 a superb new **visitor centre** opened with interactive displays and audiovisual presentations that really do bring to life the tumultuous history of the town. There are eight galleries, each depicting an aspect of life here through the ages. The highlight is the fourth gallery with its Siege Experience which takes place in a circular panoramic gallery with plenty of blood curdling screams that the kids (in particular) will love.

groups, so book well ahead; you can often find savings online.

The banquets at Knappogue Castle and Dunguaire Castle (in Galway) are similar but more sedate.

Kilkee

POP 1100

Kilkee's wide beach has the kind of white, powdery sand that's made the Caribbean, well, the Caribbean. Granted the waters are chilly and the winds often brisk, but in summer the strand is thronged with day-trippers and holidaymakers. The sweeping semicircular bay has high cliffs on the north end and weathered rocks to the south. The waters are very tidal, with wide-open sandy expanses replaced by pounding waves in just a few hours.

❶ Getting There & Away

Bus Éireann has three to four buses daily to Kilkee from Limerick (€19, two hours) and Ennis (€15, 1¼ hours). Both routes pass through Kilrush.

Kilkee to Lahinch

DOONBEG

POP 300

Doonbeg (An Dún Beag) is a tiny seaside village about halfway between Kilkee and Quilty. Another Spanish Armada ship, the *San Esteban*, was wrecked on

20 September 1588 near the mouth of the River Doonbeg. The survivors were later executed at Spanish Point. Note the surviving wee little 16th-century **castle tower** next to the graceful seven-arch stone bridge over the river.

White Strand (Trá Bán) is a quiet beach, 2km long and backed by dunes. It's north of town and hard to miss, as it's now been surrounded by the Doonbeg Golf Club. From the public car park, you follow a break in the dunes to a perfect sweep of sand.

Doonbeg also has some decent **surfing**. For golf, the economic collapse means that the **Doonbeg Golf Club** (✆065-905 5600; www.doonbeglodge.com; green fees from €170, r from €200) has lost a load of its previous snoot. The championship course is laid out amid the bare, rolling dunes; the lodge has luxurious rooms.

🛏 Sleeping & Eating

Morrissey's   Inn €€
(✆065-905 5304; www.morrisseysdoonbeg.com; Main St; s/d from €55/90, mains €12-25; ⏱Mar-Oct; ❷🐾) Under its fourth-generation owner, this old pub is a stylish coastal haven. The six rooms feature king-size beds and large soaking tubs. The pub's restaurant is renowned for its casual but enticing seafood, from fish and chips to succulent local crab claws. Outside there's a terrace overlooking the river.

236

MILTOWN MALBAY

POP 800

A classically friendly place in the chatty Irish way, Miltown Malbay has a thriving music scene. Every year it hosts the Willie Clancy Summer School, one of Ireland's great traditional music events.

🛏 Sleeping & Eating

An Gleann B&B   B&B €€

(☎ 065-708 4281; www.angleann.net; Ennis Rd; s/d from €30/60; 🛜) Possibly the friendliest welcome in town is at this B&B off the R474 about 1km from the centre. The five rooms are basic and comfy and owners Mary and Harry Hughes are a delight. Cyclists are catered for.

Old Bake House   Irish €

(Main St; mains €5-15; ⏱ noon-9pm) In a region of great seafood chowder, some of the best is at the Old Bake House, which serves Irish classics in humble surrounds.

🍷 Drinking & Nightlife

O'Friel's Bar (Lynch's; The Square) is one of a couple of genuine old-style places with occasional trad music sessions. The other is the dapper **Hillery's** (Main St).

ⓘ Getting There & Away

Bus Éireann service is paltry. Expect one or two buses Monday to Saturday north and south along the coast and inland to Ennis.

LAHINCH

POP 650

Lahinch (Leacht Uí Chonchubhair) has always owed its living to beach-seeking tourists. The town sits on protected Liscannor Bay and has a fine beach. Free-spending mobs descend in summer, many wielding golf clubs for play at the famous traditional-style **Lahinch Golf Club** (☎ 065-708 1003; www.lahinchgolf.com; green fees from €120). It dates from 1892 when it was laid out amid the dunes by Scottish soldiers.

Clare's Best Music Festival

Half the population of Miltown Malbay seems to be part of the annual **Willie Clancy Summer School** (☎ 065-708 4148; www.scoilsamhraidhwillieclancy.com), a tribute to a native son and one of Ireland's greatest pipers. The nine-day festival usually begins in the first or second week in July, when impromptu sessions occur day and night, the pubs are packed and Guinness is consumed by the barrel.

Workshops and classes underpin the event; don't be surprised to attend a recital with 40 noted fiddlers. Asked how such a huge affair has happened for almost four decades, a local who teaches fiddle said: 'No one knows, it just does.'

🛏 Sleeping & Eating

West Coast Lodge   Inn €

(☎ 065-708 2000; www.lahinchaccommodation.com; Station Rd; dm/r from €20/50; @ 🛜) Flashpackers will cheer this stylish and downright plush hostel and inn in the heart of Lahinch. Power showers, fine cotton sheets and down duvets are just some of the touches found throughout the seven- to 12-bed dorms and private rooms. Check out the surf from the roof deck and rent a bike to go exploring.

Barrtra Seafood Restaurant   Seafood €€

(☎ 065-708 1280; www.barrtra.com; Miltown Malbay Rd; mains €15-28; ⏱ 1-10pm daily Jul & Aug, fewer days rest of year) The 'Seafood Symphony' menu item says it all at this rural repose 3.5km south of Lahinch. Enjoy views over pastures to the sea from this lovely country cottage, surrounded by pretty kitchen gardens. The lavish €35 set meal is great value.

ⓘ Getting There & Away

Bus Éireann runs two to four buses daily through Lahinch on the Doolin–Ennis/Limerick routes and one or two Monday to Saturday south along the coast to Doonbeg in summer.

Cliffs of Moher

Star of a million tourist brochures, the Cliffs of Moher (Aillte an Mothair, or Ailltreacha Mothair) are one of the most popular sights in Ireland. But like many an ageing star, you have to look beyond the famous facade to appreciate its inherent attributes.

The entirely vertical cliffs rise to a height of 203m, their edge falling away abruptly into the constantly churning sea. A series of heads, the dark limestone seems to march in a rigid formation that amazes, no matter how many times you look. On a clear day you'll channel Barbara Streisand as you can see forever;

the Aran Islands stand etched on the waters of Galway Bay, and beyond lie the hills of Connemara in western Galway.

Such appeal comes at a price: mobs. This is check-off tourism big time and busloads come and go constantly in summer. A vast visitor centre is set back into the side of a hill; it's impressively unimpressive – it blends right in. As part of the development, however, the main walkways and viewing areas along the cliffs have been surrounded by a 1.5m-high wall that's too high and set too far back from the edge.

But there are good rewards if you're willing to walk for 10 minutes as you quickly escape the crowds. Past the end of the 'Moher Wall' south, a **trail** runs along the cliffs to Hag's Head (about 5.5km) – few venture this far, yet the views are uninhibited. From here you can continue on to Liscannor for a total walk of 12km (about 3.5 hours). To the north, you can follow the **Doolin Trail** via O'Brien's Tower right to the village of Doolin (about 7km and 2.5 hours). The entire Liscannor to Doolin walking path via the cliffs is now signposted, note that there are a lot of ups and downs and narrow, cliff-edge stretches.

With binoculars you can spot the more than 30 species of **birds** – including darling little puffins – that make their homes among the fissure-filled cliff faces.

The roads leading to the cliffs pass through refreshingly undeveloped lands, the rolling hills giving no hint of the dramatic vistas just over the edge.

For awe-inspiring views of the cliffs and wildlife you might consider a **cruise**. The boat operators in Doolin offer popular tours of the cliffs.

Cliffs of Moher
SLOW IMAGES/GETTY IMAGES ©

ℹ Information

Visitor Centre (www.cliffsofmoher.ie; admission to site adult/child €6/free; ⏱9am-9.30pm Jul & Aug, 9am-7pm May, Jun & Sep, 9am-6pm Mar, Apr & Oct, 9.15am-5pm Nov-Feb) Actually, revealingly, it's called the 'Cliffs of Moher Visitor Experience', and has glitzy exhibitions about the cliffs and the environment called the *Atlantic Edge*.

ℹ Getting There & Away

Bus Éireann runs two to four buses daily past the cliffs on the Doolin–Ennis/Limerick routes. Waits between buses may exceed your ability to enjoy the spectacle, so you might combine a bus with a walk. Numerous private tour operators run tours to the cliffs from Galway and the region.

The Burren

The Burren region is rocky and windswept, an apt metaphor for the hardscrabble lives of those who've eked out an existence here. Stretching across northern Clare, from the Atlantic coast to Kinvara in County Galway, it's a unique striated limestone landscape that was shaped beneath ancient seas, then forced high and dry by a great geological cataclysm.

This is not the green Ireland of postcards. But there are wildflowers in spring, giving the 560-sq-km Burren brilliant, if ephemeral, colour amid the arid beauty. There are also intriguing villages to enjoy. These include the music hub of Doolin on the west coast, Kilfenora inland and Ballyvaughan in the north, on the shores of Galway Bay.

FLORA & FAUNA

Soil may be scarce on the Burren, but the small amount that gathers in the cracks is well drained and rich in nutrients. This, together with the mild Atlantic climate, supports an extraordinary mix of Mediterranean, Arctic and alpine plants. Of Ireland's native wildflowers, 75% are found here, including 24 species of beautiful orchids, the creamy-white burnet rose, the little

---

💛 If You Like...
Traditional Music Festivals

If you enjoy the **Willie Clancy Irish Summer School** (☎065-708 4281; www.oac.ie), you'll like these other great celebrations of trad music.

1 CRAICEANN INIS OÍRR INTERNATIONAL BODHRÁN SUMMER SCHOOL
(www.craiceann.com) A weeklong festival in late June on Inisheer that keeps the focus strictly on the bodhrán (circular drum made with goat skin), includes masterclasses and workshops as well as great music.

2 ENNIS TRAD FESTIVAL
(www.ennistradfestival.com) Traditional music in venues across this County Clare town for one week in mid-November.

3 FLEADH NUA
(www.fleadhnua.com) A lively traditional music festival held in Ennis in late May, with singing, dancing and workshops.

4 MICHO RUSSELL FESTIVAL
(www.doolin-tourism.com; ⏱Feb) Held on the last weekend in February, this festival celebrates the work of a legendary Doolin musician and attracts top trad talent.

---

starry flowers of mossy saxifrage and the magenta-coloured bloody cranesbill.

The Burren is a stronghold of Ireland's most elusive mammal, the rather shy weasel-like pine marten. Badgers, foxes and even stoats are common throughout the region. Otters and seals haunt the shores around Bell Harbour, New Quay and Finavarra Point.

🏃 Activities

The Burren is a walkers paradise. The bizarre, beautiful landscape, numerous trails and many ancient sites are best explored on foot. 'Green roads' are the old

Right: The Burren (p239)
Below: Ashford Castle (p244)

(RIGHT) GARETH McCORMACK/GETTY IMAGES ©; (BELOW) EOIN CLARKE/GETTY IMAGES ©

highways of the Burren, crossing hills and valleys to some of the remotest corners of the region. Many of these unpaved ways were built during the Famine as part of relief work, while some date back possibly thousands of years. They're now used mostly by hikers and the occasional farmer. Some are signposted.

The **Burren Way** is a 123km network of marked hiking routes throughout the region.

Guided nature, history, archaeology and wilderness **walks** are great ways to appreciate the Burren. Typically the cost of the walks averages €10 to €25 and there are many options, including individual trips. Confirm times and walk locations.

Burren Guided Walks & Hikes
Walking Tour

(☎ 087 244 6807, 065-707 6100; www.burrenguid-edwalks.com) Long-time guide Mary Howard leads groups on a variety of itineraries.

Burren Wild Tours
Walking Tour

(☎ 087 877 9565; www.burrenwalks.com) John Connolly offers a broad range of walks, including gentle options as well as more strenuous ones.

Heart of Burren Walks
Walking Tour

(☎ 065-682 7707; www.heartofburrenwalks.com) Local Burren author Tony Kirby leads walks and archaeology hikes.

Getting There & Away

A few **Bus Éireann** (www.buseireann.ie) services pass through the Burren. The main routes include one from Limerick and Ennis to Corofin, Ennistymon, Lahinch, Liscannor, the Cliffs of Moher, Doolin and Lisdoonvarna; another connects Galway with Ballyvaughan, Lisdoonvarna and Doolin. Usually there are one to four buses daily, with the most in summer.

DOOLIN

POP 250

Doolin gets plenty of press and chatter as a centre of Irish traditional music, owing to a trio of pubs that have sessions throughout the year. It's also known for its setting – 6km north of the Cliffs of Moher and down near the ever-unsettled sea, the land is windblown, with huge rocks exposed by the long-vanished top soil.

Given all its attributes, you might be surprised when you realise that Doolin as it's known barely exists. Rather, you might be forgiven for exclaiming, 'There's no there here!' For Doolin is really three infinitesimally small neighbouring villages. **Fisherstreet** is right on the water, **Doolin** itself is about 1km east on the little River Aille, and **Roadford** is another 1km east. None has more than a handful of buildings, which results in a scattered appearance, without a centre.

Still, the area is hugely popular with music-seeking tourists. There are scores of good-value hostels and B&Bs spread about the rough landscape. It's also a place to get boats to the offshore Aran Islands.

Sleeping

O'Connors Guesthouse　Inn €€

(☑065-707 4498; www.oconnorsdoolin.com; Doolin; s/d from €45/70; ☺Feb-Oct; ☎) On a bend in the Aille, this working farm has 10 largish rooms in a rather plush farmhouse-style inn. It's near the main crossroads and is utterly spotless.

Dounroman House　B&B €€

(☑065-707 4774; www.doolinbedandbreakfast. com; Doolin; s/d from €45/70; ☎) Near the main Doolin crossroads, this two-storey B&B has views over the rough, grassy countryside. The rooms are large; some are good for families. Breakfast options include locally smoked salmon and potato waffles.

Finding Traditional Music in County Clare

From atmospheric small pubs in tiny villages where non-instrument-playing patrons are a minority to rollicking urban boozers in Ennis, Clare is one of Ireland's best counties for traditional music. Eschewing any modern influences from rock or even polkas (as is heard elsewhere), Clare's musicians stick resolutely to the jigs and reels of old, often with little vocal accompaniment.

Although you can find pubs with trad sessions at least one night a week in almost every town and village, the following are our picks for where to start:

Doolin Offers a much-hyped collection of pubs with nightly trad music sessions. However, tourist crowds can erase any sense of intimacy or even enjoyment.

Ennis You can bounce from one music-filled pub to another on most nights, especially in the summer. Musicians from around the county come here to show off and there are good venues for serious trad pursuits.

Ennistymon A low-key farming village inland from Doolin with a couple of ancient pubs that attract top local talent.

Kilfenora Small village with a big musical heritage on show at the great local pub Vaughan's.

Miltown Malbay This tiny village hosts the annual Willie Clancy Summer School, one of Ireland's best music festivals. The talented locals can be heard performing throughout the year in several old pubs.

🍷 Drinking & Nightlife

Doolin's rep is largely based on music. A lot of musicians live in the area, and they have a symbiotic relationship with the tourists: each desires the other and each year things grow a little larger.

McGann's   Pub
(www.mcgannspubdoolin.com; Roadford)
McGann's has all the classic touches of a full-on Irish music pub; the action often spills out onto the street. The food here is the best of Doolin's three famous pubs (get the crab claws!). Inside you'll find locals playing darts in its warren of small rooms, some with peat fires. There's a small outside covered area.

O'Connor's   Pub
(www.gusoconnorsdoolin.com; Fisherstreet)
Right on the water, this sprawling favourite packs them in and has a rollicking atmosphere when the music is in full swing. It gets the most crowded and has the highest tourist quotient; on some summer nights you won't squeeze inside and trying to eat is like playing the fiddle for the first time.

MacDiarmada's   Pub
(www.mcdermottspubdoolin.com; Roadford)
Also known as McDermott's, this simple red-and-white old pub is the rowdy favourite of locals. The inside is pretty basic, as is the menu of sandwiches and roasts. There's an outside area.

ℹ️ Getting There & Away

Boat
Doolin is one of two ferry departure points to the Aran Islands from mid-March to October. Sailings are often cancelled due to high seas or tides which make the small dock inaccessible. The boats also offer Cliffs of Moher tours (about €15 for one

hour) which are best done late in the afternoon when the light is from the west.

Doolin 2 Aran Ferries (087 245 3239, 065-707 5949; www.doolin2aranferries.com; Doolin Pier; mid-Mar–Oct) Has a full schedule to the Aran islands plus Cliffs of Moher cruises.

O'Brien Line (065-707 5555; www.obrienline.com) Usually has the most sailings to the Arans; also offers cliff cruises and combo tickets.

Bus

Bus Éireann runs one to four buses daily to Doolin from Ennis (€12, 1½ hours) and Limerick (€18, 2½ hours) via Corofin, Lahinch and the Cliffs of Moher. Buses also go to Galway (€16, 1½ hours, one or two daily) via Ballyvaughan.

In summer, various backpacker shuttles often serve Doolin from Galway and other points in Clare. These shuttle services are amply marketed in hostels.

BALLYVAUGHAN & AROUND
POP 260

Something of a hub for the otherwise dispersed charms of the Burren, Ballyvaughan (Baile Uí Bheacháin) sits between the hard land of the hills and a quiet leafy corner of Galway Bay. It makes an excellent base for visiting the northern reaches of the Burren.

◉ Sights

Aillwee Caves Caves
(www.aillweecave.ie; off R480; combined ticket adult/child €17/10; 10am-5.30pm, to 6.30pm Jul & Aug) Send the kids underground. The main cave penetrates 600m into the mountain, widening into larger caverns, one with its own waterfall. The caves were carved out by water some two million years ago. Near the entrance are the remains of a brown bear,

extinct in Ireland for more than 10,000 years.

Often crowded in summer, the site has a cafe, and a large raptor exhibit has captive hawks, owls and more. A shop sells the excellent locally produced Burren Gold cheese.

🛏 Sleeping

Gregan's Castle Hotel Hotel €€€
(065-707 7005; www.gregans.ie; N67; r from €200;) This hidden Clare gem is housed in a grand estate dating to the 19th century. The 20 rooms and suites have a plush, stylish feel with just enough modern touches to keep you from feeling you've bedded down in a waxworks. The restaurant specialises in inventive fresh fare sourced locally while the bar is the kind of place to sip something brown and let hours roll away in genteel comfort. The grounds are a fantasy of gardens and when you're not walking in the Burren, there's croquet. The estate is some 6km south of Ballyvaughan at Corkscrew Hill.

Pub in Ballyvaughan
RICHARD CUMMINS/GETTY IMAGES ©

⭐ Entertainment

Ólólainn
Pub

(Coast Rd) A tiny family-run place on the left as you head out to the pier, Ólólainn (o-*loch*-lain) is the place for a timeless moment or two in old-fashioned snugs. Look for the old whiskey bottles in the window but save all your energy for the amazing selection of rare whiskeys within.

ℹ️ Getting There & Away

Bus Éireann runs one to three buses daily from Galway through Ballyvaughan and around Black Head to Lisdoonvarna and Doolin.

COUNTY MAYO

Cong

Sitting on a sliver-thin isthmus between Lough Corrib and Lough Mask, twee-little Cong complies with romantic notions of a traditional Irish village. Time appears to

have stood still ever since the evergreen classic *The Quiet Man* was filmed here in 1951. In fact a lot of effort has been made to preserve Cong as it looked for the filming of the movie – even though that was largely the work of Hollywood set designers.

◎ Sights

Cong Abbey
Historic Site

(admission free; ⊙dawn-dusk) An evocative reminder of ecclesiastical times past, the weathered shell of Cong's 12th-century Augustinian abbey is scored by wizened lines from centuries of exposure to the elements. Nevertheless, several finely sculpted features have survived, including a carved doorway, windows and lovely medieval arches (touched up in the 19th century).

Ashford Castle
Historic Building

(☎094-954 6003; www.ashford.ie; grounds adult/child €5/3.50; ⊙9am-dusk) Just beyond Cong Abbey, the village abruptly ends and the woodlands surround-ing Ashford Castle begin. First built in

Walkers on Croagh Patrick (p246)

EOIN CLARKE/GETTY IMAGES ©

Detour:
Killaloe & Ballina

Facing each other across a narrow channel, Killaloe and Ballina are really one destination, even if they have different personalities (and counties). A fine 1770 13-arch one-lane bridge spans the river, linking the pair. You can walk it in five minutes or drive it in about 20 (a Byzantine system of lights controls the traffic).

Killaloe (Cill Da Lúa) is picturesque Clare at its finest. It lies on the western banks of lower Loch Deirgeirt, the southern extension of Lough Derg, where the lough narrows at one of the principal crossings of the River Shannon. The village lies snugly against the Slieve Bernagh Hills that rise abruptly to the west. The Arra Mountains create a fine balance to the east and all of Lough Derg is at hand.

Not as quaint as Killaloe, Ballina (Béal an Átha) is in County Tipperary and has some of the better pubs and restaurants. It lies at the end of a scenic drive from Nenagh along Lough Derg on the R494.

1228 as the seat of the de Burgo family, owners over the years included the Guinness family (of stout fame). Arthur Guinness turned the castle into a regal hunting and fishing lodge, which it remains today.

Quiet Man Museum Museum
(Circular Rd; admission €5, location tour €15; ◎10am-4pm Mar-Oct) Modelled on Sean Thornton's White O' Mornin' Cottage from the film, the Quiet Man Museum also squeezes in a fascinating regional archaeological and historical exhibition of items from 7000 BC to the 19th century. Film fanatics (or those with a postmodern fascination for the way reality and fiction blur) can take a 75-minute **location tour** (time varies), which includes museum entry.

Sleeping

Michaeleen's Manor B&B €€
(✆094-954 6089; www.congbb.com; Quay Rd, Lisloughrey; s/d from €55/65; �) This large, modern home is something of a shrine to The Quiet Man. Each of its 12 sparkling rooms is named after a character in the film and decorated with memorabilia and

quotations. There's also a sauna, outdoor hot tub and a large fountain replica of the Quiet Man Bridge.

Ashford Castle Hotel €€€
(✆094-954 6003; www.ashford.ie; r from €380; @奈) Old-world elegance, 83 exquisite rooms and faultless service are on tap at Ashford Castle. It easily the grandest of the grand in Ireland. Even if you're staying elsewhere, you can come for dinner (from €70) at the **George V Dining Room** (be sure to dress up as it's rather posh).

Getting There & Away

Bus Éireann (www.buseireann.ie; Main St) has three buses to Galway (€12, one hour) Monday to Saturday and four to Westport (€11, one hour).

Westport

Bright and vibrant even in the depths of winter, Westport is a photogenic Georgian town with tree-lined streets, a riverside mall and a great vibe. With an excellent choice of accommodation, restaurants and pubs renowned for their music, it's an extremely popular spot yet has never sold its soul to tourism.

Detour:
Croagh Patrick

St Patrick couldn't have picked a better spot for a pilgrimage than this conical mountain (also known as 'the Reek'). It was on Croagh Patrick that Ireland's patron saint fasted for 40 days and nights, and where he reputedly banished venomous snakes. Climbing the 772m holy mountain is an act of penance for thousands of pilgrims on the last Sunday of July (Reek Sunday). The truly contrite take the original 40km route from **Ballintubber Abbey** (www. ballintubberabbey.ie; Ballintubber; admission free; ☺9am-midnight) FREE, Tóchar Phádraig (Patrick's Causeway), and ascend the mountain barefoot.

The **main trail** ascends the mountain from the car park in Murrisk. You can rent walking sticks for €1.50 for the steep trail which is rocky in parts. The average return trip takes three to four hours and it gets crowded on sunny weekends. At the summit you'll find a 1905 whitewashed church and a 9th-century **oratory fountain.** Views are sublime.

Opposite the car park is the National Famine Memorial, a spine-chilling sculpture of a three-masted ghost ship wreathed in swirling skeletons, commemorating the lives lost on so-called 'coffin ships' employed to help people escape the Famine. A path down past the memorial leads to the scant remains of **Murrisk Abbey,** founded by the O'Malleys in 1547.

Murrisk is 8km southwest of Westport. The best way to get here is along the lovely bayside bike and walking path. Otherwise there are daily buses.

◉ Sights

Westport House   Historic Building
(☏098-27766; www.westporthouse.ie; Quay Rd; house-only adult/child €12/6.50, house & pirate adventure park €20/16.50; ☺11am-6pm Jul & Aug, times vary greatly rest of year; 👶) Built in 1730 on the ruins of Grace O'Malley's 16th-century castle, this charming Georgian mansion retains much of its original contents and has some stunning period-styled rooms.

The house is set in glorious gardens but the overall effect is marred by its commercial focus. Children will love it however, and the **Pirate Adventure Park**, complete with a swinging pirate ship, a 'pirate's playground' and a roller-coaster-style flume ride through a water channel are big hits. The house is located 3km west of the centre.

🛏 Sleeping

St Anthony's   B&B €€
(☏087 630 1550; www.st-anthonys.com; Distillery Rd; s/d from €50/70; 🛜) This genteel B&B sits under cover of a large hedge and thick, twisted vines inhabited by birds' nests. Rooms have clean lines and restful, light colours. Bathrooms have Jacuzzi tubs or power showers. Breakfast is excellent.

Eating

Pantry &
Corkscrew   Modern Irish €€
(☏098-26977; www.thepantryandcorkscrew. com; The Octogon; lunch mains €8-15, dinner mains €12-25; ☺noon-3.30pm, 5.30-10pm Tue Sun) The heart of Mayo's Slow Food movement is found here at this narrow little storefront. The kitchen has huge talent as the changing menu shows, with dishes sourced from local and organic producers.

🍷 Drinking & Nightlife

Matt Molloy's   Pub
(Bridge St) Matt Malloy, the fife player from the Chieftains, opened this old-school pub years ago and the good times haven't let up. Head to the back room around 9pm and you'll catch live *céilidh* (traditional music and dancing). Or perhaps an old man will simply slide into a chair and croon a few classics.

ℹ️ Getting There & Away

Bus

Bus Éireann services include Dublin (€19, 4½ hours, two daily), Galway (€15, two hours, three daily) and Sligo (€20, 2½ hours, one daily). Buses depart from Mill St.

Train

There are five daily trains to Dublin (€35, 3¼ hours).

Counties Sligo & Donegal

The northwestern counties of Sligo and Donegal match any other part of the country for **sheer beauty.** Packing poetry, myth and folklore into their broody, dramatic landscapes, they have no equal when it comes to wildness.

County Sligo is Yeats country, as in William Butler (1865–1939) and Jack Butler (1871–1957), who helped cement its pastoral reputation through verse and paintbrush, respectively.

County Donegal is the wild child of the Irish family. Its rugged landscapes, relative isolation and impetuous weather have all served to forge the county's distinctly stubborn character. It has plenty to offer the visitor, including magnificent coastlines, great surfing and its wonderfully photogenic interior.

Fanad Head (p273)

GARETH MCCORMACK/GETTY IMAGES ©

249

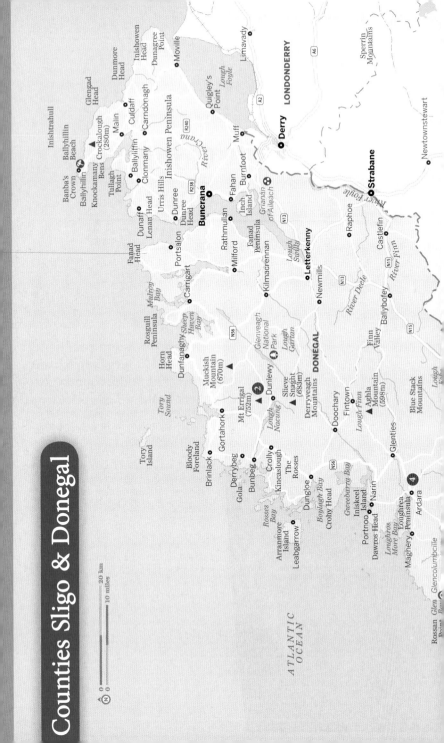

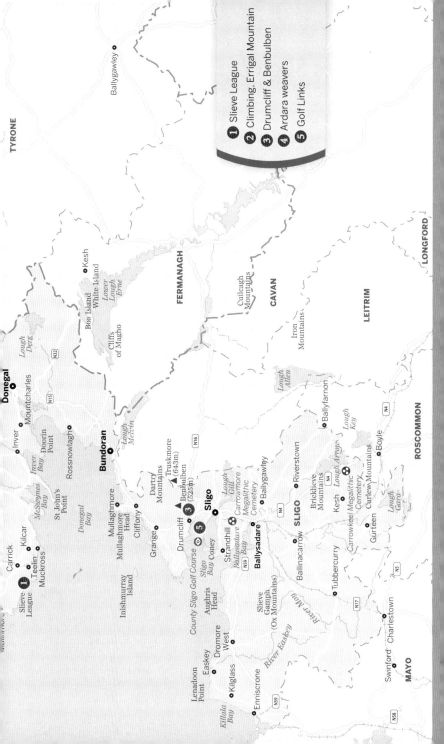

1 Slieve League
2 Climbing, Errigal Mountain
3 Drumcliff & Benbulben
4 Ardara weavers
5 Golf Links

TYRONE

Ballygawley

Donegal
Mountcharles
Inver
Doorin Point
Traver Bay
St John's Point
McSwynes Bay
Muckross
Teelin
Kilcar
Carrick
Slieve League
1

Rossnowlagh

Lough Derg
N32
N15

Bundoran

Lough Melvin

Boa Island
White Island
Kesh
Lower Lough Erne

FERMANAGH

Cliffs of Magho

Cuilcagh Mountains

CAVAN

LEITRIM

Iron Mountains

Lough Allen

LONGFORD

Mullaghmore
Mullaghmore Head
Cliffony
Grange
Drumcliff
3
Dartry Mountains
Truskmore (643m)
Benbulben (525m)

Sligo
5
Strandhill
Coney
Sligo Bay
Ballysadare Bay
County Sligo Golf Course
Inishmurray Island
Aughris Head

Lough Gill
Carrowmore Megalithic Cemetery
Ballygawley
Ballysadare
Ballinacarrow
N4
N59
N16

Riverstown
Brickieve Mountains
N4
Lough Arrow
Kesh
Carrowkeel Megalithic Cemetery
Curlew Mountains
Gurteen
Lough Gara
N5

SLIGO

Ballyfarnon
Lough Key
Boyle
N4
ROSCOMMON

Slieve Gamph (Ox Mountains)
River Moy
Tubbercurry
N17

Lenadoon Point
Easkey
Kilglass
Dromore West
River Easkey
Enniscrone
Killala Bay
N59

Swinford
Charlestown
N58

MAYO

Counties Sligo & Donegal's Highlights

Slieve League

The Cliffs of Moher might draw greater numbers, but that's the only concession Slieve League (p266) makes to its southern rival. Plunging some 600 vertical metres into an often wild and raging sea, these sea cliffs are the tallest and most spectacular in Europe, and with viewing locations like the aptly named One Man's Pass, they can be quite treacherous, too.

Climbing Errigal Mountain

At a very manageable 752m, Donegal's highest peak (p271) might not seem that impressive, but this stunning pyramid-shaped peak will leave you breathless... with the sheer beauty of its summit views, which take in most of the coast-line and the offshore islands. Otherwise it's a relatively easy climb up either of two routes, unless of course it's misty or raining, and then the climb is far more challenging.

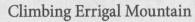

GARETH MCCORMACK/GETTY IMAGES ©

Drumcliff & Benbulben

Ireland's greatest poet, WB Yeats, lies buried in the graveyard of the small Protestant church in Drumcliff (p262), County Sligo. His final resting place lies in the shadow of the magnificent Benbulben, as beautiful a bit of raised earth as you'll see anywhere on your Irish travels. Benbulben

GARETH MCCORMACK/GETTY IMAGES ©

PAUL HARRIS/GETTY IMAGES ©

4 Ardara Weavers

Sure, you can buy an Irish-made woollen or tweed pretty much anywhere in the world these days, but how often do you get the chance to see it hand-woven at the source? The pretty Donegal town of Ardara (p267) is the heart of Donegal's traditional knitwear and hand-woven tweed, and virtually all of the town's manufacturers will gladly let you observe the process – before gently inviting you to purchase the fruit of their looms!

5 Golf Links

You play most of the holes on the links at County Sligo Golf Course (p259) within sight of Ireland's most distinctive peak, Benbulben. This would be reason enough to play, but the world-famous course, at Rosses Point, also happens to be one of the best courses in Ireland. Other golf courses in the area include those at Buncrana, Ballyliffin, Portsalon and Rosapenna. Golf course, Buncrana (p274)

Counties Sligo & Donegal's Best...

Beauty Spots

⊙ **The Glengesh Pass** A touch of the Alps in southwestern Donegal. (p265)

⊙ **Poisoned Glen** Stunning ice-carved rock face overshadowing the glen. (p269)

⊙ **Horn Head** A towering headland with superb views. (p270)

⊙ **Benbulben** A mountain so beautiful that Yeats wanted to be buried in its shadow. (p262)

⊙ **Rosguill Peninsula** Its rugged splendour is best appreciated by car. (p273)

Walking Beaches

⊙ **Portsalon** Ireland's most beautiful beach. (p274)

⊙ **Enniscrone** The 5km Hollow is probably Sligo's most beautiful beach.

⊙ **Mullaghmore** Sligo's only Blue Flag beach has safe shallow waters lapping up to its sweeping arc of golden sand.

⊙ **Tramore** This stunning beach was recently voted the second-best walking beach in Ireland. (p270)

⊙ **Trá na Rossan** A gorgeous, secluded beach just by the village of Carrigart.

Historic Sites

⊙ **Glencolumbcille** Ruins of a 6th-century monastic settlement. (p267)

⊙ **Carrowkeel Megalithic Cemetery** Cairns, dolmens and graves from the late Stone Age. (p260)

⊙ **Carrowmore Megalithic Cemetery** Ireland's largest Stone Age cemetery. (p259)

⊙ **Glenveagh National Park** Where the pain of Irish history still resonates. (p272)

⊙ **Grianán of Aileách** A pre-Celtic site with an amphitheatre-shaped stone fort. (p276)

Restaurants

o **Olde Glen Bar & Restaurant** Low ceilings, slate floor, great beer... perfect. (p273)

o **Mill Restaurant & Guesthouse** Old converted flax mill, now a superb restaurant. (p270)

o **Beach House** Cafe that takes surf-and-turf to a whole new level of goodness. (p275)

Need to Know

ADVANCE PLANNING

o **Two months before** Learn some basic Irish words to impress in Donegal's Gaeltacht.

o **One month before** Book a surf lesson.

o **Two weeks before** Check out the weather forecast, then ignore it.

o **Upon arrival** Realise that Donegal Irish sounds nothing like what you heard on those tapes.

RESOURCES

o **Donegal Tourism** (www.donegaldirect.ie) Donegal Tourism's official website.

o **Fáilte Ireland** (www. discoverireland.ie) The national tourism authority.

o **John McGinley Bus** (www.johnmcginley.com) Bus operator serving northwestern Donegal from Dublin.

GETTING AROUND

o **Bus** There are excellent national services to main towns. You'll have to rely on private operators for transport between smaller towns.

o **Train** Good for Sligo, but service in Donegal is nonexistent.

o **Car** The best way of getting around; watch out for sheep and boy racers!

BE FOREWARNED

o **Roads** Tortuous winding narrow roads can make travel in the northwest quite slow so it's a good thing there's plenty of scenery to keep you occupied!

o **Seasonal tourism** Many hotels and restaurants shut down between December and Easter.

o **Weather** Warm, sunny summers and ferocious winters make the northwest a place of extremes.

Left: Glengesh Pass (p265);
Above: Poisoned Glen (p269)

(LEFT) STEPHEN SAKS/GETTY IMAGES ©;
(ABOVE) GARETH McCORMACK/GETTY IMAGES ©

Counties Sligo & Donegal Itineraries

Two neighbouring counties, two distinct personalities: the first itinerary explores the artistically inspiring Sligo, the other gives you the best of awe-inspiring Donegal, so wild in parts that art just can't imitate nature.

ROSGUILL PENINSULA

DUNFANAGHY ⑤

⑦

⑧ **BUNCRANA**

⑥

GLENVEAGH NATIONAL PARK

IRELAND

④ **GLENCOLUMBCILLE**

NORTHERN IRELAND

③

① **DONEGAL**

SLIEVE LEAGUE

② **ROSSNOWLAGH**

COUNTY SLIGO GOLF COURSE ③

② **DRUMCLIFF**

① **SLIGO**

STRANDHILL ④

⑥ **CARROWMORE**

IRELAND

CARROWKEEL ⑤

5 DAYS

DONEGAL TOWN TO BUNCRANA
DELIGHTS OF DONEGAL

Five days is barely enough time to make a dent in what Donegal has to offer, but the following itinerary should whet your appetite for a longer visit. Start in the southwest, perhaps basing yourself in ① **Donegal Town** (p263) for visits to the beach at ② **Rossnowlagh** (p264) – a surfing mecca for beginners and advanced surfers alike – and the sea cliffs at ③ **Slieve League** (p266), best appreciated from below aboard a tour boat. On day three, move in a northwesterly arc around the county, checking out the monastic ruins at ④ **Glencolumbcille** (p267)before heading toward ⑤ **Dunfanaghy** (p269), which is a fine base from which to explore the county's northern coasts. Your remaining two days could include ⑥ **Glenveagh National Park** (p272) and the ⑦ **Rosguill Peninsula's** (p273) superbly scenic Atlantic Drive. Finally, the remote beauty of the Inishowen Peninsula will leave you in Ireland's northernmost point; the seaside resort of ⑧ **Buncrana** (p274) is very popular with summer visitors from Derry, but in the off-season it is a quiet resort.

Top Left: Donegal Town (p263);
Top Right: *WB Yeats* statue, Sligo Town (p258)

(TOP LEFT) © RICK STRANGE/ALAMY; (TOP RIGHT) WB YEATS 1990 BY ROWAN GILLESPIE.
BRONZE, HEIGHT 240CM; WAYNE WALTON/GETTY IMAGES ©

5 DAYS

SLIGO TOWN & AROUND
SLIGO SURROUNDS

The northwest's most dynamic town is unquestionably ❶ **Sligo Town** (p258), a pleasant spot on the River Garavogue that has its own distractions but is also a fine base from which to explore the surrounding area. The Yeats connection is everywhere, from the room devoted to the two brothers, poet and dramatist William Butler and painter Jack Butler, in the Sligo County Museum, to WB Yeats' final resting place in ❷ **Drumcliff** (p262), under the shadow of the memorable Benbulben, carefully chosen by Yeats so as to forever reside in the shadow of the distinctive peak. You can appreciate the majesty of the mountain and spoil a good walk by playing the stunning ❸ **County Sligo Golf Course** (p259), designed in such a way that almost every hole is in view of the peak. Unwind by immersing yourself in a traditional seaweed bath in ❹ **Strandhill** before returning to Sligo Town, but don't forget the county's prehistoric heritage, at ❺ **Carrowkeel** (p260) and ❻ **Carrowmore** (p259).

Discover Counties Sligo & Donegal

COUNTY SLIGO

Sligo Town

POP 17,600

Pedestrian streets lined with inviting shop fronts, stone bridges spanning the River Garavogue, and *céilidh* (traditional music and dancing) sessions spilling from pubs contrast with contemporary art and glass towers rising from prominent corners of compact Sligo. It makes a good and low-key choice for exploring Yeats country.

◎ Sights

Sligo County Museum   Museum
(Stephen St; ⊙9.30am-12.30pm & 2-4.45pm Tue-Sat May-Sep, 9.30am-12.30pm Tue-Sat Oct-Apr) **FREE** The major draw of Sligo's county museum is the Yeats room, which features photographs, letters and news-paper cuttings connected with WB Yeats, as well as drawings by Jack B Yeats.

✸ Festivals

Tread Softly   Cultural
(www.yeats-sligo.com; ⊙late Jul) Part of Sligo's 'Season of Yeats', this series of events over two weeks celebrates the iconic man with tours, perfromances and more.

🛏 Sleeping

Sligo City Hotel   Hotel €€
(☏071-914 4000; www.sligocityhotel.com; Quay St; r from €60; 🛜) Recently renovated, this four-storey hotel could not be better located. The 60 rooms have a simple

River Garavogue, Sligo Town
GARETH MCCORMACK/GETTY IMAGES ©

Sligo Town

corporate colour scheme. The manager wins plaudits for helpfulness.

🍴 Eating

Source   Irish €€

(☏ 071-914 7605; www.sourcesligo.ie; 1 John St; mains €11-23; ⏱ restaurant 9.30am-9pm Mon-Sat, wine bar 3pm-late Wed-Sat; 🛜)
High-profile Source champions local suppliers and food-stuffs. Arty photos of its favourite fishermen, farmers and cheese producers grace the walls of the buzzy ground-floor restaurant with its open kitchen, while upstairs the **wine bar** serves tipples from the owners' vineyard in France and plates of Irish-style tapas. The top floor is a **cookery school**.

ℹ️ Getting There & Away

Bus

Bus Éireann (☏ 071-916 0066; www.buseireann. ie; Lord Edward St) leaves from the bus station situated below the train station. Destinations include Ballina (€16, 1½ hours, one daily), Westport (€20, two hours, one daily) and Donegal town €14, one hour, seven daily). Local buses run to Strandhill and to Rosses Point.

Train

Trains leave the station for Dublin (€22, three hours, seven daily) via Boyle, Carrick-on-Shannon and Mullingar.

Around Sligo Town

ROSSES POINT

POP 830

Rosses Point is a picturesque seaside town with grassy dunes rolling down to the golden strand. Benbulben (525m), Sligo's most recognisable landmark, looms in the distance. Offshore, the unusual – and jaunty – 1821 **Metal Man** beacon points the way into harbour. In the distance are ride-free **Coney Island** and **Oyster Island**.

Rosses Point has two wonderful **beaches** and one of Ireland's most challenging and renowned golf links, **County Sligo Golf Course** (www.countysligogolfclub.ie; green fees €45-95; ⏱ Apr-Oct), which attracts golfers from all over the world. Fringed by the Atlantic and lying in the shadow of Benbulben, this is possibly Ireland's greatest and most picturesque golf links.

Rosses Point is 8km northwest of Sligo on the R291. There are regular buses from Sligo.

CARROWMORE MEGALITHIC CEMETERY

One of the largest Stone Age cemeteries in Europe, **Carrowmore** (www.heritageireland.ie; adult/child €3/1; ⏱ 10am-6pm Easter- early Oct, final admission 5pm) is slowly getting the fame it deserves and is truly a must-see Sligo attraction.

Some 60 monuments including stone circles, passage tombs and dolmens adorn the rolling hills of this haunting site, which is thought to pre-date Newgrange in County Meath by 700 years. Although over the centuries, many of the stones have been destroyed, ongoing excavations continue to uncover more sites both within the public site and on adjoining private land.

To get here, follow the N4 south from Sligo for 5km and follow the signposts.

South of Sligo Town

RIVERSTOWN

The endearing **Sligo Folk Park** (☏ 071-916 5001; www.sligofolkpark.com; Millview House; adult/child €6/4; ☺ 10am-5pm May-Sep) revolves around a restored 19th-century cottage. Humble, thatched structures complement this centrepiece, along with scattered farm tools and other old things. A peacock sounds off as he strolls.

For more heritage charm, albeit with a heavy dose of posh, head for **Coopershill House** (☏ 071-916 5108; www.coopershill.com; Riverstown; s/d from €145/220; ☺ Apr-Oct; @) an idyllic Georgian retreat in an estate alive with wildflowers, birdsong and deer. Most of the eight bedrooms have original antiques and oil paintings. It's been in the same family since it was built in 1774. Drinking water comes from its own spring.

Riverstown is 2km east of the N4 at Drumfin.

CARROWKEEL MEGALITHIC CEMETERY

With a bird's-eye view of the county from high in the Bricklieve Mountains, it's little wonder this hilltop **site** was sacred in prehistoric times. This windswept and lonely location is simultaneously eerie and uplifting. But for a few sheep (you drive though a sheep gate), it's undeveloped and spectacular. Dotted with around 14 cairns, dolmens and the scattered remnants of other graves, the site dates from the late Stone Age (3000 to 2000 BC).

Carrowmore Megalithic Cemetery (p259)

GARETH MCCORMACK/GETTY IMAGES ©

Just the sweeping views down to South Sligo county from the car park make the journey worthwhile. It's a 1km walk to the first ancient site, Cairn G. Above its entrance is a roof-box aligned with the midsummer sunset which illuminates the inner chamber. The only other such roof-box known in Ireland is that at Newgrange in County Meath. Everywhere you look across the surrounding hills you'll see evidence of early life here, including about 140 stone circles, all that remain of the foundations of a large village thought to have been inhabited by the builders of the tombs.

Carrowkeel is closer to Boyle than Sligo town. It's about 5km from either the R295 in the west or the N4 in the east. Follow the signs.

LOUGH GILL

The mirrorlike 'Lake of Brightness', Lough Gill was a place of great inspiration for Yeats.

The lake, southeast of Sligo town, is shaded by two magical swaths of woodland, **Hazelwood** and **Slish Wood**, which have loop trails; there are good views of Innisfree Island from the latter.

You can take a **cruise** on the lake from atmospheric Parke's Castle, in nearby County Leitrim.

🛈 Getting There & Away

The lake is immediately east of Sligo town. Take the R286 along the north shore for the most interesting views, whether you are driving or riding. The southern route on the R287 is less interesting until you reach Dooney Rock.

Dooney Rock

Immortalised by Yeats in *The Fiddler of Dooney*, this huge fissured limestone knoll bulges awkwardly upward by the lough's southern shore. There's a great lake view from the top.

It's 7km southwest of Sligo town on the R287.

Innisfree Island

This pint-sized island lies tantalisingly close to the lough's southeastern shore,

Local Knowledge

Yeats' Sligo

RECOMMENDATIONS BY IAN KENNEDY, DIRECTOR OF THE YEATS SOCIETY.

1 **DRUMCLIFFE CHURCH**
On the site of an ancient monastery founded by Columbcille, Drumcliffe was where Yeats wanted to be buried, in the shadow of Benbulben and in the church yard where his ancestor had once been rector. Although he died in 1939, his wishes weren't fulfilled until almost a decade later, when he was given a state funeral.

2 **LOUGH GILL**
Stretching from Dromahair, Co. Leitrim to Sligo Bay a tour of Lough Gill, by boat, bus or car, is a great way to see some of the places associated with Yeats. View the beauty of the hillside of Dooney Rock, Slish Wood, Innisfree and Hazelwood.

3 **ROSSES POINT**
The Yeats family spent many summer holidays in Rosses Point. The most notable landmark associated with the family is the ivy-clad ruin of Elsinore Lodge, built by local smuggler John 'Black' Jack and later occupied by Yeats' cousin Henry Middleton. It's next to Sligo Yacht Club overlooking Sligo Bay.

4 **INNISFREE**
It was while walking down Fleet Street in London that WB Yeats was inspired by the sound of a fountain with the immortal lines that would become his signature poem, the *Lake Isle of Innisfree*. Innisfree, that place where *peace comes dropping slow*, is a small uninhabited Island on Lough Gill.

5 **DOONEY ROCK**
The inspiration for the poem *The Fiddler of Dooney*, Dooney Rock is on the road from Carraroe to Ballintogher. Along the way is Tobernalt, a holy well that was used in penal times to secretly baptise Catholics. Yeats drew huge inspiration from walking the woods in the area.

Detour:
Drumcliff & Benbulben

A stolid greenish-grey eminence visible all along Sligo's northern coast, **Benbulben** (525m), often written Ben Bulben, resembles a table covered by a pleated cloth: its limestone plateau is uncommonly flat, and its near-vertical sides are scored by earthen ribs. Walking here is not for the uninitiated.

Benbulben's beauty was not lost on WB Yeats. Before the poet died in Menton, France, in 1939, he had requested: 'If I die here, bury me up there on the mountain, and then after a year or so, dig me up and bring me privately to Sligo'. His wishes were honoured in 1948, when his body was interred in the churchyard at **Drumcliff**, where his great-grandfather had been rector.

Yeats' grave is next to the doorway of the Protestant church, and his youthful bride Georgie Hyde-Lee is buried alongside. Almost three decades her senior, Yeats was 52 when they married. The poet's epitaph is from his poem 'Under Ben Bulben':

> Cast a cold eye
> On life, on death.
> Horseman, pass by!

There's a small **cafe and crafts shop** (mains from €4; ⊙9am-5pm) beside the church. It is popular with locals at lunch and has a good selection of books. Nearby is a fine little gallery.

In the 6th century, St Colmcille chose this location for a monastery. You can still see the stumpy remains of a round tower, which was struck by lightning in 1396, on the main road nearby. Also in the churchyard is an extraordinary 9th-century high cross, etched with intricate biblical scenes that include Adam and Eve as well as Daniel in the Lion's Den.

Buses run from Sligo to Drumcliff (€5, 10 minutes, seven to eight daily) and stop at the post office.

but alas, can't be accessed. Still, it's visible from the shore. Its air of tranquillity so moved Yeats that he famously wrote *The Lake Isle of Innisfree*:

> I will arise and go now, and go to Innisfree,
> And a small cabin build there, of clay and wattles made;
> Nine bean rows will I have there, a hive for the honey bee,
> And live alone in the bee-loud glade.

Access the best vantage point of the island from a small road that starts at the junction of the R287 and the R290. Follow the winding lane for 4.2km to a small parking area by the water.

COUNTY DONEGAL

ⓘ Getting There & Away

Donegal Airport (www.donegalairport.ie) Runs flights to and from Dublin (50 minutes, two daily) and to Glasgow Prestwick (50 minutes, four weekly). The airport is about 3km northwest of Annagry on the northwestern coast. There's no public transport to the airport, but there are car-rental desks in the terminal.

City of Derry Airport (www.cityofderryairport. com) Just beyond the county's eastern border, in Northern Ireland.

Donegal Town

Pretty Donegal town occupies a strategic spot at the mouth of Donegal Bay. With a backdrop of the Blue Stack Mountains, a handsome and well-preserved castle, friendly locals and a good choice of places to eat and sleep, it makes an excellent base for exploring the wild coastline nearby.

Sights & Activities

Donegal Castle Historic Building
(www.heritageireland.ie; Castle St; adult/child €4/2; ⏰10am-6pm daily Easter–mid-Sep, 9.30am-4.30pm Thu-Mon mid-Sep–Easter)
Guarding a picturesque bend of the River Eske, Donegal Castle remains an imperious monument to both Irish and English might.

Built by the O'Donnells in 1474, it served as the seat of their formidable power until 1607, when the English decided to rid themselves of pesky Irish chieftains once and for all. Rory O'Donnell was no pushover, though, torching his own castle before fleeing to France in the infamous Flight of the Earls. Their defeat paved the way for the Plantation of Ulster by thousands of newly arrived Scots and English Protestants, sowing the seeds of the divisions that still afflict Ireland to this day.

The castle was rebuilt in 1623 by Sir Basil Brooke, along with the adjacent three-storey Jacobean house. Further restoration in the 1990s has made it a wonderfully atmospheric place to visit, with rooms furnished with French tapestries and Persian rugs. There are guided tours every hour.

Sleeping & Eating

Ard na Breatha B&B €€
(☎074-972 2288; www.ardnabreatha.com; Drumrooske Middle; d/f €118/139; ⏰Feb-Oct; 🛜) In an elevated setting 1.5km north of town, this boutique guesthouse on a working farm has tasteful rooms with pine furniture and wrought-iron beds. It's an incredibly warm and welcoming place, with a full bar and restaurant (three-course dinner €39).

Food is organic and sourced from the farm or its neighbours where possible. Dinner is available at least Friday to Sunday by reservation.

Olde Castle Bar Seafood €€
(☎074-972 1262; www.oldecastlebar.com; Castle St; mains €9-24; ⏰bar noon-8pm; 👶) This old-world boozer just off the Diamond serves upmarket pub classics such as venison pie, Donegal Bay oysters, Irish stew, seafood platters and good old bacon and cabbage. The restaurant opens at weekends and has excellent seafood and steaks; the two-course early-bird menu (6pm to 8pm) costs €20 .

Getting There & Away

Bus Éireann (☎074-913 1008; www.buseireann. ie) Services connect Donegal with Sligo (€14.50, one hour, six daily), Galway (€20, four hours, four daily), Killybegs (€8.50, 35 minutes, three daily), Derry (€17, 1½ hours, seven Monday to Saturday, six Sunday) and Dublin (€21, 4½ hours, nine daily). The bus stop is on the western side of the Diamond.

Feda O'Donnell (☎074-954 8114; www. fedaodonnell.com) Buses run to Galway (€20, four hours, twice daily, three on Friday and Sunday) via Bundoran and Sligo (€12). Call to

Donegal

If You Like...
Beaches

If you like the beach at Rossnowlagh, you should explore some other beaches along Donegal's wild and rugged coastline:

1 TRAMORE
Hike through the dunes west of Dunfanaghy and you'll be rewarded with pristine sands on this secluded stretch of coast.

2 CARRICK FINN
A gorgeous sweep of undeveloped sand near Donegal Airport.

3 PORTNOO
A wishbone-shaped sheltered cove backed by undulating hills on the Loughrea Peninsula.

4 BALLYMASTOCKER BAY
An idyllic stretch of sand lapped by turquoise water.

5 CULDAFF
A long stretch of golden sand on the Inishowen Peninsula, popular with families.

confirm departure point. Heading north, buses call at Dungloe, Gweedore and Dunfanaghy (all €10).

Around Donegal Town
LOUGH ESKE

Almost surrounded by the Blue Stack Mountains, tranquil Lough Eske is a scenic spot perfect for walking, cycling or fishing. Lough Eske translates as 'Lake of the Fish' and is a popular angling centre. The season runs from May to September and there's a purpose-built angling centre on the shore where you can buy permits and hire boats.

There is no public transport to the lake.

Sleeping & Eating

Lough Eske Castle — Hotel €€€
(☎ 074-972 5100; www.solisloughneskecastle. com; Lough Eske; d from €245; ☒ closed Sun-Wed Nov-Mar; @ ☎ ☒) Set in vast grounds, this imposing 19th-century castle was all but razed by fire in 1939 but has been painstakingly rebuilt and restored and is now the epitome of elegant country living. Most of the complex, including the minimalist rooms, decadent spa and smart restaurant, is spanking new but exudes a sense of classic sophistication mixed with impeccable contemporary style.

ROSSNOWLAGH
POP 50

Rossnowlagh's spectacular 3km-long Blue Flag beach is a broad, sandy stretch of heaven that attracts families, surfers, kitesurfers and walkers throughout the year. The gentle rollers are great for learning to surf or honing your skills, and Ireland's largest and longest-running surfing competition, the **Rossnowlagh Intercounty Surf Contest**, is held here in late October. It's popularly known as the most sociable event in Ireland's surfing calendar.

Sights & Activities

Franciscan Friary — Monastery
(www.franciscans.ie; ☒ 10am-8pm Mon-Sat) FREE Hidden deep in a forest at the southern end of the beach, this modern friary is set in beautiful, tranquil gardens which are open to the public. There's also a small museum and a wonderful signed walk, The Way of the Cross, which meanders up a hillside smothered with rhododendrons for spectacular views.

Fin McCool Surf School — Surfing
(☎ 071-985 9020; www.finmccoolsurfschool. com; Beach Rd; gear rental per 3hr €29, 2hr lesson incl gear €35; ☒ 10am-7pm daily Easter-Oct, 10am-7pm Sat & Sun mid-Mar–Easter & Nov-Christmas) Tuition, gear rental and

SLAWEK STASZCZUK/GETTY IMAGES ©

★ Don't Miss
The Glengesh Pass

A remote, 25km single-track road leads from Glencolumbcille to Ardara via the **Glengesh Pass** (Glean Géis; meaning 'Glen of the Swans'), one of Donegal's most scenic driving routes; the cascade of hairpin bends descending into the head of the glen is almost alpine in appearance.

On the northern coast of the Glencolumbcille peninsula, 9km west of Ardara, tiny **Maghery** has a picturesque waterfront. If you follow the strand westward, you'll get to a rocky promontory full of caves. During Cromwell's 17th-century destruction, 100 villagers sought refuge here but all except one were discovered and massacred. About 1.5km east of Maghery is the enchanting **Assarancagh Waterfall**.

accommodation are available at this friendly surf lodge run by Pro Tour surf judge Neil Britton with the help of his extended family, most of who have competed on the international circuit. The three- and four-bed dorms cost €20 per night, doubles €50.

🛏 Sleeping

Smugglers Creek　　　B&B **€€**
(☎071-985 2367; www.smugglerscreekinn. com; Cliff Rd; s/d from €45/70; ☺daily Apr- Sep, Thu-Sun Oct-Mar; 🛜) This combined pub-restaurant-guesthouse perches on the hillside above the bay. It's justifiably popular for its excellent food (mains €13-25) and sweeping views (room 4 has the best vantage point and a balcony into the bargain).

There's live music on summer weekends.

ℹ Getting There & Away

Rossnowlagh is 17km southwest of Donegal town; there's no public transport.

GARETH MCCORMACK/GETTY IMAGES ©

★ Don't Miss
Slieve League

The Cliffs of Moher get more publicity, but the cliffs of **Slieve League** are higher. In fact, these spectacular polychrome cliffs are thought to be the highest in Europe, plunging some 600m to the sea (although they're not vertical). Looking down, you'll see two rocks nicknamed the 'school desk and chair' for reasons that are immediately obvious.

The narrow road beyond the Slieve League Cliffs Centre (being widened at the time of research) leads to the lower car park beside a gate in the road; you can drive another 1.5km beyond the gate (cars only) to the upper car park (often full) right beside the viewpoint. The cliffs are particularly scenic at sunset when the waves crash dramatically far below and the ocean reflects the last rays of the day.

From the upper car park, a rough and eroded footpath leads up and along the top of the near-vertical cliffs to the aptly named **One Man's Pass**, a narrow ridge that leads to the summit of Slieve League (595m; 10km round trip). Be aware that mist and rain can roll in unexpectedly and rapidly, making conditions treacherous.

It's also possible to hike to the summit of Slieve League from Carrick via the **Pilgrim Path** (signposted along the minor road on the right before the Slieve League cliffs road), returning via One Man's Pass and the viewpoint road (12km; allow four to six hours).

Sightseeing boat trips along the Slieve League cliffs can be arranged by contacting **Nuala Star Teelin** (☎074-973 9365; www.sliabhleagueboattrips.com; ☺Apr-Oct). Prices are €20 to €25 per person, depending on numbers, with reductions for children. Boats depart from Teelin pier every two hours (weather permitting). Sea angling and diving trips can also be arranged.

BUNDORAN
POP 2140

Blinking amusement arcades, hurdy-gurdy fairground rides and fast-food diners are Bundoran's stock-in-trade. But Donegal's best-known seaside resort also has superb surf, and attracts a mixed crowd of young families, pensioners and beach dudes. Outside summer, the carnival atmosphere abates and the town can be quite desolate.

···

Southwestern Donegal

KILCAR, CARRICK & AROUND
POP 260

Kilcar (Cill Chártha) and its more attractive neighbour Carrick (An Charraig) are good bases for exploring the breathtaking coastline of southwestern Donegal, especially the stunning sea cliffs at Slieve League.

Bus Éireann services run from Donegal to Kilcar (€9.80) and from Kilcar to Carrick (€2.90) and Glencolumbcille (€5.50) three times daily Monday to Saturday and once on Sunday.

GLENCOLUMBCILLE & AROUND
POP 255

'There's nothing feckin' here!' say the locals, in an endearingly blunt forewarning to visitors. But once you've sampled Glencolumbcille's three-pub village, scalloped beaches, stunning walks and fine little folk museum, chances are you'll disagree.

Approaching Glencolumbcille (Gleann Cholm Cille) via the Glengesh Pass does, however, reinforce just how isolated this starkly beautiful coastal haven is. You drive past miles and miles of hills and bogs before

the ocean appears, followed by a narrow, green valley and the small Gaeltacht village within it. This spot has been inhabited since 3000 BC and you'll find lots of Stone Age remains scattered among the cluster of tiny settlements.

ARDARA
POP 570

Gateway to the switchbacks of the Glengesh Pass, the heritage town of Ardara (arda-rah) is the heart of Donegal's tweed and knitwear industry. You can visit the weavers at work and see the region's most traditional crafts in action.

◉ Sights

Ardara Heritage Centre Museum
(☏ 074-954 1704; Main St; adult/child €3/1.20; ☺10am-6pm Mon-Sat, 2-6pm Sun Easter-Sep) Set in the old courthouse, this centre traces the story of Donegal tweed from sheep shearing to dye production and weaving. A weaver is usually present to demonstrate how a loom works and explain the stitches used in traditional garments.

Lough Eske (p264) and the Blue Stack Mountains
GARETH MCCORMACK/GETTY IMAGES ©

Right: Coastal fields, Dunfanaghy;
Below: Ruined church, Poisoned Glen

(RIGHT) TRISH PUNCH/GETTY IMAGES ©; (BELOW) RELIGIOUS IMAGES/UIG/GETTY IMAGES ©

the best place in town for a sociable pint or two.

🛏 Sleeping & Eating

Gort na Móna   B&B €€
(📞074-953 7777; www.gortnamonabandb.com; Donegal Rd, Cronkeerin; s/d €50/70; 🛜) Huge but cosy and colourful rooms with ortho-paedic mattresses, knotty pine furniture and silky throws make this a real home from home. With excellent home baking and preserves for breakfast, mountain views and a pristine beach just down the road, you won't want to leave. Gort na Móna is 2km southeast of town on the old Donegal road.

Nancy's Bar   Irish €
(Front St; mains €7-13) This old-fashioned pub-restaurant, in the same family for seven generations, makes its guests feel as if they're sitting in Nancy's living room. It serves superb seafood and chowder with hearty wheaten bread and is also

🔒 Shopping

Signs in the town centre point you to the town's knitwear producers.

Eddie Doherty   Clothing
(www.handwoventweed.com; Front St) Behind Doherty's bar, you can usually catch Eddie Doherty hand-weaving here on a traditional loom.

John Molloy   Clothing
(www.johnmolloy.com; Killybegs Rd) Handmade and machine-knitted woollies are availa-ble here at the flagship establishment and at the factory outlet in Glencolumbcille.

Kennedy's   Clothing
(Front St) In business for over a century, Kennedy's helped establish Ardara's reputation as a sweater mecca.

Northwestern Donegal

DUNLEWEY & AROUND

POP 700

Blink and chances are you'll miss the tiny hamlet of Dunlewey (Dún Lúiche). You won't miss the spectacular scenery, however, or quartzite cone of Errigal Mountain, whose craggy peak dominates the surrounding area. Plan enough time to get out of your car and do some walking here, as it's a magical spot.

🏃 Activities

Poisoned Glen   Walking

Legend has it that the huge ice-carved hollow of the Poisoned Glen got its sinister name when the ancient one-eyed giant king of Tory, Balor, was killed here by his exiled grandson, Lughaidh, whereupon the poison from his eye split the rock and poisoned the glen. The less interesting truth, however, lies in a cartographic gaffe.

Locals were inspired to name it An Gleann Neamhe (The Heavenly Glen), but when an English cartographer mapped the area, he carelessly marked it An Gleann Neimhe – The Poisoned Glen.

Two kilometres east of the Dunlewey Lakeside Centre turn-off, a minor road leads down through the hamlet of Dunlewey, past a ruined church, to limited roadside parking at a hairpin bend. From here, a rough walking path leads into the rocky fastness of the glen (4km round-trip). Watch out for the green lady – the resident ghost!

DUNFANAGHY & AROUND

The attractive little town of Dunfanaghy, clustered along the southern shore of a sandly inlet, is at the centre of one of the most varied and attractive parts of Donegal. Moors and meadows, sea cliffs and sandy beaches, forest and lake lie scattered below the humpbacked hill of Muckish, all waiting to be explored.

⊙ Sights

Horn Head
Viewpoint

The towering headland of Horn Head has spectacular coastal scenery, with dramatic quartzite cliffs, topped with bog and heather, rearing over 180m high. The narrow road from Dunfanaghy ends at a small parking area. where you can walk 150m to a WWII lookout point or 1.5km to Horn Head proper. On a fine day you'll encounter tremendous views of Tory, Inishbofin, Inishdooey and tiny Inishbeg islands to the west; Sheep Haven Bay and the Rosguill Peninsula to the east; Malin Head to the northeast; and the coast of Scotland beyond. Take care in bad weather as the cliff edge can be perilous.

Beaches
Beaches

The wide, sandy and virtually empty **Killahoey Beach** leads right into the heart of Dunfanaghy village. **Marble Hill Strand**, about 5km east of town in Port-na-Blagh, is backed by static caravans and is often crammed in summer. Reaching Dunfanaghy's loveliest beach, **Tramore**, requires hiking through the grassy dunes to the west of the village.

🛏 Sleeping & Eating

Whins
B&B €€

(📞 074-913 6481; www.thewhins.com; Dunfanaghy; s/d €52/74; 📶) 🅿 The colourful rooms have patchwork quilts, quality furniture and a real sense of character. A wide choice of superb breakfasts is served upstairs in a room with a view towards Horn Head. The B&B is about 750m east of the town centre opposite the golf course.

Mill Restaurant & Guesthouse
Irish €€€

(📞 074-913 6985; www.themillrestaurant.com; Figart, Dunfanaghy; 4-course dinner €41; ⊙dinner Tue-Sun mid-Mar-mid-Dec) An exquisite country setting and perfectly composed meals make dining at this restaurant a treat. Set in an old flax mill that was for many years the home of renowned watercolour artist Frank Eggington, it also has six high-class guest rooms (singles/doubles €60/96). The mill is just south of town on the N56 road. Book in advance.

ℹ Getting There & Away

Feda O'Donnell (📞 074-954 8114; www.feda.ie) Buses between Crolly (€7, 40 minutes) and Galway (€20, five hours) stop in Dunfanaghy Sq twice daily Monday to Saturday and three times on Friday and Sunday.

John McGinley (📞 074-913 5201; www.johnmcginley.com) Buses stop in Dunfanaghy two to four times daily en route to Letterkenny (€5, one hour) and Dublin (€22, five hours).

Lough Swilly (📞 028-7126 2017; www.loughswillybusco.com) The Derry–Dungloe bus (change at Letterkenny) calls at Dunfanaghy once daily Monday to Friday (£10, two to three hours).

Horn Head

GARETH MCCORMACK/GETTY IMAGES ©

GARETH MCCORMACK/GETTY IMAGES ©

★ Don't Miss
Errigal Mountain

The pinkish-grey quartzite peak of Errigal Mountain (752m) dominates the landscape of northwestern Donegal, appearing conical from some angles, from others like a ragged shark's fin ripping through the heather bogs. Its name comes from the Gaelic *earagail,* meaning 'oratory', as its shape brings to mind a preacher's pulpit.

Its looming presence seems to dare walkers to attempt the strenuous but satisfying climb to its pyramid-shaped summit. If you're keen to take on the challenge, pay close attention to the weather: it can be a dangerous climb on windy or wet days, when the mountain is shrouded in cloud and visibility is minimal.

The easiest route to the summit, a steep and badly eroded path, begins at a parking area on the R251, about 2km east of Dunlewey hamlet (4.5km round-trip; allow three hours). Details are available at the **Dunlewey Lakeside Centre** (Ionad Cois Locha; ☏ 074-953 1699; www.dunleweycentre.com; Dunlewey; cottage or boat trip adult/child/family €5.95/3.95/14, combined ticket €10/7/15; ⏱10.30am-6pm Mon-Sat, 11am-6pm Sun Easter-Oct; 👫).

....

Central Donegal

LOUGH GARTAN

The patriarch of Irish monasticism, **St Colmcille** (Columba), was born in the 6th century in a lovely setting near glassy Lough Gartan, where some relics associated with the saint can be seen. The lake is 17km northwest of Letterkenny; it's beautiful driving country, but you won't be able to get here on public transport.

CLAIRE TAKACS/GETTY IMAGES ©

⭐ Don't Miss
Glenveagh National Park

Lakes shimmer like dew in the mountainous valley of **Glenveagh National Park** (Páirc Náisiúnta Ghleann Bheatha; www.glenveaghnationalpark.ie) FREE. Alternating between great knuckles of rock, green-gold swaths of bog and scatterings of oak and birch forest, the 16,500-sq-km protected area is magnificent walking country. Its wealth of wildlife includes the golden eagle, which was hunted to extinction here in the 19th century but reintroduced in 2000.

The **Glenveagh Visitor Centre** (☎074-913 7090; ⊗9am-6pm Mar-Oct, to 5pm Nov-Feb) has a 20-minute audiovisual display on the ecology of the park and the infamous Adair. The **cafe** (⊗Easter & Jun-Sep) serves hot food and snacks, and the reception sells the necessary midge repellent, as vital in summer as walking boots and waterproofs are in winter. Camping is not allowed.

The delightfully showy **Glenveagh Castle** (adult/child €5/2) was modelled on Scotland's Balmoral Castle. Access is by guided tour only; tours last 30 minutes and take in a series of flamboyantly decorated rooms that remain as if McIlhenny has just stepped out. The most eye-catching, including the tartan-and-antler-covered music room and the pink candy-striped room demanded by Greta Garbo whenever she stayed here, are in the round tower.

The last guided tours of the castle leave about 45 minutes before closing time. Cars are not allowed beyond the Glenveagh Visitor Centre; you can walk or cycle the scenic 3.6km route to the castle or take the shuttle bus (€3 return, every 15 minutes).

⊙ Sights

Glebe House & Gallery Gallery

(www.heritageireland.ie; Church Hill; adult/child €3/1; ⊙11am-6.30pm daily Easter & Jul-Aug, Sat-Thu Jun & Sep) The English painter Derrick Hill bought this historic house in 1953, providing him with a mainland base close to his beloved Tory Island. Before Hill arrived, the house served as a rectory and then a hotel. The 1828-built mansion is sumptuously decorated with an evident love of all things exotic, but its real appeal is Hill's astonishing art collection. In addition to paintings by Hill and Tory Island's 'naive' artists are works by Picasso, Landseer, Hokusai, Jack B Yeats and Kokoschka. The woodland gardens are also wonderful. A guided tour of the house takes about 45 minutes.

....

Northeastern Donegal

ROSGUILL PENINSULA

The best way to appreciate Rosguill's rugged splendour is by driving, cycling or even walking the 15km **Atlantic Drive**, a waymarked loop on minor roads signposted to your left as you come into the sprawling village of **Carrigart** (Carraig Airt) from the south. The sea views are superb, if you can ignore the creeping blight of holiday homes and static caravans.

⊕ Activities

Rosapenna Golf Resort Golf

(☎074-915 5000; www.rosapenna.ie; Downings; green fees €80) The scenery at this renowned golf club – designed by St Andrew's Old Tom Morris in 1891 and remodelled by Harry Vardon in 1906 – is as spectacular as the layout, which can challenge even the lowest handicapper.

FANAD PENINSULA

The second-most northerly point in Donegal, Fanad Head thrusts out into the Atlantic to the east of Rosguill. The peninsula curls around the watery

Detour:
Olde Glen Bar & Restaurant

Authentic down to its original 1700s stone floor, the simply marvelous **Olde Glen Bar** (☎074-915 5130; Glen, Carrigart; mains €15-25; ⊙dinner Tue-Sat late May–mid-Sep) serves a sensational pint. Out the back, its small farmhouse-style restaurant serves outstanding blackboard specials. It doesn't take reservations and is popular with locals – turn up by 5.30pm to get a table for the 6pm seating, or by 7pm for a table at the 8pm seating. By the time you leave, you'll feel like a local yourself. Open most weekends out of season, but call to check.

expanses of Mulroy Bay to the west, and Lough Swilly to the east, the latter edged with high cliffs and sandy beaches. Most travellers stick to the peninsula's eastern flank, visiting the beautiful beach and excellent golf course at Portsalon, and the quiet heritage towns of Rathmelton and Rathmullan. Accommodation is relatively limited, so book ahead in summer.

Rathmelton

The first community you come to if you're approaching the peninsula from Derry or Letterkenny is Rathmelton (sometimes called Ramelton), a picture-perfect spot with rows of Georgian houses and rough-walled stone warehouses curving along the River Lennon.

⊕ Sleeping

Frewin House B&B €€€

(☎074-915 1246; www.frewinhouse.com; Rectory Rd; d €110-150, cottage per week €550,

Detour:
Castle Murray

Overlooking the ruins of the 15th-century McSwyne's Castle, **Castle Murray** (☏074-973 7022; www.castlemurray.com; St John's Point; s/d €75/140; ☎) is no castle itself, but a boutique hotel in a sprawling modern beach house. Each of its 10 individually decorated guest rooms is named for townlands contested by 15th-century Scottish clans, but it's best known for its superb French restaurant (four-course dinner €47). Start with the signature prawns and monkfish in garlic butter, move on to mains such as seared Donegal scallops with coconut curry, and finish off with a lime soufflé with gin sorbet. Castle Murray is 1.5km south of Dunkineely (on the N56 between Mountcharles and Killybegs), on a minor road leading to St John's Point.

dinner €45-50; � closed Christmas) This fine Victorian rectory in secluded grounds would make every weepy heroine's dreams come true. The house combines all the character you would expect from a charming period property – antique furniture, well-thumbed books and open fires – with contemporary style. The bedrooms are pretty but uncluttered, dinner is served communally and by candlelight, and the gardens just beg to be walked with a book and a parasol.

Portsalon & Fanad Head

A spectacular rollercoaster of a road hugs the sea cliffs from Rathmullan to Portsalon, passing the early 19th-century **Knockalla Fort**, one of six built to defend against a possible French invasion – the history is told at its companion, **Fort Dunree** (www.dunree.pro.ie; Dunree Head; adult/child €6/4; ☉10.30am-6pm Mon-Sat, 1-6pm Sun Jun-Sep, 10.30am-4.30pm Mon-Fri, 1-6pm Sat & Sun Oct-May) across the lough.

Once named the second most beautiful beach in the world by British newspaper the *Observer*, the tawny-coloured Blue Flag beach of **Ballymastocker Bay**, which is safe for swimming, is the principal draw of tiny Portsalon (Port an tSalainn). For golfers, however, the main attraction is the marvellously scenic **Portsalon Golf Club** (☏074-915 9459; www.portsalongolfclub.com; green fees weekdays/weekends €40/50).

From Portsalon it's another 8km to the lighthouse on the rocky tip of **Fanad Head**, the best part of which is the scenic drive there.

INISHOWEN PENINSULA

The Inishowen Peninsula reaches just far enough into the Atlantic to grab the title of northernmost point on the island of Ireland: Malin Head. It is remote, rugged, desolate and sparsely populated, making it a special and peaceful sort of place. Ancient sites and ruined castles abound, as do traditional thatched cottages that haven't yet been demoted to storage sheds.

Buncrana
POP 3400

On the tame side of the peninsula, Buncrana is a busy but appealing town with its fair share of pubs and a 5km sandy beach on the shores of Lough Swilly. You'll find all the local services you'll need here before heading into the wilds further north.

John Newton, the composer of *Amazing Grace,* was inspired to write his legendary song after his ship the *Greyhound* took refuge in the calm waters of Lough Swilly during a severe storm in 1748. He and his crew were welcomed in Buncrana after their near-death experience and his spiritual journey from slave trader to antislavery campaigner had its beginnings here. He went on to become a prolific hymn writer and later mentored William Wilberforce in his fight against slavery. For more information on the story, visit www.amazinggrace.ie.

🛏 Sleeping & Eating

Westbrook House B&B €€
(📞 074-936 1067; www.westbrookhouse.ie; Westbrook Rd; s/d €40/70; 📶) A handsome Georgian house set in beautiful gardens, Westbrook offers old-world hospitality and charm by the bucket load. Chandeliers, antique furniture and cut glass give it a refined sophistication but the little trinkets and subtle florals make it very much a lived-in and loved home.

Caldra B&B €€
(📞 074-936 3703; www.caldrabandb.com; Lisnakelly; s/d €50/80; 📶 🚃) This large, modern B&B has four spacious rooms ideal for families. Expect impressive fireplaces and gilt mirrors in the common areas but more tranquil contemporary style in the guest rooms. The garden and patio overlook Lough Swilly and the mountains.

Beach House Seafood €€
(📞 074-936 1050; www.thebeachhouse.ie; The Pier, Swilly Rd; lunch mains €11-13, 3-course dinner €30; ⏰ lunch & dinner Jun-Aug, dinner Thu-Sun, lunch Sat & Sun Sep-May; 🚃) With picture windows overlooking the lough, this aptly named cafe-restaurant projects an elegant simplicity. Although the menu is intrinsically simple, the quality and preparation are a cut above: 'surf and turf', for example, comes with fillet steak, crab claws, langoustines and creamy bisque.

Inishowen Peninsula

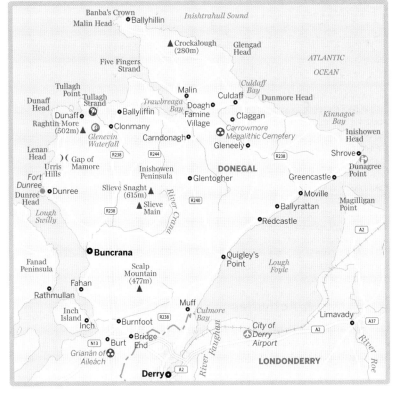

Detour:
Grianán of Aileách

This amphitheatre-like **stone fort** (admission free; ⏱24hr) encircles the top of Grianán Hill like a halo and offers eye-popping views of the surrounding loughs. On clear days you can see as far as Derry. Its mini-arena can resemble a circus whenever a tour bus rolls up and spills its load inside the 4m-thick walls.

The original fort may have existed at least 2000 years ago, but it's thought that the site itself goes back to pre-Celtic times as a temple to the god Dagda. Between the 5th and 12th centuries it was the seat of the O'Neills, before being demolished by Murtogh O'Brien, king of Munster. Most of what you see today is a reconstruction built between 1874 and 1878.

The fort is 18km south of Buncrana near Burt, signposted off the N13.

ⓘ Getting There & Away

Lough Swilly (☎028-7126 2017; www.loughswillybusco.com) Buses run from Buncrana eight times daily Monday to Friday, seven on Saturday and four on Sunday to Derry (€6.50, 1½ hours) and once daily Monday to Saturday to Carndonagh (€6, 45 minutes) via Clonmany (€4.90, 25 minutes) and Ballyliffin (€6, 30 minutes).

Lough Foyle Ferry (☎074-938 1901; www.foyleferry.com) From June to September, a car ferry operates between Buncrana and Rathmullan, with eight crossings a day on weekends only in June and September, daily in July and August. One-way fares for a car/adult/child are €15/3.50/2.50.

CLONMANY & BALLYLIFFIN
POP 700

These two quaint villages and their surrounds have plenty to occupy visitors for a day or two. Clonmany has a working atmosphere and lots of pubs, while Ballyliffin feels more upmarket with more hotels and restaurants. Both have post offices but no banks.

◉ Sights & Activities

Doagh Famine Village   Museum
(☎074-938 1901; www.doaghfaminevillage.com; Doagh Island; adult/child €7/5; ⏱10am-5pm Easter-late Sep) A walk along the dunes north of Ballyliffin brings you to Doagh Island (now part of the mainland), capped by the matchbox ruin of 16th-century Carrickabraghey Castle. Also here is the enthusiastically thrown-together Doagh Famine Village, set in a reconstructed village of thatched cottages. A bit of a coach-tour magnet, it's packed with entertaining titbits about a disappearing way of life, and insightful comparisons with famine-stricken countries today. Call ahead to book the guided tour.

Ballyliffin Golf Club   Golf
(☎074-937 6119; www.ballyliffingolfclub.com; green fees €50-90) With two championship courses, Ballyliffin Golf Club is among the best places to play a round of golf in Donegal. The scenery is so beautiful that it can distract even the most focused golfer. Its above-average restaurant, the **Links** (lunch & dinner mains €10-20), overlooks the fairways.

🛏 Sleeping & Eating

Glen House   B&B €€
(☎074-937 6745; www.glenhouse.ie; Straid, Clonmany; s/d from €55/70; 🛜🚻) Despite the grand surroundings and luxurious rooms, you'll find neither pretension nor high prices at this gem of a guesthouse. The welcome couldn't be friendlier, the rooms are a lesson in restrained sophistication, and the setting is incredibly tranquil. The

walking trail to Glenevin Waterfall starts next door to the **Rose Tea Room** (◷10am-6pm daily Jul-Aug, Sat & Sun Mar-Jun & Sep-Oct), which opens to a timber deck.

ⓘ Getting There & Away

Lough Swilly (☎074-912 2863; www.loughswillybusco.com) Buses run once daily Monday to Saturday between Clonmany and Carndonagh (€2.80, 20 minutes).

MALIN HEAD

Even if you've already seen Ireland's southernmost and westernmost points, you'll still be impressed when you clap your eyes on Malin Head, the island's northern extreme.

On the northernmost tip, called **Banba's Crown**, stands a cumbersome cliff-top **tower** that was built in 1805 by the British admiralty and later used as a Lloyds signal station. Around it are concrete huts that were used by the Irish army in WWII as lookout posts. To the west from the fort-side car park, a path leads to **Hell's Hole**, a chasm where the incoming waters crash against the rocky formations. To the east a longer headland walk leads to the **Wee House of Malin**, a hermit's cave in the cliff face.

The Plantation village of **Malin**, on Trawbreaga Bay, 14km southeast of Malin Head, has a pretty movie-set quality, set around a neat, triangular village green. Bring enough cash with you, as there are no ATMs here.

🛏 Sleeping & Eating

Village B&B   B&B €€
(☎074-937 0763; www.malinvillagebandb.com; The Green; s/d €45/70) Sitting right on the village green, this lovely B&B has a choice of cosy rooms, some traditional with antique furniture and brocade armchairs, others more contemporary with white linen and pretty floral patterns. Although you'll get a hearty breakfast here, guests also have use of a kitchen and utility room.

Belfast, Derry & the Antrim Coast

Once a byword for trouble, Northern Ireland has finally taken its place as one of the loveliest corners of the island. Emerging from nearly four decades of sectarian conflict, it now has as much to offer as any of Ireland's tourist havens.

The regional capital, Belfast, has shrugged off its bomb-scarred past and reinvented itself as one of the most exciting and dynamic cities in Britain – of which Northern Ireland remains a firm part. You can explore the tensions as they're expressed today in the iconic neighbourhoods of West Belfast or in the province's second city, Derry (or Londonderry), which is leading the north's cultural revival.

And it wouldn't be Ireland if it didn't have its fair share of stunning landscapes: from the Antrim Coast and its world-famous Giant's Causeway to the mountains of Mourne in south County Down.

Belfast, Derry & the Antrim Coast

Portrush
Portstewart
Downhill
Castlerock
Coleraine
A2

Lough
Foyle
Culmore
Bay
Burnfoot

DONEGAL

Derry/Londonderry
⑤

Limavady

DERRY/LONDONDERRY

Garvagh

River Foyle
N5
River Faughan
A6
Dungiven
Claudy
River Roe
Glenshane
Pass
Mullaghmore
(554m)
Maghera
A29

Dunnamanagh

Stranorlar
Castlefin

Strabane

Mt Sawel
(678m)
Sperrin
Mountains
Cranagh B47
Sperrin
Draperstown

Blue Stack
Mountains

Plumbridge

River Mourne

Slieve
Gallion
(528m)
Magherafelt

Castlederg
Newtownstewart
Gortin

Davagh
Forest
Park
B162
Moneymore
A29

Mullaghcarn
(542m)

River Ballinderry

River Strule

TYRONE
Creggan
Kildress
Cookstown
Coagh

Omagh

River Camowen
Pomeroy

FERMANAGH

Lower
Lough
Erne
Kesh
Dromore
A32
N5

Coalisland

Castlecaulfield
Dungannon
A4
M1

Ballygawley
Moy
Augher
Aughnacloy
Benburb
A28
Loughgall

Caledon
Emyvale
Killylea
Armagh

Monaghan

A3

Keady

MONAGHAN
Newtownhamilton
A29

Cullyhanna
Castleblayney

① Coastal Causeway Route
② Belfast
③ The Antrim Coast
④ Carrick-a-Rede Rope Bridge
⑤ Historic Derry/Londonderry

Belfast, Derry & the Antrim Coast's Highlights

Coastal Causeway Route

There is nothing better than driving along on a sunny day with the green Glens of Antrim on your left and the Irish Sea with views over to Scotland on your right – and as you turn each bend you get another spectacular view (p301). Glens of Antrim

Belfast

For three decades until the turn of the millennium, Belfast (p288) was synonymo with violence, sectarianism and the politics of hatred. And while divisions remain entrenched, the violence has long since abated and the city has turned its attentions to the business o attracting visitors. Recent history is a popular theme, as is the city's best-known creation, the *Titanic*. *Titanic* dry doc Belfast shipyards

OONAT/GETTY IMAGES ©

The Antrim Coast

3

It's a no brainer, but the number one tourist destination in Northern Ireland deserves all of the kudos it gets. The Antrim Coast, though, is about more than just coastline: from the intoxicating charms of the Bushmill's Distillery (p303) to the more sedate pleasures of Rathlin Island (p306), there's something for everyone, especially walkers, who can explore the coastline along the waymarked Causeway Coastal Route. Giant's Causeway (p305)

SIMON GREENWOOD/GETTY IMAGES ©

JOHN SONES SINGING BOWL MEDIA/GETTY IMAGES ©

4

Carrick-a-Rede Rope Bridge

Crossing the 20 swaying metres of the Carrick-a-Rede Rope Bridge (p303) to the eponymous island is either breathtaking or frightening (depending on your head for heights); it's a short, stunning clamber that will linger long in the memory. It's on the Antrim Coast, between the Giant's Causeway and Ballycastle.

5

Historic Derry/Londonderry

Northern Ireland's second city (p307) – and Ireland's only surviving walled city – is second to none in terms of history and character. A walk around the historic walls is one of the highlights of any trip, as is an exploration of the well-storied Bogside district, which, like West Belfast, was at the heart of the Troubles but is in the midst of restoring itself and its battered community to its rightful pride of place.

Belfast, Derry & the Antrim Coast's Best...

Spots to Lay Your Head

○ **Malmaison Hotel** A successful conversion of two elegant Italianate warehouses. (p296)

○ **Old Rectory** Elegant Victorian villa. (p297)

○ **Merchant's House** Superb Georgian-style B&B. (p310)

○ **Whitepark House** Handsome 18th-century home overlooking White Park Bay. (p305)

Cultural Stops

○ **Ulster Folk Museum** 18th- and 19th-century living brought to life. (p299)

○ **Ulster Transport Museum** See the ill-fated DeLorean car. (p299)

○ **Ulster Museum** Superb collection of enormous social and cultural significance. (p292)

○ **Museum of Free Derry** One of the best political museums in Europe. (p310)

Places to Eat

○ **Ginger** Small and unassuming, the food is outstanding. (p298)

○ **Brown's Restaurant** Gastronomic exploration of fine Irish dining. (p311)

○ **Barking Dog** Great food in a cosy, farmhouse-style setting. (p298)

○ **55 Degrees North** Antrim Coast's best eatery. (p302)

○ **Bushmills Inn** Superb restaurant attached to popular inn. (p303)

Scenic Walks

○ **Cushendun** Bracing coastal walks. (p306)

○ **Rathlin Island** Perfect island walk. (p306)

○ **Derry's City Walls** Walk the length of the 16th-century walls. (p307)

Need to Know

ADVANCE PLANNING

○ **Two months before** Book your accommodation, especially along the Antrim Coast.

○ **One month before** Read a book on Northern Ireland's turbulent history.

○ **Two weeks before** Make reservations for the province's top restaurants.

RESOURCES

○ **Discover Northern Ireland** (www.discovernorthernireland.com) Official website of Northern Ireland Tourism Bureau.

○ **Antrim** (www.countyantrim.com) Attractions, accommodation and restaurants in Antrim.

○ **Belfast Tourism** (www.gotobelfast.com) Belfast Welcome Centre.

○ **Derry Tourism** (www.derryvisitor.com) City's official website.

GETTING AROUND

○ **Bus** Excellent regional service on all main routes linking all towns and cities.

○ **Train** Good between Belfast and Derry, serving the Antrim Coast.

○ **Car** Probably the easiest way of getting around.

BE FOREWARNED

○ **Sectarianism** Broad divisions still exist, especially in so-called 'interface' areas in parts of Belfast; these are best avoided, as is most of the province around the marching days of 11 and 12 July, when Loyalists march throughout the province.

○ **Seasonal tourism** Many hotels and restaurants shut down between December and Easter.

Left: Giant's Causeway (p305);
Above: City walls, Derry/Londonderry (p307)

(LEFT) GARETH MCCORMACK/GETTY IMAGES ©, (ABOVE) ©
SCENICIRELAND.COM/CHRISTOPHER HILL PHOTOGRAPHIC/ALAMY

Belfast, Derry & the Antrim Coast Itineraries

Northern Ireland is fascinating and beautiful. These itineraries cover its largest, most interesting city and its most scenic and best-loved stretch of coastline.

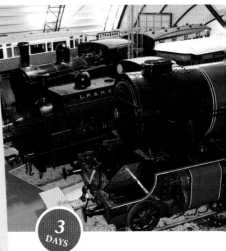

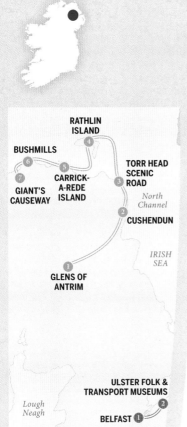

RATHLIN ISLAND

BUSHMILLS

GIANT'S CAUSEWAY

CARRICK-A-REDE ISLAND

TORR HEAD SCENIC ROAD

North Channel

CUSHENDUN

IRISH SEA

GLENS OF ANTRIM

ULSTER FOLK & TRANSPORT MUSEUMS

Lough Neagh

BELFAST

---

3 DAYS

BELFAST CITY
BEST OF BELFAST

This itinerary is all about the province's capital and biggest city, ❶ **Belfast** (p288). Start your visit with a free guided tour of City Hall. Take a black taxi tour of the West Belfast murals, then ask the taxi driver to drop you off at the Ox for lunch. Then head across the river to spend the rest of the afternoon exploring Titanic Belfast. Round off the day with dinner at Deane's Restaurant or Ginger. On your second day, explore the fascinating exhibits in the Ulster Museum. In the afternoon take a guided tour around historic Crumlin Road Gaol. Have dinner at Shu or the Barking Dog, then spend the evening crawling traditional pubs such as the Crown Liquor Saloon, Kelly's Cellars and the Duke of York. On the third day, head outside the city to visit the adjoining ❷ **Ulster Folk Museum & Ulster Transport Museum** (p299), two of the best in the province.

Top Left: Rail collection, Ulster Transport Museum (p299);
Top Right: Rathlin Island (p306)

(TOP LEFT) STEPHEN SAKS/GETTY IMAGES ©. (TOP RIGHT) © DESIGN PICS INC. · RM CONTENT/ALAMY

5 DAYS

GLENS OF ANTRIM TO GIANT'S CAUSEWAY
THE ANTRIM COAST

Most visitors naturally make their way to the Antrim Coast, the province's number one tourist destination and a favourite of many locals themselves. You could drive it in a couple of hours, but this five-day itinerary is all about taking a bit of time to enjoy it. Start north of Belfast at the **1 Glens of Antrim** (p305), making sure to visit the seaside village of **2 Cushendun** (p306), famous for its National Trust Cornish-style cottages. Take the **3 Torr Head Scenic Road** to Ballycastle, from which you can go on to explore the bird sanctuary of **4 Rathlin Island** (p306) – guillemots, kittiwakes, razorbills and puffins from mid-April to August. If you're up for it, make the short but devilishly challenging crossing to **5 Carrick-a-Rede Island** (p303), for which you'll need real sea legs! Your next stop is the historic town of **6 Bushmills** (p302), home of the famous distillery that should be a highlight of a visit here. And finally, clamber across the most famous site in all of Northern Ireland, the hexagonal natural wonders that make up the **7 Giant's Causeway** (p304). If you've taken the appropriate amount of time, five days will have flown by!

287

Discover Belfast, Derry & the Antrim Coast

At a Glance

○ **Belfast** (p288) A contemporary city growing in confidence and distractions after decades of troubled shadows.

○ **The Antrim Coast** (p301) Scenic coastline stretching virtually the length of the province's northern edge, from just north of Belfast to east of Derry.

○ **Derry/Londonderry** (p307) Northern Ireland's second city has an intimate character and plenty of history.

BELFAST

Once lumped with Beirut, Baghdad and Bosnia as one the four 'Bs' for travellers to avoid, Belfast has pulled off a remarkable transformation from bombs-and-bullets pariah to a hip-hotels-and-hedonism party town. The opening of Titanic Belfast in 2012, along with the 50th anniversary of the Belfast Festival at Queen's – the UK's second-biggest arts festival – saw visitor numbers soar by more than 40%.

◎ Sights

CITY CENTRE

City Hall   Historic Building
(Map p290; www.belfastcity.gov.uk/cityhall; Donegall Sq; ☉ guided tours 11am, 2pm & 3pm Mon-Fri, 2pm & 3pm Sat) **FREE** The Industrial Revolution transformed Belfast in the 19th century, and its rapid rise to muck-and-brass prosperity is manifested in the extravagance of City Hall. Built in classical Renaissance style in fine, white Portland stone, it was completed in 1906 and paid for from the profits of the gas supply company.

The highlights of the free, 45-minute **guided tour** of City Hall include the sumptuous, wedding-cake Italian marble and colourful stained glass of the entrance hall and rotunda; an opportunity to sit on the mayor's throne in the council chamber; and the idiosyncratic portraits of past lord mayors – each lord mayor is allowed to choose his or her own artist and the variations in personal style are intriguing.

City Hall
RICHARD CUMMINS/GETTY IMAGES ©

Crown Liquor Saloon
Historic Building

(Map p290; www.nationaltrust.org.uk; 46 Great Victoria St; ⏱11.30am-11pm Mon-Wed, to midnight Thu-Sat, 12.30-10pm Sun) **FREE** There are not too many historical monuments that you can enjoy while savouring a pint of beer, but the National Trust's Crown Liquor Saloon is one of them. Belfast's most famous bar was refurbished by Patrick Flanagan in the late 19th century and displays Victorian decorative flamboyance at its best (he was looking to pull in a posh clientele from the newfangled train station and Grand Opera House across the street).

TITANIC QUARTER
Belfast's former shipbuilding yards – the birthplace of RMS *Titanic* – stretch along the east side of the River Lagan, dominated by the towering yellow cranes known as **Samson and Goliath** (dating from the 1970s). The area is currently undergoing a £1 billion regeneration project known as **Titanic Quarter** (www.titanicquarter.com), which plans to transform the long-derelict docklands over the next 15 to 20 years.

Titanic Belfast
Exhibition

(www.titanicbelfast.com; Queen's Rd; adult/child £14.75/7.25; ⏱9am-7pm Apr-Sep, 10am-5pm Oct-Mar) The head of the slipway where the *Titanic* was built is now occupied by the gleaming, angular edifice of Titanic Belfast, an all-singing all-dancing multimedia extravaganza that charts the history of Belfast and the creation of the world's most famous ocean liner. Since

Around Belfast

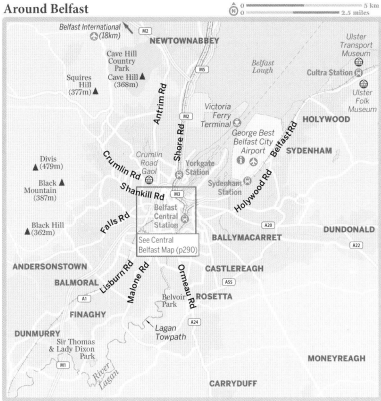

Central Belfast

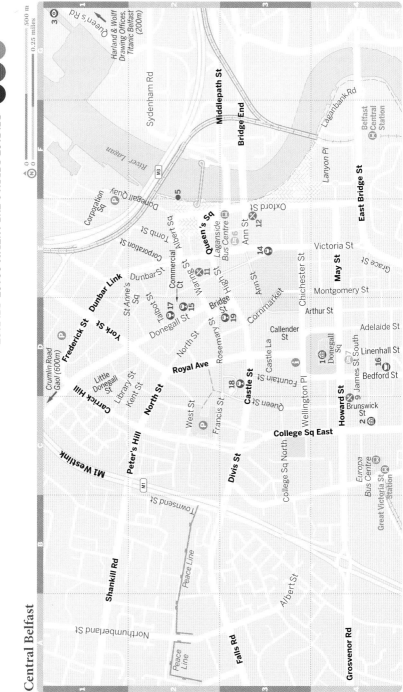

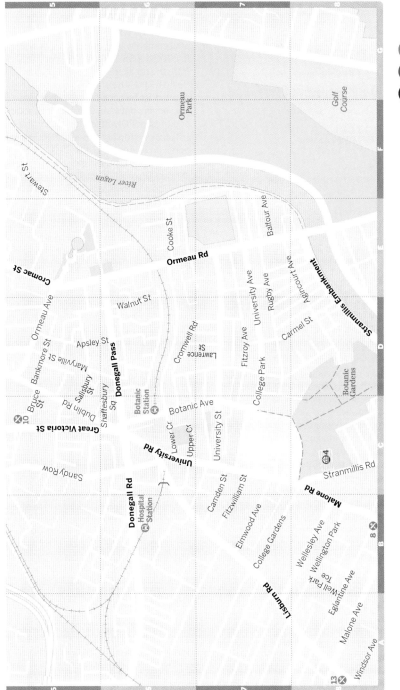

Golf
Course

Ormeau
Park

River Lagan

Stewart St

Cromac St

Ormeau Rd

Cooke St

Balfour Ave

Walnut St

Ormeau Ave

Banmore St

Maryville St

Apsley St

Salisbury St

Donegall Pass

Shaftesbury Sq

Dublin Rd

Bruce St

Cromwell Rd

Lawrence St

University Ave

Rugby Ave

Agincourt Ave

Stranmillis Embankment

Carmel St

Fitzroy Ave

Great Victoria St

Botanic Station

Botanic Ave

College Park

Botanic Gardens

Sandy Row

University Rd

Lower Cr

Upper Cr

University St

Camden St

Fitzwilliam St

College Gardens

Malone Rd

Stranmillis Rd

Donegall Rd

Hospital Station

Lisburn Rd

Elmwood Ave

Wellesley Ave

Well Park Tce

Wellington Park

Eglantine Ave

Malone Ave

Windsor Ave

291

Central Belfast

opening in April 2012, the centenary of the ship's sinking, it has rapidly become Northern Ireland's most popular tourist attraction, outstripping even the Giant's Causeway.

Cleverly designed exhibits, enlivened by historic images, animated projections and soundtracks, chart Belfast's rise to a turn-of-the- 20th-century industrial superpower. This is followed by a hi-tech ride through a noisy, smells-and-all re-creation of the city's shipyards. You can then explore every detail of the *Titanic*'s construction, from a computer 'fly-through' from keel to bridge, to replicas of the passenger accommodation. Perhaps most poignant are the few flickering images that constitute the only film footage of the ship in existence.

SS Nomadic   Historic Ship
(Map p290; www.nomadicbelfast.com; Queen's Rd; adult/child 38.50/5; ☉10am-6pm Apr-Sep, 10am-5pm Oct-Mar) The Hamilton Graving Dock, just northeast of the Odyssey Complex, is now the permanent berth of SS *Nomadic*, which is the only surviving vessel of the White Star Line (the shipping company that owned the *Titanic*). In 2006 the SS *Nomadic* was rescued from the breaker's yard and brought to Belfast. This little steamship once served as a tender ferrying 1st- and 2nd-class passengers between Cherbourg Harbour and the giant Olympic Class ocean liners (which were too big to dock at the French port); on 10 April 1912 the SS *Nomadic* delivered 142 1st-class passengers to the ill-fated *Titanic*. Now fully restored, she is home to an exhibition on the ship's history and her part in the *Titanic* story.

Harland & Wolff
Drawing Offices   Historic Building
(Queen's Rd; ☉open to guided tours only) Just along the road from the *Nomadic* are the original Harland & Wolff drawing offices, where the designs for the *Titanic* were first drawn up; you can see inside only as part of a guided tour such as Titanic Tours (p295). Behind the building, where the new Titanic Belfast attraction now sits (though best seen from a boat tour on the river), are the two massive **slipways** where the *Titanic* and her sister ship *Olympic* were built and launched.

SOUTH BELFAST (QUEEN'S QUARTER)

Ulster Museum   Museum
(Map p290; www.nmni.com/um; Stranmillis Rd; ☉10am-5pm Tue-Sun; ⊞) FREE Following a major revamp, the Ulster Museum is now one of the North's don't-miss attractions. You could spend several hours browsing the beautifully designed displays, but if you're pressed for time don't miss the Armada Room, Takabuti (a 2500-year-old Egyptian mummy), the Bann Disc and the Snapshot of an Ancient Sea Floor.

WEST BELFAST (GAELTACHT QUARTER)

Northwest of Donegall Sq, Divis St leads across the Westlink Motorway to Falls Rd and West Belfast (Gaeltacht Quarter). Though scarred by three decades of civil

ANDREW MCCONNELL/ALAMY ©

⭐ Don't Miss
Crumlin Road Gaol

Since it opened in 1846, Belfast's notorious Crumlin Road Gaol has imprisoned a whole range of historic figures, from Éamon de Valera to the Reverend Ian Paisley, and from suffragette Dorothy Evans to the 'Shankill Butcher' murderer Lenny Murphy.

The guided tour takes you from the tunnel beneath Crumlin Rd, built in 1850 to convey prisoners from the courthouse across the street (and allegedly the origin of the judge's phrase 'take him down'), through the echoing halls and cramped cells of C-Wing, to the truly chilling execution chamber – it's hard not to feel that the guide's light-hearted banter is inappropriate here and there's a genuine sense of relief at getting out in the open air again.

It's best to book tours in advance using the website.

NEED TO KNOW

📞 9074 1500; www.crumlinroadgaol.com; 53-55 Crumlin Rd; adult/child £7.50/5.50; 🕙 10am-5.30pm

---

unrest, the former battleground of West Belfast is one of the most compelling places to visit in Northern Ireland. Recent history hangs heavy in the air, but there is a noticeable spirit of optimism and hope for the future.

The main attractions in this area are the powerful murals that chart the history of the conflict (see p294), as well as the political passions of the moment and, for visitors from mainland Britain, there is a grim fascination to be found

Murals of Belfast

Belfast's tradition of political murals is a century old, dating from 1908 when images of King Billy (William III, Protestant victor over the Catholic James II at the Battle of the Boyne in 1690) were painted by Unionists protesting against home rule for Ireland. The tradition was revived in the late 1970s as the Troubles wore on, with murals used to mark out sectarian territory, make political points, commemorate historical events and glorify terrorist groups. As the 'voice of the community' the murals were rarely permanent, but changed to reflect the issues of the day. Taxi tours visit many of the more prominent murals, and the driver/guide can provide context and an explanation of the various symbols.

REPUBLICAN MURALS

The first Republican murals appeared in 1981, when the hunger strike by Republican prisoners – demanding recognition as political prisoners – at the Maze Prison saw the emergence of dozens of murals of support. In later years, Republican muralists broadened their scope to cover wider political issues, Irish legends and historical events. After the Good Friday Agreement of 1998, the murals came to demand police reform and the protection of nationalists from sectarian attacks.

The main areas for Republican murals are Falls Rd, Beechmount Ave, Donegall Rd, Shaw's Rd and the Ballymurphy district in West Belfast, New Lodge Rd in North Belfast, and Ormeau Rd in South Belfast.

LOYALIST MURALS

Loyalist murals have traditionally been more militaristic and defiant in tone than the Republican murals, which are often artistic and rich in symbolic imagery. The Loyalist battle cry of 'No Surrender!' is everywhere, along with red, white and blue painted kerbstones, paramilitary insignia and images of King Billy, usually shown on a prancing white horse.

MURALS TODAY

In recent years there has been a lot of debate about what to do with Belfast's murals. Some see them as an ugly and unpleasant reminder of a violent past, while others claim they are a vital part of Northern Ireland's history. There's no doubt they have become an important tourist attraction, but there is now a move to replace the more aggressive and militaristic images with murals dedicated to local heroes and famous figures such as footballer George Best and *Narnia* novelist CS Lewis.

If you want to find out more about Northern Ireland's murals, look out for the books *Drawing Support* (three volumes) by Bill Rolston, *The People's Gallery* by the Bogside Artists and the website of the **Mural Directory** (www.cain.ulst.ac.uk/murals).

in wandering through the former 'war zone' in their own backyard.

Despite its past reputation, the area is safe to visit. The best way to see West Belfast is on a **black taxi tour**. The cabs visit the more spectacular murals as well as the Peace Line (where you can write a message on the wall) and other significant sites, while the drivers provide a colourful commentary on the history of the area.

There's nothing to stop you visiting under your own steam, either walking or using the shared black taxis that travel along the Falls and Shankill Rds. Alternatively, buses 10A to 10F from Queen St will take you along the Falls Rd; buses 11A to 11D from Wellington Pl go along Shankill Rd.

FALLS ROAD

Although the signs of past conflict are inescapable, the Falls today is an unexpectedly lively, colourful and optimistic place. Local people are friendly and welcoming, and community ventures such as Conway Mill, the Cultúrlann centre and black taxi tours have seen tourist numbers increase dramatically.

SHANKILL ROAD

Although the Protestant Shankill district (from the Irish *sean chill,* meaning 'old church') has received less media attention than the Falls, it also contains many interesting murals. The people here are just as friendly, but the Shankill has far fewer tourists than the Falls. Loyalist communities seem to have more difficulty in presenting their side of the story than the Republicans, who have a far more polished approach to public relations.

To reach Shankill Rd on foot, set off north from City Hall along Donegall Pl and Royal Ave, then turn left on North St and continue straight on across the Westlink Motorway.

 Tours

You can find full details of organised tours at the Belfast Welcome Centre. If you want to hire a personal guide, call the Welcome Centre or contact the **Northern Ireland Tourist Guide Association** (www.bluebadgeireland.com; half-/full-day tours £80/150).

Belfast iTours (belfastitours.com) offers 10 self-guided video tours of the city that you can download to your smartphone or MP4 player; alternatively you can hire af

If You Like...
Good Food

If you enjoy the cuisine at OX (p297) and Ginger (p298) in Belfast, try these other reputable restaurants in the provincial capital.

1 **SHU**
(Map p290; 9038 1655; www.shu-restaurant. com; 253 Lisburn Rd; mains £12-23; lunch & dinner Mon-Sat) Award-winning epitome of Belfast chic – food is mostly French.

2 **DEANE'S RESTAURANT**
(Map p290; 9033 1134; www.michaeldeane. co.uk; 34-40 Howard St; mains lunch £10, dinner £17-25; lunch & dinner Mon-Sat) One of the province's best restaurants, despite losing its Michelin star.

3 **GREAT ROOM**
(Map p290; 9023 4888; www. themerchanthotel.com; 35-39 Waring St, Merchant Hotel; mains £20-29; 7am-11pm) Magnificent, decadent dining in the former banking hall of the Ulster Bank.

preloaded MP4 player (£9 for 24 hours) from the Belfast Welcome Centre.

Lagan Boat Company Boat Tour
(Map p290; 9033 0844; www.laganboatcompany.com; adult/child £10/8; 12.30pm, 2pm & 3.30pm daily Apr-Sep, 12.30 & 2pm daily Oct, 12.30 & 2pm Sat & Sun Nov-Mar) The excellent **Titanic Tour** explores the derelict docklands downstream of Lagan Weir, taking in the slipways where the liners *Titanic* and *Olympic* were launched and the huge dry dock where they could fit with just nine inches to spare; departs from Donegall Quay near the *Bigfish* sculpture.

Titanic Tours Guided Tour
(07852 716655; www.titanictours-belfast. co.uk; adult/child £30/15; on demand) A three-hour luxury tour led by the great-granddaughter of one of the *Titanic*'s

crew, visiting various *Titanic*-related sites. For groups of two to five people; includes pick-up and drop-off at your accommodation.

Belfast Pub Tours Guided Tour
(Map p290; ☏ 028-9268 3665; www.belfastpub-tours.com; per person £8; ☺7pm Thu & 4pm Sat May-Oct) A two-hour tour (not including drinks) taking in six of the city's historic pubs, departing from the Crown Dining Rooms, above the Crown Liquor Saloon on Great Victoria St.

TAXI TOURS

Black taxi tours of West Belfast's murals – known locally as the 'bombs and bullets' or 'doom and gloom' tours – are offered by a large number of taxi companies and local cabbies. These can vary in quality and content, but in general they're an intimate and entertaining way to see the sights and can be customised to suit your own interests. There are also historical taxi tours of the

city centre. For a one-hour tour expect to pay around £30 total for one or two people, and £10 per person for three to six. Call and they will pick you up from anywhere in the city centre.

The following companies are recommended:

Harpers Taxi Tours (☏ 07711 757178; www.harperstaxitours.co.nr)

Official Black Taxi Tours (☏ 9064 2264; www.belfasttours.com)

Original Belfast Black Taxi Tours (☏ 07751 565359; www.originalbelfasttours.com)

🛏 Sleeping

CITY CENTRE

Malmaison Hotel Hotel £££
(Map p290; ☏ 0844 693 0650; www.malmaison-belfast.com; 34-38 Victoria St; r from £123, ste from £269; @ 🛜) Housed in a pair of beautifully restored Italianate ware-

Left: Bar in Belfast; **Below:** Crown Liquor Saloon (p298)
(LEFT) TONY PLEAVIN/GETTY IMAGES ©. (BELOW) DOUG MCKINLAY/GETTY IMAGES ©

houses (originally built for rival firms in the 1850s), the Malmaison is a luxurious haven of king-size beds, deep leather sofas and roll-top baths big enough for two, all done up in a decadent decor of black, red, dark chocolate and cream. The massive, rock-star Samson suite has a giant bed (almost 3m long), a huge bathtub and, wait for it...a billiard table, with purple baize.

Ten Square Hotel **££££**
(Map p290; ☎ 9024 1001; www.tensquare.co.uk; 10 Donegall Sq S; r from £115; @ 🛜) A former bank building to the south of City Hall that has been given a designer feng-shui makeover, Ten Square is an opulent, Shanghai-inspired boutique hotel with friendly and attentive service. Magazines such as *Cosmopolitan* and *Conde Nast Traveller* drool over the dark lacquered wood, low-slung futon-style beds and sumptuous linen, and the list of former guests includes Bono and Brad Pitt.

SOUTH BELFAST

Old Rectory B&B **££**
(☎ 9066 7882; www.anoldrectory.co.uk; 148 Malone Rd; s/d £55/86; @ 🛜) A lovely Victorian villa with lots of original stained glass, this former rectory has five spacious bedrooms, a comfortable drawing room with leather sofa, and fancy breakfasts (wild boar sausages, scrambled eggs with smoked salmon, veggie fry-ups, freshly squeezed OJ). It's a 10-minute bus ride from the centre – the inconspicuous driveway is on the left, just past Deramore Park South. No credit cards.

Eating

CITY CENTRE

OX Irish **££**
(Map p290; ☎ 9031 4121; oxbelfast.com; 1 Oxford St; mains lunch £10, dinner £15-20; ⏱lunch & dinner Tue-Sat) A high-ceilinged space

♥ If You Like... Victorian Classics

If you like Victorian classics like the Crown Saloon, check out these other beautiful Belfast pubs.

1 BITTLE'S BAR
(Map p290; 103 Victoria St) Nineteenth-century redbrick classic decorated with paintings of Irish literary heroes.

2 DUKE OF YORK
(Map p290; 11 Commercial Ct) Sinn Fein president Gerry Adams pulled pints in this Victorian pub as a student

3 KELLY'S CELLARS
(Map p290; 1 Bank St) Belfast's oldest bar is a bit rough around the edges, but it's a popular favourite.

4 WHITE'S TAVERN
(Map p290; www.whitestavern.co.uk; 1-4 Wine Cellar Entry) An open peat fire and live traditional music make this a weekend favourite.

walled with cream-painted brick and furnished with warm golden wood creates a theatre-like ambience for the open kitchen at the back, where Michelin-trained chefs turn out some of Belfast's finest and best-value cuisine. The restaurant works with local suppliers and focuses on fine Irish beef, sustainable seafood and seasonal vegetables and fruit.

Ginger   Bistro ££
(Map p290; ☏ 9024 4421; www.gingerbistro.com; 7-8 Hope St; mains £13-23; ⊙ lunch Tue-Sat, dinner Mon-Sat; ☝) ⬤ Ginger is one of those places you could walk right past without noticing, but if you do you'll be missing out. It's a cosy and informal little bistro serving food that is anything but ordinary – the flame-haired owner/

chef (hence the name) really knows what he's doing, sourcing top-quality Irish produce and turning out exquisite dishes such as scallops with crisp black pudding and chorizo butter. The lunch and pre-theatre (5pm to 6.45pm Monday to Friday) menus offer main courses for £9 to £14.

SOUTH BELFAST

Barking Dog   Bistro ££
(Map p290; ☏ 9066 1885; www.barking-dogbelfast.com; 33-35 Malone Rd; mains £9-17; ⊙ lunch & dinner Mon-Sat, noon-9pm Sun) Chunky hardwood, bare brick, candlelight and quirky design create the atmosphere of a stylishly restored farmhouse, and the menu completes the feeling of cosiness and comfort with simple but sensational dishes such as their signature burger of meltingly tender beef shin wrapped in caramelised onion and horseradish cream. Superb service.

♉ Drinking & Nightlife

CITY CENTRE

Crown Liquor Saloon   Pub
(Map p290; www.crownbar.com; 46 Great Victoria St) Belfast's most famous bar has a wonderfully ornate Victorian interior. Despite also being a tourist attraction (p289), it still fills up with crowds of locals at lunchtime and in the early evening.

Harlem Cafe   Cafe, Bar
(Map p290; www.harlembelfast.com; 34-36 Bedford St; ☏) Cool of vibe and quirky of decor, with eclectic art and framed photos of New York city and furnished with glass-topped tables full of seashells and starfish, the Harlem is a great place for lounging over coffee and reading the Sunday papers, or relaxing with a glass of wine after hitting the shops. It also offers a full food menu from breakfast to brunch to pre-theatre dinner.

Detour:
Ulster Folk Museum &
Ulster Transport Museum

Just outside Belfast on either side of the A2 road to Bangor are two of the province's best museums. The **Ulster Folk Museum** is a hands-on exploration of the last 500 years, with farmhouses, forges, churches, mills and a completely reconstructed village. Industrial times are represented with red-brick terraces from 19th-century Belfast and Dromore. In summer, thatching and ploughing are demonstrated and there are characters dressed in period costume.

Across the street, the **Ulster Transport Museum** is a sort of automotive zoo, with displays of captive steam locomotives, rolling stock, motorcycles, trams, buses and cars. The highlight of the car collection is the stainless steel–clad prototype of the ill-fated DeLorean DMC, made in Belfast in 1981. Most popular is the new Titanica exhibit, opened in 2012, which includes the original design drawings for the *Titanic* and its sister ship *Olympic*, and photographs of the ships' construction.

CATHEDRAL QUARTER & AROUND

John Hewitt
Bar & Restaurant
Pub

(Map p290; www.thejohnhewitt.com; 51 Donegall St) Named for the Belfast poet and socialist, the John Hewitt is one of those treasured bars that has no TV and no gaming machines; the only noise here is the murmur of conversation. As well as Guinness, the bar serves Hilden real ales from nearby Lisburn, plus Hoegaarden and Erdinger wheat beers. There are regular sessions of folk, jazz and bluegrass from 9pm most nights.

ⓘ Information

Dangers & Annoyances

Even at the height of the Troubles, Belfast wasn't a particularly dangerous city for tourists, and today you're less at risk from crime here than you are in London. It's best, however, to avoid the so-called 'interface areas' – near the peace lines in West Belfast, Crumlin Rd and the Short Strand (just east of Queen's Bridge) – after dark; if in doubt about any area, ask at your hotel or hostel. You can follow the Police Service of Northern Ireland (PSNI) on Twitter (@policeserviceni) and receive immediate notification of any alerts.

If you want to take photos of fortified police stations, army posts or other military or quasi-military paraphernalia, get permission first, just to be on the safe side. In the Protestant and Catholic strongholds of West Belfast it's best not to photograph people without permissionl. Taking pictures of the murals is not a problem.

Tourist Information

Belfast Welcome Centre (Map p290; ☑9024 6609; www.visit-belfast.com; 8-9 Donegall Sq N; ☉9am-5.30pm Mon-Sat & 11am-4pm Sun year-round, to 7pm Mon-Sat Jun-Sep; @ 🕾) Provides information about the whole of Northern Ireland, and books accommodation anywhere in Ireland and Britain. Services include left luggage (not overnight), currency exchange and internet access.

ⓘ Getting There & Away

Air

Belfast International Airport (BFS; www.belfastairport.com) Located 30km northwest of the city; flights from Galway, UK, Europe and New York.

George Best Belfast City Airport

(BHD; www.belfastcityairport.com; Airport Rd)
Located 6km northeast of the city centre;
flights from the UK and Paris.

Bus

There are information desks (⊙7.45am-6.30pm
Mon-Fri, 8am-6pm Sat) at both of Belfast's bus
stations, where you can pick up regional bus
timetables. Contact Translink (☎9066 6630;
www.translink.co.uk) for timetable and fares
information.

National Express (☎08717 818 178; www.
nationalexpress.com) runs a daily coach
service between Belfast and London (£47
one way, 15 hours) via the Cairnryan ferry,
Dumfries, Carlisle, Preston, Manchester and
Birmingham. The ticket office is in the Europa
BusCentre.

Scottish Citylink (☎0871 266 3333; www.
citylink.co.uk) operates four buses a day from
Glasgow to Belfast (£32, six hours), via the
same ferry.

Europa Bus Centre (Map p290; ☎9066 6630;
Great Victoria St, Great Northern Mall) Belfast's
main bus station is behind the Europa Hotel
and next door to Great Victoria St train station;
it's reached via the Great Northern Mall beside
the hotel. It's the main terminus for buses to
Derry, Dublin and destinations in the west and
south of Northern Ireland.

Laganside Bus Centre (Map p290; ☎9066
6630; Oxford St) The smaller of Belfast's two
bus stations, Laganside is near the river and
is mainly for buses to County Antrim, eastern
County Down and eastern County Tyrone.

Train

For information on train fares and timetables, see
Translink (www.translink.co.uk). The NIR Travel
Shop (☎9023 0671; Great Victoria St Station;
⊙9am-5pm Mon-Fri, to 12.30pm Sat) books train
tickets, ferries and holiday packages.

Belfast Central Station (East Bridge St) East
of the city centre; trains run to Dublin and all
destinations in Northern Ireland. If you arrive
by train at Central Station, your rail ticket
entitles you to a free bus ride into the city
centre.

Great Victoria St Station (Great Victoria
St, Great Northern Mall) Next to the Europa
BusCentre; has trains for Portadown, Lisburn,
Bangor, Larne Harbour and Derry.

Republican murals, Falls Road (p294)

DAMIAN TULLY/ALAMY ©

ℹ Getting Around

Belfast possesses that rare but wonderful thing – an integrated public-transport system, with buses linking both airports to the central train and bus stations.

To/From the Airports

Belfast International Airport Airport Express 300 bus runs to the Europa Bus Centre (one way/return £7.50/10.50, 30 minutes) every 10 or 15 minutes between 7am and 8pm, every 30 minutes from 8pm to 11pm, and hourly through the night; a return ticket is valid for one month. A taxi costs about £30.

George Best Belfast City Airport Airport Express 600 bus runs to the Europa Bus Centre (one way/return £2.40/3.60, 15 minutes) every 15 or 20 minutes between 6am and 10pm. A return ticket is valid for one month. The taxi fare to the city centre is about £10.

THE ANTRIM COAST

Portrush

POP 6300

The bustling seaside resort of Portrush (Port Rois) bursts at the seams with holidaymakers in high season and, not surprisingly, many of its attractions are focused unashamedly on good old-fashioned family fun.

◉ Sights & Activities

Curran Strand   Beach
Portrush's main attraction is the beautiful sandy beach of Curran Strand that stretches for 3km to the east of the town, ending at the scenic chalk cliffs of White Rocks. In summer, boats depart regularly for **cruises** or **fishing trips**.

Coastal Zone   Aquarium
(8 Bath Rd; ⊙10am-5pm daily Easter week & Jun-Aug, Sat & Sun only May & Sep; 👪) **FREE** You'll find more activities for kids at the Coastal Zone, including marine-life exhibits, a touch pool, rock-pool rambles and fossil hunts.

Local Knowledge

Coastal Causeway Route

BY JASON POWELL,
CAUSEWAY COASTS & GLENS TOURISM

1 GIANT'S CAUSEWAY
The Giant's Causeway (p303) is Northern Ireland's most popular attraction and my favourite place. The 40,000 basalt columns, the 400ft cliffs and the views all show the magnificence of Mother Nature. Best time to visit? When the weather is a bit stormy and the Atlantic waves crash in on the rocks!

2 RATHLIN ISLAND
Just five miles from Ballycastle, Rathlin Island (p306) is a world away from the mainland. There are only a few cars on the island, so it is ideal for walking or cycling. It is also home to the largest sea bird colony in Northern Ireland.

3 MORTON'S FISH & CHIPS
Although tiny, **Morton's** (📞028 2076 1100; 22 Bayview Rd) serves the best fish and chips on the island. You have to wait about 10 minutes as they make it all fresh, but once you have your order, you can just sit out on the harbour and watch the fishing boats sailing around the harbour.

4 GLENARIFF FOREST PARK
Glenariff Forest Park (p310) is a great place to get back to nature with great walks that take you past three wonderful waterfalls. As you get to the higher ground, you will reach some magnificent mountain viewpoints.

5 NORTHWEST 200
When I first stood at the grid of the NorthWest 200 (wwwnorthwest200.org), with the bikes revving ready to go, I could feel the tension and adrenaline of the country's biggest sporting event. The noise was unbelievable – I could feel the vibrations going right through my body. At that moment I was converted.

🛏 Sleeping & Eating

Clarmont
B&B ££

(☎7082 2397; www.clarmontguesthouse.com; 10 Landsdowne Cres; d £80; 🚻) Our favourite among several guesthouses on Landsdowne Cres, the recently refurbished Clarmont has great views and, from polished pine floors to period fireplaces, has a decor that tastefully mixes Victorian and modern styles. Ask for one of the bay window bedrooms with sea views and spa.

55 Degrees North
International ££

(☎7082 2811; www.55-north.com; 1 Causeway St; mains £10-20; ⏱12.30-2.30pm & 5-9pm; 🔌🚻) One of the north coast's most stylish restaurants, 55 Degrees North boasts a wall of floor-to-ceiling windows allowing diners to soak up a spectacular panorama of sand and sea. The food is excellent, concentrating on clean, simple flavours and unfussy presentation. There's an early-bird menu (three courses £10 to £12) available 5pm to 6.45pm.

ℹ Getting There & Around

The bus terminal is near the Dunluce Centre. Bus 140 links Portrush with Coleraine (20 minutes) and Portstewart (£2.60, 20 to 30 minutes) every 30 minutes or so.

The train station is just south of the harbour. Portrush is served by trains from Coleraine (£2.20, 12 minutes, hourly Monday to Saturday, 10 on Sunday), where there are connections to Belfast or Derry.

For taxis, try Andy Brown's (☎7082 2223) or North West Taxis (☎7082 4446). A taxi to Kelly's Complex is around £8, and it's £15 to the Giant's Causeway.

Bushmills
POP 1350

The small town of Bushmills has long been a place of pilgrimage for connoisseurs of Irish whiskey. A good youth hostel and a restored rail link with the Giant's Causeway have also made it an attractive stop for hikers exploring the Causeway Coast.

Portrush (p301)

STEPHEN SAKS/GETTY IMAGES ©

Detour:
Carrick-a-Rede Rope Bridge

The main attraction on the stretch of coast between Ballycastle and the Giant's Causeway is the famous (or notorious, depending on your head for heights) **Carrick-a-Rede Rope Bridge** (www.nationaltrust.org.uk; Ballintoy; adult/child £5.60/2.90; ⊙10am-7pm Jun-Aug, to 6pm Mar-May, Sep & Oct). The 20m-long, 1m-wide bridge of wire rope spans the chasm between the sea cliffs and the little island of Carrick-a-Rede, swaying gently 30m above the rock-strewn water.

The island has sustained a salmon fishery for centuries; fishermen stretch their nets out from the tip of the island to intercept the passage of salmon migrating along the coast to their home rivers. The fishermen put the bridge up every spring as they have done for the last 200 years – though it's not, of course, the original bridge.

Crossing the bridge is perfectly safe, but it can be frightening if you don't have a head for heights, especially if it's breezy (in high winds the bridge is closed). Once on the island there are good views of Rathlin Island and Fair Head to the east. There's a small National Trust information centre and cafe at the car park.

BELFAST, DERRY & THE ANTRIM COAST BUSHMILLS

◉ Sights & Activities

Giant's Causeway & Bushmills Railway   Heritage Railway
(www.freewebs.com/giantscausewayrailway; adult/child return £7.50/5.50) Brought from a private line on the shores of Lough Neagh, the narrow-gauge line and locomotives (two steam and one diesel) follow the route of a 19th-century tourist tramway for 3km from Bushmills to below the Giant's Causeway visitor centre. Trains run hourly between 11am and 5.30pm, departing on the hour from the Causeway, on the half-hour from Bushmills, daily in July and August, weekends only from Easter to June and September and October.

Old Bushmills Distillery   Distillery
(www.bushmills.com; Distillery Rd; tour adult/child £7/3.50; ⊙9.15am-5pm Mon-Sat Jul-Oct, 10am-5pm Mon-Sat Nov-Jun, noon-5pm Sun year-round) Bushmills is the world's oldest legal distillery, having been granted a licence by King James I in 1608. Bushmills whiskey is made with Irish barley and water from St Columb's Rill, a tributary of the River Bush, and matured in oak barrels. During ageing, the alcohol content drops from around 60% to 40%; the spirit lost through evaporation is known, rather sweetly, as 'the angels' share'. After a tour of the distillery you're rewarded with a free sample (or a soft drink), and four lucky volunteers get a whiskey-tasting session to compare Bushmills with other brands.

🛏 Sleeping & Eating

Bushmills Inn Hotel   Hotel £££
(☏2073 3000; www.bushmillsinn.com; 9 Dunluce Rd; s/d from £158/178, ste £298; @ �{}) One of Northern Ireland's most atmospheric hotels, the Bushmills is an old coaching inn complete with peat fires, gas lamps and a round tower with a secret library. There are no longer any bedrooms in the old part of the hotel – the luxurious accommodation is in the neighbouring, modern Mill House complex.

Bushmills Inn   Irish ££
(9 Dunluce Rd; lunch mains £11-15, dinner mains £16-24; ⊙noon-9.30pm Mon-Sat, 12.30-9pm Sun; �{}) The inn's excellent restaurant, with intimate wooden booths set in the old 17th-century stables, specialises in fresh Ulster produce and serves everything from sandwiches to full à-la-carte dinners.

303

GÄWNTER GRÄWNER/GETTY IMAGES ©

⭐ Don't Miss
Giant's Causeway

When you first see it you'll understand why the ancients believed the causeway was not a natural feature. The vast expanse of regular, closely packed, hexagonal stone columns dipping gently beneath the waves looks for all the world like the handiwork of giants.

This spectacular rock formation – a national nature reserve and Northern Ireland's only Unesco World Heritage Site – is one of Ireland's most impressive and atmospheric landscape features, but it is all too often swamped by visitors – around 750,000 each year. If you can, try to visit midweek or out of season to experience it at its most evocative. Sunset in spring and autumn is the best time for photographs.

Visiting the Giant's Causeway itself is free of charge but you pay to use the car park and the impressive new **Giant's Causeway Visitor Experience** (📞 2073 1855; www.giantscausewaycentre.com; adult/child £8.50/4.25; 🕙 9am-9pm Jul & Aug, to 7pm Apr-Jun & Sep, to 6pm Feb-Mar & Oct, to 7pm Nov-Jan; 📶). (The admission fee is reduced by £1.50 if you arrive by bus, bike or on foot.) This ecofriendly visitor centre, built into the hillside and walled in tall black basalt slabs that mimic the basalt columns of the Causeway, houses an exhibition explaining the geology of the region, as well as a tourist information desk, restaurant and shop.

From the visitor centre it's an easy 1km walk from the car park down to the Causeway; minibuses with wheelchair access ply the route every 15 minutes (adult/child £2/1 return). Guided tours of the site (June to August only) cost £3.50/2.25 per adult/child.

Giant's Causeway to Ballycastle

Between the Giant's Causeway and Ballycastle lies the most scenic stretch of the Causeway Coast, with sea cliffs of contrasting black basalt and white chalk, rocky islands, picturesque little harbours and broad sweeps of sandy beach. It's best enjoyed on foot, following the 16.5km of waymarked **Causeway Coast Way** between the Carrick-a-Rede car park and the Giant's Causeway, although the main attractions can also be reached by car or bus.

About 8km east of the Giant's Causeway is the meagre ruin of 16th-century **Dunseverick Castle**, which is spectacularly sited on a grassy bluff.

Another 1.5km on is the tiny seaside hamlet of **Portbradden**, with half a dozen harbourside houses and the tiny, blue-and-white **St Gobban's Church**, said to be the smallest in Ireland.

Visible from Portbradden and accessible via the next junction off the A2 is the spectacular **White Park Bay**, which has a wide, sweeping sandy beach.

A few kilometres further on is **Ballintoy** (Baile an Tuaighe), another pretty village tumbling down the hillside to a picture-postcard harbour. The restored limekiln on the quayside once made quicklime using stone from the chalk cliffs and coal from Ballymoney.

Sleeping

Whitepark House
B&B £££

(2073 1482; www.whiteparkhouse.com; 150 White Park Rd, Ballintoy; s/d £80/120;) A beautifully restored 18th-century house overlooking White Park Bay, this B&B has traditional features such as antique furniture and a peat fire complemented by Asian artefacts gathered during the welcoming owners' oriental travels. There are three rooms – ask for one with a sea view.

Getting There & Away
Bus 172 between Ballycastle, Bushmills and Coleraine (seven daily Monday to Friday, four on Saturday and Sunday) is the main, year-round service along this coast. The bus stops at the Giant's Causeway, Ballintoy and Carrick-a-Rede.

Glens of Antrim

The northeastern corner of Antrim is a high plateau of black basalt lava overlying beds of white chalk. Along the coast, between Cushendun and Glenarm, the plateau has been dissected by a series of scenic, glacier-gouged valleys known as the Glens of Antrim.

Two waymarked footpaths traverse the region: the **Ulster Way** sticks close to the sea, passing through all the coastal villages, while the 32km **Moyle Way**

White Park Bay
WOJTEK BUSS/GETTY IMAGES ©

Detour:
Rathlin Island

In spring and summer, rugged **Rathlin Island** (Reachlainn; www.rathlincommunity.org), 6km offshore from Ballycastle, is home to hundreds of seals and thousands of nesting seabirds. An L-shaped island just 6.5km long and 4km wide, Rathlin is famous for the coastal scenery and bird life at **Kebble National Nature Reserve** at its western end.

The island's most illustrious visitor was Scottish hero **Robert the Bruce**, who spent some time here in 1306 while hiding out after being defeated by the English king. Watching a spider's resoluteness in repeatedly trying to spin a web gave him the courage to have another go at the English, whom he subsequently defeated at Bannockburn. The cave where he is said to have stayed is beneath the **East Lighthouse**, at the northeastern tip of the island.

The RSPB's **Rathlin Seabird Centre** (www.rspb.org.uk; ⏱10am-4pm Apr-Aug) FREE at Rathlin West lighthouse provides stunning views of the neighbouring sea stacks, thick with guillemots, kittiwakes, razorbills and puffins from mid-April to August. During the summer a minibus service runs there from the harbour; public toilets and binocular hire are available.

If you don't have time to visit the Kebble Nature Reserve, the best short walk on the island is through the National Trust's Ballyconagan Nature Reserve to the **Old Coastguard Lookout** on the north coast, with great views along the sea cliffs and across to the Scottish islands of Islay and Jura.

The **Boathouse Visitor Centre** (admission free; ⏱9.30am-5pm Apr-Sep) FREE, south of the harbour, details the history, culture and ecology of the island, and can give advice on walks and wildlife. **Paul Quinn** (☎07745 566924, 7032 7960; www.rathlinwalkingtours.com; per person £4-12) offers guided walking tours of the island.

Getting There & Around

A **ferry** (☎2076 9299; www.rathlinballycastleferry.com; adult/child/bicycle return £12/6/3) operates daily from Ballycastle; advance booking is recommended in spring and summer. From April to September there are eight or nine crossings a day, half of which are fast catamaran services (20 minutes), the rest via a slower car ferry (45 minutes); in winter the service is reduced.

Only residents can take their car to Rathlin (except for disabled drivers), but nowhere on the island is more than 6km (about 1½ hours' walk) from the ferry pier. You can hire a bicycle (£10 per day) from Soerneog View Hostel, or take a minibus tour with **McGinn's** (☎2076 3451; per person £5), which also shuttles visitors between the ferry and Kebble Nature Reserve (£5 return) from April to August.

---

runs inland across the high plateau from Glenariff Forest Park to Ballycastle.

CUSHENDUN
POP 350

The pretty seaside village of Cushendun is famous for its distinctive Cornish-style cottages, now owned by the National Trust. Built between 1912 and 1925 at the behest of the local landowner, Lord Cushendun, they were designed by Clough Williams-Ellis, the architect of Portmeirion in north Wales. There's a nice sandy **beach**, various short **coastal walks** (outlined on an information board beside the car park), and some impressive **caves** cut into the overhanging conglomerate sea cliffs south of the village (follow the trail around the far end of the holiday apartments south of the river mouth).

🛏 Sleeping & Eating

Villa Farmhouse
B&B ££

(☎ 2176 1252; www.thevillafarmhouse.com; 185 Torr Rd; s/d from £35/60; @) This lovely old whitewashed farmhouse is set on a hillside, 1km north of Cushendun, with great views over the bay and the warm atmosphere of a family home, decorated with photos of children and grandchidlren. The owner is an expert chef and breakfast will be a highlight of your stay – best scrambled eggs in Northern Ireland?

DERRY/LONDONDERRY

POP 83,700

Northern Ireland's second city comes as a pleasant surprise to many visitors. Derry was never the prettiest of places, and it certainly lagged behind Belfast in terms of investment and redevelopment, but in preparation for its year in the limelight as UK City of Culture 2013, the city centre was given a handsome makeover. The new Peace Bridge, Ebrington Square, and the redevelopment of the waterfront and Guildhall area make the most of the city's riverside setting, while Derry's determined air of can-do optimism has made it the powerhouse of the North's cultural revival.

⊙ Sights

WALLED CITY

Derry's walled city is Ireland's earliest example of town planning. It is thought to have been modelled on the French Renaissance town of Vitry-le-François,

designed in 1545 by Italian engineer Hieronimo Marino; both are based on the grid plan of a Roman military camp, with two main streets at right angles to each other, and four city gates, one at either end of each street.

Completed in 1619, Derry's **city walls** (www.derryswalls.com) are 8m high and 9m thick, with a circumference of about 1.5km, and are the only city walls in Ireland to survive almost intact.

Tower Museum
Museum

(www.derrycity.gov.uk/Museums; Union Hall Pl; adult/child £4.20/2.65; ⊙10am-5pm Tue-Sat year-round, plus 11am-3pm Sun Jul-Sep) Inside the Magazine Gate is this award-winning museum, housed in a replica 16th-century tower house. Allow a good two hours to do the museum justice.

St Columb's Cathedral
Cathedral

(www.stcolumbscathedral.org; London St; admission free, donation appreciated; ⊙9am-5pm Mon-Sat year-round) Built between 1628 and 1633 from the same grey-green schist as the city walls, this was the first

Tower Museum
STEPHEN SAKS/GETTY IMAGES ©

post-Reformation church to be erected in Britain and Ireland, and is Derry's oldest surviving building.

OUTSIDE THE WALLS

Guildhall
Notable Building

(www.derrycity.gov.uk/Guildhall; Guildhall Sq; 10am-5.30pm daily) FREE Standing just outside the city walls, the neo-Gothic Guildhall was originally built in 1890, then rebuilt after a fire in 1908.

The Guildhall is noted for its fine **stained-glass windows**, presented by the London Livery companies, and its clock tower which is modelled on London's Big Ben. Following a major restoration in 2012–13, the Guildhall now hosts a historical exhibition on the Plantation of Ulster, and a tourist information point.

Harbour Museum
Museum

(Harbour Sq; 10am-1pm & 2-5pm Mon-Fri) FREE The small, old-fashioned Harbour Museum, with models of ships, a replica of a *currach* (an early sailing boat of the type that carried St Colmcille to Iona) and the bosomy figurehead of the *Minnehaha*, is housed in the old Harbour Commissioner's Building next to the Guildhall.

BOGSIDE

The Bogside district, to the west of the walled city, developed in the 19th and early 20th centuries as a working-class, predominantly Catholic, residential area.

In August 1969 the three-day 'Battle of the Bogside' – a running street battle between local youths and the Royal Ulster Constabulary (RUC) – prompted the UK government to send British troops into Northern Ireland. The residents of the Bogside and neighbouring Brandywell districts – 33,000 of them – declared themselves independent of the civil authorities and barricaded the streets to keep the security forces out. 'Free Derry', as it was known, was a no-go area for the police and army, its streets patrolled by IRA volunteers. In January of 1972 the area around Rossville St witnessed the horrific events of Bloody Sunday. 'Free Derry' ended with Operation Motorman on 31 July 1972, when thousands of British troops and armoured cars moved in to occupy the Bogside.

Since then the area has been extensively redeveloped, the old houses and flats demolished and replaced with modern housing, and the population is now down to 8000. All that remains of the old Bogside is **Free Derry Corner** (intersection of Fahan & Rossville Sts), where the gable end of a house painted with the famous slogan 'You are Now Entering Free Derry' still stands. Nearby is the H-shaped **Hunger Strikers' Memorial** (Rossville St) and, a little further north along Rossville

People's Gallery mural
STEPHEN SAKS/GETTY IMAGES ©

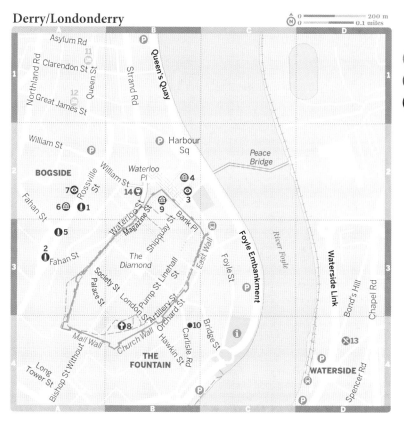

St, the **Bloody Sunday Memorial**
(Rossville St), a simple granite obelisk that
commemorates the 14 civilians who were
shot dead by the British Army on 30
January 1972.

People's Gallery Murals   Murals
(Rossville St) The 12 murals that decorate
the gable ends of houses along Rossville
St, near Free Derry Corner, are popularly
referred to as the People's Gallery. They
are the work of Tom Kelly, Will Kelly and
Kevin Hasson, known as 'the Bogside
Artists'. The three men have spent most
of their lives in the Bogside, and lived
through the worst of the Troubles.

The murals can be seen online at www.
cain.ulst.ac.uk/bogsideartists, and in
the book *The People's Gallery,* which is
available from the artists' website.

Derry/Londonderry

Detour:
Glenariff

About 9km south of Cushendun is the village of **Waterfoot**, with a 2km-long sandy beach, the best on Antrim's east coast. From here the A43 Ballymena road runs inland along Glenariff, the loveliest of Antrim's glens. Views of the valley led the writer Thackeray to exclaim that it was a 'Switzerland in miniature', a claim that makes you wonder if he'd ever been to Switzerland!

At the head of the valley is **Glenariff Forest Park** (car/motorcycle/pedestrian £4.50/2.30/1.50; ⏰10am-dusk), where the main attraction is **Ess-na-Larach Waterfall**, an 800m walk from the visitor centre. You can also walk to the waterfall from Laragh Lodge, 600m downstream. There are various good walks in the park; the longest is a 10km circular trail.

Laragh Lodge (📞2175 8221; 120 Glen Rd; mains £10-16, 4-course Sun lunch £16; ⏰11am-9pm daily Mar-Oct, Fri-Sun only Nov-Feb) is a restaurant and bar on a side road off the A43, 3km northeast of the main park entrance. A renovated Victorian tourist lodge with assorted bric-a-brac dangling from the rafters, the Laragh dates from 1890 and serves hearty pub-grub-style meals – beef and Guinness pie, fish and chips, sausage and mash (with a couple of vegetarian options) – and offers a traditional roast lunch on Sunday.

You can reach Glenariff Forest Park on Ulsterbus 150 from Cushendun (£4, 30 minutes, six daily Monday to Friday, four Saturday) and Ballymena (£4, 30 minutes).

Museum of Free Derry   Museum
(www.museumoffreederry.org; 55-61 Glenfada Park; adult/child £3/2; ⏰9.30am-4.30pm Mon-Fri, plus 1-4pm Sat Apr-Sep, 1-4pm Sun Jul-Sep) Just off Rossville St, this museum chronicles the history of the Bogside, the civil rights movement and the events of Bloody Sunday through photographs, newspaper reports, film clips and the accounts of first-hand witnesses, including some of the original photographs that inspired the murals of the People's Gallery.

🌀 Tours

Bogside Artists Tours   Art
(📞07514 052481; www.bogsideartists.com; per person £6) Guided walking tours of the famous People's Gallery murals led by the artists themselves. Book in advance by phone or on the website.

City Tours   Guided Tour
(📞7127 1996; www.irishtourguides.com; Carlisle Stores, 11 Carlisle Rd; adult/child £4/2) Runs one-hour Historic Derry walking tours starting from Carlisle Stores at 10am, noon and 2pm year-round. There are also tours of the Bogside and of Derry's murals.

Tours'n'Trails   History
(📞7136 7000; www.toursntrails.co.uk; adult/child £6/4) Offers 1½-hour guided walking tours of the walled city, starting from the tourist office at 11am and 3pm Monday to Saturday from April to October. The price includes admission to St Columb's Cathedral.

🛏 Sleeping & Eating

Merchant's House   B&B ££
(📞7126 9691; www.thesaddlershouse.com; 16 Queen St; s/d £55/80; @ 📶) This historic, Georgian-style town house is a gem of a B&B. It has an elegant lounge and dining room with marble fireplaces and antique furniture, TV, coffee-making facilities and even bathrobes in the bedrooms (only one has a private bathroom), and homemade marmalade at breakfast. Call at Saddler's House (p311) first to pick up a key.

Saddler's House

B&B ££

(☎7126 9691; www.thesaddlershouse.com; 36 Great James St; s/d £55/75; @ 📶) Centrally located within a five-minute walk of the walled city, this friendly B&B is set in a lovely Victorian town house. All seven of the rooms have private bathrooms, and you get to enjoy a huge breakfast in the family kitchen.

Brown's Restaurant

Irish ££

(☎7134 5180; brownsrestaurant.com; 1 Bond's Hill, Waterside; 3-course lunch £16.50, dinner mains £17-23; ⊙noon-3pm Tue-Fri, 5-9.30pm Tue-Sat; 👬) 🌿 From the outside Brown's Restaurant may not have the most promising appearance, but step inside and you'll find yourself in an elegant little enclave of brandy-coloured banquettes and ornate metal light fittings, with vintage monochrome prints adorning the walls. The ever-changing menu is a gastronome's delight, and makes creative use of fresh local produce.

🍷 Drinking & Nightlife

Peadar O'Donnell's

Pub

(www.peadars.com; 63 Waterloo St) A backpackers' favourite, Peadar's has traditional music sessions every night and often on weekend afternoons as well. It's done up as a typical Irish pub-cum-grocer, down to the shelves of grocery items,

shopkeepers scales on the counter and a museum's-worth of old bric-a-brac.

ℹ️ Information

Derry Tourist Information Centre (☎7126 7284; www.derryvisitor.com; 44 Foyle St; ⊙9am-6pm Mon-Sat, 11am-6pm Sun; 📶) Covers all of Northern Ireland and the Republic as well as Derry. Sells books and maps, can book accommodation throughout Ireland and has a bureau de change and free wi-fi.

ℹ️ Getting There & Away

Air

City of Derry Airport (☎7181 0784; www.cityofderryairport.com) About 13km east of Derry along the A2 towards Limavady. Direct flights daily to London Stansted, Liverpool, Birmingham and Glasgow Prestwick (Ryanair).

Bus

The **bus station** (☎7126 2261; Foyle St) is just northeast of the walled city.

Train

Derry's train station (always referred to as Londonderry in Northern Ireland timetables) is on the eastern side of the River Foyle; a free Rail Link bus connects with the bus station. There are trains to Belfast (£11.50, 2¼ hours, seven or eight daily Monday to Saturday, four on Sunday) and Coleraine (£9, 45 minutes, seven daily), with connections to Portrush (£11.50, 1¼ hours).

Ireland
In Focus

Bluebells and beech trees outside Derry/Londonderry (p307)
GARETH McCORMACK/GETTY IMAGES ©

Ireland Today

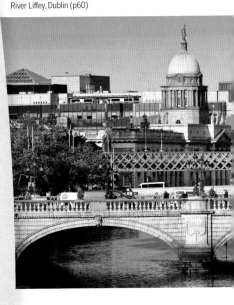

River Liffey, Dublin (p60)

> 66
> *The Irish are used to tough times and have gone to great lengths to adjust*
> 99

belief systems
(% of population)

85

3   1   3   1   7

Roman Catholic | Church of Ireland | Muslim | Other Christian | Other religion | No religion/ not stated

if Ireland were 100 people

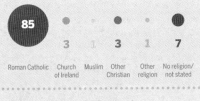

34 would be 24 years old or younger
32 would be between 25 and 44
23 would be beteen 45 and 64
11 would be 65 or older

population per sq km

♦ ≈ 25 people

IRELAND   UK   FRANCE

Times are tough, and austerity – a catch-all term for the unforgiving program of forced cuts and revenue increases that Ireland has been dealing with of late – is neither an abstract concept nor a temporary inconvenience. The Irish are used to tough times and have gone to great lengths to adjust accordingly, but the struggle is profound and ongoing.

The Cost of a Bailout

Ever since the infamous bank guarantee of October 2008 – when the six Irish pillar banks were given a blanket guarantee of *all* their liabilities (totalling €440 billion) by a panicked government – Ireland has been in profound economic crisis. The guarantee expired in 2010 and the government was forced to turn to the EU, the European Financial Stability Fund (EFSF) and the International Monetary Fund (IMF) – referred to as the 'troika' – for a bailout, totalling roughly €85 billion. All of it has to be repaid and the terms set by the troika,

Tightening Irish Belts

The harsh reality for the majority of the Irish is a rising unemployment rate – in 2013 it was just shy of 14%, the highest in 20 years – and emigration, which is bleeding Ireland of 3000 people a month, the highest rate since the Famine. Ordinary people find themselves facing acute mortgage distress, unable to make payments on properties that in some cases have lost more than half their value – in 2013, one in five mortgages were reckoned to be delinquent.

Hope for the Future

Some Irish console themselves by declaring that the country has a long history of hard times and that nothing much has changed. But something has changed, especially in the perception of that generation of Irish who've never known difficult times or recession: they grew up with the unfettered ambitions of the Celtic Tiger, inured with belief that everything was possible so long as you were willing to chase it. Rather than surrender their ambitions, many have opted to emigrate – and they seem to do so with confidence rather than a cap in hand – while the ones staying must endeavour to find new opportunities amid the mayhem. Whereas previous generations may have treated tough times as an unavoidable birthright, this generation continues to struggle in the knowledge that they deserve better.

RICHARD I'ANSON/GETTY IMAGES ©

who show up every three months for a progress report, have resulted in one draconian budget after another.

Political Rhetoric

The year 2011 saw a change of government – out went Fianna Fáil and the Green Party (blamed for the economic crisis), in came a new coalition of centre-right Fine Gael and left-leaning Labour. It was initially greeted with cautious hope, but that hope turned to despair when the pre-election rhetoric about creating jobs and making 'Ireland the best small country in the world to do business in' was revealed to be just that – rhetoric. The unemployment rate hovers stubbornly around 14%, while any downward adjustment is ascribed to skyrocketing emigration: in the year up to April 2013, 86,000 people left Ireland (a 6% increase on the previous year), 57% of whom were Irish nationals.

History

GARETH McCORMACK/GETTY

From pre-Celts to Celtic cubs, Ireland's history is a search for identity, which would be a little more straightforward if this small island hadn't been of such interest to so many invaders, especially the English. Indeed, Ireland's fractious relationship with its nearest neighbour has occupied much of the last 1000 years, and it is through the prism of that relationship that a huge part of the Irish identity is reflected.

Who the Hell are the Irish?

Hunters and gatherers may first have traversed the narrowing land bridge that once linked Ireland with Britain, but many more crossed the Irish Sea in small hide-covered boats. In the 8th century BC, Ireland came to the attention of the fearsome Celts, who, having fought their way across Central Europe, established permanent settlements on the island in the 3rd century BC.

10,000–8000 BC
After the last Ice Age ends, the first humans arrive in Ireland.

Getting into the Habit

Arguably the most significant import into Ireland came between the 3rd and 5th centuries AD, when Christian missionaries first brought the new religion of Rome. Everyone has heard of St Patrick, but he was merely the most famous of many who converted the local pagan tribes by cleverly fusing traditional pagan rituals with the new Christian teaching, creating an exciting hybrid known as Celtic (Insular) Christianity. The artistic and intellectual credentials of Ireland's Christians were the envy of Europe and led to the moniker 'the land of saints and scholars'.

More Invaders

The Celts' lack of political unity made the island easy pickings for the next wave of invaders, Danish Vikings. Over the course of the 9th and 10th centuries, they established settlements along the east coast, intermarried with the Celtic tribes and introduced red hair and freckles to the Irish gene pool.

The '800 years' of English rule in Ireland began in 1171, when the English King Henry II sent a huge invasion force, at the urging of the pope, to bring the increasingly independent Christian missionaries to heel. It was also intended to curb the growing power of the Anglo-Norman lords, who had arrived in Ireland two years before Henry's army, and who had settled quite nicely into Irish life, becoming – as the old saying went – *Hiberniores Hibernis ipsis* (more Irish than the Irish themselves). By the 16th century, they had divided the country into their own fiefdoms and the English Crown's direct control didn't extend any further than a cordon surrounding Dublin, known as 'the Pale'.

Divorce, Dissolution & Destruction

Henry VIII's failure to get the pope's blessing for his divorce augured badly for the Irish, who sided with the Vatican. Henry retaliated by ordering the dissolution of all monasteries in Britain and Ireland, and had himself declared King of Ireland. His daughter Elizabeth I went even further, establishing jurisdiction in Connaught and Munster before crushing the last of the rebels, the lords of Ulster, led by the crafty and courageous Hugh O'Neill, Earl of Tyrone.

With the native chiefs gone, Elizabeth and her successor, James I, could pursue a policy of plantation with impunity. Though confiscations took place all over the country, Ulster was most affected both because of its wealthy farmlands and as punishment for being home to the primary fomenters of rebellion.

700–300 BC

The Celtic culture and language arrive, ushering in 1000 years of cultural and political dominance.

AD 431–2

Arrival of the first Christian missionaries with Bishop Palladius and, a year later, St Patrick.

550–800

The great monastic teachers begin exporting their knowledge across Europe, ushering in Ireland's 'Golden Age'.

The Best...
Irish History
Museums

Bloody Religion

At the outset of the English Civil War in 1641, the Irish threw their support behind Charles I against the Protestant parliamentarians in the hope that victory for the king would lead to the restoration of Catholic power in Ireland. When Oliver Cromwell and his Roundheads defeated the Royalists and took Charles' head off in 1649, Cromwell then turned his attention to the disloyal Irish. His nine-month campaign was effective and brutal; yet more lands were confiscated – Cromwell's famous utterance that the Irish could 'go to hell or to Connaught' seems odd given the province's beauty, but there wasn't much arable land out there – and Catholic rights restricted even more.

The Boyne & Penal Laws

Catholic Ireland's next major setback came in 1690. Yet again the Irish had backed the wrong horse, this time supporting James II after his deposition in the Glorious Revolution by the Dutch Protestant King William of Orange (who was married to James' own daughter Mary). After James had unsuccessfully laid siege to Derry for 105 days (the loyalist cry of 'No Surrender!', in use to this day, dates from the siege), in July he fought William's armies by the banks of the Boyne in County Louth and was roundly defeated.

The final ignominy for Catholic Ireland came in 1695 with the passing of the Penal Laws, known collectively as the 'popery code', which prohibited Catholics from owning land or entering any higher profession. Irish culture, music and education were banned in the hope that Catholicism would be eradicated. Most Catholics continued to worship at secret locations, but some prosperous Irish converted to Protestantism to preserve their careers and wealth. Land was steadily transferred to Protestant owners, and a significant majority of the Catholic population became tenants living in wretched conditions. By the late 18th century, Catholics owned barely 5% of the land.

If at First You Don't Succeed...

With Catholics rendered utterly powerless, the seeds of rebellion against autocracy were planted by a handful of liberal Protestants, inspired by the ideologies of the Enlightenment and the unrest provoked by the American War of Independence and then the French Revolution.

795–841

Vikings plunder Irish monasteries before establishing settlements throughout the country.

1171

King Henry II invades Ireland and forces Anglo-Norman warlords to accept him as their overlord.

1366

Statutes of Kilkenny outlaw intermarriage and a host of Irish customs to stop Anglo-Norman assimilation.

St Patrick

Ireland's patron saint, St Patrick (AD 389–461), remembered all over the world on 17 March, wasn't even Irish. This symbol of Irish pride hailed from what is now Wales, which at the time of his birth was under Roman occupation. Kidnapped by Irish raiders when he was 16 and made a slave, he found religion, escaped captivity and returned to Britain. He returned to Ireland vowing to make Christians out of the Irish, and within 30 years of his return his dream had come true.

So next St Paddy's Day, as you're swilling Guinness, think of who the man really was.

The first of these came in 1798, when the United Irishmen, led by a young Dublin Protestant, Theobald Wolfe Tone (1763–98), took on the British at the Battle of Vinegar Hill in County Wexford – their defeat was hastened by the failure of the French to land an army of succour in 1796 in Bantry Bay.

The Liberator

The Act of Union, passed in 1801, was the British government's vain attempt to put an end to any aspirations towards Irish independence, but the nationalist genie was out of the bottle, not least in the body of a Kerry-born Catholic named Daniel O'Connell (1775–1847). In 1823 O'Connell founded the Catholic Association with the aim of achieving political equality for Catholics, which he did (in part) by forcing the passing of the 1829 Act of Catholic Emancipation, allowing some well-off Catholics voting rights and the right to be elected as MPs.

O'Connell's campaign now switched to the repeal of the Act of Union, but the 'Liberator' came to a sorry end in 1841 when he meekly stood down in face of a government order banning one of his rallies. His capitulation was deemed unforgivable given that Ireland was in the midst of the Potato Famine.

The Uncrowned King of Ireland

The baton of moderate opposition to British rule was then taken up by the extraordinary Charles Stewart Parnell (1846–91), who instigated the strategy of 'boycotting' (named after one particularly unpleasant agent named Charles Boycott) tenants, agents and landlords who didn't get on board with the demands of the Land League, an organisation set up to agitate for land reform, arguably the most important feature of the Irish struggle against British rule. The Land Act of 1881 improved life immeasurably for tenants, creating fair rents and the possibility of tenants owning their land.

1534–41

Henry VIII declares war on the Irish Church and declares himself King of Ireland.

HENRY VIII/
DE AGOSTINI/GETTY IMAGES ©

1594

Hugh O'Neill, Earl of Tyrone, instigates open conflict with England and starts the Nine Years' War.

319

Parnell's other assault on British rule was on agitating for Home Rule, a limited form of autonomy for Ireland. As leader of the Irish Parliamentary Party (IPP), he formed alliances with William Gladstone's Liberal Party in return for the introduction of a Home Rule Bill, which came (but was defeated) in 1886 and 1892 – although Parnell was not around for the second bill: in 1890 he was embroiled in a divorce scandal, was forced to resign and died a broken man in 1891.

Rebellion Once Again

Ireland's struggle for some kind of autonomy picked up pace in the second decade of the 20th century. The radicalism that had always been at the fringes of Irish nationalist aspirations was once again beginning to assert itself, partly in response to a hardening of attitudes in Ulster. Mass opposition to any kind of Irish independence had resulted in the formation of the Ulster Volunteer Force (UVF), a loyalist vigilante group whose 100,000-plus members swore to resist any attempt to impose Home Rule on Ireland. Nationalists responded by creating the Irish Volunteer Force (IVF), and a showdown seemed inevitable.

Home Rule was finally passed in 1914, but the outbreak of WWI meant that its enactment was shelved for the duration. For most Irish, the suspension was disappointing but hardly unreasonable and the majority of the volunteers enlisted to help fight the Germans.

The Easter Rising

A few, however, did not heed the call. Two small groups – a section of the Irish Volunteers under Pádraig Pearse and the Irish Citizens' Army led by James Connolly – conspired in a rebellion that took the country by surprise. A depleted Volunteer group marched into Dublin on Easter Monday 1916 and took over a number of key positions in the city, claiming the General Post Office on O'Connell St as its headquarters. From its steps, Pearse read out to passers-by a declaration that Ireland was now a republic

Beyond the Pale

The expression 'beyond the pale' came into use when the Pale – defined as a jurisdiction marked by a clear boundary – was the English-controlled part of Ireland, which stretched roughly from Dalkey, a southern suburb of Dublin, to Dundalk, north of Drogheda. Inland, the boundary extended west to Trim and Kells. The British elite considered the rest of Ireland to be uncivilised.

1601
O'Neill surrenders after the Battle of Kinsale and Irish rebellion against the Crown is broken.

1649–53
Oliver Cromwell lays waste throughout Ireland after the Irish support Charles I.

1690
Catholic King James II defeated by William of Orange in the Battle of the Boyne on 12 July.

and that his band was the provisional government. Less than a week of fighting ensued before the rebels surrendered to the superior British forces. The rebels weren't popular and had to be protected from angry Dubliners as they were marched to jail.

The Easter Rising would probably have had little impact on the Irish situation had the British not made martyrs of the rebel leaders. Of the 77 given death sentences, 15 were executed, including the injured Connolly, who was shot while strapped to a chair. This brought about a sea change in public attitudes and support for the Republicans rose dramatically.

War with Britain

By the end of WWI, Home Rule was far too little, far too late. In the 1918 general election, the Republicans stood under the banner of Sinn Féin and won a large majority of the Irish seats. Ignoring London's Parliament, where technically they were supposed to sit, the newly elected Sinn Féin deputies – many of them veterans of the 1916 Easter Rising – declared Ireland independent and formed the first Dáil Éireann (Irish assembly or lower house), which sat in Dublin's Mansion House under the leadership of Éamon de Valera (1882–1975). The Irish Volunteers became the Irish Republican

Ruined abbey, County Wexford (p145)
MARTIN MOOS/GETTY IMAGES ©

1801

The Act of Union unites Ireland politically with Britain, ending Irish 'independence'.

1845–51

Between 500,000 and one million die during Potato Famine; two million more emigrate.

FAMINE 1997 BY ROWAN GILLESPIE, BRONZE, HEIGHT 200–250CM; DOUG McKINLAY/GETTY IMAGES ©

Army (IRA) and the Dáil authorised it to wage war on British troops in Ireland.

As wars go, the War of Independence was pretty small fry. It lasted 2½ years and cost around 1200 casualties. But it was a pretty nasty affair, as the IRA fought a guerrilla-style, hit-and-run campaign against the British, and their numbers swelled by returning veterans of WWI (known as Black and Tans on account of their uniforms, a mix of army khaki and police black), most of whom were so traumatised by their wartime experiences that they were prone to all kinds of brutality.

A Kind of Freedom

A truce in July 1921 led to intense negotiations between the two sides. The resulting Treaty, signed on 6 December 1921, created the Irish Free State, made up of 26 of 32 Irish counties. The remaining six – all in Ulster – remained part of the UK. The Treaty was an imperfect document: not only did it cement the geographic divisions on the island that 50 years later would explode into the Troubles, but it caused a split among nationalists – between those who believed the Treaty to be a necessary stepping stone toward full independence and those who saw it as capitulation to the British and a betrayal of Republican ideals. This division was to determine the course of Irish political affairs for virtually the remainder of the century.

Civil War

The Treaty was ratified after a bitter debate and the June 1922 elections resulted in a victory for the pro-Treaty side. But the anti-Treaty forces rallied behind de Valera. Though president of the Dáil, de Valera had not been a member of the Treaty negotiating team – this afforded him, in the eyes of his critics and opponents, maximum deniability should the negotiations go pear-shaped – and he objected to some of the Treaty's provisions, most notably the oath of allegiance to the English monarch.

Within two weeks of the elections, civil war broke out between comrades who, a year previously, had fought alongside each other. The most prominent casualty of this particularly bitter conflict was Michael Collins (1890–1922), mastermind of the IRA's campaign during the War of Independence and a chief negotiator of the Anglo-Irish Treaty. Shot in an ambush in his native Cork, Collins himself had presaged the bitterness that would result from the Treaty: upon signing it he is said to have declared, 'I tell you, I have signed my own death warrant.'

1916

The Easter Rising rebels surrender to superior British forces in less than a week.

1919

The Irish War of Independence begins in January.

1921

War ends in a truce on 11 July; Anglo-Irish Treaty is signed on 6 December.

The Great Famine

As a result of the Great Famine of 1845–51, a staggering three million people died or were forced to emigrate from Ireland. This great tragedy is all the more inconceivable given that the scale of suffering was attributable to selfishness as much as to natural causes. Potatoes were the staple food of a rapidly growing, desperately poor population and, when a blight hit the crops, prices soared. The repressive Penal Laws ensured that farmers, already crippled with high rents, could ill afford the limited harvest of potatoes not affected by blight or imported from abroad to sell to the Irish.

Shamefully, during this time there were abundant harvests of wheat and dairy produce. The country was producing more than enough grain to feed the entire population and it's said that more cattle were sold abroad than there were people on the island.

Mass emigration continued to reduce the population during the next 100 years and huge numbers of Irish emigrants who found their way abroad, particularly to the US, carried with them a lasting bitterness.

The Making of a Republic

The Civil War ground to an exhausted halt in 1923 with the victory of the pro-Treaty side, who governed the new state until 1932. Defeated but unbowed, de Valera founded a new party in 1926 called Fianna Fáil (Soldiers of Ireland) and won a majority in the 1932 elections – they would remain in charge until 1948. In the meantime, de Valera created a new constitution in 1937 that did away with the hated oath of allegiance, reaffirmed the special position of the Catholic Church and once again laid claim to the six counties of Northern Ireland. In 1948 Ireland officially left the Commonwealth and became a Republic, but as historical irony would have it, it was Fine Gael, as the old pro-Treaty party were now known, that declared it – Fianna Fáil had surprisingly lost the election that year. After 800 years, Ireland – or at least a substantial chunk of it – was independent.

Growing Pains & Roaring Tigers

Unquestionably the most significant figure since independence, Éamon de Valera's contribution to an independent Ireland was immense but, as the 1950s stretched into the 1960s, his vision for the country was mired in a conservative and traditional

1921–22

Treaty grants independence to 26 counties; six Ulster counties remain part of Great Britain.

1922–23

Brief and bloody civil war between pro-Treaty and anti-Treaty forces results in victory for former.

1932

De Valera leads his Fianna Fáil party into government for the first time.

orthodoxy that was patently at odds with the reality of a country in desperate economic straits, where chronic unemployment and emigration were but the more visible effects of inadequate policy.

Partners in Europe

In 1972 the Republic (along with Northern Ireland) became a member of the European Economic Community (EEC), which brought an increased measure of prosperity thanks to the benefits of the Common Agricultural Policy, which set fixed prices and guaranteed quotas for Irish farming produce. Nevertheless, the broader global depression, provoked by the oil crisis of 1973, forced the country into yet another slump and emigration figures rose again, reaching a peak in the mid-1980s.

From Celtic Tiger...

In the early 1990s, European funds helped kick start economic growth. Huge sums of money were invested in education and physical infrastructure, while the policy of low corporate tax rates coupled with attractive incentives made Ireland very appealing to high-tech businesses looking for a door into EU markets. In less than a decade, Ireland

Memorial to the 1798 Rebellion, Vinegar Hill (p150)
MAURICE SAVAGE/ALAMY ©

1948
The new Fine Gael declares the Free State to be a republic.

1972
The Republic (and the UK) join the EEC; 13 civilians are killed by soldiers in Derry.

1993
Downing Street Declaration signed by British prime minister John Major and Irish *Taoiseach* Albert Reynolds.

went from being one of the poorest countries in Europe to one of the wealthiest: unemployment fell from 18% to 3.5%, the average industrial wage somersaulted to the top of the European league and the dramatic rise in GDP meant that the government had far more money than it knew what do with. Ireland became synonymous with the Celtic Tiger, an economic model of success that was the envy of the entire world.

...to Rescue Cat

From 2002, the Irish economy was kept buoyant by a gigantic construction boom that was completely out of step with any measure of responsible growth forecasting. The out-of-control international derivatives market flooded Irish banks with cheap money, and they were only too happy to lend it to anyone who wanted. And in Ireland, everyone wanted.

Then Lehman Brothers and the credit crunch happened. The Irish banks nearly went to the wall, were bailed out at the last minute and, before Ireland could draw breath, the International Monetary Fund (IMF) and the European Union held the chits of the country's mid-term economic future. Ireland found itself yet again confronting the demons of its past: high unemployment, limited opportunity and massive emigration.

The Best...
Books About Ireland

1 *The Course of Irish History* (TW Moody & FX Martin)

2 *The Great Hunger* (Cecil Woodham-Smith)

3 *The Irish in America* (Michael Coffey)

4 *For the Cause of Liberty: A Thousand Years of Ireland's Heroes* (Terry Golway)

5 *A History of Ulster* (Jonathon Bardon)

It's (Not So) Grim up North

Making sense of Northern Ireland isn't that easy. It's not because the politics are so entrenched (they are), or that the two sides are at such odds with each other (they are): it's because the fight is so old.

It began in the 16th century, with the first Plantations of Ireland ordered by the English Crown, whereby the confiscated lands of the Gaelic and Hiberno-Norman gentry were awarded to English and Scottish settlers of good Protestant stock. The policy was most effective in Ulster, where the newly arrived Protestants were given an extra leg-up by the Penal Laws, which successfully reduced the now landless Catholic population to second-class citizens with little or no rights.

1994
Sinn Féin leader Gerry Adams announces a cessation of IRA violence on 31 August.

mid-1990s
The 'Celtic Tiger' economy transforms Ireland into one of Europe's wealthiest countries.

1998
After the Good Friday Agreement, the 'Real IRA' detonates a bomb in Omagh, killing 29 people and injuring 200.

Irish Sectarianism

Fast-forward to 1921, when the notion of independent Ireland moved from aspiration to actuality. The new rump state of Northern Ireland was governed until 1972 by the Protestant-majority Ulster Unionist Party, backed up by the overwhelmingly Protestant Royal Ulster Constabulary (RUC) and the sectarian B-Specials militia. As a result of tilted economic subsidies, bias in housing allocation and wholesale gerrymandering, Northern Ireland was, in effect, a divided state, leaving the roughly 40% Catholic and Nationalist population grossly underrepresented.

Defiance of Unionist hegemony came with the Civil Rights Movement, founded in 1967 and heavily influenced by its US counterpart. In October 1968 a mainly Catholic march in Derry was violently broken up by the RUC amid rumours that the IRA had provided 'security' for the marchers. Nobody knew it at the time, but the Troubles had begun.

The Troubles

Conflict escalated quickly: clashes between the two communities increased and the police openly sided with the Loyalists against a Nationalist population made increasingly militant by the resurgence of the long-dormant IRA. In August 1969 British

Peace mural, Belfast (p294)
MARTIN MOOS/GETTY IMAGES ©

2005

The IRA orders all of its units to commit to exclusively democratic means.

2007

The Northern Ireland Assembly resumes after a five-year break as Unionists and Nationalists resolve differences.

MEMORIAL GARDEN, WEST BELFAST (P292), CARLOS SANCHEZ PEREYRA/GETTY IMAGES

troops went to Derry and then Belfast to maintain law and order; they were initially welcomed in Catholic neighbourhoods but within a short time they too were seen as an army of occupation: the killing of 13 innocent civilians in Derry on Bloody Sunday (30 January 1972) set the grim tone for the next two decades, as violence, murder and reprisal became the order of the day in the province and, occasionally, on the British mainland.

Overtures of Peace

In the 1990s external circumstances started to alter the picture. Membership of the EU, economic progress in Ireland and the declining importance of the Catholic Church in the South started to reduce differences between the North and the Republic. American interest also added an international dimension to the situation.

A series of negotiated statements between the Unionists, Nationalists and the British and Irish governments eventually resulted in the historic Good Friday Agreement of 1998, which established the power-sharing Northern Ireland Assembly.

The agreement called for the devolution of legislative power from Westminster (where it had been since 1972) to a new Northern Ireland Assembly, but posturing, disagreement, sectarianism and downright pigheadedness made slow work of progress, and the assembly was suspended four times – the last from October 2002 until May 2007.

During this period, the politics of Northern Ireland polarised dramatically, resulting in the falling away of the more moderate UUP and the emergence of the hardline Democratic Unionist Party (DUP), led by Ian Paisley; and, on the Nationalist side, the emergence of the IRA's political wing, Sinn Féin, as the main torch-bearer of Nationalist aspirations, under the leadership of Gerry Adams and Martin McGuinness.

2008
The Irish banking system is declared virtually bankrupt following the collapse of Lehman Brothers.

2010
Ireland surrenders financial sovereignty to IMF and EU in exchange for bailout package of €85bn.

2011
Queen Elizabeth II is the first British monarch to visit the Republic of Ireland.

Food & Drink

A selection of Irish cheeses

OLIVER STREWE/GETTY IMAGE

Ireland's recently acquired reputation as a gourmet destination is thoroughly deserved. A host of chefs and producers are leading a foodie revolution that, at its heart, is about bringing to the table the kind of meals that have always been taken for granted on well-run Irish farms. Coupled with the growing sophistication of the Irish palate – by now well used to the varied flavours of the world's range of cuisines – it's now relatively easy to eat well in all budgets.

Local Specialities

To Eat...

Potatoes

It's a wonder the Irish retain their good humour amid the perpetual potato-baiting they endure. But, despite the stereotyping, and however much we'd like to disprove it, potatoes are still paramount here and you'll see lots of them on your travels. The mashed potato dishes *colcannon* and *champ* (with cabbage and spring onion respectively) are two of the tastiest recipes in the country.

Meat & Seafood

Irish meals are usually meat based, with beef, lamb and pork common options. Seafood, long neglected, is finding a place on the table in Irish homes. It's widely available in restaurants and is often excellent, especially in the west. Oysters, trout and salmon are delicious, particularly if they're direct from the sea or a river rather than a fish farm. The famous Dublin Bay prawn isn't actually a prawn but a lobster. At its best, the Dublin Bay prawn is superlative, but it's priced accordingly. If you're going to splurge, do so here – but make sure you choose live Dublin Bay prawns because once these fellas die, they quickly lose their flavour.

Soda Bread

The most famous Irish bread, and one of the signature tastes of Ireland, is soda bread. Irish flour is soft and doesn't take well to yeast as a raising agent, so Irish bakers of the 19th century leavened their bread with bicarbonate of soda. Combined with buttermilk, it makes a superbly light-textured and tasty bread, and is often on the breakfast menus at B&Bs.

Cheese

Ireland has some wonderful cheeses, such as the flavoursome farmhouse Ardrahan with a rich nutty taste; the subtle Corleggy, a pasteurised goats cheese from County Cavan; Durrus, a creamy, fruity cheese; creamy Cashel Blue from Tipperary; and the award-winning Camembert-style cheese, Cooleeney.

The Fry

Perhaps the most feared Irish speciality is the fry – the heart attack on a plate that is the second part of so many B&B deals. In spite of the health concerns, the fry is still one of the most common traditional meals in the country. Who can say no to a plate of fried bacon, sausages, black pudding, white pudding, eggs and tomatoes? For the famous Ulster fry, common throughout the North, simply add *fadge* (potato bread).

Dare to Try

Ironically, while the Irish palate has become more adventurous, it is the old-fashioned Irish menu that features some fairly interesting dishes:

Black pudding Made from congealed pork blood, suet and other fillings, it is a ubiquitous part of an Irish cooked breakfast.

Boxty A Northern Irish starchy potato cake made with a half-and-half mix of cooked mashed potatoes and grated, strained raw potato.

Carrageen The typical Irish seaweed that can be found in dishes as diverse as salad and ice cream.

Corned beef tongue Usually accompanied by cabbage, this dish is still found on a traditional Irish menu.

Lough Neagh eel A speciality of Northern Ireland typically eaten around Halloween; it's usually served in chunks and with a white onion sauce.

Poitín It's rare enough that you'll be offered a drop of the 'cratur', as illegally distilled whiskey (made from malted grain or potatoes) is called here. Still, there are pockets of the country with secret stills in Donegal, Connemara and West Cork.

The Best...
Memorable Meals

1 Restaurant Patrick Guilbaud (p84)

2 Fishy Fishy Cafe (p184)

3 Tannery (p157)

4 Ginger (p298)

5 55 Degrees North (p302)

To Drink...

Stout

While Guinness has become synonymous with stout the world over, few outside Ireland realise that there are two other major producers competing for the favour of the Irish drinker: Murphy's and Beamish & Crawford, both based in Cork city.

Tea

The Irish drink more tea, per capita, than any other nation in the world and you'll be offered a cup as soon as you cross the threshold of any Irish home. Taken with milk (and sugar, if you want) rather than lemon, preferred blends are very strong, and nothing like the namby-pamby versions that pass for Irish breakfast tea elsewhere.

Whiskey

At last count, there were almost 100 different types of Irish whiskey, brewed by only three distilleries – Jameson's in Midleton, County Cork, Bushmills on the Antrim Coast, and Cooley's on the Cooley Peninsula, County Louth. A visit to Ireland reveals a depth of excellence that will make the connoisseur's palate spin, while winning over many new friends to what the Irish call *uisce beatha* (water of life).

Other Irish Beers

Beamish Ale For something a little different, try this sweet and palatable traditional red ale brewed in Cork city.

Caffrey's Irish Ale A robust cross between a stout and an ale brewed in County Antrim.

Kinsale Irish Lager A golden-coloured lager brewed in the eponymous County Cork town, with a slightly bitter taste that fades after a few sips.

McCardles Traditional Ale Hard to come by but worthy, this is a wholesome dark nutty ale.

Smithwick's A lovely refreshing full scoop brewed in Kilkenny on the site of the 14th-century St Francis Abbey, Ireland's oldest working brewery.

When to Eat

Irish eating habits have changed over the last couple of decades, and there are differences between urban and rural practices.

Breakfast

Breakfast is an important meal given the Irish tendency toward small lunches. It's usually eaten before 9am as most people rush off to work; hotels and B&Bs will serve until 11am Monday to Friday, to noon at weekends. Weekend brunch is popular in bigger towns and cities, although it pretty much copies traditional rural habits of eating a large, earthy breakfast late in the morning.

Lunch

Once the biggest meal of the day, lunch is now one of the more obvious rural/urban divides. Urban workers have succumbed to the eat-on-the-run restrictions of nine-to-five, with most eating a sandwich or a light meal between 12.30pm and 2pm (most restaurants don't begin to serve lunch until at least midday) in urban areas.

At weekends, especially Sunday, the midday lunch is skipped in favour a substantial mid-afternoon meal (called dinner), usually between 2pm and 4pm.

Tea

No, not the drink, but the evening meal – also confusingly called dinner. For urbanites, this is the main meal of the day, usually eaten around 6.30pm. Rural communities eat at the same time but a more traditional tea of bread, cold cuts and, yes, tea. Restaurants follow more international habits, with most diners not eating until at least 7.30pm.

Supper

A before-bed snack of tea and toast or sandwiches is still enjoyed by many Irish although urbanites increasingly eschew it for health reasons. Not a practice in restaurants.

Dining Etiquette

The Irish aren't big on restrictive etiquette, preferring friendly informality to any kind of stuffy formality. Still, there are a few tips to dining with the Irish.

A local repast: lobsters, bread and Guinness
OLIVER STREWE/GETTY IMAGES ©

Vegetarians & Vegans

Vegetarians can take a deep breath. And then exhale. Calmly. For Ireland has come a long, long way since the days when vegetarians were looked upon as odd creatures. Nowadays, even the most militant vegan will barely cause a ruffle in all but the most basic of rustic kitchens. Which isn't to say that travellers with plant-based diets are going to find the most imaginative range of options on menus outside the bigger towns and cities – or in the plethora of modern restaurants that have opened in the last few years – but you can rest assured that the overall quality of the homegrown vegetable is top-notch and most places will have at least one dish that you can tuck into comfortably.

All restaurants welcome kids until 7pm, but pubs and some smarter restaurants don't allow them in the evening. Family restaurants have children's menus, others have reduced portions of regular menu items.

If the food is not to your satisfaction, it's best to politely explain what's wrong with it as soon as you can; any respectable restaurant will endeavour to replace the dish immediately.

If you insist on paying the bill, be prepared for a first, second and even third refusal to countenance such an *exorbitant* act of generosity. But don't be fooled: the Irish will refuse something several times even if they're delighted with it. Insist gently but firmly and you'll get your way!

Price Ranges

Throughout this guide, cafe and restaurant listings appear in order of price range, with the cheapest budget range first.

€/£ (budget) less than €12/£12

€€/££ (midrange) €12–25/£12–20

€€€/£££ (top end) over €25/£20

Pub in Dublin (p58)

TERRY WILLIAMS/GETTY IMAGES ©

Simply put, the pub is the heart of Ireland's social existence, and we're guessing that experiencing it ranks pretty high on your list of things to do while you're here. But let's be clear: we're not just talking about a place to get a drink. Oh no. You can get a drink in a restaurant or a hotel, or wherever there's someone with a bottle of something strong. The pub is something far more than just that.

Role

The pub is the broadest window through which you can examine and experience the very essence of the nation's culture, in all its myriad of forms. It's the great leveller, where status and rank hold no sway, where generation gaps are bridged, inhibitions lowered, tongues loosened, schemes hatched, songs sung, stories told and gossip embroidered. It's a unique institution: a theatre and a cosy room, a centre stage and a hideaway, a debating chamber and a place for silent contemplation. It's whatever you want it to be, and that's the secret of a great Irish pub.

Talk

Talk – whether it is frivolous, earnest or incoherent – is the essential ingredient. Once tongues are loosened and the cogs of thought oiled, the conversation can go

IN FOCUS THE PUB

The Best... Traditional Music Pubs

1 Cobblestone (p89)

2 O'Friel's Bar (p237)

3 Peadar O'Donnell's (p311)

anywhere and you should let it flow to its natural conclusion. An old Irish adage suggests you should never talk about sport, religion or politics in unfamiliar company. But as long as you're mindful, you needn't restrict yourself too much. While it's a myth to say you can walk into any pub and be befriended, you probably won't be drinking on your own for long – unless that's what you want of course. There are few more spiritual experiences than a solitary pint in an old country pub in the mid-afternoon.

Tradition

Aesthetically, there is nothing better than the traditional haunt, populated by flat-capped pensioners bursting with delightful anecdotes and always ready to dispense a kind of wisdom distilled through generations' worth of experience. The best of them have stone floors and a peat fire; the chat barely rises above a respectful murmur save for appreciative laughter; and most of all, there's no music save the kind played by someone sitting next to you. Pubs like these are a disappearing breed, but there are still plenty of them around to ensure that you will find one, no matter where you are.

Etiquette

The rounds system – the simple custom where someone buys you a drink and you buy one back – is the bedrock of Irish pub culture. It's summed up in the Irish saying: 'It's impossible for two men to go to a pub for one drink.' Nothing will hasten your fall from social grace here like the failure to uphold this pub law.

Another golden rule about the system is that the next round starts when the first person has finished (preferably just about to finish) their drink. It doesn't matter if you're only halfway through your pint – if it's your round, get your order in.

Irish Mythological Symbols

Shamrocks

JOHN SONES/GETTY IMAGES ©

Ireland's collection of icons serves to exemplify the country – or a simplistic version of it – to an astonishing degree. It's referred to by the Irish as Oirishness, which is what happens when you take a spud, shove it in a pint of Guinness and garnish it with shamrock. You'll see it throughout the world, as the hyphenated Irish join with the nation's native sons and daughters to celebrate St Patrick's Day, their eyes made bleary by more than just emotion.

The Shamrock

Ireland's most enduring symbol is the shamrock, a three-leafed white clover known diminutively in Irish as *seamróg*, which was anglicised as 'shamrock'. According to legend, when St Patrick was trying to explain the mystery of the Holy Trinity to the recently converted Celtic chieftains, he plucked the modest little weed and used its three leaves to explain the metaphysically challenging concept of the Father, the Son and the Holy Spirit as being separate but part of the one being. This link is what makes the shamrock a ubiquitous part of the St Patrick's Day celebrations.

The Best...
Irish Crafts & Memorabilia

1 Avoca Handweavers (p91)

2 Thomas Dillon's Claddagh Gold (p219)

3 Ardara Heritage Centre (p267)

4 Long Room (p61), Trinity College

The Celtic Cross

Everywhere you go, you will see examples of the Celtic cross – basically, a cross surrounded by a ring. Its origins weren't simply a question of aesthetic design but more of practical necessity. The cross was a clever fusing of new Christian teaching (the cross itself) with established pagan beliefs – in this case, sun worship (marked by the circle).

Some of the most famous crosses in Ireland are in Monasterboice, County Louth, and Clonmacnoise, County Offaly.

The Leprechaun

The country's most enduring cliche is the myth of the mischievous leprechaun and his pot of gold, which he jealously guards from the attentions of greedy humans. Despite the twee aspect of the legend, their origin predates the Celts and belongs to the mythological Tuatha dé Danann (peoples of the Goddess Danu), who lived in Ireland 4000 years ago. When they were eventually defeated, their king Lugh (the demi-God father of Cúchulainn) was forced underground, where he became known as Lugh Chromain, or 'little stooping Lugh' – the origin of leprechaun.

The Irish can get visibly irritated if asked whether they believe in leprechauns (you might as well ask them if they're stupid), but many rural dwellers are a superstitious lot. They mightn't necessarily *believe* that malevolent sprites who dwell in faerie forts actually exist, but they're not especially keen to test the theory either, which is why there still exist trees, hills and other parts of the landscape that are deemed to have, well, supernatural qualities, and as such will never be touched.

The Harp

The Celtic harp, or *clársach*, is meant to represent the immortality of the soul, which is handy given that it's been a symbol of Ireland since the days of Henry VIII and the first organised opposition to English rule. The harp was the most popular instrument at the Celtic court, with the harpist (usually blind) being ranked only behind the chief and bard in order of importance. In times of war, the harpist played a special, jewel-encrusted harp and served as the cheerleading section for soldiers heading into battle.

During the first rebellions against the English, the harp was once again an instrument of revolutionary fervour, prompting the crown to ban it altogether. This eventually led to its decline as the instrument of choice for Irish musicians but ensured its status as a symbol of Ireland.

The Luck of the Irish?

Nearly a millennium of occupation, a long history of oppression and exploitation, a devastating famine, mass emigration… how *exactly* are the Irish 'lucky'? Well, they're not – or at least not any more so than anybody else. The expression was born in the mid-19th century in the US during the gold and silver rush, when some of the most successful miners were Irish or of Irish extraction. It didn't really seem to matter that the Irish – recent escapees from famine and destitution in Ireland – were over-represented among the miners; the expression stuck. Still, the expression was always a little derisory, as though the Irish merely stumbled across good fortune.

The Claddagh Ring

The most famous of all Irish jewellery is the Claddagh ring, made up of two hands (friendship) clasping a heart (love) and usually surmounted by a crown (loyalty). Made in the eponymous fishing village of County Galway since the 17th century, the symbolic origins are much older and belong to a broader family of rings popular since Roman times known as the *fede* rings (from *mani in fede*, or 'hands in trust'), which were used to symbolise marriage. Nevertheless, their popularity is relatively recent, and almost entirely down to their wearing by expat Americans who use them to demonstrate their ties to their Irish heritage.

Literary Ireland

A reading on Bloomsday (p43)

WAYNE WALTON/GETTY IMAGES

Of all their national characteristics and cultural expressions, it's perhaps the way the Irish speak and write that best distinguishes them. Their love of language and their great oral tradition have contributed to Ireland's legacy of world-renowned writers and storytellers. All this in a language imposed on them by a foreign invader. The Irish responded to this act of cultural piracy by mastering a magnificent hybrid – an English that has been flavoured and enriched by the rhythms, pronunciation, patterns and grammatical peculiarities of Irish.

The Mythic Cycle

Before there was anything like modern literature, there was the Ulaid (Ulster) Cycle – Ireland's version of the Homeric epic – written down from oral tradition between the 8th and 12th centuries. The chief story is the Táin Bó Cúailnge (Cattle Raid of Cooley), about a battle between Queen Maeve of Connaught and Cúchulainn, the principal hero of Irish mythology. Cúchulainn appears in the work of Irish writers right up to the present day, from Samuel Beckett to Frank McCourt.

Modern Literature

From the mythic cycle, zip forward 1000 years, past the genius of Jonathan Swift (1667–1745) and his *Gulliver's Travels;* stopping to acknowledge acclaimed dramatist Oscar Wilde (1854–1900); *Dracula* author Bram Stoker (1847–1912) – some have optimistically claimed that the name of the count may have come from the Irish *droch fhola* (bad blood); and the literary giant that was James Joyce (1882–1941), whose name and books elicit enormous pride in Ireland (although we've yet to meet five people who have read *Ulysses* in its entirety!).

The majority of Joyce's literary output came when he had left Ireland for the artistic hotbed that was Paris, which was also true for another great experimenter of language and style, Samuel Beckett (1906–89). Influenced by the Italian poet Dante and French philosopher Descartes, Beckett's work centres on fundamental existential questions about the human condition and the nature of self. He is probably best known for his play *Waiting for Godot,* but his unassailable reputation is based on a series of stark novels and plays.

Of the dozens of 20th-century Irish authors to have achieved published renown, some names to look out for include playwright and novelist Brendan Behan (1923–64), who wove tragedy, wit and a turbulent life into his best works, including *Borstal Boy, The Quare Fellow* and *The Hostage.* Inevitably, as life imitated art, Behan died young of alcoholism.

Belfast-born CS Lewis (1898–1963) died a year earlier, leaving us *The Chronicles of Narnia,* a series of allegorical children's stories, three of which have been made into films – the third (*The Voyage of the Dawn Treader*) came out in 2010. In works by other Northern writers, not surprisingly, the Troubles are featured: Bernard McLaverty's *Cal* (also made into a film) and his more recent *The Anatomy School* are both wonderful.

Contemporary Scene

'I love James Joyce. Never read him, but he's a true genius.' Yes, the stalwarts are still great, but ask your average Irish person who their favourite home-grown writer is and they'll most likely mention someone *who's still alive*.

They might mention Roddy Doyle (b 1958), whose mega-successful Barrytown quartet – *The Commitments, The Snapper, The Van* and *Paddy Clarke, Ha Ha Ha* – have all been made into films. Most recently, he's turned to social and political history with a new trilogy, beginning with *A Star Called Henry* (2000), a story of an IRA hit-man called Henry Smart, followed by *Oh, Play That Thing!* (2004) and *The Dead Republic* (2010), both of which follow Henry on his adventures in the US.

Sebastian Barry (b 1955) started his career as a poet with *The Water Colorist* (1983), became famous as a playwright, but achieved his greatest success as a novelist: he was shortlisted for the Man Booker Prize twice, in 2005 for his WWI drama *A Long Way Down* and in 2008 for the absolutely compelling *The Secret Scripture,*

The Gaelic Revival

While Home Rule was being debated and shunted, something of a revolution was taking place in Irish arts, literature and identity. The poet William Butler Yeats and his coterie of literary friends (including Lady Gregory, Douglas Hyde, John Millington Synge and George Russell) championed the Anglo-Irish literary revival, unearthing old Celtic tales and writing with fresh enthusiasm about a romantic Ireland of epic battles and warrior queens. For a country that had suffered centuries of invasion and deprivation, these images presented a much more attractive version of history.

The Best...
Contemporary
Fiction

1 *The Empty Family*
(Colm Tóibín)

2 *Ghost Light*
(Joseph O'Connor)

3 *The Forgotten Waltz*
(Anne Enright)

4 *Room*
(Emma Donoghue)

5 *John the Revelator*
(Peter Byrne)

about a 100-year-old inmate of a mental hospital who decides to write an autobiography. It was the Costa Book of the Year in 2008 and won the prestigious James Tait Black Memorial Prize in 2009.

Anne Enright (b 1962) did nab the Man Booker for *The Gathering* (2007), a zeitgeist tale of alcoholism and abuse; her latest novel is *The Forgotten Waltz* (2011). John Banville (b 1945) also won the Booker for *The Sea* (2009); we recommend either *The Book of Evidence* (1989) or the masterful roman á clef *The Untouchable* (1998). Banville's precise and often cold prose divides critics, who consider him either the English language's greatest living stylist or an unreadable intellectual; if you're of the latter inclination then you should check out his highly readable crime novels, written under the pseudonym of Benjamin Black.

Another big hitter is Wexford-born but Dublin-based Colm Tóibin (b 1955), who spent four years looking for a publisher for his first novel *The South* (1990), but has gone on to become a hugely successful novelist and scholar – *The Master* (2004) and *Brooklyn* (2009) were both very well received. His recent book, *The Empty Family* (2011), is a collection of short stories.

Of the host of younger writers making names for themselves, we recommend the work of Claire Kilroy (b 1973), whose first three novels – *All Summer* (2003), *Tenderwire* (2006) and *All the Names Have Been Changed* (2009) – established her as a genuine talent.

Like some of their famous antecedents, some Irish novelists have gone abroad to write and find success. Joseph O'Neill (b 1964) won the PEN/Faulkner Award for fiction for his post-9/11 novel *Netherland* (2009), while Colum McCann (b 1965), who also tackled 9/11 but in a far more allegorical fashion, picked up the National Book Award for *Let the Great World Spin* (2009).

Chick Lit

Authors hate the label and publishers profess to disregard it, but chick lit is big business and few have mastered it as well as the Irish. Doyenne of them all is Maeve Binchy (1940–2012), whose mastery of the style saw her outsell most of the literary greats – her last novel before she died was *A Week in Winter* (2012). Marian Keyes (b 1963) is another author with a long line of bestsellers, including *The Mystery of Mercy Close* (2012). She's a terrific storyteller with a rare ability to tackle sensitive issues such as alcoholism and depression, issues that she herself has suffered from and is admirably honest about. Former agony aunt Cathy Kelly turns out novels at the rate of one a year: a recent book is *The Honey Queen* (2013), about all not being well in the fictional town of Redstone...

Traditional Music

Traditional music session

DOUG McKINLAY/GETTY IMAGES ©

Irish music (known as traditional music, or just trad) has maintained a vibrancy not found in other traditional European forms, which have lost out to the overbearing influence of pop music. While Irish music has retained many of its traditional aspects, it has also influenced many forms of music, most notably US country and western – a fusion of Mississippi Delta blues and Irish traditional tunes, combined with other influences including Gospel, is at the root of rock and roll.

Trad music's current success is also due to the willingness of its exponents to update the way it's played (in ensembles rather than the customary *céilidh* – communal dance – bands), the habit of pub sessions (introduced by returning migrants) and the economic good times that encouraged the Irish to celebrate their culture rather than trying to replicate international trends. And then, of course, there's Riverdance, which made Irish dancing sexy and became a worldwide phenomenon, despite the fact that most aficionados of traditional music are seriously underwhelmed by its musical worth.

Instruments

Despite popular perception, the harp isn't widely used in traditional music; the *bodhrán* (*bow*-rawn) goat-skin drum is

The Best... Traditional Albums

1 *The Quiet Glen*
(Tommy Peoples)

2 *Paddy Keenan*
(Paddy Keenan)

3 *Compendium: The Best of Patrick Street*
(Various)

4 *The Chieftains 6: Bonaparte's Retreat*
(The Chieftains)

5 *Old Hag You Have Killed Me*
(The Bothy Band)

much more prevalent. The uilleann pipes, played by squeezing bellows under the elbow, provide another distinctive sound, although you're not likely to see them in a pub. The fiddle isn't unique to Ireland but it is one of the main instruments in the country's indigenous music, along with the flute, tin whistle, accordion and bouzouki (a version of the mandolin). Music fits into five main categories (jigs, reels, hornpipes, polkas and slow airs), while the old style of singing unaccompanied versions of traditional ballads and airs is called *sean-nós*.

Tunes

Traditionally, music was performed as a background to dancing, and while this has been true ever since Celtic times, the many thousands of tunes that fill up the repertoire aren't nearly as ancient as that; most aren't much older than a couple of hundred years. Because much of Irish music is handed down orally and aurally, there are myriad variations in the way a single tune is played, depending on the time and place of its playing. The blind itinerant harpist Turlough O'Carolan (1680–1738), for example, wrote more than 200 tunes – it's difficult to know how many versions their repeated learning has spawned.

Popular Bands

More folksy than traditional, the Dubliners, fronted by the distinctive gravel voice and grey beard of Ronnie Drew (1934–2008), made a career out of bawdy drinking songs that got *everybody* singing along. Other popular bands include the Fureys, comprising four brothers originally from the travelling community (no, not like the Wilburies) along with guitarist Davey Arthur. And if it's rousing renditions of Irish rebel songs you're after, you can't go past the Wolfe Tones.

Since the 1970s, various bands have tried to blend traditional with more progressive genres, with mixed success. The first band to pull it off was Moving Hearts, led by Christy Moore, who went on to become the greatest Irish folk musician ever.

Family Travel

Trim Castle (p126)

IMAGE SOURCE/GETTY IMAGES ©

Ireland is generally a pretty good place to bring kids. The Irish love them – it's not so long ago since the average Irish family numbered four, five, six or more children – and they have a pretty easygoing approach to the noise and mayhem that they often bring in their wake. The quality and availability of services for children vary, however, and can be completely lacking outside of bigger towns and cities.

Restaurants & Hotels

On the whole you'll find that restaurants and hotels will go out of their way to cater for you and your children. Hotels will provide cots at no extra charge and most restaurants have highchairs. Bear in mind that under 16s are banned from pubs after 7pm – even if they're accompanied by their parents.

Transport

Under fives travel free on all public transport and most admission prices have an under 16s reduced fee. It's always a good idea to talk to fellow travellers with (happy) children and locals on the road for tips on where to go.

Car seats (around €50/£25 per week) are mandatory for children in hire cars between

The Best...
Distractions
for Kids

1 National Museum of Ireland – Natural History (p67)

2 Titanic Belfast (p289)

3 Killary Adventure Centre (p229)

4 Aillwee Caves (p243)

5 Fin McCool Surf School (p264)

the ages of nine months and four years. Bring your own seat for infants under about nine months as only larger, forward-facing child seats are generally available. Remember not to place baby seats in the front if the car has an airbag.

Feeding & Changing

Although breast-feeding is not a common sight (Ireland has one of the lowest rates of it in the world), you can do so with impunity pretty much everywhere without getting so much as a stare. Nappy-changing facilities are generally only found in the newer, larger shopping centres – otherwise you'll have to make do with a public toilet.

Parks & Gardens

As far as parks, gardens and green spaces, Ireland has an abundance of them, but very few amenities such as designated playgrounds and other exclusively child-friendly spots. In Dublin, St Stephen's Green has a popular playground in the middle of it, but it is the exception rather than the rule.

Resources

For further general information see Lonely Planet's *Travel with Children*. Also check out www.eumom.ie for pregnant women and parents with young children; and www.babygoes2.com, a travel site about family-friendly accommodation worldwide.

Need to Know

Car seats Mandatory in hire cars for children aged nine months to four years (around €50/£25 per week).

Changing facilities Practically non-existent, even in big cities.

Cots Usually available at all accommodations but the most basic B&Bs.

Health As you would do at home.

Highchairs Ask and most restaurants will usually provide.

Nappies Sold in every supermarket and convenience store.

Pubs Children are not allowed in after 7pm.

Transport Look out for family passes and kids' discounts on trains and buses.

Survival
Guide

Sign indicating a Gaelic speaking area
TIM GRAHAM/GETTY IMAGES ©

A 'Standard' Hotel Rate?

There is no such thing. Prices vary according to demand – or have different rates for online, phone or walk-in bookings. B&B rates are more consistent, but virtually every other accommodation will charge wildly different rates depending on the time of year, day, festival schedule and even your ability to do a little negotiating. The following price ranges have been used in our reviews of places to stay. Prices are all based on a double room with private bathroom in high season.

Budget (€/£) <€60/<£50

Midrange (€€/££) €60-150/£50-120

Top end (€€€/£££) >€150/>£120

Directory

Accommodation

Options range from bare and basic to pricey and palatial. The spine of the Irish hospitality business is the ubiquitous B&B, but in recent years they have been challenged by a plethora of midrange hotels and guesthouses. Online resources for accommodation include the following:

o **www.daft.ie** Online classified paper for short- and long-term rentals.

o **www.elegant.ie** Specialises in self-catering castles, period houses and unique properties.

o **www.familyhomes.ie** Lists (you guessed it) family-run guesthouses and self-catering properties.

o **www.gulliver.ie** Fáilte Ireland and the Northern Ireland Tourist Board's web-based accommodation reservation system.

o **www.irishlandmark.com** Not-for-profit conservation group that rents self-catering properties of historical and cultural significance, such as castles, gate lodges and lighthouses.

o **www.imagineireland. com** Offers modern cottage rentals throughout the whole island, including Northern Ireland.

o **www.stayinireland.com** Lists guesthouses and self-catering options.

B&Bs & Guesthouses

Bed and breakfasts are small, family-run houses, farmhouses and period country houses with fewer than five bedrooms. Standards vary, but most have some bedrooms with private bathroom at a cost of roughly €35 to €40 (£20 to £25) per person per night. In luxurious B&Bs, expect to pay €55 (£38) or more per person. Off-season rates – usually October through to March – are usually lower, as are midweek prices.

Guesthouses are like upmarket B&Bs, but bigger (the Irish equivalent of a boutique hotel). Facilities are usually better and sometimes include a restaurant.

Other tips include the following:

o Facilities in B&Bs range from basic (bed, bathroom, kettle) to beatific (whirlpool baths, LCD TVs, wi-fi) as you go up in price.

o Most B&Bs take credit cards, but the occasional rural one might not have facilities; check when you book.

o Advance reservations are strongly recommended, especially in peak season (June to September).

Book Your Stay Online

For more accommodation reviews by Lonely Planet authors, check out http://hotels. lonelyplanet.com. You'll find independent reviews, as well as recommendations on the best places to stay. Best of all, you can book online.

o If full, B&B owners may recommend another house in the area (possibly a private house taking occasional guests, not in tourist listings).

Hotels

Hotels range from the local pub to medieval castles. In most cases, you'll get a better rate than the one published if you go online or negotiate directly with the hotel, especially out of season. The explosion of bland midrange chain hotels (many Irish-owned) has proven to be a major challenge to the traditional B&Bs and guesthouses: they might not have the same personalised service, but their rooms are clean and their facilities generally quite good.

House Swapping

There are several agencies in Ireland that, for an annual fee, facilitate international swaps. The fee pays for access to a website and a book giving house descriptions, photographs and the owner's details. After that, it's up to you to make arrangements. Use of the family car is sometimes included.

Homelink International House Exchange (www.homelink.ie)

Intervac International Holiday Service (www.intervac-homeexchange.com)

Rental Accommodation

Self-catering accommodation is often rented on a weekly basis and usually means an apartment or house where you look after yourself. The rates vary from one region and season to another. **Fáilte Ireland** (☎ Republic 1850 230 330, the UK 0800 039 7000; www.discoverireland.ie) publishes a guide for registered self-catering accommodation; you can check listings at their website.

Customs Regulations

Both the Republic of Ireland and Northern Ireland have a two-tier customs system: one for goods bought duty-free outside the EU, the other for goods bought in another EU country where tax and duty is paid. There is technically no limit to the amount of goods transportable within the EU, but customs will use certain guidelines to distinguish personal use from commercial purpose. Allowances are as follows:

Duty free For duty-free goods from outside the EU, limits include 200 cigarettes, 1L of spirits or 2L of wine, 60ml of perfume and 250ml of eau de toilette.

Tax & duty paid Amounts that officially constitute personal use include 3200 cigarettes (or 400 cigarillos, 200 cigars or 3kg of tobacco) and either 10L of spirits,

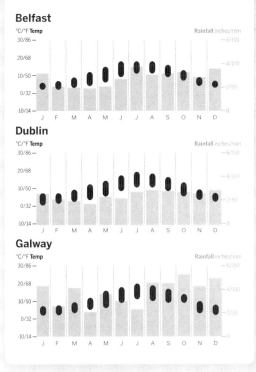

Climate

Belfast
°C/°F Temp   Rainfall inches/mm

Dublin
°C/°F Temp   Rainfall inches/mm

Galway
°C/°F Temp   Rainfall inches/mm

20L of fortified wine, 60L of sparkling wine, 90L of still wine or 110L of beer.

Cats & Dogs

Cats and dogs from anywhere outside Ireland and the UK are subject to strict quarantine laws. The EU Pet Travel Scheme, whereby animals are fitted with a micro chip, vaccinated against rabies and blood-tested six months *prior* to entry, is in force in the UK and the Republic of Ireland. No preparation or documentation is necessary for the movement of pets directly between the UK and the Republic. Contact the **Department of Agriculture, Food & Rural Development** (☎01-607 2000; www. agriculture.gov.ie) in Dublin for further details.

Electricity

120V/60Hz

Gay & Lesbian Travellers

Ireland is a pretty tolerant place for gays and lesbians. Bigger cities such as Dublin, Galway and Cork have a well-established gay scene, as does Belfast and Derry in Northern Ireland. That said, you'll still find pockets of homophobia throughout the island, particularly in smaller towns and rural areas. Resources include the following:

Gaire (www.gaire.com) Message board and info for a host of gay-related issues.

Gay & Lesbian Youth Northern Ireland (www. glyni.org.uk)

Gay Men's Health Project (☎ 01-660 2189; www.hse. ie) Practical advice on men's health issues.

National Lesbian & Gay Federation (NLGF; ☎ 01-671 9076; www.nlgf.ie) Publishes the monthly *Gay Community News* (www.gcn.ie).

Northern Ireland Gay Rights Association (Nigra; ☎ 9066 5257)

Outhouse (☎ 01-873 4932; www.outhouse.ie; 105 Capel St) Gay, lesbian and bisexual resource centre.

Health

No jabs are required to travel to Ireland. Excellent health care is readily available. For minor, self-limiting illnesses, pharmacists can give valuable advice and sell over-the-counter medication. They can also advise when more specialised help is required and point you in the right direction.

In Northern Ireland, everyone receives free emergency treatment at accident and emergency (A&E) departments of state-run NHS hospitals, irrespective of nationality.

Insurance

Insurance is important: it covers you for everything from medical expenses and luggage loss to cancellations or delays in your travel arrangements, depending on your policy.

Worldwide travel insurance is available at www.lonelyplanet.com/ travel_services. You can buy, extend and claim online at any time – even if you're already on the road.

All cars on public roads must be insured. If you are bringing your own vehicle, check that your insurance will cover you in Ireland.

Internet Access

With the advent of 3G and wi-fi networks, internet cafes are increasingly disappearing from Irish towns. The ones that are left generally charge up to €6/£5 per hour.

If you'll be using your laptop or mobile device to get online, most hotels and an increasing number of B&Bs, hostels, bars and restaurants offer wi-fi access, charging anything from nothing to €5/£5 per hour.

Otherwise, most hotels and hostels in larger towns and cities have internet access via a desktop for customer use.

Legal Matters

Illegal drugs are widely available, especially in clubs. The possession of small quantities of marijuana attracts a fine or warning, but harder drugs are treated more seriously. Public drunkenness is illegal but commonplace – the police will usually ignore it unless you're causing trouble.

Contact the following for assistance:

Legal Aid Board (066-947 1000; www.legalaidboard. ie) Has a network of local law centres.

Northern Ireland Legal Services Commission (www.nilsc.org.uk)

Money

The currency in the Republic of Ireland is the euro (€). The island's peculiar political history means that the six Ulster counties that make up Northern Ireland – Antrim, Armagh, Down, Fermanagh, Londonderry and Tyrone – use the pound sterling (£). Although notes issued by Northern Irish banks are legal tender throughout the UK, many businesses outside of Northern Ireland refuse to accept them and you'll have to swap them in British banks.

ATMs

Usually called 'cash machines', ATMs are easy to find in cities and all but the smallest of towns. Watch out for ATMs that have been tampered with; card-reader scams ('skimming') have become a real problem.

Credit & Debit Cards

Visa and MasterCard credit and debit cards are widely accepted in Ireland. American Express is only accepted by the major chains, and very few places accept Diners or JCB. Smaller businesses, such as pubs and some B&Bs, prefer debit cards (and will charge a fee for credit cards). Nearly all credit and debit cards use the chip-and-PIN system and an increasing number of places will not accept your card if you don't.

Taxes & Refunds

Non-EU residents can claim Value Added Tax (VAT, a sales tax of 21% added to the purchase price of luxury goods – excluding books, children's clothing and educational items) back on their purchases, so long as the store operates either the Cashback or Taxback refund program (they should display a sticker). You'll get a voucher with your purchase that must be stamped at the *last point of exit* from the EU. If you're travelling on to Britain or mainland Europe from Ireland, hold on to your voucher until you pass through your final customs stop in the EU; it can then be stamped and you can post it back for a refund of duty paid.

VAT in Northern Ireland is 20%; shops participating in the Tax-Free Shopping refund scheme will give you a form or invoice on request to be presented to customs when you leave. After customs have certified the form, it will be returned to the shop for a refund and the cheque sent to you at home.

Tipping

You're not obliged to tip if the service or food was unsatisfactory (even if it's been automatically added to your bill as a 'service charge').

Hotels Only for bellhops who carry luggage, then €1/£1 per bag

Pubs Not expected unless table service is provided, then €1/£1 for a round of drinks

Restaurants 10% for decent service, up to 15% in more expensive places

Taxis 10% or rounded up to the nearest euro/pound

Toilet attendants €0.50/50p

Opening Hours

Hours in both the Republic and Northern Ireland are roughly the same.

Banks 10am to 4pm Monday to Friday (to 5pm Thursday)

Offices 9am to 5pm Monday to Friday

Post offices Northern Ireland: 9am to 5.30pm

Monday to Friday, 9am to 12.30pm Saturday; Republic: 9am to 6pm Monday to Friday, 9am to 1pm Saturday. Smaller post offices may close at lunch and one day per week.

Pubs Northern Ireland: 11.30am to 11pm Monday to Saturday, 12.30pm to 10pm Sunday; pubs with late licences open until 1am Monday to Saturday and midnight Sunday. Republic: 10.30am to 11.30pm Monday to Thursday, to 12.30am Friday and Saturday, noon to 11pm Sunday (30 minutes 'drinking up' time allowed). Pubs with bar extensions open to 2.30am Thursday to Saturday. Closed Christmas Day and Good Friday.

Restaurants Noon to 10.30pm; many close one day of the week.

Shops 9am to 5.30pm or 6pm Monday to Saturday (until 8pm on Thursday and sometimes Friday), noon to 6pm Sunday (in bigger towns only). Shops in rural towns may close at lunch and one day per week.

Tourist offices 9am to 5pm Monday to Friday, 9am to 1pm Saturday. Many extend their hours in summer and open fewer hours/days or close from October to April.

Public Holidays

Public holidays can cause road chaos as everyone tries to get somewhere else for the break. It's wise to book accommodation in advance around these times.

The following are public holidays in both the Republic and Northern Ireland:

New Year's Day 1 January

St Patrick's Day 17 March

Easter (Good Friday to Easter Monday inclusive) March/April

May Holiday 1st Monday in May

Christmas Day 25 December

St Stephen's Day (Boxing Day) 26 December

St Patrick's Day and St Stephen's Day holidays are taken the following Monday if they fall on a weekend. In the Republic, nearly everywhere closes on Good Friday even though it isn't an official public holiday. In the North, most shops open on Good Friday but close the following Tuesday.

Northern Ireland

Spring Bank Holiday Last Monday in May

Orangeman's Day 12 July

August Holiday Last Monday in August

Republic

June Holiday 1st Monday in June

August Holiday 1st Monday in August

October Holiday Last Monday in October

Safe Travel

Ireland is safer than most countries in Europe, but normal precautions should be observed.

Northern Ireland is as safe as anywhere else, but there are areas where the sectarian divide is bitterly pronounced, most notably in parts of Belfast. It's probably best to ensure your visit to Northern Ireland doesn't coincide with the climax of the Orange marching season on 12 July; sectarian passions are usually inflamed and even many Northerners leave the province at this time.

Telephone

Area codes in the Republic have three digits and begin with a 0, eg ☎021 for Cork, ☎091 for Galway and ☎061 for Limerick. The only exception is Dublin, which has a two-digit code (☎01). Always use the area code if calling from a mobile phone, but you don't need it if calling from a fixed-line number within the area code.

In Northern Ireland, the area code for all fixed-line numbers is ☎028, but you only need to use it if calling from a mobile phone or from outside Northern Ireland. To call Northern Ireland from the Republic, use ☎048 instead of ☎028, without the international dialling code.

Other codes:
- ☎1550 or ☎1580 – premium rate

- 📞1890 or 📞1850 – local or shared rate

- 📞0818 – calls at local rate, wherever you're dialling from within the Republic

- 📞1800 – free calls

Free-call and low-call numbers are not accessible from outside the Republic.

Other tips include:

- Prices are lower during evenings after 6pm and weekends.

- If you can find a public phone that works, local calls in the Republic cost €0.30 for around three minutes (around €0.60 to a mobile), regardless of when you call. From Northern Ireland local calls cost about 40p, or 60p to a mobile, although this varies somewhat.

- Pre-paid phonecards can be purchased at both news agencies and post offices, and work from all payphones for both domestic and international calls.

Directory Enquiries

For directory enquiries, a number of agencies compete for your business.

- In the Republic, dial 📞11811 or 📞11850; for international enquiries it's 📞11818.

- In the North, call 📞118 118, 📞118 192, 📞118 500 or 📞118 811.

- Expect to pay at least €1/£1 from a land line and up to €2/£2 from a mobile phone.

Practicalities

- **Currency** Republic of Ireland, Euro (€); Northern Ireland, Pound Sterling (£)

- **Newspapers** *Irish Independent* (www.independent.ie), *Irish Times* (www.irishtimes.com), *Irish Examiner* (www.examiner.ie), *Belfast Telegraph* (www.belfasttelegraph.co.uk)

- **Radio** RTE Radio 1 (88-90 MHz), Today FM (100-103 MHz), Newstalk 106-108 (106-108 MHz), BBC Ulster (92-95 MHz; Northern Ireland only)

- **Weights & measures** Metric units; exception is for liquid measures of alcohol, where pints are used.

Emergency Numbers

Northern Ireland 📞999

Republic 📞112 or 📞999

International Calls

To call out from Ireland dial 📞00, then the country code (eg 📞1 for USA, 📞61 for Australia), the area code (you usually drop the initial zero) then the number. Ireland's international code is 📞353, Northern Ireland's is 📞44.

Mobile Phone

- Ireland uses the GSM 900/1800 cell phone system, which is compatible with European and Australian phones, but not North American or Japanese.

- Pay-as-you-go mobile phone packages with any of the main providers start at around €40 and usually include a basic handset and credit of around €10.

- SIM-only packages are available, but make sure your phone is compatible with the local provider.

Time

In winter, Ireland is on Greenwich Mean Time (GMT), also known as Universal Time Coordinated (UTC), the same as Britain. In summer, the clock shifts to GMT plus one hour, so when it's noon in Dublin and London, it's 4am in Los Angeles and Vancouver, 7am in New York and Toronto, 1pm in Paris, 7pm in Singapore, and 9pm in Sydney.

Tourist Information

In both the Republic and Northern Ireland you will be able to find a tourist office or information point in almost every big town. Most can offer a variety of services, ranging from accommodation and attraction reservations and currency-changing services, to map and guidebook sales, and free publication hand outs.

In the Republic, the tourism purview falls to **Fáilte Ireland** (www.discoverireland.ie); in Northern Ireland, it's the **Northern Irish Tourist Board** (NITB; ☏ head office 028-9023 1221; www.discovernorthernireland.com). Outside Ireland, Fáilte Ireland and the NITB unite under the banner **Tourism Ireland** (www.tourismireland.com).

The main branches of Fáilte Ireland in the Republic:

Cork Discover Ireland Centre (☏ 021-425 5100; Grand Pde, Cork) For Counties Cork and Kerry.

Discover Ireland Dublin Tourism Centre (☏ 01-605 7700; www.visitdublin.com; St Andrew's Church, 2 Suffolk St, Dublin)

Donegal Discover Ireland Centre (The Quay, Donegal Town)

Galway Discover Ireland Centre (☏ 091-537 700; Forster St) For Galway, Roscommon and Mayo.

Mullingar Discover Ireland Centre (☏ 044-934 8761; Market Sq, Mullingar) For Kildare, Laois, Longford, Louth, Meath, North Offaly, Westmeath and Wicklow.

Sligo Discover Ireland Centre (☏ 071-916 1201; Old Bank Bldg, O'Connell St) For Cavan, Donegal, Leitrim, Monaghan and Sligo.

Waterford Discover Ireland Centre (☏ 051-875 823; The Granary, 41 The Quay) For Carlow, Kilkenny, South Tipperary, Waterford and Wexford.

Travellers with Disabilities

All new buildings have wheelchair access, and many hotels have installed lifts, ramps and other facilities. Others, especially B&Bs, have not adapted as successfully so you'll have far less choice. Fáilte Ireland and NITB's accommodation guides indicate which places are wheelchair accessible.

In big cities, most buses have low-floor access and priority space on board, but the number of kneeling buses on regional routes is still relatively small.

Trains are accessible with help. In theory, if you call ahead, an employee of Irish Rail (Iarnród Éireann) will arrange to accompany you to the train. Newer trains have audio and visual information systems for visually impaired and hearing-impaired passengers.

The **Citizens' Information Board** (☏ 01-605 9000; www.citizensinformationboard.ie) in the Republic and **Disability Action** (☏ 028-9066 1252; www.disabilityaction.org) in Northern Ireland can give some advice to travellers with disabilities. Travellers to Northern Ireland can also check out the website www.allgohere.com.

Visas

If you're a European Economic Area (EEA) national, you don't need a visa to visit (or work in) either the Republic or Northern Ireland. Citizens of Australia, Canada, New Zealand, South Africa and the US can visit the Republic for up to three months, and Northern Ireland for up to six months. They are not allowed to work unless sponsored by an employer.

Full visa requirements for visiting the Republic are available online at www.dfa.ie; for Northern Ireland's visa requirements see www.ukvisas.gov.uk.

Women Travellers

Ireland should pose no problems for women travellers. Finding contraception is not the problem it once was, although anyone on the pill should bring adequate supplies.

Rape Crisis Network Ireland (☏ 1800-77 88 88; www.rcni.ie) In the Republic. Runs a 24-hour helpline.

Rape Crisis & Sexual Abuse Centre (☏ 028-9032 9002; www.rapecrisisni.com) In Northern Ireland. Operates a 24-hour helpline.

Transport

●●●●
Getting There & Away

Entering the Country

Dublin is the main point of entry for most visitors. In recent years, the growth of no-frills airlines means more routes and cheaper prices between Ireland and other European countries. If arriving in the Republic of Ireland:

o The overwhelming majority of airlines serving Ireland fly into the capital.

o Dublin is home to two seaports that serve as the main points of sea transport with Britain; ferries from France arrive in the southern port of Rosslare.

o Dublin is also the nation's premier rail hub.

Flights, tours and rail tickets can be booked online at www.lonelyplanet.com/bookings.

✈ Air

Airports
Ireland's main airports:

Cork Airport (ORK; ☎ 021-431 3131; www.corkairport.com)

Dublin Airport (DUB; ☎ 01-814 1111; www.dublinairport.com)

Shannon Airport (SNN; ☎ 061-712 000; www.shannonairport.com; 🛜)

Other airports in the Republic with scheduled services from Britain:

Donegal Airport (CFN; ☎ 074-954 8284; www.donegalairport.ie)

Ireland West Airport Knock (NOC; ☎ 094-936 8100; www.irelandwestairport.com; off N17) Fifteen kilometres north of Knock just off the N17, Ireland West Airport Knock has daily flights to seven cities in the UK and less frequent services to Portugal, Spain, Germany, Italy and the Canaries.

Kerry Airport (KIR; ☎ 066-976 4644; www.kerryairport.ie; Farranfore)

Waterford Airport (WAT; ☎ 051-875 589; www.flywaterford. com)

Northern Ireland's airports:

Belfast International Airport (BFS; ☎ 028-9448 4848; www.belfastairport.com)

Climate Change & Travel

Every form of transport that relies on carbon-based fuel generates CO_2, the main cause of human-induced climate change. Modern travel is dependent on aeroplanes, which might use less fuel per kilometre per person than most cars but travel much greater distances. The altitude at which aircraft emit gases (including CO_2) and particles also contributes to their climate change impact. Many websites offer 'carbon calculators' that allow people to estimate the carbon emissions generated by their journey and, for those who wish to do so, to offset the impact of the greenhouse gases emitted with contributions to portfolios of climate-friendly initiatives throughout the world. Lonely Planet offsets the carbon footprint of all staff and author travel.

Flights from Britain, Europe and the USA.

City of Derry Airport (LDY; ☎ 028-7181 0784; www.cityofderryairport.com)

George Best Belfast City Airport (BHD; ☎ 028-9093 9093; www.belfastcityairport.com)

Land

Eurolines (www.eurolines.com) has a thrice-daily coach and ferry service from London's Victoria Station to Dublin Busáras.

Ferry & Fast Boat Routes

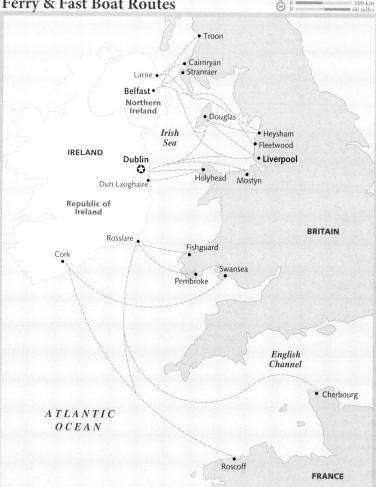

Sea

The main ferry routes between Ireland and the UK and mainland Europe:

○ Belfast to Liverpool (England; 8½ hours)

○ Belfast to Stranraer (Scotland; 1¾ hours)

○ Cork to Roscoff (France; 14 hours)

○ Dublin to Liverpool (England; fast/slow four/8½ hours)

○ Dublin & Dun Laoghaire to Holyhead (Wales; fast/slow 1½/three hours)

○ Larne to Cairnryan (Scotland; 1½ hours)

○ Larne to Fleetwood (England; six hours)

○ Rosslare to Cherbourg & Roscoff (France; 20½ hours)

○ Rosslare to Fishguard & Pembroke (Wales; 3½ hours)

Competition from budget airlines has forced ferry operators to discount heavily and offer flexible fares, meaning great bargains at quiet times of the day or year. For example, the popular route across the Irish Sea between Dublin and Holyhead can be had for as little as €15 for a foot passenger and €90 for a car plus up to four passengers.

A very useful online tool is www.ferrybooker.com, a single site covering all sea-ferry routes and operators out of the UK (the mainstay of sea travel to Ireland).

Main operators include the following:

Brittany Ferries (www.brittanyferries.com) Every Saturday April to October.

Irish Ferries (www.irishferries.com) Holyhead ferries up to four a day year-round; from France to Rosslare three times a week, mid-February to December.

Isle of Man Steam Packet Company/Sea Cat (www.steam-packet.com)

Norfolkline (www.norfolkline.com) Daily sailings year-round.

P&O Irish Sea (www.poirishsea.com) Daily sailings year-round.

Stena Line (www.stenaline.com)

Getting Around

The big decision in getting around Ireland is to go by car or use public transport. Your own car will make the best use of your time and help you reach even the most remote of places via the spidery network of secondary and tertiary roads, but hire and fuel costs can be expensive

Bus & Ferry Combo

It's possible to combine bus and ferry tickets from major UK centres to all Irish towns on the bus network, which mightn't be as convenient as flying on a budget airline but leaves less of a carbon footprint. The journey between London and Dublin takes about 12 hours; the London to Belfast trip takes 13 to 16 hours. Both can be had for as little as £40 return. Contact **Eurolines** (www.eurolines.com).

for budget travellers – while parking hassles and traffic jams in most urban centres affect everyone – so public transport is often the better choice.

The bus network, made up of a mix of public and private operators, is extensive and generally quite competitive (although journey times can be slow). The rail network is quicker but more limited, serving only major towns and cities, and can be quite costly. Both buses and trains get busy during peak times; you'll need to book in advance to be guaranteed a seat.

✈ Air

Ireland's size makes domestic flying unnecessary unless you're in a hurry, but there are flights between Dublin and Belfast, Cork, Derry, Donegal, Galway, Kerry, Shannon and Sligo, as well as a Belfast–Cork service. Most flights within Ireland take around 30 to 50 minutes.

Domestic carriers:

Aer Lingus (www.aerlingus.com)

Aer Lingus Regional (www.aerarann.com)

Ryanair (www.ryanair.com)

ᚒᚑ Bicycle

Ireland's compact size, relative flatness and scenic landscapes make it an ideal cycling destination. Dodgy weather and the occasional uneven road surface are the only concerns. A good tip for cyclists in the west is that the prevailing winds make it easier to cycle from south to north.

Buses will carry bikes, but only if there's room. For trains, bear in mind:

○ Intercity trains charge up to €10 per bike.

○ Bikes are transported in the passenger compartment.

○ Book in advance (www.irishrail.ie), as there's only room for three bikes per service.

Organisations that arrange cycle tours throughout Ireland:

Go Ireland (☏ 066-976 2094; www.govisitireland.com; Old Orchard House, Killorglin, Co Kerry)

Irish Cycling Safaris (☏ 01-260 0749; www.cyclingsafaris.com; Belfield Bike Shop, UCD, Dublin 4) Irish Cycling Safaris organises tours for groups of cyclists in the southwest, the southeast, Connemara and Counties Clare, Donegal and Antrim.

🚢 Boat

Ireland's offshore islands are all served by boat, including the Aran and Skellig Islands to the west, the Saltee Islands to the southeast, and Tory and Rathlin Islands to the north.

Ferries also operate across rivers, inlets and loughs, providing useful short cuts, particularly for cyclists.

Cruises are very popular on the 258km-long Shannon–Erne Waterway and on a variety of other lakes and loughs. The tourist offices only recommend operators that are registered with them. Details of non-tourist-board-affiliated boat trips are given under the relevant sections throughout this book.

Border Crossings

Security has been progressively scaled down in Northern Ireland in recent years and all border crossings with the Republic are now open and generally unstaffed. Permanent checkpoints have been removed and ramps levelled. On major routes your only indication that you have crossed the border will be a change in road signs and the colour of number plates and postboxes.

🚌 Bus

Private buses compete – often very favourably – with Bus Éireann in the Republic and also run where the national buses are irregular or absent.

Distances are not especially long: no bus journey will last longer than five hours. A typical fare on a popular route like Dublin to Cork is about €12 one way; distance and competitiveness will reflect pricing, but you can also find higher fares on routes that are shorter but less frequented.

Bus Éireann bookings can be made online, but you can't reserve a seat for a particular service.

The main bus services in Ireland:

Bus Éireann (☎ 01-836 6111; www.buseireann.ie) The Republic's bus line.

Dublin Bus (www.dublinbus.ie) Dublin's bus service.

Metro (☎ 028-9066 6630; www.translink.co.uk) Belfast's bus service.

Ulsterbus (☎ 028-9066 6600; www.ulsterbus.co.uk) Northern Ireland's bus service.

🚗 Car & Motorcycle

Travelling by car or motorbike means greater flexibility and independence. The road system is extensive, and the constantly growing network of motorways has cut driving

Bus & Rail Passes

There are a number of bus- or train-only and bus-and-rail passes worth considering if you plan on doing a lot of travel using public transport. All of the following passes are issued by Bus Éireann.

Emerald Card (Bus & Rail) Eight days' travel out of 15 consecutive days (€218) to 15 days out of 30 (€375) on all national and local services within the Republic and Northern Ireland.

Irish Rambler (Bus) Three days' travel out of eight consecutive days (€53) to 15 days out of 30 (€168) on all Bus Éireann services.

Irish Rover (Bus) Three days' travel out of eight consecutive days (€68) to 15 days out of 30 on all Bus Éireann and Ulster Bus services, as well as local services in Cork, Galway, Limerick, Waterford and Belfast.

Irish Explorer (Bus & Rail) Eight days' travel out of 15 consecutive days (€194) on trains and buses within the Republic.

Irish Explorer (Rail) Five days' travel out of 15 consecutive days (€115.50) on trains in the Republic.

Children aged under 16 pay half-price for all these passes and for all normal tickets. Children aged under three travel for free on public transport. You can buy the above passes at most major train and bus stations in Ireland.

times considerably. Downsides include traffic jams, problems with parking in urban centres and the high cost of petrol.

Hire

Compared with many countries (especially the USA), hire rates are expensive in Ireland; you should expect to pay around €250 a week for a small car (unlimited mileage) but rates go up at busy times and drop off in quieter seasons.

The major car-hire companies have different web pages on their websites for different countries, so the price of a car on the Irish page can differ from the same car's price on the USA or Australia page. You have to surf a lot of sites to get the best deals. **Nova Car Hire** (www.novacarhire.com) acts as an agent for Alamo, Budget, European and National, and offers greatly discounted rates.

Other tips:

o Most cars are manual; automatic cars are available, but they're more expensive to hire.

o If you're travelling from the Republic into Northern Ireland, it's important to be sure that your insurance covers journeys to the North.

o The majority of hire companies won't rent you a car if you're under 23 and haven't had a valid driving licence for at least a year.

o Some companies in the Republic won't rent to you if you're aged 74 or over; there's no upper age limit in the North.

o Motorbikes and mopeds are not available for rent in Ireland.

The main car-hire companies:

Avis (www.avis.ie)

Budget (www.budget.ie)

Europcar (www.europcar.ie)

Hertz (www.hertz.ie)

Sixt (www.sixt.ie)

Thrifty Car Rental (☎ 1800 515 800; www.thrifty.ie)

Parking

All big towns and cities have covered short-stay car parks that are conveniently signposted.

o On-street parking is usually by 'pay and display' tickets available from on-street machines or disc parking (discs, which rotate to display the time you park your car, are available from newsagencies). Costs range from €1.50 to €4.50 per hour; all-day parking in a car park will cost around €24.

o Yellow lines (single or double) along the edge of the road indicate restrictions. Usually you can park on single yellow lines between 7pm and 8am while double yellow lines means no parking at any time. Always look for the nearby sign that spells out when you can and cannot park.

o In Dublin, Cork and Galway, clamping is rigorously enforced: it'll cost you €85 to have the yellow beast removed. In Northern Ireland, the fee is £100 for removal.

Roads & Rules

Motorways (marked by M+number on a blue background) and primary

Fare Go

Travel costs throughout this book are for single (one-way) adult fares, unless otherwise stated.

roads (N+number on a green background) are the fastest way to get around and will deliver you quickly from one end of the country to another. Secondary and tertiary roads (marked as R+number) are much more scenic and fun, but they can be very winding and exceedingly narrow – perfect for going slowly and enjoying the views.

o EU licences are treated like Irish licences.

o Non-EU licences are valid in Ireland for up to 12 months.

o You must carry your driving licence at all times.

o If you plan to bring a car from Europe, it's illegal to drive without at least third-party insurance.

The basic rules of the road:

o Drive on the left; overtake to the right.

o Safety belts must be worn by the driver and all passengers.

o Children aged under 12 aren't allowed to sit in the front passenger seat.

o Motorcyclists and their passengers must wear helmets.

o When entering a roundabout, give way to the right.

o In the Republic, speed-limit and distance signs are in kilometres (although the

Motoring Organisations

The two main motoring organisations:

Automobile Association (AA; www.aaireland.ie) Republic (📞 breakdown assistance 1800 667 788, in Cork 021-425 2444, in Dublin 01-617 9999; www.aaireland.ie); Northern Ireland (📞 0870-950 0600, breakdown assistance 0800 667 788; www.aaireland.ie)

Royal Automobile Club (RAC; www.rac.ie) Republic (📞 1890 483 483; www.rac.ie); Northern Ireland (📞 0800 029 029, breakdown assistance 0800 828 282; www.rac.ie)

occasional older white sign shows distances in miles); in the North, speed-limit and distance signs are in miles. Speed limits:

Republic 120km/h on motorways, 100km/h on national roads, 80km/h on regional and local roads, and 50km/h or as signposted in towns.

Northern Ireland 70mph on motorways, 60mph on main roads, 30mph in built-up areas.

Drinking and driving is taken very seriously; in both the Republic and Northern Ireland you're allowed a maximum blood-alcohol level of 80mg/100mL (0.08%) – and campaigners want it reduced to 50mg/100mL.

Hitching

Hitching is becoming increasingly less popular in Ireland, even though it's still pretty easy compared to other European countries. Travellers who decide to hitch should understand that they are taking a small but potentially serious risk, and we don't recommend it. If you do plan to travel by thumb, remember it's illegal to hitch on motorways.

Local Transport

Dublin and Belfast have comprehensive local bus networks, as do some other larger towns.

○ The Dublin Area Rapid Transport (DART) rail line runs roughly the length of Dublin's coastline, while the Luas tram system has two popular lines.

○ Taxis tend to be expensive. For daytime rates, flagfall is €4.10 and fares start at €1.03 per km after that (night-time rates are a bit higher).

Tours

Organised tours are a convenient way of exploring the country's main highlights if your time is limited. Tours can be booked through travel agencies, tourist offices in the major cities, or directly through the tour companies themselves. Some of the most reputable operators:

Bus Éireann (www.buseireann.ie) Runs day tours to various parts of the Republic and the North.

CIE Tours International (www.cietours.ie) Runs four- to 11-day coach tours of the Republic and the North,

including accommodation and meals.

Grayline Tours (www.irishcitytours.com) Dublin-based company offering half- and full-day tours of attractions around Dublin as well as the Ring of Kerry.

Paddywagon Tours (www.paddywagontours.com) Activity-filled three- and six-day tours all over Ireland with friendly tour guides. Accommodation is in IHH hostels.

Railtours Ireland (📞 01-856 0045; www.railtoursireland.com) For train enthusiasts. Organises a series of one- and two-day train trips in association with Iarnród Éireann.

Ulsterbus Tours (www.ulsterbus.co.uk) Runs a large number of day trips throughout the North and the Republic.

🚆 Train

Given Ireland's relatively small size, train travel is an expensive luxury. All of the Republic's major towns and cities are on the limited rail network, which is operated by **Irish Rail** (Iarnród Éireann; 📞 1850 366 222; www.irishrail.ie) and fans out from Dublin in such a way that connections between destinations not on the same line usually involve an out-of-the-way trip to the capital. There's no north–south route along the western coast, no network in Donegal and no direct connections from Waterford to Cork or Killarney.

Fares are high. A mid-week one-way ticket from Dublin to Cork will cost around €65. The return fare is only marginally

Train Routes

more expensive – a feature designed to offer an incentive for rail travel but making for poor-value one-way fares. The cheapest fares are always online.

Northern Ireland Railways (NIR; ☎028-9089 9411; www.nirailways.co.uk; Belfast Central Station) runs four routes from Belfast: one links with the system in the Republic via Newry to Dublin; the other three go east to Bangor, northeast to Larne and northwest to Derry via Coleraine.

a b c

Language

Irish (Gaeilge) is Ireland's official language. In 2003 the government introduced the Official Languages Act, whereby all official documents, street signs and official titles must be either in Irish or in both Irish and English. Despite its official status, Irish is really only spoken in pockets of rural Ireland known as the Gaeltacht, the main ones being Cork (*Corcaigh*), Donegal (*Dún na nGall*), Galway (*Gaillimh*), Kerry (*Ciarraí*) and Mayo (*Maigh Eo*).

Ask people outside the Gaeltacht if they can speak Irish and nine out of 10 of them will probably reply *'ah, cupla focal'* (a couple of words) – and they generally mean it. Irish is a compulsory subject in schools for those aged six to 15, but Irish classes have traditionally been rather academic and unimaginative, leading many students to resent it as a waste of time. As a result, many adults regret not having a greater grasp of it. In recent times, at long last, a new Irish curriculum has been introduced cutting the hours devoted to the subject but making the lessons more fun, practical and celebratory.

For in-depth language information and a witty insight into the quirks of language in Ireland, check out Lonely Planet's *Irish Language & Culture*. To enhance your trip with this title or a phrasebook, visit **lonelyplanet.com**. Lonely Planet iPhone phrasebooks are available through the Apple App store.

PRONUNCIATION

Irish divides vowels into long (those with an accent) and short (those without an accent), and distinguishes between broad (**a**, **á**, **o**, **ó**, **u**) and slender (**e**, **é**, **i** and **í**) vowels, which can affect the pronunciation of preceding consonants.

Other than a few odd-looking clusters, like **mh** and **bhf** (both pronounced as 'w'), consonants are generally pronounced as they are in English.

Irish has three main dialects: Connaught Irish (in Galway and northern Mayo), Munster Irish (in Cork, Kerry and Waterford) and Ulster Irish (in Donegal). The pronunciation guides given here are an anglicised version of modern standard Irish, which is essentially an amalgam of the three – if you read them as if they were English, you'll be able to get your point across in Gaeilge without even having to think about the specifics of Irish pronunciation or spelling.

BASICS

Hello. (greeting)
Dia duit.   deea gwit

Hello. (reply)
Dia is Muire duit.   deeas moyra gwit

Good morning.
Maidin mhaith.   mawjin wah

Good night.
Oíche mhaith.   eekheh wah

Goodbye. (when leaving)
Slán leat.   slawn lyat

Goodbye. (when staying)
Slán agat.   slawn agut

Excuse me.
Gabh mo leithscéal.   gamoh lesh scale

I'm sorry.
Tá brón orm.   taw brohn oruhm

Thank you (very) much.
Go raibh (míle)   goh rev (meela)
maith agat.   mah agut

Do you speak Irish?
An bhfuil Gaeilge agat?   on wil gaylge oguht

I don't understand.
Ní thuigim.   nee higgim

What is this?
Cad é seo?   kod ay shoh

What is that?
Cad é sin?   kod ay shin

I'd like to go to ...
Ba mhaith liom   baw wah lohm
dul go dtí ...   dull go dee ...

I'd like to buy ...
Ba mhaith liom ...   bah wah lohm ...
a cheannach.   a kyanukh

..., (if you) please.
... más é do thoil é.   ... maws ay do hall ay

Yes.	*Tá.*	taw
No.	*Níl.*	neel
It is.	*Sea.*	sheh
It isn't.	*Ní hea.*	nee heh
another/ one more	*ceann eile*	kyawn ella
nice	*go deas*	goh dyass

MAKING CONVERSATION

Welcome.
Ceád míle fáilte. kade meela fawlcha
(lit: 100,000 welcomes)

How are you?
Conas a tá tú? kunas aw taw too

I'm fine.
Táim go maith. thawm go mah

What's your name?
Cad is ainm duit? kod is anim dwit

My name is (Sean Frayne).
(Sean Frayne) is (shawn frain) is
ainm dom. anim dohm

Impossible!
Ní féidir é! nee faydir ay

Nonsense!
Ráiméis! rawmaysh

That's terrible!
Go huafásach! guh hoofawsokh

Take it easy.
Tóg é gobogé. tohg ay gobogay

Cheers!
Slainte! slawncha

I'm never ever drinking again!
Ní ólfaidh mé go knee ohlhee mey gu
brách arís! brawkh ureeshch

Bon voyage!
Go n-éirí an bóthar leat! go nairee on bohhar lat

SIGNS

Fir	*fear*	Men
Gardaí	*gardee*	Police
Leithreas	*lehrass*	Toilet
Mna	*mnaw*	Women
Oifig An Phoist	*iffig ohn fwisht*	Post Office

Happy Christmas!
Nollaig shona! nuhlig hona

Happy Easter!
Cáisc shona! kawshk hona

DAYS OF THE WEEK

Monday	*Dé Luaín*	day loon
Tuesday	*Dé Máirt*	day maart
Wednesday	*Dé Ceádaoin*	day kaydeen
Thursday	*Déardaoin*	daredeen
Friday	*Dé hAoine*	day heeneh
Saturday	*Dé Sathairn*	day sahern
Sunday	*Dé Domhnaigh*	day downick

NUMBERS

1	*haon*	hayin
2	*dó*	doe
3	*trí*	tree
4	*ceathaír*	kahirr
5	*cúig*	kooig
6	*sé*	shay
7	*seacht*	shocked
8	*hocht*	hukt
9	*naoi*	nay
10	*deich*	jeh
20	*fiche*	feekhe

Behind the Scenes

Our Readers

Many thanks to the travellers who used the last edition and wrote to us with helpful hints, useful advice and interesting anecdotes:

Carla Coyle, Raymond Boyes and Silvia Grönroos-Pada.

Author Thanks

Fionn Davenport

Thanks to Cliff, Gina and all the format boffins at Lonely Planet who answered my every query – no matter what time of day or night. Thanks to my fellow authors Catherine, Ryan, Neil and Josephine, whose sterling work has improved this book even more. Cheers also to everyone in Dublin and Ireland for all of their suggestions, critiques and helpful hints: your advice wasn't always sought, but it was always appreciated!

Acknowledgments

Climate map data adapted from Peel MC, Finlayson BL & McMahon TA (2007) 'Updated World Map of the Köppen-Geiger Climate Classification', Hydrology and Earth System Sciences, 11, 163344.
Illustrations pp62-3, pp72-3 and pp110-11 by Javier Zarracina. Illustrations pp120-1 and pp164-5 by Michael Weldon.
Transport map data adapted from DART Commuter Network Map © Iarnród Éireann; Dublin Transport Map © Irish Rail.

Cover photographs
Front: Giant's Causeway, Riccardo Spila / 4Corners; Back: Christ Church Cathedral, Dublin, John Harper / Corbis

This Book

This 3rd edition of *Discover Ireland* was researched and written by Fionn Davenport, Catherine Le Nevez, Josephine Quintero, Ryan Ver Berkmoes and Neil Wilson. This guidebook was commissioned in Lonely Planet's London office, and produced by the following:

Commissioning Editor Clifton Wilkinson
Coordinating Editors Gabby Innes, Kate Mathews
Senior Cartographer Jennifer Johnston
Book Designer Wendy Wright
Assisting Editors Ross Taylor, Jeanette Wall
Assisting Book Designer Mazzy Prinsep, Wibowo Rus
Cartographer James Leversha
Cover & Internal Image Research Naomi Parker
Language Content Branislava Vladisavljevic
Thanks to Brendan Dempsey, Samantha Forge, Anna Harris, Elizabeth Jones, Catherine Naghten, Gráinne Quinn, Angela Tinson, Amanda Williamson

SEND US YOUR FEEDBACK

We love to hear from travellers – your comments keep us on our toes and help make our books better. Our well-travelled team reads every word on what you loved or loathed about this book. Although we cannot reply individually to postal submissions, we always guarantee that your feedback goes straight to the appropriate authors, in time for the next edition. Each person who sends us information is thanked in the next edition, the most useful submissions are rewarded with a selection of digital PDF chapters.

Visit **lonelyplanet.com/contact** to submit your updates and suggestions or to ask for help. Our award-winning website also features inspirational travel stories, news and discussions.

Note: We may edit, reproduce and incorporate your comments in Lonely Planet products such as guidebooks, websites and digital products, so let us know if you don't want your comments reproduced or your name acknowledged. For a copy of our privacy policy visit lonelyplanet.com/privacy.

Index

000 Map pages

N

O

P

NOTES

How to Use This Book

These symbols give you the vital information for each listing:

☏	Telephone Numbers	☎	Wi-Fi Access	☒	Bus
☺	Opening Hours	☒	Swimming Pool	☒	Ferry
P	Parking	☒	Vegetarian Selection	M	Metro
☒	Nonsmoking	☒	English-Language Menu	S	Subway
☀	Air-Conditioning	☒	Family-Friendly	☒	London Tube
@	Internet Access	☒	Pet-Friendly	☒	Tram

Look out for these icons:

FREE No payment required

🌿 A green or sustainable option

Our authors have nominated these places as demonstrating a strong commitment to sustainability – for example by supporting local communities and producers, operating in an environmentally friendly way, or supporting conservation projects.

All reviews are ordered in our authors' preference, starting with their most preferred option. Additionally:

Sights are arranged in the geographic order that we suggest you visit them, and within this order, by author preference.

Eating and Sleeping reviews are ordered by price range (budget, mid-range, top end) and within these ranges, by author preference.

Map Legend

Sights
- ☻ Beach
- ☻ Buddhist
- ☻ Castle
- ☻ Christian
- ☻ Hindu
- ☻ Islamic
- ☻ Jewish
- ☻ Monument
- ☻ Museum/Gallery
- ☻ Ruin
- ☻ Winery/Vineyard
- ☻ Zoo
- ☻ Other Sight

Activities, Courses & Tours
- ☻ Diving/Snorkelling
- ☻ Canoeing/Kayaking
- ☻ Skiing
- ☻ Surfing
- ☻ Swimming/Pool
- ☻ Walking
- ☻ Windsurfing
- ☻ Other Activity/Course/Tour

Sleeping
- ☻ Sleeping
- ☻ Camping

Eating
- ☻ Eating

Drinking
- ☻ Drinking
- ☻ Cafe

Entertainment
- ☻ Entertainment

Shopping
- ☻ Shopping

Information
- ☻ Post Office
- ☻ Tourist Information

Transport
- ☻ Airport
- ☻ Border Crossing
- ☻ Bus
- ☻ Cable Car/Funicular
- ☻ Cycling
- ☻ Ferry
- ☻ Monorail
- P Parking
- ☻ S-Bahn
- ☻ Taxi
- ☻ Train/Railway
- ☻ Tram
- ☻ Tube Station
- ☻ U-Bahn
- ☻ Underground Train Station
- ● Other Transport

Routes
- Tollway
- Freeway
- Primary
- Secondary
- Tertiary
- Lane
- Unsealed Road
- Plaza/Mall
- Steps
- Tunnel
- Pedestrian Overpass
- Walking Tour
- Walking Tour Detour
- Path

Boundaries
- International
- State/Province
- Disputed
- Regional/Suburb
- Marine Park
- Cliff
- Wall

Population
- ☻ Capital (National)
- ◉ Capital (State/Province)
- ● City/Large Town
- ● Town/Village

Geographic
- ☻ Hut/Shelter
- ☻ Lighthouse
- ☻ Lookout
- ▲ Mountain/Volcano
- ☻ Oasis
- ☻ Park
-)(Pass
- ☻ Picnic Area
- ☻ Waterfall

Hydrography
- River/Creek
- Intermittent River
- Swamp/Mangrove
- Reef
- Canal
- Water
- Dry/Salt/Intermittent Lake
- Glacier

Areas
- Beach/Desert
- Cemetery (Christian)
- Cemetery (Other)
- Park/Forest
- Sportsground
- Sight (Building)
- Top Sight (Building)

NEIL WILSON

County Donegal, Belfast, Counties Londonderry & Antrim Neil's first visit to Northern Ireland was in 1994, during the first flush of post-ceasefire optimism, and his interest in the history and politics of the place intensified when he found out that most of his mum's ancestors were from Ulster. Working on the *Ireland* guidebook has allowed him to witness first-hand the progress being made towards a lasting peace. Neil is a full-time travel writer based in Scotland, and has written more than 50 guidebooks for half a dozen publishers.

Read more about Neil at:
lonelyplanet.com/members/neilwilson

Our Story

A beat-up old car, a few dollars in the pocket and a sense of adventure. In 1972 that's all Tony and Maureen Wheeler needed for the trip of a lifetime – across Europe and Asia overland to Australia. It took several months, and at the end – broke but inspired – they sat at their kitchen table writing and stapling together their first travel guide, *Across Asia on the Cheap*. Within a week they'd sold 1500 copies. Lonely Planet was born.

Today, Lonely Planet has offices in Melbourne, London and Oakland, with more than 600 staff and writers. We share Tony's belief that 'a great guidebook should do three things: inform, educate and amuse'.

Our Writers

FIONN DAVENPORT

Coordinating Author, Dublin, Counties Wicklow & Kildare A Dubliner by birth and by persuasion, Fionn has worked on at least seven editions of Lonely Planet's *Ireland* guide, and more and more is reminded of Tancredi's aphorism in The Leopard: 'everything needs to change, so everything can stay the same.' Everything has changed in Ireland, but it has managed to hold on to its traditional strengths – beautiful landscapes, a friendly people and a general conviviality that makes a repeat trip unavoidable.

CATHERINE LE NEVEZ

Counties Cork, Kerry & Tipperary Catherine's wanderlust kicked in when she road-tripped across Europe aged four. She's been hitting the road at every opportunity since, completing her Doctorate of Creative Arts in Writing, Masters in Professional Writing, and post-grad qualifications in Editing and Publishing along the way. Catherine's Celtic connections include Irish and Breton heritage (and a love of Guinness!). She's travelled throughout every county in the Emerald Isle, and covered the majority of them for Lonely Planet, including several editions of Lonely Planet's *Ireland* guide.

JOSEPHINE QUINTERO

Counties Wexford, Waterford, Meath, Lough & Kilkenny Exploring some of the lesser visited counties Josephine discovered such delights as mystical caves, a belief in the little people and restaurant food so retro it included jelly and cream. Throughout these counties, history reverberated in the castles, landscape and evocative ruins, while a spell in the wonderfully vibrant cities of Waterford and Kilkenny was the ideal antidote to those more rural terrains. Josephine has contributed to more than 35 guides for Lonely Planet and her delight in Ireland increases with every trip.

Read more about Josephine at: lonelyplanet.com/members/josephinequintero

RYAN VER BERKMOES

Counties Clare, Galway, Mayo & Sligo From Loop Head to Sligo, with plenty of pleasures in between, Ryan has delighted in the great swath of Ireland. He first visited Galway in 1985 when he remembers a grey place where the locals wandered the muddy tidal flats for fun and frolic. Times have changed! From lost rural pubs to lost memory, he's revelled in a place where his first name brings a smile and his surname brings a 'huh?'. Follow him at ryanverberkmoes.com; and on Twitter @ryanvb.

More Writers

Published by Lonely Planet Publications Pty Ltd
ABN 36 005 607 983
3rd edition – May 2014
ISBN 978 1 74220 748 3
© Lonely Planet 2014   Photographs © as indicated 2014
10 9 8 7 6 5 4 3 2 1
Printed in China

Although the authors and Lonely Planet have taken all reasonable care in preparing this book, we make no warranty about the accuracy or completeness of its content and, to the maximum extent permitted, disclaim all liability arising from its use.

All rights reserved. No part of this publication may be copied, stored in a retrieval system, or transmitted in any form by any means, electronic, mechanical, recording or otherwise, except brief extracts for the purpose of review, and no part of this publication may be sold or hired, without the written permission of the publisher. Lonely Planet and the Lonely Planet logo are trademarks of Lonely Planet and are registered in the US Patent and Trademark Office and in other countries. Lonely Planet does not allow its name or logo to be appropriated by commercial establishments, such as retailers, restaurants or hotels. Please let us know of any misuses: lonelyplanet.com/ip.